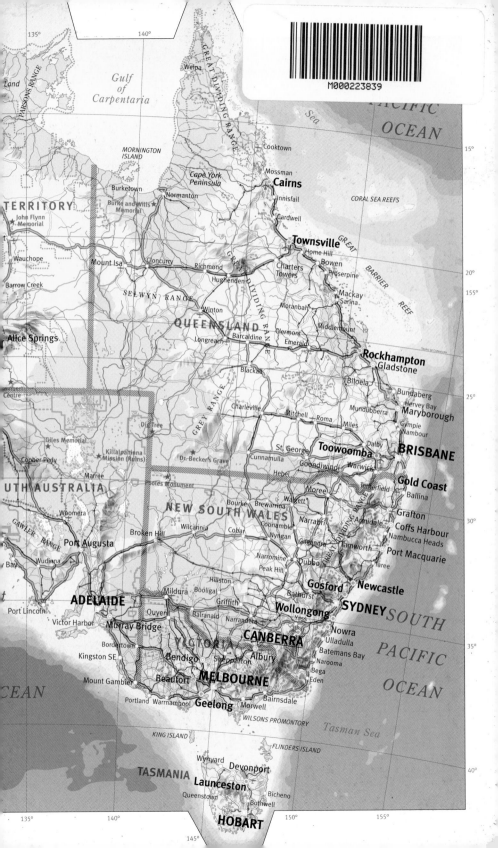

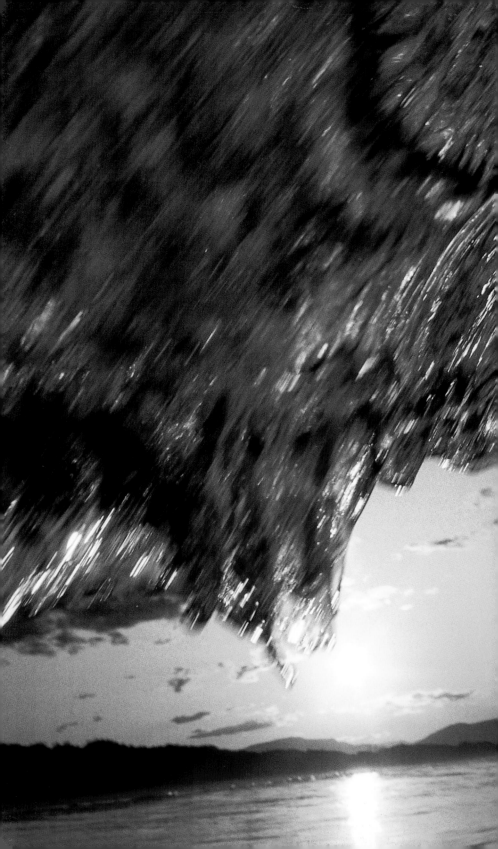

SURFING AUSTRALIA

written and edited by
Mark Thornley and Veda Dante

photo editing by
Mark Thornley

chief photographer
Peter Wilson

*with editorial and
photographic contributions by*

Wayne "Rabbit" Bartholomew, Andrew Buckley,
Conti, Simon De Salis, Rick Eaves, Albert Falzon,
Dick Hoole, Ben Horvath, Greg Keegan, Jane Lewis,
Mick McCormack, David Miller, Bill Morris,
Shaun Munro, Wayne Murphy, Mark Newsham,
Shane Peel, Neal Purchase Jnr, Eric Reginard,
Ian Reginard, Chris Rennie, Glyndon Ringrose,
Wayne Ryan, Glenn Saltmarsh, Paul Sargeant,
Deborah Sciffer, Kevin Sharland, Peter Simons,
Craig Stroh, Barrie Sutherland, Brian Taylor,
Dadee Taylor and Terry Willcocks

PERIPLUS

Published by Periplus Editions (HK) Ltd

ISBN 962-593-322-0
Printed in Singapore

Publisher: Eric Oey
Editors: Mark Thornley, Veda Dante, Rod Ritchie, Julia Walkden
Production: Rod Ritchie, Mary Chia
Cartography: Violet Wong

Distributors:

Asia-Pacific: Berkeley Books Pte Ltd., 5 Little Road, #08-01, Singapore 536983

Indonesia: PT Wira Mandala Pustaka (Java Books – Indonesia),
Jl. Kelapa Gading Kirana, Blok A-14 No. 17, Jakarta 14240

Japan: Tuttle Shokai Ltd., 21-13, Seki 1-Chome, Tama-ku, Kawasaki,
Kanagawa-ken 214

USA: Charles E. Tuttle, RRI Box 231-5, North Clarendon, VT 05759-9700

Cover: Luke Nolan hasn't lost that Woonona feeling. *Photo: Mark Newsham*

Pages 4-5: The rarely-ridden Gnaraloo Bombie, WA. *Photo: Paul Sargeant*

Pages 6-7: Zen Gold. *Photo: Terry Willcocks*

Pages 8-9: Koby Abberton living the future—now. *Photo: Bill Morris*

Pages 10-11: Melanie Redman loving it on a large one. *Photo: Peter Wilson*

Pages 12-13: Wiser than a Buddhist owl, the ocean keeps rolling. *Photo: Mick McCormack*

Pages 14-15: Mick Lowe vertigo—Winkipop. *Photo: Peter Wilson*

Pages 16-17 (Title Page): Wes Laine's cool head in hot water. *Photo: Mick McCormack*

Page 19 (Opposite Copyright Page): Taj Burrow enjoys the natural high. *Photo: Twiggy*

Pages 20-21: John Clout as deep as it gets. *Photo: Mick McCormack*

Pages 22-23: (Contents Page) Every day that ends with a wave will be a good one. *Photo: Peter Wilson*

Above: Luke Nolan hasn't lost that Woonona feeling.

Photo: Mark Newsham

SURFING AUSTRALIA

CONTENTS

Surfing in Australia

Now and Zen

By Wayne "Rabbit" Bartholomew
1978 World Surfing Champion and
National Coaching Director, Surfing Australia Inc.

Surf Season

Access

Sea Bottom

Special Gear

Hazards

Medical

Highlights

Long before beach culture was popularised, Australians were always enchanted by the oceans that lapped and pounded our golden beaches. However, until early this century, our rite of passage to the magical, spiralling waves, was blocked by ultra conservative legislation which barred beachgoers from entering the surf. But in a famous act of defiance, one Sydney gentleman thumbed his nose at the authorities and media representatives as he boldly marched into Bondi's surging shorebreak. That simple act—although rewarded with arrest and a subsequent charge—paved the way for all Australians to indulge in a newly-gained liberty and to participate in a sporting lifestyle that has distinguished this nation above the rest.

The Duke

A recreation that has evolved into a potent sub culture, surfboard riding is inextricably linked to the Olympic movement. When the 1912 Stockholm gold medallist swimmer Duke Paoa Kahanamoku visited our shores in 1914, he packed his surfboard in with his togs, and on a sparkling summer's day, turned Australia onto the ancient sport of Hawaiian kings.

As they say in the classics, the rest is history, but it certainly didn't happen overnight. A couple of World Wars and a Great Depression provided major distractions for the youth of the day, however a small core of dedicated enthusiasts managed to keep the Duke's legacy alive.

Claude West, Isobel Latham and Snowy McAllister were all present at Freshwater Beach that famous summer's day: in fact, Isobel had the distinction of being the first Aussie to ride a board with the Duke himself! Meanwhile, Claude West somehow got his hands on the Duke's board and made a replica, while Snowy McAllister went on to win the 1928 and 1930 Australian Championships, performing a headstand on his longboard to secure his comeback win in 1930.

Trailblazing

By 1945, the end of the Second World War, Australians were taking to the beach like never before. The automobile opened up our remote coastline, and small parties of pioneering surfers were soon piling into FJ Holdens. With crude equipment, and an inherent spirit of adventure, they began trailblazing and paddling their way to what are now some of the most revered surfing locations on the planet.

The metropolitan beaches such as Bondi and Manly were already famous, but by the beginning of the '50s, a new breed of surfer was emerging from backwater areas such as Newcastle, southeast Queensland, northern New South Wales and the rugged Victorian coastline.

Local Torquay identities China Gilbert, Owen Yateman, Dick Gerrard and Joe Sweeney were hellbent on braving the foreboding cliffs to surf the now famous Bells Beach. Gerard actually cut his way through the thick scrub from the south, while the others, who had all been baptised in the weaker surf close to home, donned their football

Opposite: Steve Clements finds his rhythm, breaks the shackles and hoists up and over a Forster lip.
Photos: Andrew Buckley

Phil Edwards visited Bells after the 1956 Olympics, they stunned the locals with their technique and revolutionary surfboards. Fortunately, a few boards were left behind and news of the board design breakthrough spread like wildfire.

The second watershed development occurred around 1958–1960. Many surfers had joined the surf lifesaving movement to learn watermanship and gain access to the clubhouses which sprung up in every coastal town. Free accommodation on the weekend was a great attraction to our cash-strapped, though mostly working youth, but an undercurrent of animosity was growing between the non-surfing clubbies and the free-spirited surfing fraternity. The rift was highlighted at Broadbeach in the summer of '58–'59. Peter Drouyn, Paul and Rick Neilsen and several others were enjoying the waves so much this one particular Sunday that they failed to meet their posts for beach duties and patrols. Furious, the club captain was soon on the bull-horn demanding they return to shore and dutifully pull on their red and yellow caps. The sets kept rolling in and the boys knew they were at the crossroads. After a meeting in the line-up, they surfed on and knowing they faced disciplinary action beachside, decided to resign from the club. This set the stage for a long period of disdain between clubbies and surfers.

Above: Three of Australia's most influential surfers. From left: Peter Drouyn, Nat Young and "Midget" Farrelly.
Photo: Barrie Sutherland

Below: Rabbit in his burrow.
Photo: Jane Lewis

guernseys to ward off the cold as they braved the Torquay waters for the four-mile paddle.

Surfers and Clubbies

Before air travel was part of life, Australia was virtually isolated from the rest of the world and blissfully unaware of the surfboard evolution occurring throughout California and Hawaii.

So when a troupe of demonstration surfers including the legendary Greg "Da Bull" Noll and

Everybody's goin' surfin'

The Beach Boys, Gidget movies, Fabian and Annette Funicello, Ride the Wild Surf, Mickey Dora and Phil Edwards all contributed to a fermenting '60s youth culture keen to change the world. When *Endless Summer* hit the silver screen, everyone went surf crazy, and Australia's youth spent their summers surfing by day and 'stomping' at beach parties on weekends. It was a simple but heady time.

The single most significant event that would shape Australia's surfing future was played out at Manly Beach in 1964. Loosely formatted competition had been around for a couple of years, but when the ISF (International Surfing Federation) chose Australia as the site of the first official World Championship, the best of the best descended upon Sydney.

Australian champion Midget Farrelly had already lifted the coveted Makaha International (a prophecy of things to come in this sport's mecca, Hawaii), but when he staved off an international field including American greats like Mike Doyle and Joey Cabell, Australia went berko!

Gold Coaster Phyllis O'Donell also took the women's crown, and so began a proud tradition of winning for Aussie surfers. Midget was a hero, becoming a household name in the process. He gave a

huge boost to the fledgling surfing industry by the fact that every kid wanted to emulate the world champ, right down to his iridescent pink baggies and signature model surfboard.

The competitive surf evolution

Air travel was still beyond the reach of most Australians and amazing tales of Aussies stowing away on ships for the six-week journey to Hawaii are woven into our folklore. One such stowaway was Bob McTavish. A brilliant surfer in his own right, he became part of a new breed of master shapers who would help Australia step out of California's shadow and contribute to the surfboard evolution.

Around the same time, groups of local surfers began banding together informally. This usually occurred after a happy day's surfing, while sitting around a campfire enjoying a few snags and a beer. And so the social fabric of beach culture evolved concurrently in different parts of the country, sometimes thousands of miles apart.

It wasn't long before surfers decided to form their own clubs and soon North Narrabeen, Newcastle's Merewether, Kirra, Snapper Rocks on the Gold Coast, Manly-Pacific, Windensea, Maroubra, Bondi and Cronulla all established surf riding institutions that would breed future world champions. With vivid scenes

Above: Simon Anderson shows off the first thruster design at Bells Beach during his historic title win in 1981.
Photo: Peter Simons

Short boards, long rides and the birth of an industry

The short board revolution happened virtually overnight. Again, a universal reaction took hold as surfers up and down the coast dragged longboards into the shaping bay to be guillotined. What emerged into the light of day was a new world order. Like the dinosaurs —one minute the line-up was littered with 9'6" beasts, the next second, walls were being carved by 5'10" boards. The long board was gone, but unlike the dinosaurs, not extinct.

With surfboard shapers and test pilots entering uncharted waters, the early '70s was an incredibly dynamic period. Designs were refined to cater for Queensland's long-walled point breaks and adapted to suit NSW and Victoria's punchy peaks.

It was also a time of transition for the surfing industry, as they applied their vision to products and marketing. Surf shops and beach clothing labels began to sweep through surf-crazy towns. Barry Bennett in Sydney's north, Gordon and Smith to the south, Joe Larkin, Ken Adler and Haydn Kenny in Queensland, Klonm-Bell and Pat Morgan in Victoria were some of the major players, while Platts and Hang Ten began pumpin' out the board shorts for the retail outlets. Bells Beach surfer Alan Green aspired to make the world's best board shorts, and Quiksilver was born shortly after. Just down the road in a humble factory in the back blocks of Torquay, Brian Singer and Doug Warbrick began making Rip Curl wetsuits and in 1973, Gordon and Rena Merchant (Billabong) made durable board shorts in their spare room and sold them out of Gordon's station wagon.

From those humble beginnings rose the big three of the surfing industry as Rip Curl, Quiksilver and Billabong rode a wave of success on the coat-tails of an extraordinary group of Australian surfing superstars.

Above: Isobel Latham with her board at Freshwater Beach, just two years after her legendary ride with the Duke. Circa 1917. *Photo: Isobel Latham Collection, Warringah Library Service, NSW.*

from *Ride the Wild Surf* and *Endless Summer* still fresh in his mind, Australian filmmaker Bob Evans set about recording the classic waves of Noosa, Kirra, Lennox, Angourie, Fairy Bower, Bells Beach and WA's Margaret River for Australian consumption.

Free, challenging and alive, this brave new world was sent into perpetual orbit when Australia's Nat Young travelled to San Diego and stamped himself as the world's premier surfer at the 1966 World Titles. While Midget had put us on the map, Nat set in place a domination that would inspire an entire generation to seek greatness.

Influential surfers became icons of the flower power era; growing their hair long and pursuing a soulful existence while taking a stand against involvement in Vietnam. Dictating fashion amongst the beach culture, they took their place at the helm of a global youth rebellion.

Living the legends at surfing's Mecca

Blessed with the world's most challenging big-wave arena and an impressive list of lucrative professional meets, Hawaii soon became the focus of a new breed of competitive animal which came to embody the unique Aussie spirit. These pioneers laid down the gauntlet to future generations with barnstorming sessions at Sunset Beach, Haleiwa, Big Pipeline and Waimea Bay. The likes of Mark Richards, Michael Peterson, Dan Cairns, Rabbit Bartholomew, Peter Townend, Mark Warren, Terry Fitzgerald, Paul Neilsen and Bruce Raymond have since stood the test of time. In fact, many of those performers are yardsticks for the ages.

Back in Australia, professional surfing evolved through a loosely knit network of individual events that upgraded from amateur to professional status. When the Rip Curl Pro offered $1,000 first prize in 1973, mavericks such as Michael Peterson and Terry Fitzgerald turned pro. In 1974, Sydney journalist Graham Cassidy established the inaugural Coca Cola Surfabout, allowing surfing mainstream media coverage and respect for the first time.

Amazing stories came out of Hawaii in the winter of 1975-76. The Aussies, along with South Africans Shaun and Mike Tomson, dominated the north shore events, while waging individual kamikaze assaults on Big Sunset, Outside Pipe and Waimea. High performance surfing, the antics of the characters themselves, the growing industry and an explosion of magazine coverage dedicated to this generation helped set the stage for international professional surfing.

Surfing turns Pro

Seizing the opportunity, the ASP (Australian Surfing Professionals) was established in 1976, and for the first time the world's best could follow a global circuit in the pursuit of a world crown. Sure there were teething problems, and the sport was badly in need of full-time pro-moters, administrators and media directors. But the sheer passion with which the original vanguard carried themselves around the globe as paid athletes, assured the sport a golden potential.

As a new decade unfolded, the circuit was consolidated and the industry gathered momentum. A watershed event occurred beneath the hallowed cliffs of Bells Beach in 1981. On Easter Monday, the world's best surfers awoke to the sight of 15 ft lines of swell. Most of them were caught on the hop, but Sydney professional Simon Anderson seized the moment to usher in his new thruster design. Big Simon not only mastered the radical conditions but went on to win the Bells' trophy, the Narrabeen Coke Classic and the Pipeline Masters in Hawaii that same year.

Within months, most of the world's top surfers had moved across to the thruster with only four-time world champion Mark Richards holding out on his twin fin, and four-time runner-up Cheyne Horan, sticking grimly to his McCoy single fin. Not since the McTavish V-bottom had one design turned the sport on its ear. An everlasting legacy to Simon, the thruster remains the equipment staple nearly two decades later.

A quantum leap in design and a new generation ready to seize the moment

When Quiksilver signed up Tom Carroll to a $1,000,000 multi-year contract in 1985, the bidding wars began. Offers came rolling in for the hot, new blood who could push the limits. Goofy footers Damien Hardman, Barton Lynch, Mark Occhilupo and of course, Tom Carroll, who went on to win two world titles, would effectively close the chapter on the legendary Mark Richards and the Bronzed Aussies. These new sensations, including fellow Aussie Gary Elkerton and American Tom Curren, would go on to dominate the sport, the fashion, and the rankings, for almost a decade before future king Kelly

Slater ascended to the throne and assumed the mantle as the world's pre-eminent surfer.

The future

The nineties saw the sport accepted in many other countries, including Japan and Brazil, and explode demographically. This led to burgeoning numbers in Australia's junior ranks.

Junior surfing institutions such as the Pro Junior, the Billabong Junior Series and the Australian Championship Circuit (ACC) were quickly established as annual blooding grounds for a hotbed of young grommets. The world's richest junior tour, the ACC is a fertile ground for aspiring surf stars.

WA's Taj Burrow, Australia's leading world title hope, is a former ACC competitor, and is joined in the elite World Top 44 by fellow graduates Danny Wills, Jake Paterson, Luke Hitchings, Nathan Webster, Michael Lowe, Shane Bevan and Shane Wehner. With future stars such as Joel Parkinson, Grant Hudson, Dean Morrison, Mick Fanning and Adrian Buchan waiting in the wings, Australia can look forward to a prime future.

As part of Surfing Australia Inc.'s undertaking to develop the sport in Australia and the Australasia region, both junior and women's development programs absorb a great deal of its resources. Surfing Australia Inc.'s Level 1 and 2 coaching accreditation is a world leader and we now export our programs to countries such as Brazil, Portugal, Japan, Argentina, Peru and Italy.

The Surfrider Surf Schools were also implemented several years ago, with the combined talents of a dedicated group of surfing instructors, so Australian's can rest assured that their juniors are getting the good oil.

The best part is that the waves and the legends keep coming!

Right: Glen McEwan eases off the bottom and waits for the crystal wrap at Summercloud Bay in New South Wales.
Photo: Mick McCormack

Over page: Artwork by Steve Dixon courtesy of Doolagahs.

TIMOR
SEA

DAR
KAKA

BROOME
SANDFIRE

GREAT SANDY
DESERT

TANAM
DESER

BARROW ISLAND

INDIAN OCEAN

COCOS ISLANDS

SHIP WRECKS

TURTLES

CAMP OF THE
MOON

GIBSON DESERT

SIMP

SURF POINTS

BLUE HOLE

JAKES POINT

HELLS GATE

FLAT ROCKS

HEAD BUTTS

STRICKLAND BAY

CATHEDRAL ROCK

TRIGG POINT

STARK BAY

YALLINGUP

MARGARET RIVER

SUICIDES

HUSH HUSH BEACH

GREAT VICTORIA
DESERT

Wave
Rock

COCKLEBIDDY

PERTH

TWILIGHT COVE

GREAT AUSTRAL
BIGHT

MUNGLINUP
BEACH

CRAZIES

KOORI
SURF ART

SOUTHER

TORRES STRAIT
THURSDAY ISLAND
SEA
CORAL SEA
NORTH
EAST
SOUTH
WEST
GULF OF CARPENTARIA
CAPE YORK PENINSULA
GREAT BARRIER REEF
CAIRNS
HOOK ISLAND
DAYDREAM ISLAND
SOUTH PACIFIC OCEAN
INDIAN HEAD
DOUBLE ISLAND POINT
NOOSA HEADS
PLATFORMS
NORTH STRADBROKE ISLAND
BRISBANE
BURLEIGH HEADS
KIRRA
STONY DESERT
DURANBAH
THE PASS
SOUTH WALL
BALLINA
ANGOURIE
POINT PLOMER
BOOMERANG BEACH
YAGEN
WINDA WOPPA
GHOSTIES
CRACKNECK
SYDNEY
SHARK ISLAND
MYSTICS
TUBES
BLACK ROCK
ADELAIDE
MERIMBULA
AVOID BAY
SALTWATER
KANGAROO ISLAND
BASTION POINT
CAPE CONRAN
MELBOURNE
OBERON BAY
ELEVATORS
BELLS BEACH
WATERLOO BAY
WINKIPOP
PHILLIP ISLAND
BINALONG BAY
HOBART
TRIAL HARBOUR
DEVILS POINT
BUNDOOLA
ROARING BEACH
DIXON '98

What's on at the Movies?

Oz Surf Filmmakers

by Albert Falzon and Dick Hoole

Surf Movies began as home movies in the early Fifties. Without any real experience, surfers filmed their friends surfing along the Californian coast. They would then splice the films together, invite everyone around and have a wild night. The out-of-the-ocean antics were usually filmed in fast forward speed giving the images a Chaplin-esque feel. These films were innovative, raw and humorous. Word spread, and pretty soon the films were screened in small theatres up and down the Californian coast. A whole new world for surfing had opened up.

With the technology available today, anyone can make a movie. It's relatively inexpensive; high quality,

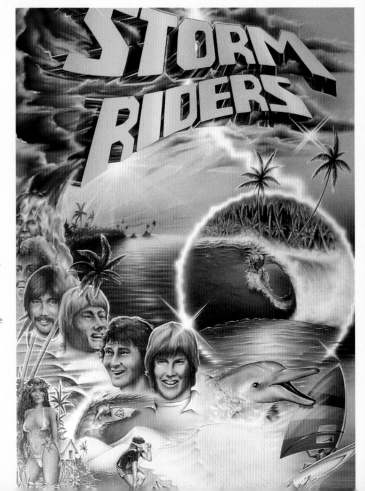

Preceding pages:
Luke Eagan crouching for the Kirra Express.
Photo: Peter Wilson

Right: Riders on the storm. Rabbit, MR, Lopez, Ho and Carroll.
Photo: Dick Hoole

Opposite:
Promotional poster for *Locked In*, a film by Bud Browne.
Photo: Courtesy Albert Falzon

computer-driven images enable movies to be produced for a fraction of the cost of "Hollywood" productions. American director Francis Ford Coppola once said that the creative future for films and filmmakers will develop not so much from Hollywood but from the "High 8" end. Forty years ago surfers did exactly that, and today hundreds of films are made by surfers who've had no previous experience in filmmaking.

You can borrow a camera, spend a few bucks on tape, cut loose with your ideas and away you go—it's that simple. And with the Internet you've got access to worldwide distribution. The Surf film has come of age—now it's time to appreciate it as an art form.

Bob Evans, the grandfather of Australian surf filmmakers, made thirteen feature-length surf movies before he died at the age of 44. He filmed, edited and self-funded most of these. Undoubtedly Australia's most prolific film producer of his time, he left a legacy of invaluable historic films documenting the early years of our country's short board evolution.

Evans also toured the eastern and southern coasts of Australia showing American Bud Browne's early surfing films of Hawaii and California. Australian surf film's great grandfather, Bud led the way in documenting the formative years of surfing, and laid the foundations of what is today a sport enjoyed by millions.

1959: Bob Evans' High on a Cool Wave

The importance of Bud Browne's silver screen images of early surfing stylists cannot be underestimated. Australian surfers were just beginning to get their feet, when Bud's films were being shown up and down the coast by Evans. Surfers were able to appreciate the classic and individual surfing styles of Dewey Weber, Kemp Aaberg, Mike Doyle and Phil Edwards, and were mesmerized by the incredible surfing of Ricky Gregg, Jose Angel, Pat Curren and Greg Noll as they dropped into the massive swells at Hawaii's Waimea Bay.

1967: Bud Browne's Cat on a Hot Foam Board

Screened in halls and cinemas up and down the coast, these early surf films played to packed houses. Occasionally when the projector broke down—which it did more often than not—the audience of over-enthusiastic surfers would go wild. Subsequently, Evans and crew always had their exits planned well in advance, should the projector lamp blow and a hasty retreat be necessary.

1971: Greg McGillivry and Jim Freeman's Five Summer Stories

In 1963 a young Australian surfer called Midget Farrelly travelled to Hawaii with Evans and won the prestigious Makaha Surfing

Championships. His victory made world headlines and set the scene for what was to become Australia's dominance in surfing. It also attracted a new breed of adventurous filmmakers keen to capture their passion on celluloid.

1965: Bruce Browne's Endless Summer

Paul Witzig, along with a hot young group of Australian surfers, produced *The Hot Generation* and *Evolution*. These were amazing, new, dynamic, rebel-rousing and raw surfing films which made the surfing world sit up and take notice. The tables turned and the international surfing elite witnessed, through Witzig's films, an undeniably aggressive Australian surfing movement. These movies shifted the focus from the fluid style of the classic Hawaiian surfers, and, in particular, the California surfers, to the raw dynamics of Australia's aggressive and radical kids. It was the beginning of an exciting new surfing era and a filmmaking era which was charting new territory.

1971: Albert Falzon's Morning of the Earth

Morning of the Earth was filmed in Hawaii, Australia, and the newly discovered Bali. Capturing the lifestyle of surfers, it adopted a more laid-back and adventurous approach which included an original soundtrack. The film extended its reach beyond the surfing world and entered a new beach generation to become an Australian hit. *Morning of the Earth* opened the door to surfing the idyllic waves of the Indonesian Archipelago, and to this day remains one of surfing's cult classics.

1975: Dick Hoole and Jack McCoy Tubular Swells

Dick Hoole and Jack McCoy then formed a partnership to produce *Tubular Swells*. This established the foundations for McCoy's later work with the Billabong crew. Experimenting with a new, super high quality 16 mm format, hi 8 digtal camera, he produced a series of creatively hip, state-of-the-art surfing videos. *Bunyip Dreaming* and the *Green Iguana* set the scene for what is today a profuse showcase of homegrown filmmakers.

The 16 mm Evolution

Travelling the world, Californian and Australian surfing entrepreneurs enjoyed a 16 mm heyday throughout the late 1980's.

But with the dawn of the '90s, attendances at the Sydney Opera House main venue were diminishing as new video technology allowed many new players from both sides of the Pacific to enter the market. Subsidised by major clothing companies, high budget 16 mm feature productions created an exclusive club of filmmakers as corporate videos at give away prices changed audience viewing habits forever.

American director Taylor Steele was influential in this environment, mainly through his exclusive access to Kelly Slater, Rob Machado, Shane Dorian and the rest of the US talent pool who monopolised surfing's evolution during the next five years.

Oz Young Guns Become Directors

Young Australian filmmakers Tim Bonython and Jason Muir responded by producing the *Hawaii 90-Hawaii 97* series for Surf Video Magazine plus bodyboarding titles. Brooke Sylvester got lost in Indonesia for several seasons producing his programs. On the beach in Australia, Justin Gain, Mat Gye, Peter Kirkhouse, Ron Gorringe and Chris Fowler focused on what was happening Down Under and in Indonesia. Paul Sargent produced eight episodes of *Sarge's Surfing Scrapbook* over as many years, effectively archiving pro surfing's antics along with the demise of the ASP World Tour.

The Corporate Video Series

Around the same time Rip Curl invented *The Search* and Quiksilver created *The G'Land Pro* in Java, while Billabong developed an annual Junior Series and Invitational Challenge. Over six years Jack McCoy's team of camera and production people have set the standard of quality.

As each summer approaches, a flood of videos hit the surf shops, their slick packaging complemented by full-scale marketing campaigns and colour magazine advertisments.

Surfing on the Big Screen

Gone are the days of the scratchy 16 mm prints screened in coastal halls and cinemas. Now it's fast forward time. Very few of today's grommets have seen a surfing film in a theatre. They've never felt the rush as the lights go down and the audience goes wild with anticipation as huge swells fill the screen and a surfer freefalls down the face of a monster wave.

It's a pity. Surfing belongs on the big screen—those wide open places and full barrel rides; the adventure, the mystery, the magic, the beauty and absolute perfection of riding waves off some remote, majestic island. The big screen, hit surfing movie—it's still waiting to be made.

PHOTOGRAPH OF BEARER
PHOTOGRAPHIE DU TITULAIRE

The Sunshine State

Fun, Sun and Surf

Previous pages: Australia's "Raging Bull" Mark Occhilupo takes a slice out of the Kirra speed train. *Photo: Jane Lewis*

Opposite: Jay Phillips free and amped on a fun Queensland beach. *Photo: Peter Wilson*

Australia's second largest state occupies the nation's entire north-west corner (1,727,000 sq km to be exact). An exotic blend of idyllic palm fringed beaches, breathtaking Barrier Reef islands and sky-scraping resort development, the coastline is a leading international tourist drawcard and an aquatic playground often referred to as Australia's California. Queensland's agricultural industries, including sugar, pineapples, peanuts and wheat, bow to tourism, its biggest industry earner.

Blessed with world-class point breaks as hollow and fast as anywhere on the planet, the Gold Coast's 70 kilometres of pristine beaches are a hive of activity with high speed chases and traffic jams both in and out of the water. Burleigh Heads, Snapper Rocks, Greenmount and Kirra (the site of the prestigious Billabong Pro), really are a surfers' paradise treating the wave hungry masses with warm water and endless barrels throughout the year.

Australia's theme park capital, Queensland is home to Sea World, which turns on the action with the support of playful seals, dolphins and penguins. Or if you're after a rush, try Dreamworld's majorly gut-wrenching Tower of Terror, which claims to be the fastest, tallest trip in the world. A roller coaster ride which rockets from zero to 160 km/h in seven seconds, the Tower of Terror soars up to 38 storeys high then surrenders to gravity, free-falling backwards to a heart-stopping conclusion.

When the surf sucks, there's always Cable Sports World, the largest water ski park on the planet, which covers 36 ha and offers five freshwater lakes to ski and wakeboard on.

Then there's Movieworld, the Big Pineapple, para-sailing, water-skiing, hang gliding, bungee jumping and hot air ballooning. But if that's all making you feel a bit dizzy, maybe you'd prefer something more mellow like whale watching or sailing the Whitsundays. Whatever your choice, you'll find plenty of hot action to be had.

Taking the frenetic edge off the dynamic Gold Coast lifestyle, the Moreton Bay islands, including the World Heritage-listed Fraser Island (the world's largest sand island), provide more sedate settings. Pristine national parks offer uncrowded perfection to the keen wave hunter.

Bright sunny days and balmy nights provide a warm welcome for visitors to Brisbane. Australia's only sub-tropical capital city, Brisbane is pretty laid back, trading the "big city" vibe of Sydney and Melbourne for a true urban reflection of the Australian beach culture. You'll find botanical gardens, parkways and virgin bushland all within a ten kilometre radius of this modern metropolis, situated on the Brisbane River 33 km upstream from Moreton Bay. Its local seafood is famous—you must try the internationally-renowned, locally-sourced Moreton Bay Bugs.

Perhaps the world's premier diving destination, the Great Barrier Reef has been relatively unexplored by surfers. The largest living coral

Above: Looking north over the classic Gold Coast beaches.
Photo: Peter Wilson

reef in the world, its 2000 km of outer reefs and islands offer plenty of surf if you hook up with an adventurous crew and a knowledgeable skipper.

If you happen to be in the right place at the right time, don't miss the annual Great Barrier Reef coral spawning, in either October or November, when the corals release millions of radiant red, pink, blue and green eggs into the surrounding waters in a kaleidoscopic "snowstorm".

There are also hundreds of shipwrecks to explore along the Reef and coast, from the Torres Strait islands in the far north, to Tweed Heads on Queensland's southern border.

The most popular destinations enroute to the Great Barrier Reef include the Whitsunday Islands, Dunk and Hinchinbrook, which offer a relaxing distraction for travellers seeking a bit of sailing solitude. Get together a group of friends and take your pick of five star resorts or simply pitch a tent on your own slice of paradise.

In the heart of the Tropical North you'll find Cairns, gateway to Northern Australia. A world class gamefishing mecca, keen anglers travel from every corner of the planet in their bid to wrestle the huge Black Marlin that frequent the local waters.

North of Cairns arelocated the spectacular Daintree and Cape Tribulation National Parks. A cruise up the Daintree River, bordered by ancient rainforests and inhabited by crocodiles, will blow your mind.

But beware when swimming in the crystal coastal waters. From November to April each year, the deadly Box Jellyfish frequent North Queensland's rivermouths and offshore islands. One of the world's most venomous creatures, it has been responsible for over 40 human fatalities. Although some beaches now have protected stinger enclosures, it is not advisable to swim anywhere else along the northern coast during these months.

Further north is Cape York Peninsula where forests, swamps, rivers and forests co-exist as they did millions of years ago. Avoid travelling here in the wet season as up to two metres of rain can flood the major roads.

—*Mark Thornley*

The Sunshine Coast

Balmy Beaches and Long Righthand Points

November–April. (Cyclone Season)

Relatively easy drive or walk to many breaks. 4WD and boat access in places.

Predominantly sand covered reef but occasionally sharp reef.

Hotdog boards plus good tube riding sticks.

Sharks, point break traffic jams and strong rips.

Reef cuts, sharks and stingers.

Long point breaks, fun beachies and picturesque rainforest backdrops.

The Sunshine Coast lies about three hours' drive north of the Queensland border and consists of five major surfing areas—Noosa, Coolum, Maroochydore, Maloolaba and Caloundra. Like the Gold Coast, the Sunshine Coast has an abundance of sun-drenched beach breaks and long right-hand points to drool over.

A quiet coastal strip with quaint inland country towns like Eumundi, the Sunshine Coast offers a great alternative to the more commercialized Gold Coast. Because of its location, just north of the protruding islands of Moreton and Straddie, the Sunshine Coast is sheltered from the predominant SE swells that march up the coast and is usually a foot or two smaller than the Gold Coast. During the months from December to May, when the cyclones are raging to the north, is generally the best time to sample the walled-up perfection of the local point and beach breaks. There's accommodation to suit all tastes and budgets, from beachfront caravan parks to luxury five-star resorts.

Noosa

Drive into Hastings Street in Noosa Heads and you'll instantly feel like you're on vacation. The up-market accommodation, cafes and restaurants engulfed by the surrounding hills and national parks create a unique Queensland scene. Some people call it yuppie-ville, others think it's paradise. One thing's for certain, when there's a southerly wind and a solid swell, Noosa's idyllic points crank!

First Point, **National Park**, **Ti-Tree, Johnsons** and **Granite Bay** are located on Noosa's main headland. Each has its own unique power and inviting sections. The car park at National is as far as you can drive and is a great place to be when the swell's up. On a good day it's possible to take off at the rocky **Boiling Pot**, (which is the tip of National), and ride past Johnsons, into the sandy walls of First Point, but it can get crowded. To reach Ti-Tree requires a scenic walk through the national park's coastal tracks which usually ends in a surf-frenzied, toe-stubbing race to get out there. It picks up slightly more swell than its other counterparts and is a great wave, which bowls over a rocky bottom and peels into a beautiful tree-lined bay. What more could you ask for?

Wrapping around the extremity of Noosa's bay-linked headland, **Granites** is another wave that churns mechanically over a rock bottom. Slightly more exposed to the wind and swell and usually less crowded than Ti-Tree, it can be a good call when the pack gets a whiff that the waves are going off.

Below: Scott Wilden—walkin' on Sunshine, cos it makes you feel good.
Photo: Peter Wilson

Yes, if there's swell, Noosa is the place to be. However, if conditions aren't so ideal there's always Saturday's Eumundi markets.

If you don't mind a drive and the wind is NE on a small to moderate swell, then a 4WD trip up to **Double Island Point** for surfing and fishing should prove worthwhile. There are usually some great left and right peaks around the shipwreck and sometimes an insane righthander winds the length of a footy field down the lush green headland before finding its resting place in the wide bay.

Just south of Noosa, **Sunshine Beach** picks up the most swell in the area. Depending on the condition of the banks, it can produce some superb beach breaks but needs light or westerly winds to stay smooth—a basic rule for most of the beach breaks on the Sunshine Coast.

Coolum

Head south along the David Low Highway where you'll drive past the beaches of **Peregian** and **Marcus**. The waves here can turn on in westerly winds and a small to medium swell. It's even possible to find your own quiet peak here. If there's southerly in the wind then the sleepy town of Coolum will be fairly protected and should have some playful waves in front of the surf club. Coolum picks up the swell but the points rarely offer much, due to a lack of sand to line their rocky shores.

Next stop is the quiet town of **Mudjimba**, which offers some more fun beach breaks. The waves here need light or westerly winds and are usually nice and peaky due to the favourable diffraction in swells caused by the mystical **Mudjimba Island**. Home to a heavy left and an intense right that breaks into deep water, there's a pot of gold out there—but that's all I'm going to say!

Maroochydore

The Sunshine Coast's largest town, Maroochydore is a handy pit stop to restock supplies, catch a movie or go skating in the huge shopping mall. There are consistent beachbreaks along Alexandra Parade from the Maroochy River right down to **Alexandra Headland**, although they need a moderate swell with a south to westerly wind. You'll find in a southerly swell that the further you surf towards the river, the better the waves will be.

Alexandra Headland is another righthand point that produces a walling, high performance wave. On a moderate to large swell with southerly winds, it can really stack up and has some fun long-boarding sections when the swell is small. Because this beach is patrolled and is great for families, the crowds can be a big deterrent on the sunny days.

Sunshine Coast

Mooloolaba

Just south over the headland is Mooloolaba. Not much surf here, just a bunch of nightclubs, pubs and restaurants; perfect for those hot Queensland nights. If you look out towards the ocean from Mooloolaba Beach then you should see **Point Cartwright** in the distance with its lighthouse perched at the top of the hill. This is probably the best wave in the area. To get there you need to drive on the David Low Highway then turn into Point Cartwright Drive before following it to the top of the headland.

Along the way you'll see the northern end of the **Buddina** beaches. They pick up heaps of swell and are worth a look on NW–W winds. The point needs medium to solid swell with a SW wind, and has heaps of grunt with a nice hollow take-off and long walls. Unfortunately the waves are cut short of their full potential because of an annoying break wall which can also cause major backwash. Out the back, just below the lighthouse is the **Platform**. This place pumps over a dredging rock shelf and is a great alternative to the point for those with more confidence. The consistent beach breaks of Buddina,

Warana and **Wurtulla** are easily checked by driving down the suburban beach streets of Pacific Boulevard and Oceanic Drive. These beach breaks pick up heaps of swell and are best surfed on a light or westerly wind.

Caloundra

Anne Street at Caloundra is a rock, shelf-sand bottom wave that works in the same conditions as Warana and Wurtulla. There are some fun left and right peaks to be had here and it's a great place to spend the day at the beach. If the winds are light and you feel like a paddle, consider a session at the outer reefs of **Dicky Beach** which can be fun. When there's a medium to solid swell and southerly wind, then **Moffats Point** will have some nice cascading rights peeling along its rock shelf. Located on a hill, the town itself has heaps of cheap accommodation, pubs and take-aways especially on the main street and around **Kings Beach**. Worth a check on a moderate swell with northerly winds, Kings regularly has quality sand banks.

—*Neal Purchase Jnr*

Above: All down the line, the Double Island Point righthander can literally make you surf till ya drop.
Photo: Dick Hoole

Over page: Andrew Murphy doin' his stuff at Duranbah.
Photo: Peter Wilson

Offshore Sand Islands
& The Great Barrier Reef

by Dadee Taylor

Stretching 125 km from the northern tip of the Gold Coast north to Caloundra, Moreton Bay Marine Park lies directly east of Brisbane. An aquatic wonderland, this serene bay is protected by the four largest islands along Queensland's eastern coastline. South Stradbroke, North Stradbroke, Moreton and Bribie Islands buffer the smaller, more fragile islands and wetlands from the full force of the Pacific Ocean swells. The northernmost of these, Fraser Island, is the largest sand island in the world.

South Stradbroke Island

South Straddie, is easily accessed by ferry or paddling the Southport seaway. A true barrier island, it is 21 km long and composed of vegetated beach ridges barely more than a few metres high. South Straddie has a small resort called Tipplers Tavern, with a modest settlement on the western shores.

The most popular surfing spot traditionally known as **Dolphin Point**, is protected from dominant winds by the northern seaway wall. The bypass sand pump helps to keep the

Formed by the continuous build-up of sand pushed northward by ocean currents and prevailing southerly winds from as far south as Sydney, every island has the classic, reverse J-curve, eastern beach, where the northern-most point is also the eastern-most. In other words, the northern extremities of these beaches are offshore in NW–W winds while also providing protection from SW–W conditions. Fringing most of the northern coastline, the Great Barrier Reef also offers a variety of surfing opportunities for the dedicated few.

banks well shaped, with ideal conditions being in S or W winds. South Straddie can get extremely crowded in a very short zone. Take a walk and you'll find great banks somewhere along the 21 km of beachbreaks, particularly in westerly breezes.

South Stradbroke was once connected to North Stradbroke but separated during fierce storms that occurred in 1896. It is popularly accepted that the island divided at this time where the cargo of the shipwrecked Cambus Wallace was exploded.

North Stradbroke Island

North Straddie occupies the biggest area of the Moreton Bay islands. Accessed by water taxis or vehicular barges from Cleveland or Redland Bay. These services connect with Brisbane's local trains and buses.

Point Lookout, Queensland's easternmost point, has one of Australia's prettiest headland walks. Below the headland, Main Beach stretches 34 km to the south with punchy beachbreaks that are best on NW winds, although they can handle W–SW and NE winds reasonably well. Most people surf in the northernmost half-kilometre, so heaps of good waves go unexplored further along the beach. **Main Beach** and **Frenchmans** are the easternmost breaks in Australia and are pretty raw demanding lots of paddling on a rising swell. Frenchmans is the more workable wave with good take-offs. Best on SW–S and W winds, when it can be both fun and frustrating.

Cylinder and **Deadmans** are offshore on SE and S winds respectively. Although lacking the consistency of the more open beaches, they occasionally produce magic conditions. Both breaks have a killer rip that won't let you stop paddling on NE–SE swells so be ready to work for your waves. North Stradbroke and Moreton have fair-sized surfing populations and well-established pecking orders. So bring your manners and take only a fair share of waves. If you get in tight with the crew they'll show you the scenery and fill you in on a rich island history that you would otherwise miss.

Moreton Island

Accessible by vehicular barge from Lytton, Redland Bay and Scarborough, Moreton is surprisingly close to Brisbane. However, Moreton and North Stradbroke are worlds apart. Moreton is 38 km long and 8 km at its widest. The second longest sand island in the world, it also has the two highest sand dunes in the world, with Mt Tempest at 280 m and Storm Mountain at 274 m.

Moreton is a back-to-basics surfing experience similar to Fraser Island. Although settlements exist, it is better to take everything you need and set up a good base camp near fresh water on the ocean beach. Moreton is much better if you're in walking distance to waves. 4WD's are required if you're planning to drive but local island taxis can drop you at appropriate camping spots for easy surfing. Swell direction doesn't matter too much.

Moreton has good waves along its eastern beaches, while the southern end handles mainly light SSW–W to light NW winds. The top end needs W or NW winds, but the banks are generally a bit shifty. Ideal swell size is from 3–6 ft.

Yellow Patch can handle huge swells

Above: Jake Spooner gives Frenchmans Beach at North Stradbroke Island a bit of backhand stick. *Photo: Peter Wilson*

Left: North Stradbroke Island line-up overview. *Photo: Peter Wilson*

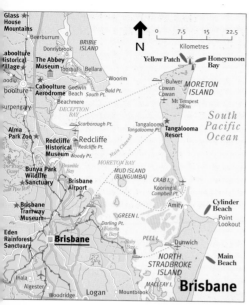

(when they eventually come), while Double Island's long inside beach is another popular location with knee-buckling rights running off the point. But a lack of swell, and abundance of sharks can be testing.

Double Island Point

Double Island Point can be found north of Noosa's rivermouth. The beach spreads NNE to the point for over 45 km. Along the beach, the shipwrecked *Cherry Venture* stands as testiment to the ocean's moods. The eastern beach features the renowned tinted sand cliffs and good beach breaks similar to Stradbroke and Moreton Islands. Beach camping is available from Little Freshwater Creek south for about 15 km to the coloured sands.

Excellent waves can be had along the eastern beach. Just north of the *Cherry Venture,* a boarded track crosses to **Rainbow Beach** about 2 km south of the point. Rainbow has a setup to match most breaks. However, like

Yellow Patch on Moreton, the lack of swell leaves the waves dormant for most of the year. The wait can drive the keen surfer batty. Still, when it's on, it's really on.

Fraser Island

All 184,000 ha of this beautiful island is World Heritage listed. The exposed eastern beach is 120 km long, with a fickle assortment of beach-breaks. Along the northern third of the beach, two quality righthanders wrap around **Indian Head** and **Waddy Point** but try to avoid peak holiday seasons—it's a long way to travel for a crowded wave.

Surrounded by crystal clear waters, Fraser is part of the **Great Sandy National Park** and the jewel in the crown of the five barrier islands that comprise the largest sand deposit in the world. The local wildlife, including inquisitive dingoes (seriously, be careful) and the spectacular beaches reward the effort required to explore this 350-km chain of surfable islands.

The Great Barrier Reef

The **Capricorn Coast**, named for the Tropic of Capricorn, stretches from Gladstone to Rockhampton, and marks the southern-most boundary of the Great Barrier Reef, which is comprised of 2,500 individual reefs, and covers a staggering area of 349,000 sq km. Adventurous surfers and local charter boat operators suggest there are literally thousands of surfable waves scattered amongst this spectacular maze of tropical cays and coral islands.

Exposed to the full fury of the predominant southeast winds, the shallow reef breaks are extremely fickle but a trip to the southern end of the **Swain Reefs** or a variety of other locations throughout the **Capricorn** and **Bunker Groups** can offer some pleasant surprises. Best surfed on larger ground swells, during January to June (cyclone season) the waves are usually fun, 2–4 ft peaks with the odd barrel. Occasionally the reef breaks take on a new dimension when 10–12 ft tubes steam over razor-sharp coral.

If you score it on, there's nothing quite like surfing by yourself in the middle of the Pacific Ocean, but unpredictable weather patterns, below deck accommodation, sea snakes, coral cuts and packs of reef sharks make it a trip for the committed seadog.

Left: South Straddie Island provides a consistent option for tube junkies in search of a fix. *Photo: Jane Lewis*

Below: There are literally hundreds of hollow peaks scattered throughout the Great Barrier Reef. *Photo: Simon Williams*

December–April.
(Cyclone Season)

All the best locations are next to each other. Drive or walk to all spots—a tube-riding heaven.

Mainly sand-covered reef with a forgiving bottom.

Boards for hollow waves. Remote control shark fin to keep the crowds at bay.

Drop-ins on double suck tube sections, nightclub benders.

Fin chops from flying surfboards or heavy barrel rolls. Safe sex!

World class point breaks, surfing in board shorts.

Below: Two worlds collide—the Burleigh Heads' tunnel of love and the Gold Coast highrizon.
Photo: Peter Wilson

The Gold Coast
A Surfer's Paradise

Situated just north of the Queensland/New South Wales border, the Gold Coast stretches for 42 km, from Coolangatta to Stradbroke Island. This region has some of the most perfect point and beach breaks in the world, and is recognised as the tourist capital of Australia.

A remarkable variety of man-made and natural attractions lure tourists from all corners of the globe, especially during the months from November to April. At this time the Queensland coast is hit by big swells created by cyclones in the Coral Sea. Unfortunately, catching your fair share of waves can involve a great deal of patience in crowded line-ups. Finding these waves is as easy as driving up or down the Gold Coast highway. There are no secrets on the Gold Coast—just good timing.

South Stradbroke Island

Situated at the northern extremity of this surf-rich coastline is South Stradbroke Island, or as the locals like to call it, TOS (The Other Side). Famous for its shallow, wedging barrels, it is best surfed on a small to moderate SE swell, with SW–W winds. On a southerly swell TOS is usually a foot or two higher than the rest of the Coast which is a saviour in the winter months or on flat days. The surf is most consistent around the sand dredging pipe but if you don't mind walking north a few hundred metres you can find your own spitting peaks. To get to TOS, drive to the far end of the **Southport Spit**, past Seaworld theme park. You will arrive at a large car park with cafe and toilet facilities. From here you can either paddle across or catch the rubber ducky for $6 return.

Southport Seaway

When the swell is huge the Southport Seaway is worth a check. Situated next to the northern wall in the rivermouth, this thundering lefthander is easily viewed from The Spit's northern car park and relies on dead tides to break at its optimum. Misjudge these tides and you may find yourself about a mile out to sea in shark-infested waters, so take care. The Seaway works in most winds and should usually be ridden on a longer board because of its intense take-off and long, powerful walls.

When the wind is NE your best bet for waves is at the **Southport Spit** on the southern side of the Southport Seaway. Take the sandy track situated next to the cafe, and you will usually find a fun wedging righthander peeling into the pier, and a long, winding left up the northern end of the beach, against the wall.

"Surfers" and South

Venturing south into the suburban concrete jungle, **Main Beach** and **Surfers Paradise** typifies most people's preconceived images of the Gold Coast. Surfers' long, sun-drenched, sandy beaches, night clubs, strip joints, restaurants, cafes and cheap tourist shops will keep you busy day and night if you're into that scene. Gold Coast's best shopping centre, Pacific Fair, and the famous Conrad Jupiters Casino are located here. You can find quite good beach breaks here on a moderate swell and northerly winds. These waves are worth checking for an uncrowded alternative to **The Spit**.

Another good call are the beach breaks from around **Broadbeach to Miami** which work in the same surf conditions as Surfers Paradise. It's definitely worth detouring off the Gold Coast Highway and checking along the beach road for some fun sandbanks.

Further south is **Nobbys Headland**, which is basically a continuation of the northern beach. It breaks (with the exception of the waves in the northern corner), handling more of a southerly wind. On the southern side of the headland the waves obviously prefer a northerly wind and occasionally boast a peaky lefthander. There are more waves along this beach heading down to **North Burleigh** which are liable to turn on every now and then.

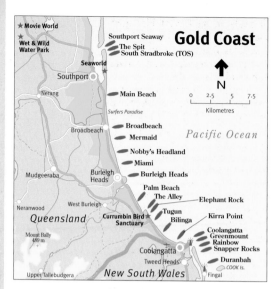

Burleigh Heads

Some of my earliest surfing memories are of days sitting under a Pandanus tree, freaking out at pros like Shaun Thompson and M.R. casually getting barrel after barrel in magical conditions at the sun-drenched Stubbies surfing contest. Obviously if you have surfed, you have heard of the mythical Burleigh barrel. **Burleigh Headland** probably handles the most size (up to 12 ft) on the coast and has the most power to back it up. Best surfed with a SW wind and a strong swell, Burleigh has perfect steep walls for big gouges and long tubing sections. The localism here is intense, so if you're an aggressive hassler, watch out! When the swell is big, it is worth your while running around the point and paddling out from the **Tallebudgera** rivermouth for a better chance of getting into the line up. On the other hand, when the swell is non-existent, head inland to Tallebudgera Valley for a hit of golf on the many cheap and cheerful courses.

South of the Tallebudgera River lies the surf-shacked avenues of **Palm Beach**. There are usually plenty of consistent banks around the many groynes of this area. A good bank with a healthy crowd can be found at both **25th Ave** and **15th Ave**. Best surfed on a moderate swell with N–SW winds, Palm Beach only handles up to 5 ft. It also has the tendency to develop an annoying rip in the larger swells.

Situated on the Currumbin Creek mouth, **The Alley** is a long, righthand point break, which breaks along a shallow sand bar, producing extensive walls to play on. The waves are deceiving in size from the car park, because of its distance. So if you see some lucky bastard weaving down the point on a walling wave into Laceys Lane, just past the river, then it's guaranteed fun.

Currumbin

Currumbin is perfect for that sneaky, quiet surf, when the swell is solid with a southerly wind and the other points like Burleigh and Kirra are saturated with crowds and aggro. On a moderate swell with light SW–NW winds, Currumbin and **Elephant Rock** beach breaks have some fun peaks. For a cool change, head inland 12 km, along the Currumbin Creek Road, for a refreshing swim in the natural environment of the Currumbin Rock Pools.

A couple of kilometres south of Currumbin is **Tugun**. Working in the same conditions as Elephant Rock and **Currumbin Beach**, Tugun doesn't quite pick up as much swell but is worth a check for the chance of an uncrowded peak. Usually best around **Flat Rock**, via Wagawn Street or in front of Breakers pub.

The next stop south is **Bilinga**, which shares the same beach and surf conditions but lacks slightly in the swell department. Worth a check if you're a beginner. Sometimes Bilinga breaks just a few times a year and requires a heavy swell and southerly wind.

Kirra Point

This famous break is a must for any competent surfer, and is worth the wait. Consisting of the **Big Groyne**, **The Point** and **Little Groyne**, Kirra guarantees you a lot of barrel time. Dropping in is a definite no-no out here and common sense goes a long way when it is crowded. Paddling out at Coolangatta, next to the Big Groyne is best, and before you know it, Kirra will conceal you within her magical, frothing blue womb. On a good day you can catch a wave all the way from the **Big Groyne** down to the Kirra Bakery and the Healthy Bee, which are great spots for a munch.

On the other side of the Big Groyne is **Coolangatta Beach** which stretches all the way down to the lush **Greenmount Headland**. Sometimes there are fun peaks along Coolangatta but usually if this beach is good, the points are better. Greenmount Headland on the other hand loves a moderate swell and southerly wind. It is best surfed at 2–5 ft and is perfect for long boarders and learners, but its long walls can prove playful for the competent surfer. On top of the headland you will find a great lookout and BBQ facilities for those hot, lazy surfed-out afternoons.

Rainbow Bay

Rainbow Bay, the next beach south, is perfect for learning to surf and has a definite family feeling about it. Here you will usually encounter all sorts of surf craft like goat-boaters, kids on boogie boards and mal riders. Rainbow's waves wall up best in a moderate to large swell with southerly winds.

Around the corner from Rainbow Bay is **Snapper Rocks**. Snapper picks up slightly more swell than the other southern points and works in the same conditions. There is a sucky, back washing take-off behind the rocks, and a long wall, which in a large swell can be ridden through Rainbow and into Greenmount. Snapper's boardwalk is a great auditorium for surveying the surf.

Sitting 100 m above the ocean at **Point Danger** with the car stereo blaring is the perfect way to check the waves and sand banks at **Duranbah**. Along with TOS, Duranbah picks up the most swell on the coast, especially from the south, and has a bunch of left and right wedging peaks breaking along its 200-m sandy shore. When the banks are good and the wind is a light southerly, Duranbah will have multiple spitting barrels from the southern wall to **Lovers** (the northern end of Duranbah). If not, there will be enough power to keep you happy, that's if the crowds don't get to you first.

—*Neal Purchase Jnr*

Over page: Rossi Phillips cruising in a Burleigh Heads barrel.
Photo: Simon Williams

Below: The Kirra corduroy. If you can handle the drop, the barrels are a perfect fit.
Photo: Simon Williams

The Premier State

Surfing Sites Galore

Preceding pages:
A legend in the making, young Aussie surf star Mick Campbell jams it up there high and fast.
Photo: Andrew Buckley

Opposite:
When you drop into a wave like this you realise you really don't give a damn about anything else. A secret North Coast haunt looking bloody perfect.
Photo: Bosko

New South Wales, lying between tropical Queensland and temperate Victoria in the southeast of the Australian landmass, has a pleasant sub tropical climate which favours all kinds of watersports. The bonus for surfers is that the Pacific Ocean and the Tasman Sea, caressing over 1,300 km of headlands and bays, delivers some of the most consistent swells in the country.

The state capital, Sydney, is Australia's first city and will be host for the 2000 Olympics. It is situated on Port Jackson, one of the world's finest natural harbours. The city is no stranger to big events, with the annual Sydney to Hobart Yacht Race, the internationally-acclaimed Gay and Lesbian Mardis Gras along with regular performances from the world's leading musicians and entertainers, attracting hundreds of thousands of visitors to the city each year. As Australia's premier tourist destination, Sydney takes it all in its stride, with the distinctive roof of its icon, the exquisite Opera House, mirroring the sails of the yachts which can be found sailing on the protected harbour waters.

Getting around Sydney's downtown area is easy. Good public transport and ample taxis service all the shopping and eating hot spots so sought after by international and domestic visitors. It is only a short walk from the city centre to infamous Kings Cross, with its strip joints and late-night restaurants, while the vibrant Bondi Beach is only a ten-minute train ride. Another short walk from the city is trendy Oxford Street, a shopping and fashion mecca.

Over 3.5 million people call the Sydney metropolitan area home, and the city's sprawling urban area has plenty to offer, including bustling bars and clubs, large entertainment venues, excellent harbourside restaurants and high rollin' trimmings such as the Star City casino.

There are 42 beaches within easy reach of the CBD, including Australian surfing's founding home at Freshwater Beach in the north. Sydneysiders spend a great deal of their time either surfing or soaking up the sun's rays on the beaches.

Right along the coastline, New South Wales is the state of origin for almost all of Australia's surfing World Champions and continues to produce the majority of the country's top competitive prospects.

The northern beaches, Manly and Narrabeen in particular, have bred many famous boardriders including Midget Farrelly, Simon Anderson, Damien Hardman, Barton Lynch, Tom Carroll, Pam Burridge and Layne Beachley. Narrabeen's Coke Classic and prestigious Pro Junior events along with Manly's Cleanwater Classic are big drawcards on the international surfing circuit, showcasing world surfing's future stars throughout the year.

Scenic Avalon, Newport and Whale Beach also have strong surfing traditions, as do Bondi and Bronte in the eastern suburbs. But once you've had enough of congested lineups, shopping and partying, the rest of New South Wales offers some magnificent scenery, surfing and other outdoor experiences.

Above: Sydney rocket scientist and frequent flyer, Koby Abberton uses waves as launching pads to other worlds.
Photo: Bill Morris

In less than 90 minutes you can reach the majestic Blue Mountains, although you'll need a lot longer to explore its deep gorges and dramatic surroundings. Named after the blue hue created by evaporating eucalyptus oil, the Blue Mountains National Park offers excellent hiking, mountain biking, base jumping and caving opportunities. Awesome locations such as the Three Sisters, Echo Point and Wentworth Falls are easily accessed and have-viewing platforms, while many other tracks lead deep into the park's 200,000 rugged hectares.

Heading north from Sydney to the industrial centre of Newcastle (home to the teenage rock supergroup silverchair and former four-times world surfing champion Mark Richards), a variety of great waves await, backdropped by steelworks smokestacks. Host of the annual Steel City Surfing Pro, this densely populated Central Coast port enjoys consistent waves and over 40 local pubs offer a colourful nightlife.

In contrast, the Holiday Coast, which stretches from the sprawling Great Lakes area to Byron Bay, is a popular destination for surfers seeking laid-back barrels in pristine sub-tropical settings. Classic point break setups such as Lennox Head, Broken Head and Angourie are truly spectacular when they pump and

there's plenty of rainforest and golden beaches to explore on calm days.

An hour's drive to the south of Sydney will bring you to the Royal National Park and surfing strongholds such as Cronulla, Garie Beach, Wombarra and Wollongong, where quality point, reef and beach breaks abound. You can't beat the national park's Stanwell Tops for a panoramic view of the coast—people flock to this classic hang-gliding site.

Further to the south lie hardcore surfing destinations such as Huskison and Ulladulla, where some of Australia's most perfect waves such as the Black Rock lefthander and a variety of semi-secret reefs and point breaks have to be ridden to be believed. The water's a little cooler but the crowds are minimal and the waves can be unbelievable—a surf trip just waiting to happen.

During the winter months, from June to August, the Snowy Mountains entice both snowboard and ski devotees to Australia's highest point, Mt Kosciusko (2,228 m). The Snowy Mountains offer world-class resort facilities and great ski runs at Perisher-Blue and Thredbo.

Wherever you chose to travel in this diverse state you are sure to be made welcome—even the grumpiest local wave-hogs loosen up by the end of the day!

—*Mark Thornley*

The North Coast
Classic Righthand Points

NSW's North Coast is the less glamorous but more groovy cousin to the Gold Coast. It's hairier, hippier and far more brooding, but can still produce the flawless perfection that Queensland's points are famous for.

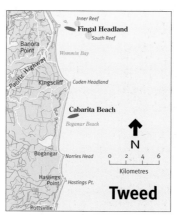

Below: Lennox Head is renowned for its gaping barrels and down-the-line walls. Here, Michelle Donoghue splays a nice fan off the inside section. *Photo: Terry Willcocks*

The Tweed

Beginning at Tweed Heads, which is so close to the Gold Coast that you could piss into a nor'easter and still make it across the Tweed River to Duranbah, you will immediately notice that the surfing vibe is super mellow.

The nearby **Fingal Headland** works in most swells with a SW wind and is reasonably protected in a SE wind. Although the headland can produce some excellent waves, the place is extremely fickle and you need to be aware of the condition of the banks. Home to a large Aboriginal community, you should respect their turf as they are locals in the truest sense. During summer the back beach can be heaps of fun and its ideal conditions are simply opposite to the main beach.

Home to Top 44 surfer Shane Bevan and legendary '80s surf band

The Sunnyboys, **Kingscliff** is renowned for its classic breakwall righthander that on rare occasions peels like Kirra. The back beach can also deliver some fun waves on northerly breezes. Host to the 1983 Australian Titles, **Cabarita** has a point break that can occasionally crank. Who could forget that shot of Gary Elkerton coming out of a barrel giving the two finger salute for victory? That was Cabarita at its finest, but to be honest I can't say I've seen it like that since. But hey, this time the banks could happen, you'll never know until you check it out. It's good in SW and SE winds

January–July.

Good roads and signage to most locations. Some 4WD and boat access to more remote waves.

Sand-covered reef, soft sand bottoms, breakwalls and sharp reefs.

A full quiver of boards. Spring suits in summer; a light steamer in winter.

Suck rocks, strong currents, and first setwave wipeouts in some impact zones.

Reef cuts and fin chops inside closeout beachbreak barrels.

Some of Australia's classic righthand point breaks. Cool beachside hangs and cultural festivals.

and the swell direction depends on the banks. The back beach can be excellent on its day too.

Hastings Point and **Pottsville** are very similar—both have potential for a good right point, both have back beaches and both have caravan parks full of beautiful young girls throughout the summer holidays.

The coast road south of Pottsville also offers plenty of potential for exploration. **New Brighton** and **Brunswick Heads** are sleepy looking places, but if you take a look around you'd be surprised by what you find. Both the south and north sides produce solid peaks and the river mouth breakwall can also reel off a few slashable waves. North winds for the southside and south winds for the northside, it's pretty obvious when you're there.

Byron Bay

Byron Bay is for the surfer who enjoys the luxuries of the city and simply cannot enjoy a hardcore surf trip without them. Cafes abound, providing vibrant meeting places for a melting pot of people. Most of the waves ridden at **The Pass** are on mals. A good option in cyclone swells, most of the region's point and beach breaks enjoy good protection from southerly winds. Banks permitting, **Tallows** is absolutely awesome with north winds and a solid south swell turning the hollow righthanders into liquid magic. **Suffolk Park** has good left and many right beachies and lots of hippies. Another quality righthander, **Broken Head** can also have incredible waves and is flanked by beautiful rainforest that covered most of the coast before the farmers and cows took to it.

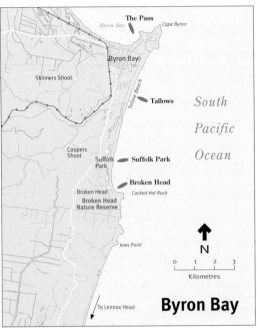

Byron Bay

Lennox Head/Ballina

Open to a little more swell, the Lennox-Ballina area is generally gruntier than Byron. There are no cafe lattes after surfing here, only meat pies, chocolate milk and cream buns! **Lennox Head**, one of the Holiday Coast's premier locations, can handle big swells with ease. NE swells and SW winds are the best, but a southerly swell can be good too. When the long righthander is in full cry, there's plenty of room for big top-turns and down-the-line barrels.

Between Lennox and Ballina there are a few spots that are definitely worth having a look at if you are feeling adventurous. For a start, **North Wall Ballina** can pack some

Ballina

hollow pits. Breaking a bit like Duranbah, it works under the same conditions and actually picks up more swell than its Queensland counterpart.

Similarly, **South Wall Ballina** is also a treat. Northerly winds and an E–SE swell are perfect for the rebound wedges that jack up against the groyne before spiralling down the beach.

Evans Head is another quiet town with some well-guarded secrets. Conditions here are much the same as for Byron, Broken Head and Lennox.

Iluka/Angourie

Further south, the **Iluka Breakwall** on the northern side of the Clarence River can produce some chunky peaks and is most famous, in my opinion, for the Bad Billies Billabong video footage of Matt Branson and Jason Buttonshaw shredding in the late '80s. South winds and north or southerly swells are what is required to ensure some uncrowded joy.

On the southside of the Clarence is **Yamba**. Look around and you'll find many surfing nooks and crannies, but ideally you'll want to surf **Angourie**, one of the finest wave locations on the north coast. Here you'll find a bowly, extremely

workable righthander, and a crafty pack of talented older generation surfers that tend to preside over the best waves at the Point, so watch your step.

Most notorious of all is one Baddy Treloar. He shapes, he rips and if he tells you to beat it, you take heed. "Anga", as it's parochially known, is also home to surfing identities such as Rod Dahlberg and Nat Young who runs his own tourist resort called Nat's Place, catering specifically for surfers.
—*Shaun Munro*

Above: Chris Slattery doesn't let the audience down and pulls into a screaming blue Byron Bay barrel. *Photo: Terry Willcocks*

Overleaf: Craig Cornish projects off the bottom on an overhead day at North Ballina breakwall. *Photo: Terry Willcocks*

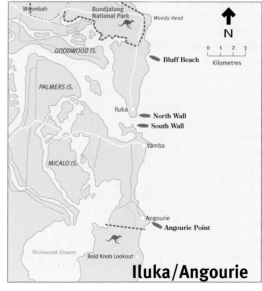

Iluka/Angourie

Surfing THE Dreamtime
WITH Australia's Vibe Tribe

by Mark Thornley

Like the early Hawaiian Kings, Australia's surfing ancients were undoubtedly indigenous. While no official evidence exists of the Kooris and Noongahs "shooting the curl", the country's coastal Aborigines must have surfed for eons, riding the waves with crude craft used to fish and navigate the surrounding waters. Like any adventurous surfers, many tribespeople would have seen the potential to transform dugout canoes or buoyant flora into hours of fun. We're talkin' the Originals, the pioneers of extreme sports.

Embodying the fundamental forces of land and sea, wind and the fire, generations of Aboriginal storytellers have preserved the epic struggles of the Dreamtime spirits. Uluru (Ayers Rock) and the Bungle Bungles are spectacular visible shrines of these subtle balances. But in surfing terms, perhaps, Wave Rock located near Hyden in Western Australia—a 50 ft high, radioactive-red rock looming ominously like a tsunami Pipeline barrel—is the most striking ancient symbol of this popular Australian pastime.

Over the past decades, Aboriginal people have excelled at many pro sports, including tennis, athletics and football, however, surfboard riding is a relatively new sport. In the '80s, Coffs Harbour's Andrew Ferguson and Cabarita's Gavin Dickinson paved the way for young indigenous surfers with outstanding performances in a variety of national junior surfing competitions. Later, in 1991, WA's Ken Dann became the first Aborigine to represent Australia in the surfing World Championships, touring Tahiti and Barbados.

But it was in 1993, when Billabong held the inaugural Indigenous Pro Surfing Invitational, that Aboriginal surfing truly exploded at Wreck Bay on NSW's south coast. Competing in hollow lefthanders, regarded as Australia's equivalent to Hawaii's Pipeline, over 60 of Australia's best Koori surfers blew the minds of local spectators, the OZ surf media and even surprised themselves.

Seminal Aboriginal boardrider Stephen Williams, who began surfing in 1973, remembers that day of colourful culture and full-blooded tube rides that changed many of his friends' lives.

"Being an Aboriginal, I've learnt that the only time you'd get to see your cousins or relatives was at funerals or weddings—mainly funerals, because you didn't have to be invited.

"Then one day I heard about this Koori Surf Comp. I thought to myself, how many Koori

surfers are there really? Finally when the big day arrived, I climbed out of my car with tears in my eyes. What I saw, words can't describe; as far as the eye can see, Koori brothers shaking hands, talking about surfing, and everyone had the biggest smiles on their faces", he said.

Since then, Stephen and fellow Aboriginal surfer Kevin Slabb have been instrumental in co-ordinating a variety of indigenous surfing events which led to the formation of a national Aboriginal surfing body named Indigenous Surf (IS).

Working in close association with Surfing Australia Inc, IS was incorporated during 1998 and is currently developing its own circuit of Aboriginal events. With literally thousands of keen Koori surfers ready to rip, IS is already planning to expand the current Billabong Indigenous Invitational competitions throughout NSW and WA. Further contests are proposed for Newcastle's Surfest and the original Koori Invitational venue at Wreck Bay.

IS was originally established to assist talented Koori juniors make the transition to the super competitive professional ranks, but no one predicted it would become a focal point for what is fast becoming a burgeoning new industry amidst the already vibrant Australian beach culture.

Aboriginal surf bands, clothing companies, artists and board shapers have not only emerged from the aftermath of the world music sensation Yothu Yindi, but are also thriving alongside a growing indigenous surfing population.

Doolagahs Surfwear, the brainchild of Wreck Bay surfer Shane Martin, is a clothing company marketing indigenous designs from Steve Dixon and other Aboriginal artists. Doolagahs raises cultural awareness by passing on Koori legends to tourists, school kids and politicians. Reaching deep into Koori culture, the Doolagah is a Dreamtime legend of the Wildman, a spirit figure that lived in the bush while caring for the forest and the sea. Consolidating Aboriginal surfing's identity and sponsorship, Doolagahs is fast gaining momentum in the Australian surfing mainstream, and has recently received export inquiries from a variety of European surf merchandisers.

Fusing contemporary surfing with an ancient culture, the prestigious Billabong Indigenous Surfing Invitational event serves

Opposite: Fingal Dancers. *Photo: Peter Wilson*

Above: Top Koori competitor, Gavin Dickinson flies through the song line of a Wreck Bay reform. *Photo: Peter Wilson*

Below: Joey Brown, one of many hot indigenous surfers who are flying the Aboriginal flag out in the surf. *Photo: Peter Wilson*

as both a contest and a gathering—a rich cultural exchange back-dropped by ceremonial dancers and didgeridoos. The cream of Australia's Aboriginal and Torres Strait Island juniors compete in the main event, while hot surfing talent from five other Pacific nations including Papua New Guinea, Indonesia, Hawaii, New Zealand and Fiji vie for the other individual and teams titles.

Nominated for one of the 6th Aboriginal and Torres Strait Islander Awards, this annual contest has helped many young indigenous surfers gain self-esteem, sponsorship and some handy prize money. The prestigious Billabong event based at Fingal Headland, in northern NSW,

now carries a prize purse of $10,000.

Kevin Slabb, the recently appointed president of Indigenous Surf, is in a unique position to appreciate the full significance of competitive and recreational surfing for Aboriginal communities throughout Australia. The father of three surf-mad and successful sons—Kyle, Joel and Josh—Slabb Snr dances a fine line between heaven and hell. A devoted surfer of 40 years, he washes his own problems away in the ocean before travelling to work each day to immerse himself in the turmoils of others. A drug and alcohol counsellor with the NSW Health Department, he knows full well the perils of boredom amidst cultural isolation.

Kevin believes surfing is an opportunity for young Aborigines to overcome the associated pressures of racial prejudice and drug abuse. By enjoying a potential career that is not only fun and exciting, he believes surfing can help guide generations of children away from booze and domestic violence and back to an ocean of heritage.

"I've seen so much trauma amongst my people that I thank God every time I see my boys out in the surf", he said.

"It's not just a healthy lifestyle. It's respecting life. They're not out taking drugs. Whenever they know there's going to be surf, they're up before it's light and heading for the waves. I know where they are and that they're lovin' it. What more could I ask for?"

Renowned for their radical surfing, the Slabb family is a tight unit and continue to perform their well-known dance and didgeridoo presentations at many surfing events.

Inspired by a 1995 international surfing cul-

tural exchange with Hawaii's notorious Hui O He'e Nalu, the most feared and famous board-riding club in the world, the Slabbs and other leading indigenous surfers, including Andrew Ferguson and Gavin Dickinson (two times winner Billabong Indigenous Invitational), returned to Australia with renewed enthusiasm.

After riding Pipeline, Haliewa and Sunset (to themselves), their surfing improved dramatically. Spurred on by the encouragement of the Da Hui "Blackshorts", they began spreading the vision of an exciting future for indigenous surfing both as a sport and a career.

Josh, who was recently honoured as a United Nations' Marine Ambassador for the International Year of the Ocean, also travelled to Fiji's famous Cloudbreak to contest the 1998 Rip Curl Oceania Surfing Cup.

Joined by outstanding indigenous juniors such as Ty Arnold, Paul Evans and Ken Dann, Aboriginal surfers are now attracting significant sponsorship from large companies. By lobbying the Australian Sports Commission and Indigenous Sports Unit for scholarships and support for international competition, Surfing Australia Inc has already raised close to $47,000 to help many wide-eyed kids celebrate their Aboriginality through surfing tournaments.

Andrew Ferguson, winner of the 1996 Billabong Indigenous Classic, continues his surfing globetrotting with Billabong, having honed a radical style that invites comparisons with Mark Occhilupo and has won him wide-ranging financial support. His reputation is right up there alongside Ken Dann's and Gavin Dickinson's as one of indigenous surfing's premier competitive talents.

Of course there are a host of other hot Aboriginal locals, including Nick Carter, Todd Roberts and Barrie Chanell, who make pulling into a dredging 6 ft barrel over dry reef look ridiculously easy. Epitomising the fluid, loose-limbed approach that distinguishes the swelling ranks of Australia's Koori surfers, they sure look like they've been doing it for thousands of years.

Opposite above: Ken Dann's radical backhand attack has established him as one of Australia's premier surfers. *Photo: Peter Wilson*

Opposite below: Frozen in time like 50 ft Pipeline about to pitch and barrel, Wave Rock at Hyden, WA is a fascinating example of the millennial forces that shaped our landscapes and oceans. Imagine getting clubbed by the lip after dropping into this monster. *Photo: WATC*

Above: Andrew Ferguson's radical moves and fine-tuned vertical control have taken him wave dreaming all over the world. *Photo: Peter Wilson*

Below: Len Collard summons the swell at Rottnest Island, WA. *Photo: Peter Wilson*

The Mid North Coast
Super Mellow Surfing Vibes

Preceding pages:
A Coffs Harbour
deep throat dredge
that keeps you pad-
dling back for more.
Photo: Bill Morris

Literally hundreds of quality breaks occur around these parts. I can't even begin to give you a run-down of them all— so feel free to explore. It's a great region for camping out and even attempting to catch your own fish for supper.

Coffs Harbour/ Crescent Head

At Coffs Harbour the focus shifts from point breaks to beach breaks. Here, **Arrawarra**, **Mullaway** and **Moonee Creek** can all produce

good waves on a variety of condi- tions but perhaps the pick of the waves are found at **Sawtell** and **Valla** which can offer excellent bar- rels during offshore conditions and a reasonable swell.

Scotts Head is a fantastic spot. A superb righthand point break, Scotts starts crackin' on a solid SE swell and SW winds. It's guaranteed to get you stoked and if you're polite to the locals, you'll get your share of waves.

Crescent Head is another great righthand point break that is steeped in surfing mysticism as a result of its popularity with pioneer- ing surfers during the '50s. A long wave offering some fun sections, it prefers conditions similar to Scotts Head, but tends to line up better on swells with an easterly bent.

Port Macquarie/Old Bar

From here, you can go in search of your own secret spots by following the dirt road that runs along the coast from Crescent Head to Port Macquarie. Unless conditions are extraordinary you'll probably only find the odd peak here although **Plomers Point** can offer OK waves.

Port Macquarie is a fairly hap- pening place with lots of good quali- ty beach breaks on shallow sandbars and a rivermouth that can produce long, rifling barrels. Best on a solid north swell and south winds, **Lighthouse Beach** has good peaky waves and is protected from the summer NE breeze.

Taree doesn't have any waves at all, but the locals do run an annual speed boat race on the river, which is adjacent to the main street. Good

Coffs Harbour

Red Rock

Dirty Ck.

BREAKER ROCKS

Corindy River
Corindi Beach

Solitary Islands
Marine Reserve

Arrawarra
Arrawarra Ck.
● Arrawarra

● Mullaway

Woolgoolga Reef
Woolgoolga T.S.
244m
● **Woolgoolga Beach**
Woolgoolga
Woolgoolga Ck.
Flat Top Pt.

Bare Bluff

Emerald Beach
Look At Me Now Headland

Monee Beach
● **Moonee Creek**
Green Bluff
Woody Hill
209m
Mid Saphire Beach

End Peak
365m
Korora
Diggers Head
MacCauleys Headland
● **Coffs Harbour**

Coffs Harbour
Coffs Ck.
Coffs Harbour
✈
Boambee

★ **Bayside Gallery**
● **Sawtell Beach**
Sawtell

South Pacific Ocean

7.5

↑
N

0   2.5   5   7.5
Kilometres

value if you happen to catch it. Thirty minutes from Taree is trusty **Old Bar**, home to many surfers, with some good back beaches in northerly winds. There is also **Saltwater Point**, a chunky, rock-bottom point that peels for 200 m or so when it's good. If you're in the area, and a solid south or east swell combines with southerly winds, you could find yourself threading some powerful barrels at this wave haunt.

___

Forster/Tuncurry

Tuncurry is your next stop and the rivermouth has quite a reputation for converting large NE cyclone swells into long, 8 ft-plus power pits. It's also notorious for the old, "you shoulda been here yesterday mate" statement. Don't you hate it when someone tells you that?

Between the clear, green waters of **Forster** and **Seal Rocks**, there are a host of good back beaches and southerly corners. A short drive out of town, **One Mile Beach** kicks off an excellent stretch of beach breaks including **Boomerang**, **Bluey's** and **Sandbar** or **Stiletto's**. It's simply a matter of surfing the back beaches in northerly winds and the southerly corners when the wind swings around to the south. There are plenty of Bazzas on offer, including one particularly insane righthand setup that has a well-defined takeoff zone

and can get extremely hollow.

All of the beaches are easily accessible except for southern Sandbar, but if you're keen and

Above: Angourie locals lead the pack.
Photo: Dick Hoole

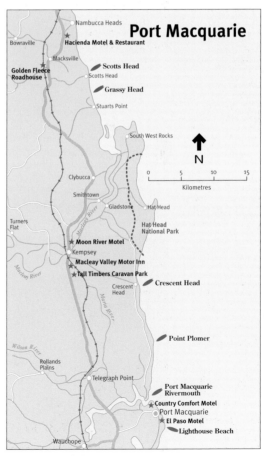

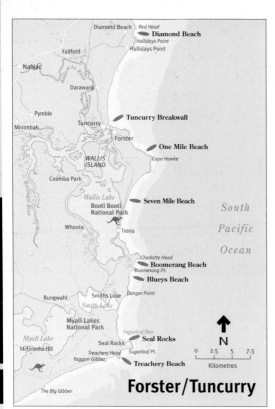

Diamond Beach
Red Head
Diamond Beach
Hallidays Point
Hallidays Point
Failford
Nabiac
Darawank
Pymble
Tuncurry Breakwall
Minimbah
Tuncurry
Forster
One Mile Beach
WALLIS ISLAND
Cape Hawke
Coomba Park
Wallis Lake
Booti Booti
National Park
Seven Mile Beach
South
Pacific
Ocean
Whoota
Tiona
Charlotte Head
Boomerang Beach
Boomerang Pt.
Blueys Beach
Bungwahl
Smiths Lake
Danger Point
Smith Lake
Myall Lakes
National Park
Sugarloaf Bay
Myall Lake
Seal Rocks
Seal Rocks
N
McGranths Hill
Treachery Head
Sugarloaf Pt.
0   2.5   5   7.5
Yaggon Gibber
Treachery Beach
Kilometres
The Big Gibber

Forster/Tuncurry

Below: Tequilla sunrise.
Photo: Terry Willcocks

January–July.

Good roads and signs to most locations. Some 4WD and boat access to more remote waves.

Sand-covered reef, soft sand bottoms, breakwalls and reefs.

A full quiver of boards. Spring suits in summer; a light steamer in winter.

Suck rocks, strong currents, cyclones.

Reef cuts and fin chops inside shallow beachbreak barrels.

Excellent, uncrowded hollow beach breaks.

astute enough, you'll find your own way there. There's also a nudist beach between One Mile and Boomerang.

Travelling further south, **Seal Rocks** is a famous venue for the timeless Australian tradition of spending the long weekend on a family camping expedition. A favourite place for beach parties, it's usually a good time and place to meet people. According to my father, I was conceived at such a gathering, on the bonnet of an old HQ station wagon. With regards to the surf, though, the point at Seal Rocks is generally slow, with a fat right-hander that requires lots of northerly swell and a southerly wind, but it can occasionally produce decent waves. If you're into swimming with sharks, there's some great diving to be had in the nearby Grey Nurse breeding grounds under the guidance of local charter operators.

A short drive from Seal Rocks along a gravel and sand road, **Treachery Beach** is the ideal back beach. Offshore in a NE wind, it picks up more swell than most places along this stretch and produces idyllic A-frame peaks up and down the beach. There's even a few reef wedges and bombies to explore if you walk further south.

A great place to surf, fish and chill, Treachery has an idyllic caravan park nestled behind the large sand dunes. The subject of local mythology, apparently something known as the Yagen Monster prowls Treachery's surrounding sandhills. Maybe it's true or maybe the creature is the product of too much dope and mushrooms during the '60s, who knows? Sounds like a local surfing crowd deterrent to me.
—*Shaun Munro*

The following two locations are a tad outside the shores of New South Wales proper, but are superb spots.

Lord Howe Island

A subtropical paradise situated less than 600 km east of Port Macquarie, Lord Howe Island offers some good surfing on the world's southern-most coral reefs. Backdropped by spectacular volcanic peaks, lush rainforest and a tranquil coral lagoon, hollow left and right peaks can be accessed by boat at mid tide with easterly winds. The outer reefs of the **Jetty** and **Lovers Bay** can be particularly good on a moderate swell.

The **Blinky Beach** righthander at **Half Moon Reef** can also get very challenging as can a righthand reef break at **Middle Beach**. Since a maximum of 400 visitors is allowed on the island at any one time (mostly non-surfers, thank goodness), there is a good chance that just you and a few locals will be threading some palm-fringed barrels. There's also some amazing diving, hiking and gamefishing to experience. Eastern Airlines have regular flights departing from Sydney to Lord Howe Island. Check it out!

Norfolk Island

Located 1600 km NE of Sydney, Norfolk Island has truly evolved in isolation. Tax free and with local residents listing their nicknames in the phonebook, the island has its own unique cuisine, laws, rare wildlife and empty lineups. Since the island is almost encircled by steep cliffs, the southern end is virtually the only place to surf and swim, but there are variety of crowd-free and consistent breaks to enjoy. The island's official language is English but locals also speak Norfolk. Ansett Airlines flies to Norfolk Island daily from Sydney and Brisbane.

—*Mark Thornley*

Above: One of NSW's few outer islands, Lord Howe offers a variety of uncrowded reef and beach breaks. This is Half Moon Reef at Blinkys Beach. *Photo: PoWWow*

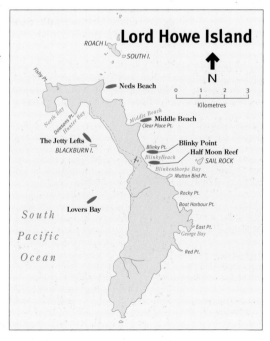

Lord Howe Island map showing: ROACH I., SOUTH I., Fishy Pt., Neds Beach, North Bay, Dowsons Pt., Hunter Bay, Middle Beach, Clear Place Pt., The Jetty Lefts, BLACKBURN I., Blinky Pt., BlinkyBeach, Blinky Point, Half Moon Reef, SAIL ROCK, Blinkenthorpe Bay, Mutton Bird Pt., Rocky Pt., Boat Harbour Pt., Lovers Bay, East Pt., George Bay, Red Pt., South Pacific Ocean. Scale 0–3 Kilometres. N (north arrow).

Newcastle and the Central Coast

Home to Champions

The densely populated industrial city of Newcastle and the service centre of Gosford are the focal points of the Central Coast. This 150-km stretch of coastline offers a vast assortment of consistent point, reef and beach breaks.

The region supports a hardcore surfing population more interested in double tube rides than the latest fashions, and has spawned some of Australia's most respected surfers. Four-times world champion Mark Richards, and contemporary power-houses such as Luke Egan, Nick Wood, Simon Law and Matt Hoy, all honed their skills in the local waves that, on a good day, can exceed 8 ft.

Nelson Bay

A small 150 m wide sand strip that loves small NE and SE swells, **Box Beach** produces quality shore-breaks that wedge at either end and provide short, round waves that are a ton of fun in SW to SE winds.

Fingal Spit, 500 m further south, is an island and sand spit that provides a natural formation to funnel NE swells accompanied by SW winds. Fingal's long righthanders can break up to 10 ft but are ideally surfed around 6–8 ft.

Perhaps the most popular beach in the Nelson Bay area is **One Mile.** A lefthand point at the north-ern end winds off down the line in a good NE swell, while a rocky out-crop in the middle is consistently surfable in small to medium SE–NE swells. There's also a right point at the other end that allows an easter-ly swell to wrap 90° around it to mould some well-formed waves.

Further south is **Morna Point**, a spot that makes summer a tad more enjoyable because it's off-shore in NE winds and loves small to medium-sized NE swells. It's a good fun wave that's frequented by touring pro and big wave legend Simon Law.

Stockton

Fifteen kilometres south of Morna Point lies **Stockton**, one of the longest stretches of uninterrupted beach in the area. Roughly in the middle lies half of the coal ship *The Sigma*, a victim of the 1975 cyclone. Either side of the wreck, great sand banks can offer hollow left and rights, but be prepared to share the waves with the local sharks who live in the guts of the nearby rusty hull. The Stockton end has produced some great surfers including '60s vintage Ron Rudder and, more recently, three-time state champ Damien Iredale. All have cut their teeth on the consistent beach breaks that are generally at their best during NE swells and W–SW winds.

Newcastle

In the heart of this steel city is **Nobbys Beach**, situated near the lighthouse at the harbour entrance. It's home to a multitude of breaks, including a wedging left that comes off the breakwall, a sand spit left, a lefthand rock reef, a surging right-hand rock shelf and finally **Nobbys Bank**. This is a sand-dredging left which honed the legendary tube-riding skills of the likes of Peter

January–July.

Good roads and carpark convenience to most breaks.

Cungie reef, sand-covered reef, and sand bottoms on beachbreaks.

Mid-range boards for 3–5 ft waves and a good big gun for larger swells.

Strong currents, sting rays, dumped effluent and some sharky areas.

Reef cuts, ear infec-tions and horren-dous shorebreak closeouts.

Uncrowded beaches. Excellent, hollow beach breaks.

McCabe and Roger Clements in the '70s.

To the south lies **Newcastle Beach**, the home of Surfest, Newcastle's contribution to pro-surfing. In a good NE swell and NW winds this lefthand point can produce waves that will hold up to 12 ft if the swell is clean. "Newie's" main beach offers consistent beach breaks that love the summer months as NE winds blow cross-shore.

The next stretch to the south comprises Bar Beach, **Dixon Park** and the ever-reliable Merewether. At the northern end lies **Bar Beach**, a rock, cungie reef that provides good running lefts in NE swells and NW winds. This left may not hold great size, but it does pack some punch.

Next down the line is **Dixon Park Beach**, which has been known to handle the odd 10–12 ft NE swell. Apart from big NE swells, it's possibly one of the most consistent areas for good banks in varying swells. Dixon is the home of '70s tube-demon Peter Cornish.

At the southern end is **Merewether**, a prominent righthander that breaks on three separate rock shelves. Holding the biggest of swells—up to 15 ft, Merewether offers consistent waves in most conditions. The high-performance faces make it a popular choice with many local and travelling surfers.

Next down the coast is **Dudley Beach**, a beach break that enjoys small NE swells and NW winds, often providing fun peaks all the way along its shores. There is also a lefthand rock shelf at the northern end and an obscured right that holds big south swells.

Above: Brenden "Margo" Margieson body-torques through a backhand snap at The Entrance. *Photo: Mark Newsham*

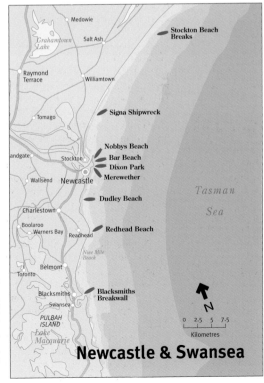

Newcastle & Swansea

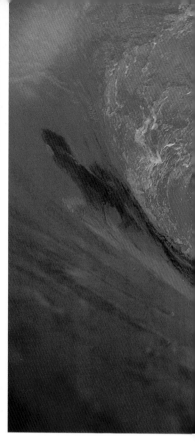

Central Coast

Doyalson
Wyee
Munmorah Lake
Budgewoi
Toukley
Norah Head
Norahville
Tuggerah Beach
Jilliby
Wyong
Tuggerah Lake
Entrance North
Pelican Beach
The Entrance
The Entrance
Wyong Creek
Tuggerah
Shelly Beach
Tasman
Sea
Ourimbah
Forresters Beach
Terrigal
Terrigal
Erina
Avoca Point
Gosford
Copacabana
Avoca Beach
McMasters Beach
MacMasters Beach
N
Brisbane Water National Park
Woy Woy
Ettalong
Box Head
Kilometres
Umina
Bouddi National Park
0   5   10   15
Broken Bay

Redhead

At the north of a 15-km stretch of beach is **Redhead**, which provides year-round waves of all shapes and sizes. Once home to the late Col Smith, who made his mark at Hawaii's Pipeline towards the end of the '70s and early '80s, this beach attracts the best of any NE swell, as Nelson Bay prevents it from fully entering the area. This provides some great long-running lefts aided by two creeks that deposit sand further down the beach.

The other end of the stretch is **Blacksmiths**, a beach generally lacking quality-shaped waves. However when a decent 6–8 ft NE swell squeezes through the wave window, the breakwall that shelters the entrance to Lake Macquarie can go off, both in the channel itself and beside the wall. This is where MR first put his feet on a surfboard and it's still a great place to learn those basic skills.

Caves Beach

On the other side of the entrance to Lake Macquarie are **Hams Beach** and **Caves Beach**. Hams has consistent beach breaks, working best in NW swells and NW winds, with Caves preferring a southerly swell, as an outside reef between the two beaches prevents a NE swell from entering.

Catherine Hill Bay

Ten kilometres south is the mining town of **Catherine Hill Bay**, with boasts one of the most consistent southern beaches, due mainly to its half-moon shape. Capable of handling swells up to 8 ft, with NE and SE directions, accompanied by SW–NW winds, it's very versatile, consistent and powerful at times.

Fraser Park

Eight kilometres further south is **Fraser Park**, a 300 m-wide national park beach that has a consistent left and right at opposite ends of the beach. Arrive on any small NE or SE swell, and a NW wind, and you'll find one of these breaks going off. Just south of here and still in the national park is **Birdie Beach**, which works in similar conditions to Fraser, but is around 6 km longer. Both breaks are great fun through the summer months, but be prepared to pay the daily national park fee (otherwise get yourself a park pass which is valid for a year and gives you access to all NSW parks).

Norah Head

Norah Head is a breeding ground for great surfers. With places like **Boat Ramps** and the **Bombie** blowing offshore in S–SE winds, and **Soldiers** doing the same in NE winds, just about any swell will provide good surfable waves somewhere within the area.

Opposite: Simon Law doin' his thing at a Newcastle beach.
Photo: Peter Wilson

Above: Luke Hitchings eases off the throttle and waits for the hot breath of the foamball.
Photo: Bill Morris

The Entrance

A little further south you'll find **Pelican Beach**, another NE offshore locale providing good beach breaks year-round. At the southern end of the beach is the popular tourist town of The Entrance. This place blows offshore in NW winds and prefers more swell from the east or south.

Five kilometres south is **Shelley Beach**, which offers a lefthand rock shelf and sometimes superb beach breaks that spit some awesome barrels. Blowing offshore in NW winds, this location is best surfed on NE or SE swells.

Wamberal/Terrigal

Forresters Beach has an outside bombie capable of holding up to 10–15 ft southerly swells, while a smattering of quality beach breaks provide consistent surfing. Up over the hill is **Wamberal Beach**, which enjoys some good beach breaks in E–NE swells and NW offshore winds.

The same stretch of beach has a bow in it, and at the other end is the pretty town of **Terrigal**. The surf at **Terrigal Haven** is renowned for holding big southerly swells that pump solid rights down and around the point, keeping the local talent pool more than happy.

Avoca

North Avoca requires NE swells and NW winds, while **Avoca** itself enjoys SE–S swells and southerly winds that get scenic the righthand point happening. Avoca's consistent waves have nurtured many a pro surfer and when conditions click there are no shortage of quality pits.

Copacabana/Ocean Beach

Further south is another pointbreak at **McMasters Beach**, which loves an easterly swell and SW winds to get it happening.

Copacabana prefers a southerly swell and a NE–NW wind. Both breaks are frequented by the Avoca boys when they want a bit of variety.

Last but not least, **Ocean Beach** thrives on southerly swells and NW winds. There is also a semi-secret rivermouth break out on the northern headland so a bit of exploring around here will reveal a few surprises.

—*Greg Keegan*

Sydney's Northern Beaches

Fast Waves, Fast Times

Preceding pages: Wetsuit free, a relaxed surfer confronts a frothy North Avalon peak. *Photo: Peter Wilson*

A surfing creche for generations of hot young Aussie boardriders, Sydney's northern beaches offer a huge variety of waves for surfers of all levels. After hours you can catch the action at heaps of surf pubs where touring bands hit the rhythm sticks until all hours.

Palm Beach/Whale Beach

Palm Beach is probably best known for its exclusive houses and as the location for a popular TV soap opera. Also home to the rich and famous,

Northern Sydney

Patonga
LION I.
Brooklyn
Barrenjoeys Head
Palm Beach
Barrenjoey
The Wedge
Whale Beach
Ku-Ring-Gai Chase National Park
Avalon
North Avalon
Little Avalon
Church Point
Bilgola
Bilgola Beach
Newport
Newport Peak
Bungan Beach
Mona Vale
Mona Vale
South
Terrey Hills
Turimetta Beach
Pacific
Bobbin Ferry
Narrabeen
The Alley
Carpark Rights
Ocean
Collaroy
Long Reef
No Man's Land
Pymble
Dee Why
Dee Why Point
Curl Curl Beach
Queenscliff
Manly
North Steyne
Fairy Bower
Chatswood
North Head
South Head
N
Watson's Bay
0 2 4 6
Kilometres
Drummoyne
Dover Heights
Sydney
Bondi

"Palmy" is not renowned for epic surf but rather the 500-metre closeout. However, there can be value south of **Elephant Rock**—towards **Kiddies Corner**—in an E–NE or a strong southerly swell. The Corner itself can be worth checking on a reasonable swell when the sand is packed in tight. At the end of the northern corner at **Barrenjoey** a nice bank can produce long lefthanders on a NE swell and NE winds. Keep an eye on these spots as they can provide fun, uncrowded alternatives.

In the north cove of **Whale Beach** is a wave called **The Wedge**. Given a predominant easterly swell and a W–NE wind, you should score some great waves. It's called the Wedge because the swell bounces up off the rocks and lets loose a filthy lefthander; not a long wave, but an intense one. At the take-off point, the lefts can be twice the size of most other Sydney peaks. During winter, there can also be a right bank at **South Whaley**, in clean, south ground swells.

Avalon Beach

Avalon is an ideal surf beach because it works on both north and south swells and has a variety of waves, generally with good power behind them. In a north or east swell (even a cyclone swell), **North Avalon** produces insane lefts that wheel down the beach—one of Sydney's best. In a S–SE swell with W–S winds, **South Avalon** produces great righthanders that break over a deep rock platform. These waves can also be some of Sydney's finest. And then there's **Little**

Avalon, a righthand tube that explodes over a shallow rock platform at the base of the cliff at South Avalon. Nearby **Bilgola Beach**, one of Sydney's more scenic beaches, can often produce great waves on small to medium peaky E–NE swells with NW–NE winds and is generally a good place for less experienced waveriders.

Newport Beach

The stomping ground of former world champ Tom Carroll, Newport also boasts a wide variety of waves, although none as consistently good as its neighbour Avalon. **The Peak**, on the northern end, can produce excellent top to bottom lefts and rights, with a good bank to base your bottom turn from. Occasionally, on a reasonable north swell, you'll find good waves off the northern headland at Newport and perhaps at **Thompsons**, a right bank just south of here, but The Peak is the mainstay location.

Working on any swell up to 6 ft, the wave quality is not necessarily destroyed with an onshore wind. In fact, it can be most fun in a light SE wind. At the southern end of Newport, some really good waves can be had off **Newport Reef** which breaks out the back of the Pool. This will happen in an E–NE swell and a southerly wind. Offering a relatively easy take-off, it's a good place to ease into some larger surf. After a good session, head up to the famous Newport Arms pub where you'll find a great Australian beer garden.

A little further south, **Bungan Beach** can also handle some size on E–NE swells and is generally overlooked by the roving northern beach surf hordes. Best in prevailing W–NE winds.

Mona Vale is best in summer with NE swells and N–W winds. Given a good northerly swell, the fast lefthand waves will run along the beach, producing great, and sometimes classic, rides.

Warriewood comes into its own during a strong southerly. It will often be one of the only places producing decent rideable waves in a southerly wind. From close to the cliff base, good righthanders break and run down the beach. Although rarely epic, Warriewood can surprise you with some fun surfable rights when all the other beaches are written off.

 December–April.

 Carparks which allow easy surf checks and convenient viewing at all the hotspots.

 Sand-covered reef, exposed lava reef, cungie rock shelfs and sand bottoms.

 Crowd repellent and full board quiver.

 Strong rips in some locations. Future world champions hungry for waves.

 Pollution and ear infections from stormwater runoffs.

 Heaps of quality barrels. Live surf bands, some of Australia's best board shapers.

Narrabeen

North Narrabeen is undisputedly the best wave location in Sydney, especially in a E–NE swell and W–NE winds. The secret behind the legend is Narrabeen Lake, which deposits sand year-round into the ocean ensuring shallow, well-formed banks. Although the North Narrabeen surf does not suffer much in a light E–SE wind, strong south swells with accompanying southerly winds are a worry.

North Narrabeen's place in Sydney surfing has long been documented, and its list of world champion surfers is longer than most surfing nations, let alone individual beaches. My tip is surf it when it doesn't look so classic and you'll have a blast. Surf the main break left on a perfect 6–8 ft north swell with favourable winds and you'll be waiting in line with half of the world's top 30 surfers plus a major contingent of hot Narrabeen carvers—a recipe for major frustration. **The Alley** rights are usually a tad less crowded than the more famous lefts that barrel, wall and barrel again for up to 100 m. Then there's **The Point**, a gnarly left with a heavy rock ledge takeoff that rarely works, but on classic days can link up with the main peak at The Alley.

Quite often a better option is found further south at **Carpark Rights**, which can also turn on hollow pits in a medium south swell, or even at **South Narrabeen** where shifty banks can produce some blinding barrels with W–SW light offshore winds and a reasonable E–NE swell.

About five minutes drive further south, **Collaroy** is a last-resort surf spot, that can provide some novelty right peaks off the pool during a huge E–NE storm swell but even then you'll have to contend with some stormwater drain runoffs.

Long Reef

Heading along the shoreline towards the headland that announces Long Reef there aren't many consistent locations, however **Brownwater** lefts can get half decent during NE swell and south wind combinations. The **White Rock** righthander can also deliver hollow waves over a semi shallow reef on a big E–NE swell with SW–S winds. The fabled **Butterbox** lefthander located on the southern side of the golf course can also churn out excellent, long lefthanders and is worth checking on a heavy south swell with NE winds.

A more reliable location, **Long**

Reef has some great reef and beach break waves that work on any swell direction. It's offshore in a W–NW wind and is also protected in a NE wind. The good thing about Long Reef is that generally at the point of take off, the peak is about twice the size of any comparable wave hitting Sydney's beaches at that time. The Long Reef wave is a good left and a good right on two bombie peaks that can often shift around. The waves also have a large surface area with a lot of face to explore. It's a really fun wave, generally better towards the low tide. There are some good waves off **Long Reef Headland**, but you really have to know them and be familiar with the way they break. More myth and legend than fact! Just down from Long Reef is a series of beach breaks that can, and often do, produce good quality waves. However, as with most beach breaks, you get to hear about the great waves more often than you get to surf them.

Dee Why

Dee Why's most famous wave is **Dee Why Point**. This ledging, sucking and reasonably serious wave breaks on submerged rock ledges not too far from an exposed rock ledge. The Point is a wave you either love or hate. It's a difficult wave to ride as you have to take off

before it hits the first inside section, the problem being that the perfect takeoff point is just a few metres from dry rock and is quite a small zone when it's crowded. Of course the local boys know instinctively where to position themselves.

Too often in the tube, the bottom will drop out as the wave passes over one particularly shallow rock ledge and, just as you're negotiating your way out of the barrel, you'll find yourself in midair. Dee Why Point is one of those places where you're either a local or you surf it uncrowded if you want a few waves. It works in a strong southerly swell with a southerly wind best on midtide coming in. The nearby beach breaks are also fairly consistent and a lot of fun. The better peaks are usually found just north of the point but are susceptible to onshore winds and shifting sand banks. **No Man's Land** is a typical stretch of fickle waves running north towards Long Reef, but like many beach breaks this stretch can sometimes turn it on if you're in the right place at the right time.

Curl Curl often produces great beach breaks and on any given day they can be some of the best sand bank waves in Sydney. **South Curl Curl** works best in a W–SW wind, but **"North Curlie"**, as it is known, is also reasonably protected in a NE breeze. The beach is open to most

swell directions so the waves are usually as big as you'll find anywhere in Sydney.

Manly

Freshwater Beach, the founding site of Australian surfing, where the "Duke" rode the country's first official wave, is renowned as a clubbie hang and has a reputation for consistent closeouts. But on a small south swell with NE winds it can have peaky lefts and rights in the southern corner.

Queenscliff is probably second only to Narrabeen in producing world-class surfers. Marking the northern end of Sydney's famous **Manly Beach**, it picks up a lot of NE swell and works best on a W–SW wind. **South Steyne**, the southernmost end of the beach, is famous for producing top to bottom lefthanders that can be hundreds of metres long. Queenscliff is one of those places that always has a wave—sometimes it can be disgusting in quality but at other times it can be the best in Sydney. It is generally crowded and the locals are, in most cases, competent surfers, so there are not too many spare waves.

When the swell jumps over 3 m,

the **Queenscliff Bombora** located about a kilometre offshore begins to show but this huge bombie is rarely ridden.

Two hundred metres along the beach from Queenscliff is **North Steyne**, which can also produce great lefthanders as well as high quality rights in a southerly swell and wind direction. North Steyne is reasonably protected in a southerly wind and can usually be one of the few reliable places given large south swell/south wind weather patterns. It's a beach break though, so there are no guarantees.

Fairy Bower is a ripping righthand reef break that works on an E–NE swell and a W–SW to S wind direction. It is a really good wave but can be fickle. A huge southerly swell, for example, is more likely to march straight past and up the coast, missing Fairy Bower. It definitely needs east in the swell and works best on a low to medium incoming tide. Now that the city's sewerage discharge is directed further up the coast, it's much more fun to ride and definitely a place to check given the above conditions, because as a reef break it's quite a consistent wave to ride.

—*Ben Horvath*

Sydney's Southern Beaches

Easy Surf Checks and Paddle-outs

Preceding pages: Tamarama or "Glamarama" as it's known to men with binoculars, attracts a fair amount of Baywatch-style bikini models . Oh yeah, there's also some surf on offer. The left can get very long and very crowded. *Photo: Bill Morris*

The southside of Sydney can be traditionally divided into two distinct regions—the Eastern suburb beaches (Bondi to La Perouse) and Bate Bay (Cronulla). Generally pretty consistent wave zones, most days somewhere in the south is rideable. If you can handle the crowds, southern Sydney can provide an interesting surfing lifestyle. We surf a lot of slop but also get our fair share of quality waves—particularly on the reef breaks. Despite the media myth, south of the Sydney Harbour Bridge probably scores more quality surf than the famous northern beaches during winter—and that's a fact!

Protected from a wide range of wind directions, a handy mid-latitude position also means the southern beaches experience regular swell activity from all directions. Whether the swells are cyclone season-generated from the north, midwinter southern Tasman groundswells, or local SE or NE wind swell, southern Sydney certainly doesn't lack variety.

Bondi Beach

Australia's most famous beach, **Bondi**, is less than 20 minutes by car or public transport from the city centre and so is insanely crowded during the summer months. For pure entertainment though, Bondi can be an all-time freak show and one of Sydney's best people-watching options. The food, the girls, the culture—they're all accessible and the surf is quite consistent. While many beaches are blown out during summer, Bondi is perfectly protected, being offshore in a W–NW to NE wind, though the punch-drunk backpacker and kook factor can be out of control at times. If you're patient, Bondi does get a lot of swell, especially from the south, with the left and right peaks at the southern end of this colourful capital city bay providing the most consistent options.

Best surfed a couple of hours either side of high tide, Bondi is at

Map labels

Watson's Bay
Drummoyne
Sydney
Dover Heights
Bondi
South Bondi
MacKenzies
Tamarama
Bronte Reef
Coogee
Wedding Cake Island
Maroubra
Maroubra
Canterbury
Rockdale
La Pérouse
Botany Bay
Hurstville
Kurnell
South Pacific Ocean
Voodoo
Cronulla
Cronulla Beach
Wanda
The Alley
Elouera Beach
Cronulla Point
Shark Island
Sandshoes
Audley
Warumbul
Bundeena
Bundeena
Royal National Park
Marley Beach
Wattamolla
0 3 6 9
Kilometres
Garie Beach Breaks
Garie Beach
North Era
South Era

Southern Sydney

its optimum at around 3–4 ft with south swells, and north winds on a mid to high tide. It can also be fun in peaky onshore 4–6 ft chop with SE winds. On an extremely large northerly swell, **Ben Buckler**, located at Bondi's northern point, can occasionally turn it on with some big, loping lefthanders that break off a shallow rock shelf into deep water.

MacKenzies/Tamarama

Just around the corner, **MacKenzies Bay** is a small rock-lined cove that imitates the Whale Beach Wedge. Here the swell refracts off the exposed rock ledge then pushes back into the water moving shorewards, forming a wave that, at take-off point, is twice the size of the swell hitting other beaches. MacKenzies works on a S–SE swell and is best on a NE wind, but can be worth checking in a small to medium E–NE swell. Forget it if the wind's up from the south or the swell is over 6 ft.

Tamarama works best on a NE swell, with great waves to be had off the point and occasionally right across the bay. The best winds are W–NW to NE. Tamarama can also work on SE–E swells, but breaks best on a swell with northerly influ-

ence. The waves are generally pretty short and intense, though this can vary. Given the right conditions "Glamarama"—named after the hordes of beautiful G-stringed women that regularly sunbake there each summer—can hold a swell up to 8 ft and sometimes wraps perfectly, producing some of the best left beach break waves on the southern beaches.

Bronte Beach

Bronte works best in a W–SW to southerly wind, ensuring it's reasonably sheltered. It has two consistent breaks, **Bronte Reef**, which can be great on a handful of days a year, running from the outside boil section right across the bay. However, the best break is the righthander in the middle of the bay. This breaks really well when there's a 6-ft plus S–SE swell, and also offers a decent left running into the shoreline channel. In fact, besides Cronulla Point, Bronte is virtually southern Sydney's only protected break in a strong southerly.

Coogee is a non-wave, except in huge storm swells. On an extremely large northerly swell (generally a cyclone swell), the northern side of **Wedding Cake Island** looks very

April–September.

 Carparks for easy surf checks, and headland paddle-outs for easy access to the main peaks.

 Sand-covered reefs, shallow rock shelves, and sand bottoms.

 Small-wave hotdog board through to tube-threading semi-gun for hollow reef break barrels.

 Heavy crowds and localism, rips, car thieves.

 Reef cuts, sea urchins, blue bottle stings and ear infections.

 Consistent waves, beach-loving models and partying on tap.

much like Sunset, Hawaii. However catching this place on is virtually impossible as the beach break is usually guttered.

Maroubra

During E–NE swells, great left-handers grace the northern end of Maroubra Beach which works best on a W–NW or NE wind. The south end can produce good to excellent waves on W–SW or south winds during both northerly or southerly swells. On a day-to-day basis and given any easterly in the swell, Maroubra is, in my opinion, the outstanding city beach and is even better now that the human waste is being discharged 2.5 km out to sea.

Cronulla

The southern most beachside suburb of Sydney, Cronulla is flanked to the north by Botany Bay and to the south by Port Hacking and the Royal National Park.

With the disappearance of the surrounding sand hills (a casualty of short-sighted sandmining projects), surfers who once frequented the classy **Wanda** and **Greenhills** beach breaks now endure summer midmorning blowouts and a drastic reduction in bank quality.

Before the flattening of the towering dunes, the prevailing summer NE seabreeze funnelled almost straight offshore, which often meant uncrowded all-day surfing. Nowadays, a 20-knot NE renders the beach breaks unrideable, reserving Wanda for wave-sailors on many summer afternoons. There are, however, many positive aspects when considering the surfing possibilities around Cronulla. During autumn, winter, and often even in spring, Cronulla can really turn it on.

A variety of surf can be found, ranging from poor to perfect beach breaks. Cronulla's beachies from **The Alley** to **Hills** and encompassing **Elouera**, **Midway**, **John Davey** and **Wanda** are more consistent than most of Sydney's beach breaks. The waves from Elouera North through to Greenhills are generally best in small to medium-sized E–S swells around 3-6 ft, rarely bigger these days, with offshore SW–NW winds.

Wanda and Elouera can handle solid swells occasionally, but they must be peaky, not straight groundswell lines, unless there's a rare outer bank. The Alley and The

Wall beach breaks are semi-sheltered from southerly winds and occasionally get mindless. Alley rights sometimes line up in a direct south or SE swell, while the consistent inside left has honed many well-known goofy footers' styles over the years. Behind the rockpool can be good in NE swells or in big, clean southerlies, while **South Cronulla** lefts can provide a solid alternative if the point's too crowded on really big days.

Voodoo/The Reefs
On the NE tip of Bate Bay lies Voodoo. There's a short, hollow reef just north of "Vooey" called **Suck Rock**, or **The Wamp**, but it's generally a bodyboarders' haven—a short, intense, gnarly barrel best in small to medium-size SE swells with offshore west or north winds.

Voodoo is one mean, thick mother of a wave that can handle a solid 15 ft south swell. It's a juice magnet and when the beaches are 6 ft in the south, Voodoo is 8–10 ft and packing Hawaiian-style punch. Best in NW winds, it also handles the afternoon NE, but forget it during strong westerlies. Straight S or SE swells and low to mid tides are the go unless it's huge. The take-off is a gnarly, ledgy bowl and the inside actually gets larger as it heads down the line.

The Reefs are semi-secret, so it's not really cool to say anything other than there are an assortment of lefts and rights varying in quality. The wider you go, the more swell they handle. The 5th left really only gets ridden a couple of times a year. The first right, second right and second lefts are the most frequented breaks that operate best in small to medium E–SE swells, with W–NW winds and the tide dropping.

Cronulla Point
At the southern end of the beach break lies the legendary **Cronulla Point**. The Point consists of two separate reef sections, **First and Second Reef**. First breaks on small days and is a hollow fun section that backs off into a cutback wave until the final drain section. Second Reef comes into play when the swell hits the 5–6 ft mark and handles a solid 12-ft swell easily.

On solid days the Point is a serious wave that rapidly barrels across the reef with awesome power and class. Of course, as in most locales, there's a close-knit community who dominate on the bigger days. Best in a solid SE or south swell with west or even SW–S winds, the Point is

Below: Danny Maloney leaves a kinetic tattoo on a top-to-bottom Voodoo's lefthander. *Photo: Chris Stroh*

Above: The reef snaps below while water shoots up the face with an eerie thunder. Be sure of yourself inside the jaws of the Shark Island barrel.
Photo: Craig Stroh

rideable in any swell direction but is actually more performance-oriented in an E–NE swell.

Shark Island

Just 150 m SE, and outside of the Point to the SE, lies the world-famous and notorious **Shark Island**. In recent years the Island has become a bodyboarding haven simply because they can take it in all conditions, even when the swell has north in it. The surf's best in a straight SE swell with light offshore winds from the W–SW. Swell direction is critical. If it's too south, the end section doesn't barrel, but if it's too east there is a shutdown factor. Medium to large, clean E–SE swells are probably the ideal direction and 4–8 ft is generally accepted as the optimum size, although it can handle 10–12 ft if conditions are perfect. Definitely only a mid to high tide break. Only committed surfers need paddle out, as one wrong move can land you on bone-dry reef.

South of **Island Rights**, you have **Island Lefts**, which can be worth investigating in a NE swell. Then there's **Shelley** (a fat, rarely worthwhile reef break), **Pipeline** (a complete embarrassment to its namesake) and **Windy Point**, which can be an interesting, though sectioning barrel when the swell is big. **Sandshoes** is an urchin-infested peak that can occasionally get insane. Best in small to medium peaky NE swell combined with W–SW winds or large south swell. It should be surfed on a mid to high tide only.

During winter (surfers' season), the local tribes dominate their breaks and you won't see better hard core surfing on many beaches in Oz.

The Royal National Park

With over 15,000 ha of deep river gorges, rare flora, relatively untouched beaches and awe-inspiring vertical cliff structures, Sydney's Royal National Park is one of the oldest national parks in the world.

Thousands of surfers, fishermen and stressed individuals take the opportunity to escape from the pollution and crowds of the city beaches to unwind in the serenity of the park which is under an hour's drive from Sydney's hustle.

A scenic drive through the park takes between 12–25 minutes with

the northern entrance found at Sutherland, followed by other entry points at Waterfall and Stanwell Tops as you move further south. In the warmer months, rangers occupy the various entrance gates from around 8 am till 4 pm, and charge a fee of $7 to use the park. If you wake up late and want to surf one of the breaks you'll have to pay for the pleasure or think of a convincing excuse. If you're planning regular visits, purchase a season sticker that will also give you access to NSW's many other national parks, including the snowfields, for a very reasonable sum.

There are several high quality breaks, the most popular being **Garie Beach** due to its easy access by car. Garie is a consistent beach break (particularly during the summer and autumn months), offering a fine array of wedgey peaks, especially lefts. Its outer banks can hold medium-sized swells and there's usually a fine left and right shorebreak up the northern end. The one and only Garie kiosk is pretty average in the supply stakes, so you're best advised to travel armed with your own food and drinks.

Garies cranks on a medium E–NE swell or a small south, providing the winds are from the West or North, but you should avoid surfing in a southerly. On a good day you can usually guarantee Garie will be a foot or two bigger than most Sydney metro coast beach breaks. At the same time, Garie rarely handles anything over the 8 ft mark, which usually means the banks are badly chewed up after the heavy winter swells.

The same could be said of **North Era,** which can produce the occasional hollow lefthander off the point and, if you're lucky, a fickle but occasionally awesome righthander on the beach. Access to Era is by foot only, but the long walk is worth it if the conditions are right.

North Era, South Era, Burning Palms, Little Garie and some of the more secret reef breaks up towards **Bundeena** are relatively isolated and accessible only by foot. The only other known break within the park is the novelty break of **Bundeena,** a sandspit lying inside Port Hacking that only breaks in huge swells; even then, it's totally dependent on sand build-up.

Had enough of the crowds? Try heading to Wollongong and beyond.
—*Ben Horvath*

Wollongong

Coal Mining and Crystal Cylinders

Preceding pages:
Luke Nolan hasn't lost that Woonona feeling.
Photo: Mark Newsham

The majority of Wollongong's population live on a narrow floodplain wedged between the Illawarra Ranges and the Tasman Sea, an hour's drive south of Sydney.

Over the years I have formed two vivid, contrasting images of Wollongong. My first and favourite picture is arriving at Stanwell Tops, on an early winter's morning drive down the coast, to be greeted by the sight of a strong southerly groundswell fanned by a stiff, cold westerly. In the distance you can clearly make out the white water outlines of various breaks, with industrial Wollongong, the mountain range and the sunrise provid-

ing an inspiring backdrop. The other more alarming image I have of this region is an ageing, industrial Port Kembla, legacy-lined with BHP smokestacks, rusting sheds and vacant factories.

Whichever way you see Wollongong, there's a huge variety of surf spots, from the northern fringe suburbs of Stanwell Park through the city metropolitan breaks and all the way down to Windang Island in the south. With such easy access to so much surf, the Leisure Coast has spawned generations of outstanding surfers.

The northern suburbs, stretching from **Stanwell** through to **Coledale**, basically offer shifting beach breaks that rarely cope with too much swell size. Stanwell is best in E–NE swells when the northern end lefts can fire and occasionally the southern end gets classic, but you have to be lucky. Stanwell can be fun in small peaky swells with offshore winds.

Coalcliff offers some protection from southerly winds and generally produces average beach breaks. There's a fickle bombie left that requires north swell and offshore winds. The south end reef break can also appear surfable but is a hoax.

Scarborough can get good in NE swells when lefts run down the beach, but generally the banks are straight. This wave requires offshore NW–SW winds. At the other end of the beach, **Wombarra** can be epic a couple of times a year when the sand packs in on the southern end rocks producing hollow left and right peaks. Usually autumn's the go when SW–S winds blow offshore.

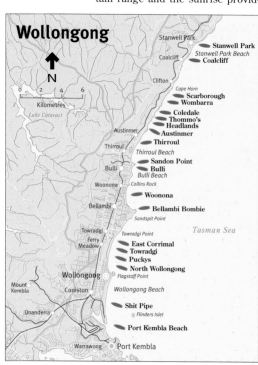

Wollongong

N

0 2 4 6
Kilometres
Lake Cataract

Stanwell Park
Coalcliff
Clifton

Austinmer

Thirroul

Bulli

Woonona

Bellambi

Towradgi
Ferry
Meadow

Wollongong

Mount
Kembla

Coniston

Unanderra

Warrawong   Port Kembla

Stanwell Park
Stanwell Park Beach
Coalcliff

Cape Horn
Scarborough
Wombarra
Coledale
Thommo's
Headlands
Austinmer
Thirroul
Thirroul Beach
Sandon Point
Bulli
Bulli Beach
Collins Rock
Woonona
Bellambi Bombie
Sandspit Point

Tasman Sea

Towradgi Point
East Corrimal
Towradgi
Puckys
North Wollongong
Flagstaff Point
Wollongong Beach

Shit Pipe
Flinders Islet

Port Kembla Beach

Above:
Powerarcing on a
Wollongong beach-
break.
Photo: Bill Morris

Coledale often has a peaky, wedging righthander just north of the southern end rocks, entirely dependent on sand build-up. It's well worth a check in small to medium E–S swells with W–S winds.

Thommo's is a strange bombie-type left that can be good on low tides in solid E–NE swells with offshore NW–SW winds. The right can be a less crowded option too. Next up, **Sharkies** can be a fat, pregnant sort of sand reef lefthander that occasionally gets really good, but it's dependent on northerly winds all the way around to the SW. Again the rights can sometimes be a better, less crowded option.

Just to the south of Sharkies lies **Headlands.** Headies is a serious right-hand, horse-shoeing, barrel set-up that is ideally ridden during clean E–NE swells with W–SW winds. On south swells it can still be a powerful, more performance-oriented right, but in a north it can be world-class.

Austinmer and **Thirroul** offer fun beach break surf up to 5–6 ft. Thirroul and **Macauleys** operate in peaky E–NE swells, though both "Austy" and Thirroul can be worth a check in small to medium south swells.

Sandon Point, in my opinion, is the best point break on the New South Wales coast, at least until you get up to Angourie, and even then it holds its own easily. Rideable from 3ft–15 ft, Sandon has many moods. One thing's for sure it's best in W–S winds. East swells in the 4–8 ft range can provide an epic balance of hollow sections and performance faces while NE swells can mean freight-train barrels, and huge souths can be awesome. Check it out, make up your own mind, but respect the locals. Hang back and you might pick up a few of the best waves you'll ever find. Low to mid tides are for experienced surfers only. Kooks will be savaged by the locals (I've been paid to say that). Crowds are already hideous. If you're not sure, stay away.

Peggy's, further south, is another interesting reef/point break. It's fickle, unpredictable and weird, but it can and does get classic in medium SE–NE swells. Paddle out at low tide only, with W–S winds required. **Bulli** is an uncrowded beach break option that can produce the goods, particularly at the southern end.

Woonona is The Gong's Narrabeen, a real swell magnet that often produces long, walling lefts and shorter punchy rights. It's best in

April–September.

Sealed roads to the majority of breaks. Short beach walks to primo breaks.

Sand-covered reef, breakwalls, sharp reef and outer bombies.

Mid-range board for 2–5 ft waves and big-wave gun for bombies, beachies and reef breaks.

Strong currents and collapsing sand-banks causing heavy undertows.

Reef cuts and sea urchins.

Consistent, quality surf with marginal crowds at many excellent breaks.

Above: Not Hawaii, but Wollongong's 16th Hole.
Photo: Mick McCormack

Opposite: John Craig on a collapsing section at Sandon Point.
Photo: Mark Newsham

Below: An empty Shit Pipe barrel goes unridden—but not for long.
Photo: Mark Newsham

SW–N winds and an E–NE swell. **Belambi** is a desperate southerly option, though it does have an interesting bombie that can get good in big, clean swells accompanied by light offshore NW–SW winds.

East Corrimal has a fickle reef set-up that occasionally pumps. It's best in a small to medium SE–NE swell with W–N winds. **Corrimal** beach breaks similarly can be good in any small to medium-size swell, again with W–N winds. **Towradgi** has a shifting, peaky sand-on-reef set-up that can link with the inside banks. Best with NW–S winds, it handles up to about 6 ft.

Further south, **Puckys** can be a worthwhile right reef break, peeling into the creek entrance just to the north of North Beach. W–S winds are required for maximum surfing stoke.

North Beach at Wollongong can be fun in peaky NE swells or larger south swells. Protected from south winds, the lefts in the northern corner or rights in front of the southern end rocks are the more consistent banks. **South Beach** offers great NE wind protection on the southern side of the headland. There is often a decent left bank situated in the more sheltered northern corner. **South Pipe**, or **Shitties**, as it's more affectionately known, lies near the golf course and ropes in any NE swell. Although this place can get exceptionally good, it's also exposed to all winds except offshore westerlies.

Down towards the **Port Kembla Coal Loader**, there are some sheltered southerly options near the groynes. **Port Kembla Beach** also harbours a serious left reef off the northern end and some excellent summer beach breaks. It's also totally protected in NE winds.

—Ben Horvath

The South Coast
A Surf Adventurer's Dream

Much has been written about the South Coast in recent years, particularly about South Coast Pipeline and Black Rock. The hype is justified when you see just how perfect. Pipe gets on occasions, but there are numerous other breaks in the region that can be just as perfect.

The South Coast enjoys a minimal surfing population, with approximately 600 km of highly surfable terrain following the Tasman Sea all the way to the Victorian border. This area is a surf explorer's dream and nearly every town and dirt road leading off the highway has waves with a

variety of beach breaks, bombies, reefs, small islands and points catering for both goofies and naturals in almost any swell or wind direction.

No one gives away anything—especially the locals—while radio surf reporters rarely mention particular spots. Note that overly bright wetsuits or sticker-covered cars stand out and loud-mouthed blow-ins are soon singled out. There are plenty of soul surfers as well as an emerging crew of competitive surfers.

Shellharbour

People call anywhere south of the Royal National Park the South Coast, but most genuine surf adventurers will tell you it begins at **Windang Island** just north of Shellharbour. It's here that a solid, lefthand, big wave option works best in a clean, solid E–NE groundswell between 6–12 ft. NW–NE winds are ideal and a mid to low tide is premium, but south swells don't do the place much justice.

Between Windang and Shell Harbour central there's a fickle big wave option Michael Lowe made famous a couple of years ago called **Insanities** or **Mads**, but realistically it's best left as a locals-only wave unless you're game. Shellharbour has some great southerly wind E–NE swell options. Of course, big south swells also wrap into **Cowries, the Pool** and even **Redsands** or the way softer **Shallows**. Psyche yourself for these waves—we're talking solid, throaty, hollow death pit righthanders offshore in SW to SE winds. Think 6'8" boards minimum. Think commitment. Think tube city. Enough.

Windang Island

Warilla Beach
Insanities/Mads
Cowries
The Pool

Albion Pk

Shellharbour

Mystics Beach
The Farm
Boneyard
Bombo Beach

Barren Grounds
Nature Reserve

Kiama

Tasman Sea

Werri Beach

Gerringong

Berry

Black Pt.
Chips
Seven Mile Beach

N

Shoalhaven
Heads

Shoalhaven

0   2   4   6
Kilometres

Comerong

Callala

Greenwell
Point   *Bight*   **Shellharbour/Kiama**

Crookhaven

Above: Dylan Longbottom making it look way too easy on a flawless day at Bombo Beach. *Photo: Conti*

Kiama

Heading south a couple of kms you have the south swell mecca called **The Farm**. Offshore in northerlies, the Farm can get good in small to medium S–SE swells on mid to high tide in north winds. But then again it can also be Cornwall revisited—flakey and weak—go figure. Just to the south again, **Mystics** funnels every swell it receives into a wedge. Short, sharp, peaky, hollow and intense sand bottom runners is the description that immediately comes to mind. W, NW or even N winds are cool. Peaky E–NE swells are best. Just north of Kiama lies **Boneyard**, another seriously sheltered southerly option. Again E–NE swells or a huge southerly swell is the go. SW–SE winds are not a problem. Best in NE swells up to 10 ft, this place can really hold the juice and packs a whallop!

Bombo picks up the best of both south and north swells. It also enjoys reasonable wind shelter from both southerlies and NE winds. Shifty, occasionally insane beachies are the order of the day, depending on the sand build-up. Having sampled this spot, the real scenery and swell begins, with miles of natural bushland and lush, rolling green hills, interrupted only by the Princes Highway as it winds its way through surf-rich townships.

Gerringong

Continuing south, **Werri** is a quality surf check option. Great banks, a fun right point that is sheltered from southerlies, and winding lefts up the northern end in northerly breezes provide plenty of options. The left and right peak in the southern corner of the beach is also quite dependable and has been known to handle some size.

Gerroa just south of Gerringong, overlooks Seven Mile Beach. North or NE winds blow offshore at Seven Mile, and **Chips**, the left-hand point/reef in the northern corner, can even handle an easterly wind. South swells pour into Seven Mile, Chips and the outside Bombies. Chips is best at 6 ft-plus of south swell.

On the northern side of the Gerroa headland and further to the SE there are one or two fickle, quieter spots that I'll leave for you to explore. The beachies at **Seven**

February–September.

Sealed, gravel and dirt roads to car-parks and camping grounds at a multitude of breaks.

Cungie-covered reefs, soft sand bottoms on the beachies.

National Park permits and mid-range boards.

Sting rays, sea urchins, remote wipeouts and Great White Sharks.

Reef cuts, blue bottle stings.

Relatively unexplored regions rich with surf. World-class hollow reef breaks with minimal crowds.

Above: Aussie Pipeline, Black Rock or Summercloud Bay, call it what you like. Despite all the media hype the place still defies description.
Photo: Bill Morris

Mile can often prove a good uncrowded option, but they have a nasty habit of developing into straighthanders. Peaky swells as opposed to lined-up groundswells are best.

The **Comerong Island-Crookhaven Heads-Currarong** region is well worth exploring in NE swell and southerly wind combinations. On the northern side of **Jervis Bay**, there are some interesting beachies and seriously under-

ground hollow right reef breaks in the vicinity. In fact, inside the bay there's an infamous, quality left reef break set-up named **Callala**, that requires a large SE swell to start showing.

Wreck Bay

Some of the better, more popular spots lie south of Jervis Bay because they tend to be more exposed to powerful southerly swells. On the southern side of the bay **Sailors** and **Husky Bombie** are quality novelty breaks when the swell outside is mega.

Just south of Jervis Bay lies **Wreck Bay**, home of the infamous **South Coast Pipe**. Pipe is a hollow, intense left tube, offering a shorter, punchy right. Best anywhere from 3–8 ft from the south with NW–E winds, Pipe will hold 10, even 12 ft tubes, if conditions are perfect. It's a very consistent wave as far as reef breaks go, accepting any hint of south swell and blowing offshore in the prevailing summer NE seabreezes.

Sussex Inlet

Further south, **Sussex Inlet** can occasionally offer some interesting beach breaks and one or two fickle though worthwhile reef breaks, again best in W–N winds. **Conneeleys** and **Berrara Point** require moderate swells and offshore westerly winds to get any good.

Bendalong is one of the East Coast's most consistent beach breaks—always has been, always will be. Bendy often has well-formed banks and picks up the smallest of swells from all directions, particularly the south. It's best in west through to north winds.

Just north of Bendalong, in an impenetrable region known as **Panther Country**, lies a series of uncrowded reef breaks that work best during SW winds and E–NE swells. To the south awaits the majestic **Green Island** set-up—a popular but slightly overrated spot, that again blows offshore in

Jervis Bay

Crookhaven Heads

Warrain Beach

Currarong — Beecroft Head

Callala Beach

Huskisson — Jervis Bay

Collingwood Beach — **Sailors**

Plantation Pt.

Vincentia

Hymans Beach — Governor Head

Green Patch

Jervis Bay National Park

Cave Beach — Wreck Bay

Black Point

St Georges Head — Steamers Beach

Steamers Beach

To Sussex Inlet

Tasman Sea

N

0   3   6   9
Kilometres

NW–NE winds, it accepts any hint of south swell. The long left-handers are best at 6 ft and remain rideable, but often fat up to 10, even 12, ft.

and some excellent peaky and hollow beachies on offer. There's also one or two great semi secretive reef/point set-ups that are well worth searching out.

Above: American tourist Wes Laine looking right at home at Redsands. *Photo: Mick McCormack*

Ulladulla

Continuing southwards still, the Ulladulla region remains a world-class wave haven with an assortment of quality beach breaks and hideous reef breaks to accommodate all swell and wind combinations. Quality abounds and certain locations, such as the Bombie in town, are swell power stations.

The Bombie works best in clean 4–10 ft, S–SE swells with NW–NE winds. It's a truly challenging, powerful, shifting and often tubular open ocean right-hander, for experienced crew only. Best at low to mid-tide.

Seek out those perfect little beachies at **Rennies Beach** in town, or if the southerly's howling, head for protection at **Golfcourse Reef** (a playful left just south of Mollymook Golf Club). **Mollymook Beach** or **Narrawallee**, just north, can also produce fun waves in favourable southerly conditions. Just south of Ulladulla you'll find **Wairo**

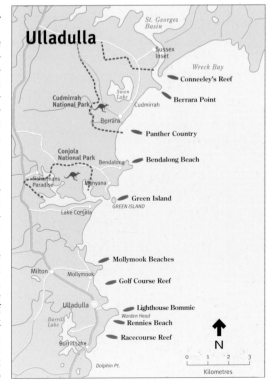

Overleaf: An inside-out view of a secretive South Coast reef.
Photo: Mick McCormack

Opposite: The Moruya Breakwall lefthander moves into full swing as the offshore blows a big plume of spray off the top.
Photo: Terry Willcocks

Below: Ominously named Guillotines, don't lose your head in the Bawley Point barrel.
Photo: Peter Wilson

Bawley Point

The **Bawley Point** region boasts a couple of gnarly rock reef/point set-ups that again produce in the E–NE swell-south wind combination. Otherwise try a large south swell accompanied by a southerly wind for more potent wave affect. There's also an interesting rivermouth set-up and one or two beachies worth checking in the vicinity. Hunt around.

Just south of Bawley the crowds really start to thin out with heaps of surfing claims to be staked especially around **Depot Beach**. The picturesque camping grounds at **Pebbly** and **Pretty Beach** are well worth a check even if only to feed the kangaroos, but believe me there are a whole bunch of sly beachies and fun little reef breaks in the area offering plenty of stoke and wind protection. **Batemans Bay** itself is a big town that's pretty much a hoax, wave wise, as it misses out on a lot of swell. However, in epic swells there are some novelty options.

Broulee

Further south towards **Broulee** there are a couple of well-known quality breaks. **Tomalga rivermouth** can turn on punchy peaks in medium sized E–SE swells with W–S winds. North from Tomalga, back towards Batemans Bay, is also worth a check as well for some uncrowded action when the swell's maxing.

Another big wave location, not scared of a bit of juice, **Pink Rocks** at Broulee Island is a quality right-hand reef/point set-up. In solid E–NE swells or a huge south, Pink Rocks offers everything—performance-orientated wally sections and some tube action. Sheltered from strong southerly winds, put this place high on your priority list.

Moruya Breakwall is the next quality buzz. Often compared to North Coast breakwalls such as Nth Wall Ballina or Nth Wall at Port Macquarie, Moruya serves up powerful rights off the wall up to 6 or 7 ft. There can be the added bonus of good lefts at the entrance to the river if you're game. Best in SW–S winds, on a low to mid tide, in medium east swells or big southerlies.

Narooma

Heading south, check the waves at **Congo** and **Potato Point** before you come across another righthand

breakwall set up at **Narooma**. From here keep your eyes open for **Camel Rock** and **Bunga**, which is another nice right point (10–15 minutes south of Bermagui). There are also some fun beachies at **Tathra**.

Finally, the two jewels in the south coast crown, the Merimbula and Pambula Rivermouths—both world class setups in their own right. **Merimbula Bar** has been compared to Mundaka in Spain. A long hollow lefthander that requires a solid SE swell to get going. It's best in west to NE winds and can get very crowded once the word is out. Beautiful wave. Beautiful town.

Right down at the other end of the long, sweeping bay lies **Pambula Rivermouth,** a Kirra-like freight train righthander of epic proportions when it's breaking. Both Michael and Tommy Peterson are on record citing Pambula as more perfect than the world-famous Kirra Point when it's on.

The only problem is, you need a huge E–NE swell to get in there or a massive SE swell. Once again southerly winds are the go. Do yourself a favour and catch it on at least once in your surfing life.

—*Ben Horvath*

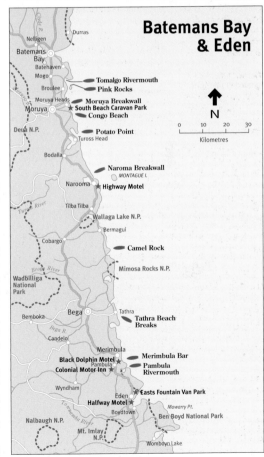

Batemans Bay & Eden

N

0   10   20   30
Kilometres

Clyde R.

Nelligen
Durras
Batemans Bay
Batehaven
Mogo
Broulee
Tomalgo Rivermouth
Pink Rocks
Moruya Heads
Moruya Breakwall
Moruya
★ South Beach Caravan Park
Congo Beach
Deua N.P.
Potato Point
Tuross Head
Bodalla
Naroma Breakwall
MONTAGUE I.
Narooma
★ Highway Motel
Tuross River
Tilba Tilba
Wallaga Lake N.P.
Bermagui
Cobargo
Camel Rock
Brogo River
Mimosa Rocks N.P.
Wadbilliga National Park
Bega
Tathra
Bemboka
Tathra Beach Breaks
Bega R.
Candelo
Merimbula
Merimbula Bar
Black Dolphin Motel ★
Pambula
Colonial Motor Inn ★
Pambula Rivermouth
Wyndham
★ Easts Fountain Van Park
Eden
Mowarry Pt.
Halfway Motel ★
Boydtown
Ben Boyd National Park
Nalbaugh N.P.
Mt. Imlay N.P.
To Wombalana River
Womboyn Lake

Home of the Brave

Dramatic Surfing and Great Coastal Scenery

Home to 4.4 million people (of which 3.1 million live in its capital Melbourne), and with an area the size of Great Britain, Victoria lies in Australia's southeast corner bordering South Australia and New South Wales.

The State's harsh desert interior contrasts with the snow-capped peaks of the Great Dividing Range. These mountains split the state and shelter the fertile plains which run down to the rugged, and scenic coastline.

Victoria has a colourful colonial past, which includes a major gold rush in the middle of the last century. This influx of fortune seekers formed the basis for what is today, Australia's most densely populated state. Travellers wanting to make a quick buck now head to Australia's largest casino which is found in the Crown Entertainment Complex on the south bank of the Yarra River in Melbourne.

On the northern side of the city, slick high-rise monoliths soar above what remains of its opulent Victorian architecture. Melbourne is also recognised as Australia's cultural and fashion capital and claims to have more than 3000 restaurants serving over 70 national cuisines. The city is famous for its trams which criss-cross the central business district and service the inner suburbs.

Each year, Melbourne plays host to international sporting events such as Albert Park's Formula One motor races, Grand Slam tennis at the Australian Open, and the world-famous Melbourne Cup. The city is the founding home of Australian Rules Football, a fast-moving, high-flying game which attracts huge crowds of keen fans.

Driving along Victoria's Great Ocean Road, with its towering cliffs and huge Southern Ocean seas crashing along the shores, is a fantastic experience. The raw open ocean swells attract many surfers from all over the country, and towns like Torquay are the gathering places for riders out to catch the best waves on offer.

At Torquay, the first surfing site found along Australia's most famous stretch of quality big-wave locations, are Bells Beach and Winkipop, where surfing legends were born and reputations forged in some of Australia's most perfect and challenging waves.

Surfworld, Australia's largest surfing museum is also found at Torquay. This beach culture shrine houses a variety of Australian surfing artefacts, and recognises the country's most influential surfers through the Surfing Hall of Fame. Torquay's laid-back surfing lifestyle is a focal point for industry giants such as Rip Curl, Quiksilver and Beachcrew. These influential companies continue to refine their wetsuit and clothing technologies in the cold and treacherous waters that pound Victoria's surf-rich coastline.

With a backdrop of temperate rainforest, rolling green hills and fertile farmland, the Great Ocean Road snakes its way from Geelong to Nelson near the South Australian border. Diverse and ever-changing, the 337-kilometre trip is truly captivating. Flawless point breaks, giant limestone rock outcrops, rugged

Opposite:
Taking the plunge into the icy keyhole at The Well.
Photo: Steve Ryan

cliffs, sheltered bays, playful beach breaks and giant 20–30 ft waves at remote outer bombies—the unpredictable scenery is surpassed only by the volatile weather. Driving through the scenic Otway Ranges and continuing further west, you begin to really appreciate Victoria's wealth of natural wonders.

Port Campbell National Park showcases some excellent waves as well as the Twelve Apostles, magnificent rock pillars said to be more than two million years old. Also in the area are Loch Ard Gorge, Gibson's Steps, London Bridge, The Grotto and the Blowhole. All of these sites are set in spectacular coastal surroundings and offer a bird's-eye perspective of many potential surf spots. There's also an historical shipwreck trail of 25 coastal wrecks.

To the east of Melbourne, Wilsons Promontory National Park protects some 50,000 hectares of rare native flora and fauna. This fascinating region along with the boot-shaped Mornington Peninsula provides plenty of empty waves and awesome wilderness to explore.

Connected to the mainland at San Remo, Phillip Island has a variety of great surf locations and some amazing wildlife including the Little Penguins which gather at sunset and return to their burrows at Summerland Beach. Like most of Victoria's popular coastal resorts, this area can get a little crowded during the school holiday period from December to January but enjoys consistent surf all year-round, particularly during the winter months of April to September.

Further east, a network of roads runs off the Princes Highway, the main arterial connecting any number of completely isolated surf locations. At the prime times of the year you are likely to encounter plenty of content travelling surfers who have taken up the challenge to explore this isolated coastline.

If by chance the surf doesn't co-operate, during winter there are always snowboarding and skiing. Some of the best slopes in Australia can be found at the Mount Buller, Mount Hotham and Falls Creek snowfields, which have great runs to practise your bottom turns and full rail carves. Excellent surfing, good winter snow and spectacular scenery—just keep moving and you'll beat the cold.

Opposite: After visiting 13th Beach and riding waves like this, Shane Bevan reckons the devil's advocate is his lucky number.
Photo: Peter Wilson

Below: One of the world's most famous right-handers is at Bells Beach. This is one of those places where surfers claim the best waves of their lives.
Photo: Peter Wilson

The Torquay Coast

Home to the World's First Surfing Reserve

Bells Beach, declared the world's first surfing recreation reserve, hosts the annual Rip Curl Pro each Easter. Its leg-sapping walls continue to attract surfers from every part of the globe.

Point Lonsdale

Point Lonsdale has several breaks worth mentioning and although the area's waves can often prove inconsistent, there are some fun breaks when the swell is pumping through the more famous beaches to the west.

On a northerly it can be advantageous to check the banks at **Lighthouse**, not as a primo surfing option, but rather as a useful swell indicator for conditions at **Glenuyes**. Located at the end of Glenuyes Road, when the swell runs up to the 6 ft mark, a pitching lefthand reef break will do its thing. From here to **Barwon Heads** some tame beach breaks provide ideal waves for beginners who want to hone their skills before taking on more challenging surf. Probably the best known of these waves, **Raffs** is found at the western end of Ocean Grove Beach.

13th Beach

Located south of Barwon Heads, the famous **13th Beach** can look like the end of the earth on a cold July day when a strong SW breeze whips the ocean into a frenzy. However, on a light NE wind and a S–SW swell, it's a refreshingly different scenario with perfect left and right peaks producing long, work-

able walls and powerful tube rides that can really make your day.

Just west of Point Flinders, **The Hole** breaks on swells up to 9 ft and throws out a real challenge for those willing to take it on. Read your tide chart for this location, because if conditions are too full, the wave shape will be flat and lacklustre. On the other hand, a miscalculation on low tide may see you hitting up the local pharmacist for a band-aid sponsorship after bouncing your head on the reef.

Driving further west, an old shipping marker in the dunes gave **The Beacon** its name. This is a popular location that shares many similarities with The Hole. Once again ideal conditions are a S–SW swell and light NE winds, which will perfectly fan the incoming 6-footers, making for an incredibly smooth take-off and a glassy, rippable wall that just makes you want to go surfing all day, everyday.

April–September.

Most of the primo sites have carparks and are linked by the Great Ocean Rd. Sand-covered reef on the beach breaks and sharp reef bottoms on the points and reef breaks.

Big wave guns, booties, spare boards and long leashes.

Crowds, rips, locals.

Some pollution at 13th Beach.

Some of the longest rides and best barrels of your life.

Above: There are no girls but plenty of waves at the shallow Boobs lefthander.
Photo: Steve Ryan

Turd Rock lies at the westernmost end of 13th Beach and is generally a bit smaller than its easterly counterparts. Unfortunately this location and a significant section of 13th Beach suffer from pollution courtesy of the Geelong sewer pipe. If you're not keen on a severe bout of gastro, it might pay to give this place a miss. However when 13th is cranking there's usually a variety of different peaks that will spring up further along the beach and those without the sheep mentality can enjoy a barrel to themselves (although this is a rarity during summer).

Torquay

If you've left your longer boards at home, or if the swell steaming through Bells is ridiculously large, then salvation lies off **Fishos** or **Fishermen's Reef**. Breaking off the point to the right of the boat ramp, a sand-covered reef can provide a fun session and maybe even a coverup or two on days when you prefer not to challenge the heavier Southern Ocean juice. If your resolve is strong and you don't get distracted by the surf industry retail sales mecca that is **Surf Coast Plaza**, you're bound to find some excellent waves. If you prefer sand rather than reef beneath your feet, you're best advised to head for either **Torquay Back Beach** or **Jan Juc**.

Linking the notorious wave-jumping haven of **Point Danger** with the westerly extremity at **Haystacks**, Torquay can often have quality waves breaking over the **Point Danger** reef, but when the wind's up and the wave sailors are out in force, a wise man searches a little further.

Continue west along the beach and you will stumble across some scattered rocks in amongst the shorebreak. If you see what appears to be a quality beach break, you've found **Drainoes** where a lefthander will most commonly provide the longer and better option.

Drainoes is a protected haven that could not have been better constructed to provide an easy introduction to larger waves. You can paddle out from the Life Saving Club and have plenty of fun on days

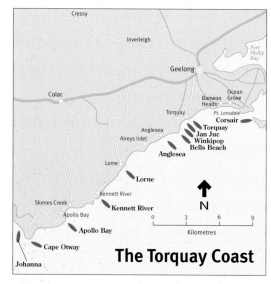

The Torquay Coast

when the surf is up to about 5 ft. When the swells are a bit bigger, a reasonable wave will sometimes break right off the point. Just around the corner, the long cliff-lined expanse of **Jan Juc** beckons and fun beach breaks abound. On a good day, peaks will triangle all along the beach, particularly out in front of the favoured southern-end carpark that forms a popular arena for the latest radical and experimental manoeuvres.

At the far SW end of Jan Juc is a submerged point known as **Bird Rock**. A shallow righthand reef, it can turn on excellent waves, particularly on bigger swells when deep, hollow pits are licked clean by light NE winds. You'll want to get up early to catch this place when it's really cranking because the local pack well and truly has it wired.

If you can find the unmarked carpark SW of here and make it down the dirt tracks unscathed, you should come across three shallow reef breaks that can provide fantastic surf and a perfect venue for photography off the rocky cliffs. **Steps, Evos** and **Boobs** run SW respectively and despite receiving less swell than the more famous duo of Bells and Winkipop, these shapely waves provide some challenging sections that will keep most surfers entertained.

Bells and Winkipop

Winkipop and Bells Beach have been well-publicised in the pages of surfing magazines throughout the world for good reasons. **Winkipop**, to the left of Bells, can produce unbelievable rides up to 300 m long. The wave is racy, the take-off critical and the local crew make it their business to try to snaffle every set wave. If this sounds like fun, you could end up snagging the ride of your life, but you'll need a mid to high tide, unless you're suicidal.

In the late '40s, Dick Garrard would paddle around the point at Jan Juc and surf what we now know as **Bells Beach**. When these early pioneers were able to drive around in Dick's old army jeep, they would have to pass through Martha Bell's farm, hence the naming of the now famous location.

Bells can be a very intimidating place when the swell is running. The waves seem so wide, carrying

Below: Troy Brooks rips the top off a playful Jan Juc peak.
Photo: Steve Ryan

Above: Precision
surfing in perfect
waves. World
champ Kelly Slater
goes rail to rail at
Bells Beach.
Photo: Steve Ryan

a huge force of energy. Although
Bells is renowned for its size, it can
also be enormous fun at 3 ft.
Working best on SW swells and
NW winds, when the swell is maxing you can take-off from **Outside
Rincon** before surfing through the
Bells Bowl and into the shore. On
the headland there are two quality
waves. **Centreside** is a punchy
right, then off to the west is
Southside, a rare lefthander on
this stretch of coast. Both need a SE
swell to really fire. To the west, but
still in the same bay, lies **Pt Addis**.
A performance right, it offers plenty of protection from the SE winds
that destroy the majority of the
nearby beach breaks.

Anglesea/Aireys Inlet

The next spot worth checking is
Point Roadnight (just follow the
Point Roadknight turn-off). The
swell has to be pretty big for this
spot to get a look-in but it can be
fun, particularly for malibu riders.

From here to **Aireys Inlet**, and
indeed all the way to **Apollo Bay**,
surfers are treated to a very rare
phenomenon—a road that follows
the coastline the entire way. This
makes finding the waves extremely easy, although from most vantage points it's very difficult to
judge the size and power of the
waves. Home to many reclusive
surf legends and excellent shapers
such as Wayne Lynch, the region
can be quite deceptive when
assessing the swell. It's possible to
stare out to sea many times and
think that the surf looks fairly tame
and fun until a lone figure plummets down the face of a foaming
beast, further and deeper, the wave
2–3 times his height. It's then you
realise that this place requires
some serious consideration.

One of the hotspots to watch
for is **Fairhaven**, a beach break
that scoops up more swell than
most of the surrounding beaches
and delivers great waves right out
the front of the local surf lifesaving
club. The quality relies heavily on
the condition of the sand banks
and takes NW–NE winds and
swells from the S–SW to ensure a
good session. A few good options
further south are **Moggs Creek**,
and **Spout Creek** but these can be
pretty fickle.

Lorne

The next class wave is found at **Cathedral Rock**, which shares many characteristics with Winkipop. The paddle out here can be hell, as the place rarely gets happening unless the swell is over the 6 ft mark. An extremely long righthander with several hollow sections, the challenge lies in the fact that it works best on low tide which brings you perilously close to some flesh-eating jagged rocks. As usual though, fortune favours the brave.

Five minutes down the road is the thriving town of Lorne. Take a look around and you might see some fun beachies, but the point is the main wave here. The swell has to be huge or directly from the east (which is very rare) for this place to get epic. Well protected from E–SE winds, **Lorne Point** is generally reserved for low tide surfing and judging by the photos adorning the walls of the local surf shop, it can be an extremely long ride when conditions come together. From Lorne to Apollo Bay the coastline assumes a more rugged appearance with less surfers, although generally more swell. There are a variety of waves around the **Cumberland River** and **Back Point** which can often outshine and hold bigger swells than Cathedral Rock, so don't be afraid to look around.

Apollo Bay

Searching further afield, **Wye River**, **Kennett River** and **Skeenes Creek** can all produce good waves. They work best on S–SW swells with N–NW winds. If you score a good session, why not keep buzzing with a great night out at Kennet River's famous Rookery Nook (the pub that overlooks the point). Interspersing these "name" breaks are a myriad of tiny bays guarding powerful, hollow waves such as **Boneyards** and the superb **Massacres** righthander which can both offer uncrowded, quality waves. The good thing is that most locations are accessible from the road and more often than not, you can watch the waves from the car—a real bonus during the colder months.

So how secret can these spots be? Well the locals won't tell you very much, so just keep your eyes open and study the forecasts as you're likely to find some incredible breaks through here. It's a beautiful area and the waves certainly compare with the best the state has to offer.

—*Chris Rennie*

Overleaf: A stoked surfer prepares to spray a mate at the Lorne Point righthander.
Photo: Steve Ryan

Below: Cool water and cooler waves. Nigel Muscroft fits snugly into a Wye River tube.
Photo: Steve Ryan

THE Australian
Surfing Big Top

Oz Surfing Competitions

by Mark Thornley

THE YEAR IS 1973. GATHERED ALONG THE BEACH is an eclectic mix of people with long hair and beards, bell-bottoms and flares. Malibus, shortboards, beaten-up Volkswagons and FJ Holdens line a grassy headland on a classic Easter's day. The shortboard revolution is in full swing and despite harsh social criticism of the contestants as "druggies and bludgers", surfing's simplicity is riding an increasing groundswell of popularity.

Cult icons for independence and self-realisation, Nat Young, Michael Peterson and some of the world's best surfers have gathered at Victoria's Bells Beach to transcend romanticism into competition.

These surfers were oblivious to the fact they were the catalyst that would lead to the transformation of an art form into a sport—a way of life into a way of making a living.

Today, the professional world surfing circuit involves 900 male competitors, 80 female competitors and over $3 million worth of prize money.

The Australian leg of the Association of Surfing Professionals' World Tour is comprised of three major events—the Billabong Pro, Rip Curl Pro and Coca Cola Surf Classic. Each event carries a prize purse of $US120,600 for the men, and $US30,000 for the women. There are also two Four Star World Qualifying Series events held annually.

The Mark Richards Newcastle City Pro, held at NSW's Newcastle Beach during late March, and the Coca Cola Masters which is usually blessed with epic surf at WA's Margaret River during early April, are both fantastic events offering $US80,000 respectively.

With superb waves close to each contest site, these events are a great way to see the latest in contemporary surfing while partying your head off with some true surfing legends.

The Rip Curl Pro
The Bells Women's Classic
Venue: Bells Beach or
Johanna Beach
Date: April 7-16

First held over a quarter of a century ago, the Rip Curl Pro is the longest-running event on the world professional surfing tour.

The incomparable surfing of Queensland's Michael Peterson, who took three consecutive titles from the event's inception 1973–1975, attracted growing crowds each year as young people realised how spectacular and accessible the sport of surfing really was. News of Bells Beach's double-storey righthanders sped around the world with the dawn of each new swell, bringing hordes of American surfers bitten by the surfing bug.

It was at Bells Beach, which consistently produces Australia's largest competition waves, that Mark Richards began a four-year national and world title surfing reign by winning three consecutive titles from 1978–80. This feat remains unsurpassed by an Australian surfer to date.

A year later, in 1981, the Rip Curl Pro provided the arena for top Narrabeen surfer and shaper Simon Anderson to showcase his strange three-fin "thruster" design to the world. Doubts that the weird-looking craft

would even float were soon dispelled, when Simon caught his first wave and carved radical lines nobody had ever seen before. He went on to win the event and his design fundamentals still remain the staple template for today's high-performance surfing.

In the ensuing years, Bells hosted some titanic Australia-USA struggles with Tom Curren and Tom Carroll going carve-for-carve in solid surf. In 1987, Mark Richards' nephew and child surfing prodigy, Nick Wood, startled everybody by winning the event with some awesome surfing at the tender age of 16.

A women's contest was incorporated into the Rip Curl Pro program during 1989, when Wendy Botha and a determined group of female pro surfers showed they, too, could tame some of Australia's largest surf. Since then the Bells' Women's Classic has been an on-going duel between Florida's Lisa Andersen and Australia's Pauline Menczer, who seem to save their best big-wave performances for the Bell's righthanders each year.

A high-performance wave, offering tubes and wide open, manoeuvre-oriented walls, Bells has always suited powerful, precise surfers with heaps of style in larger surf. Australians such as Damien Hardman, Barton Lynch—and in more recent years Americans Kelly Slater and Sunny Garcia—have all excelled at Bells.

Solid 6–8 ft waves have been enjoyed here for the past two years of competition, and radical Australian surfers Matt Hoy and Mark Occhilupo have once again wrestled the Bells title balance back from the Americans in a see-sawing battle for one of the world tour's most prestigious big-wave competition titles. There's plenty of action on the land as well with an annual surf music festival and celebration held at Torquay to cap off a great week of surfing.

The Coca-Cola Surf Classic
The Diet Coke Women's Classic
Venue: Manly Beach
Date: April 20-26

Conceived by Sydney newspaper journalist and surfer Graham Cassidy, the first Coke event began nervously from the back of a VW combi van, where judges pioneered a make-shift scoring system. Cassidy, aided by surfing colleagues Geoff Luton, Midget Farrelly and Terry Fitzgerald, persuaded Coca Cola to back up their psychedelic surf advertising with a board-riding contest. Based at NSW's North Narrabeen Beach, the first Coke Surfabout event in 1974 enjoyed great waves with perfect Narrabeen and big Fairy Bower turning on insane barrels. Surfers such as Nat Young and Michael Peterson gave the sporting media their first real look at tube-riding and inspired an entire generation of young surfers, who had taken the day off school to watch their heroes pull in.

Tom Carroll, Cheyne Horan and contest reserves Mark Richards and Wayne "Rabbit" Bartholomew were among those whose lives had been changed forever.

Fronted by the articulate Richards, a number of true surfing characters began to emerge, and in 1978, when the Coke Surfabout scored mind-blowing waves at Manly's North

Steyne, a cheeky Larry Blair laid the foundations for an award-winning televised surfing documentary that cemented modern-day surfing's acceptance.

That same year, the Coke Surfabout offered a women's professional surfing division that was eventually won by Hawaii's Lynne Boyer, although it was not until 1982 that women's competitive surfing really began in earnest.

Even then, it took courageous big-wave performances from talented surfers such as Manly's Pam Burridge, WA's Jodie Cooper and South Africa's Wendy Botha (three times Coke Classic winner) to attract solid sponsorship to the premier Australian events.

During 1982–83 the "kids" became men, Rabbit Bartholomew decimated Dee Why Point and Tom Carroll ripped North Steyne, to set the international surfing standard with searing roundhouse cutbacks and full rail turns that previously were thought impossible.

However, as men and women's pro surfing stepped up a notch and headed for what appeared an inevitable sponsorship boom time, the unthinkable happened and the Coke Surfabout collapsed.

By 1986 the Coke Surfabout had been resurrected by Coca Cola Bottlers as the Coke Classic—a decision that marked pro surfing's coming of age. Over the ensuing years, the event has produced many surfing world title winners including Tom Carroll, Damien Hardman, Martin Potter and the five-times surfing world champion, Kelly Slater.

Keeping a stranglehold on the women's title from 1989–91, South African, now Australian citizen, Wendy Botha felt right at home in the peaky Narrabeen rights and lefts. She used Coke Classic wins to launch her world title bids, as did Australian's Pam Burridge and Pauline Menczer, who won in 1992 and 1994 respectively.

In recent years, NSW's Kylie Webb has dominated the event with some explosive surfing from 1996–97 to take two consecutive women's titles.

The Coca Cola Surf Classic, which was moved from Narrabeen to its present location at Manly during 1998, is a big crowd pleaser and always generates plenty of action at the Narrabeen Sands Hotel and other beach-side watering holes.

The Billabong Pro
Men's and Women's event
Venue: Kirra Point or
Burleigh Heads
Date: March 12-22

Billabong founder Gordon Merchant entered the international surfing stakes during the inaugural Billabong Pro in 1984. Staged at Duranbah Beach on Queensland's Gold Coast, the event introduced the world-class point breaks of Kirra and Burleigh Heads to many overseas surfers for the first time.

A solid tube rider, Hawaiian Hans Hedeman threaded his way through Duranbah's hollow beach break pits, taking the honours over a super-competitive field.

Following the event's success, Merchant cited plans to stage the richest event in surfing history, and so was born the 5A-rated Billabong Pro, a mobile contest that shifted the focus to Oahu's North Shore. From 1985–88 the event enjoyed many great highlights including an epic day at 25-ft Waimea Bay that saw some dramatic rescues and Barton Lynch's emotional world title victory at the Banzai Pipeline.

In 1989, the Billabong Pro offered a world-record US$50,000 first prize and in a miraculous display of backdoor tube riding, Australian veteran, Cheyne Horan, mastered the challenging Sunset Beach righthanders to take home the hefty winner's cheque. The following year, a struggling Nick Wood put it all together at Sunset Beach to resurrect his career.

The Coke Classic's re-birth, in 1986, saw the suspension of the Billabong Pro in 1991, as political wrangles and restrictions with the event's mobility forced Gordon Merchant to put the Hawaiian competition on hold.

It wasn't until 1996 that the Billabong Pro returned, this time to the Queensland Gold Coast where Hawaiian Kaipo Jaquias outpointed American Jeff Booth with some inspirational tube riding at North Stradbroke Island.

Held during the peak of Queensland's cyclone season, the 1997 tournament demonstrated why the event is one of the most respected competitions on the pro circuit. Blessed with perfect 6–8 ft waves at Kirra and Burleigh Heads, the star-studded surfing field gorged themselves on filthy tuberides for an entire week with Florida's Kelly Slater putting on a flawless display of barrel mastery to take the title.

Similarly, Hawaiian gidget Rochelle Ballard created professional surfing history when she scored two perfect tens in her semi-final against Sydney's Layne Beachley. Riding some of the deepest tube rides of the entire contest, Ballard beat the radical USA charger Lisa Andersen to grab the spoils.

Although the tournament is based at Burleigh Heads, the Billabong Pro's preferred venue is Kirra Point, since it offers fantastic waves and spectator vantage points. The contest also takes advantage of the waves around North Stradbroke Island, Ballina and northern NSW, should the swell be scarce. There's also plenty of post-contest partying at the surrounding pubs and clubs including Billy's Beach House, the Miami Hotel and Friday's.

Page 127: Power and perfect timing. Shane Powell always pushes the limits at Bells Beach. *Photo: Steve Ryan*

Opposite: One of Australia's all time competitive greats, former world champ Tom Carroll heaves into a massive cutback at his beloved North Narrabeen lefts. *Photo: Andrew Buckley*

Below: Four times Women's Surfing World Champion, Florida's Lisa Andersen prepares to be swallowed by Kirra's sandy cyclone chamber. *Photo: Andrew Christie*

The Shipwreck Coast
Busted Ships—Busted Surfers

December–March.

Some cliff climbs and beach hikes.

Sand-covered reef and rock-shelf bottoms.

7 ft-plus boards, spare boards and limbs, Marine Boy oxygen gum, super-glue for booties.

Fanatical localism, strong currents and 20–30 ft wipeouts kms out to sea.

Reef cuts and broken bones.

Some of the largest and most challeng-ing rideable surf anywhere in the world.

The Shipwreck Coast has become infamous for obvious reasons. The treacherous waters between Apollo Bay and Portland have claimed many ships, their twisted anchors and assorted debris embedded in the surrounding reefs serve as a bitter reminder of the awesome power of the Southern Ocean. Holding gnarly swells of 25 ft plus, this largely inaccessible coastline guards some of Australia's best big wave locations.

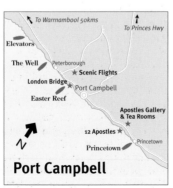

Apollo Bay

As you pass through Apollo Bay and head towards Port Campbell you will often find that wind direc-tions change and the swell jumps accordingly. If **Torquay** (you pass through it on your way here, just past Geelong) is flat then you can expect many of the Shipwreck Coast locations to be breaking at around 4–5 ft. If it's 4–6 ft at Tor-quay it'll be too heavy for all but the crazed big wave maniacs that don't mind copping a couple of 20–30 footers on the head!

Beginning with a beautiful mean-dering drive through the Otway Ranges, once you pass through this scenic area, the real action begins. The first accessible wave is **Castles** which can offer a variety of excel-lent lefthand and righthand waves all of which can be viewed from the carpark. The best time to surf this coast is during Summer when it takes on new appeal as the rest of Victoria's coastline is hampered by a general lack of swell.

Johanna is a popular pitstop and has great camping facilities located next to some of the best beach breaks in the state. There is plenty of area for BYO accommoda-tion and this often draws the crowds. Consequently, there is sometimes a strong 'locals only' type attitude. This has been bred out of the disrespect that some visi-tors display, but generally speaking the vibe is pretty mellow. Just be friendly and keep the area pristine and you'll have a great time.

Johanna is a very powerful break, even at 3–4 ft it's punishing,

so beware! The set-up is pretty obvious once you get to the viewing spot. The trick to this place, and indeed anywhere you surf, is to use the rips to your advantage. Johanna is particularly renowned for its fierce currents and it's important you continually read the ocean to avoid a very frustrating surf or placing yourself in a potentially dangerous situation.

NE winds are generally offshore, perhaps the result of the adjacent Otway Ranges which have a profound affect on this small stretch of tube-rich coastline!

Port Campbell

Continue on past Lavers Hill, still heading towards Port Campbell, and you'll bump into **Moonlight Head**, one of the few locations that works on a SE breeze. The local waves are ferocious but can be a real buzz when the swell has time to settle. While you're waiting there are some great wrecks and Aboriginal caves to check out. **Princetown** can also produce good waves with a nice right point set-up, plus camping nearby.

One of Victoria's visual highlights, **Gibson's Steps** is clearly marked as a tourist attraction for spectacular views of the coast. Even more attractive from a surfer's perspective are the long, grinding waves that break down below the 90 odd steps. The peaks usually look very inviting but don't ever be

fooled into believing that they don't look that big, because they're always a lot bigger than you think.

Searching further afield, **Port Campbell** is a beautiful town with a thriving fishing and tourist trade. The harbour can have some great waves when big swells are closing out other surfing options. I've surfed the left across the bay at 6 ft when there was a solid 15–20 ft swell running—pretty eerie waiting for the reform of one of those beasts! Directly out from the harbour is **Easter Reef** which would have to rate as one of the most powerful bomboras around. Holding huge, rideable righthanders, it is up there with Western Australia's Margaret River as an all-time thrill. There has been quite a bit of coverage about the place, but you need a boat, willing buddies and guts—plenty of 'em.

Warrnambool

The next name break is **The Well**, located just outside Peterborough. If there was an instruction manual for this place it would read something like this—throw your board into a foaming 2 m square ocean keyhole, 5 m below. Next, hurl your body with an outgoing swell, paddle with all your strength to a grinding righthand reef break, making take-off essential, paddle back to keyhole, wait for incoming swell, launch onto tiny reef shelf, scramble to safety!!

Above: A deserted Portland line-up just asking to be ridden. *Photo: Steve Ryan*

Opposite: The dramatic Shipwreck Coast has provided much pleasure and pain. *Photo: Steve Ryan*

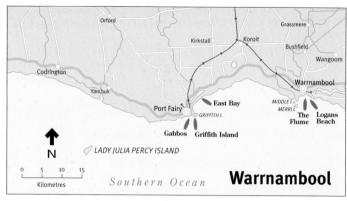

What more can I say, except try it on the lower tides and a NE wind.

Elevators has an even more God-fearing reputation, when 12–15 ft waves batter the coast. When everywhere else is too big, this big wave magnet will hold its own and is best tackled on low tides. From here to Warrnambool there are a host of good surf spots. Much of the enjoyment is in finding them yourself. Some of the places to look out for are: the **Bay of Martyrs**, a big righthander in the **Bay of Isles** and **Lake Gillear**. These spots often have quality big wave surf but the paddles are long and over deep, dark, cold water which of course is a party house for sharks and a host of other rather large, marine life.

Warrnambool is about three hours drive from Melbourne (four-and-a-half hours via the coast) and hosts some fun waves. To the east of the rivermouth there is **Logans Beach** which often has a good left-hander. If you're there between January and April you might also witness the spectacular antics of the Southern Right Whale. **The Flume** is the name break which you will find west of the rivermouth and close to the town.

Port Fairy

On the way to Port Fairy there is a break known as **The Cutting**, directly south of Tower Hill. It can have classic lefthanders with a consistent sandbar. One of Victoria's oldest ports, Port Fairy retains much of its historic charm. An annual folk festival attracts thousands. **East Bay** is best for mellow waves with NW winds being offshore. **Griffith Island** is the big wave location in the area which holds the most bohemoth swells the ocean can deliver. Hence, there is never a problem with overcrowding. The best spot is known as **The Passage,** a powerhouse righthand point break that comes with a fairly aggressive local attitude. Northerly winds are offshore and a rising tide is best. About a kilometre west from here is a break called **Gabbos** which is a lefthander that has a pretty heavy guillotine lip. It works on the same conditions as the Passage.

Portland

Portland has some great waves all within close proximity to each other. A versatile and historic surfing village, it plays host to good quality waves that work on a variety of swells and wind directions. **Narrawong** is at its best on a light N–NW wind and many quality beach break peaks can provide a great session with swells up to 5 ft. Anything larger has a tendency to provide some challenging closeout take-offs.

A trio of delectable righthand point breaks, within coooeee of each other, will work during a large swell and SW winds. Those same SW winds, that blow out many favoured west coast breaks, make **Crumpets** and its big brother **Blacknose Point** work well. The waves can be so long and so much fun that quite often it's preferable to paddle in and hoof it

back to the take-off zone. The third of these point breaks, **Rifle Range** picks up more swell but is usually a little messier. **Yellow Rock** on a north wind will ensure good beach breaks but a titanic struggle against the rips can wreak havoc on your session. If you have reliable transportation, preferably a good 4WD, take the punt on northerly winds and seek out **Crayfish Bay,** a superb lefthand reef that will make all that effort to get there seem meagre. Don't forget your booties or you'll be in for an urchin surprise. Ouch!

Murrels Beach also favours the bold, with some sizeable lefts over a shallow rock bottom. **Bridgewater Bay** plays host to **Bombers Beach, Blowholes, Shelly Beach** and **The Boatshed's** big kelp-lined waves. **Discovery Bay** offers a range of beach breaks with a quality lefthand reef thrown in. Nearby **Whites Beach** will also provide a challenging session and works best on a big S–SW swell with E–NE winds, which allow the righthand reef break to lineup for maximum buzz.

—*Chris Rennie*

Above: Martin Potter wrenches a nice snap in the pocket at inside Elevators.
Photo: Steve Ryan

Overleaf: Shaun Brooks puts the pedal to the metal with his back to the wall at Logans Beach.
Photo: Steve Ryan

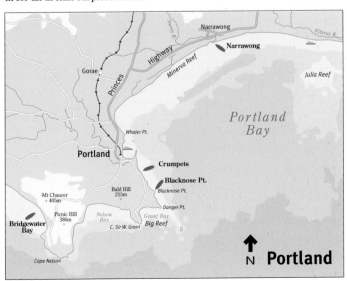

Phillip Island

Penguins and Powerful Waves

Below: One of Victoria's most consistent wave windows, Woolamai Beach crafts raw groundswell into surfing masterpieces. Who knows what surfers would give to own this art. *Photo: Steve Ryan*

One of Victoria's top tourist destinations, Phillip Island is home to the diminutive Little Penguin. The island's main attraction, these peculiar birds have assumed legendary status for their spectacular parades and cheeky antics. Gathering in their thousands, just after sunset each night, they march across the sand dunes to their burrows at the back of Summerland Beach.

Phillip Island also hosts the Australian 500cc Motorcycle Grand Prix, which attracts hordes of local and international visitors each year.

Oblivious to the hype, Phillip Island surfers are a hardy breed, braving icy waters and sharky Bass Strait line-ups in pursuit of the perfect barrel. Since the island is surrounded by long sandy beaches and a rugged coastline sprinkled with an assortment of excellent reef and point breaks, the surfers don't have to travel too far to find good waves.

After a 90-minute drive from Melbourne, the island is reached via the bridge that links mainland San Remo to Newhaven and the small towns of **Cowes** and **Rhyll**. Popular with city surfers looking for a weekend escape and keen boardriders from the nearby Mornington Peninsula, **Woolamai Beach** is one of Victoria's most consistent swell magnets.

Woolamai

When everywhere else is flat, Woolamai will usually be churning out some perfect right and lefthand peaks. A long beach with a variety of breaks including **Magic Lands**, **1st Carpark**, **2nd Carpark** and **Ocean Reach**, you'll find 'V' banks all the way along, which change from week to week depending on the rips and swell. The currents are strong but they make the waves stand up and barrel, so a little pad-

December–Sept.

Roads to most breaks. Short walks.

Rounded and flat reefs. Sand-covered reef and sand bottoms.

Boards for fast, hollow sections.

Strong currents. Largest currents in Australia.

Reef cuts and cold-water cramps.

Powerful waves, relatively uncrowded. Offshore in southerly winds— a rarity in Victoria.

dling can go a long way. Best surfed on E–NW winds with a medium to high tide and a 2–6 ft swell.

A similar setup to Woolamai, **Forest Caves** offers a series of beach break peaks scattered over a long beach. A taxing hike over a big sand dune, it tends to handle the NW winds better than its popular neighbour and when a southerly swell is running it can really crank.

Heading west along Back Beach Rd, you'll come to a carpark overlooking the headland at **Surfers Point**. Best surfed on a low tide, the wave has a big drop and a short wall that reforms on the inside. Be prepared to turn around a shallow rock that sucks dry on a low tide. In northerly to westerly winds, Surfers Point can handle 4–10 ft on a mid to high tide.

Phillip Island's premier wave, **Express Point** or 'EP' as it is affectionately known to locals, is a classic righthand reef break that demands commitment.

A heavy take-off over shallow reef followed by an intense inside tube section reserves it for competent surfers only. If you wipeout you'll usually visit some sharp rocks and if you drop in on one of the heavy locals something worse could happen.

Above: Phillip Island's Little Penguins put on their dinner suits and get ready for a big night out. *Photo: Scancolour*

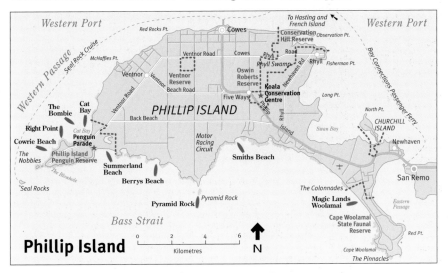

Requiring medium to large S–SW swells, Express Point is generally a fickle break handling waves from 4–8 ft with light N–NW winds. EP has a reputation for eating surfboards so remember surf it on a high tide only!

Smiths Beach

In contrast, Smiths Beach offers a fun and safe surfing environment with right and left peaks. Unlike most breaks, it's best surfed during an onshore breeze which makes the waves peak up before peeling. Offshore winds tend to make the place closeout. A good back stop when nowhere else is working, it's best surfed on a mid to low tide with SE–SW winds.

Pyramid Rock/Cowries

If the wind is NE, Pyramid Rock could have some nice left and right peaks over a sand bottom, but more than likely **Berry's Beach**, a little further west, will be a better option. Requiring about 2–4 ft swell, it can sometimes resemble Woolamai's quality A frames, only there are a lot more rocks. A high tide with NE–NW winds is ideal.

Beachfront real estate for thousand's of Little Penguins, **Summerland** located near Phillip Island's western point, offers two breaks. At high tide the waves will break

around the point with many sections. It's a slow wave but has a few sweet spots. On a mid to low tide, the inside section called **Centre Crack** can be a great wave. A very sucky take-off over a shallow rock will get the adrenaline pumping before you negotiate a barrel or a good wall. Sometimes the sand lines

up parallel with the coast and the wave goes all the way to the beach. SW–N winds and a medium swell are best for the point while Center Crack requires about a 3–6 ft swell.

Just around the corner lies **Cowrie Beach**. When surfing this big, wally lefthander you can see **Nobbies** and **Seal Rocks**. It's a good place to try out your 7 ft gun so you can keep your feet out of the water. If you're lucky you'll spot a seal—and if you're unlucky a White Pointer. S–E winds with a medium to large swell and 4–10 ft waves are best.

Cat Bay

Located inside Cat Bay, **Right Point** has a fast barrel section and a high performance wall to do whatever. It's only a short ride but it's pretty intense. On a 4–6 ft swell, the inside reform at **Thistles** can get quite long and fast but a little flat. Sometimes you can link it from out the back to the inside. If the swell is smaller, the tide higher and it stops breaking out the back, surf **The Bowl**—it's a fun little reef break.

Even sharkier is the **Bombie**, a big lefthander a long way out to sea off Cat Bay. It starts breaking from 8 ft but can handle 15 ft plus. You'll need your big boards, some friends for company and maybe even a boat. Working on a low tide and a SE wind, when it's big and barreling, the Bombie requires some serious courage.

A mid to high tide with southerly winds is best. **Shelly Beach** is also a gentle wave best for beginners and mals. You'll find some good left and right peaks breaking over a soft reef. It can handle any swell because it's so protected but is best on SE–SW winds with a medium to high tide.

One of the island's most consistent and popular spots, **Flynn's Reef** offers a good righthander with a fast wall to do some big turns. At times resembling the Bells' Bowl, Flynn's likes S–NE winds with a medium to large swell. Even when the wind is onshore the waves are still good.

—*Glyndon Ringrose*

Above: The unforgiving Express Point lip.
Photo: Andrew Buckley

Opposite: Glyndon Ringrose floats weightlessly over a foamy Phillip Island section.
Photo: Steve Ryan

Mornington Peninsula

*Fickle Surf and
Prime Beach Breaks*

Preceding pages:
Victorian big-wave
legend Tony Ray
slides into some
liquid candy.
Photo: Steve Ryan

Below: Gash
Surfboards shaper,
Greg Brown sets a
deep line in the
Gunamatta pit.
Photo: Steve Ryan

February–June.

Via farmlands and
roads. Some boat
access.

Sand-covered reef,
reef and sand bot-
toms.

Medium wave
boards, a friend
with a boat, 4 mm
wetsuit.

Military police and
sharks.

Reef cuts and rips.

Relatively uncrowd-
ed and sometimes
excellent waves.

About as close to the city of
Melbourne as you can get for a
surf, Mornington Peninsula has
plenty of great wave locations.

Point Leo

In my 15 years of surfing the
Mornington Peninsula, I have never seen any rideable waves at
Balnarring Point. Many of my
friends have boasted about the quality of surf this far inside Western-
port Bay, but I'm yet to be con-
vinced. I certainly wouldn't pin the
hope of a quality session on the
hearsay of pub talk.

Really the first quality reef break,
some say the only one, that you will
encounter in this area is **Point Leo**.
Indicative of this surf region, beach
access was, until recently, through
the farm lands and although there's
been much subdivision, Point Leo
still retains that rural feel.

The peak months for this coastline are during autumn and winter
with Spring still providing the odd
classic session. The premier break
known as **Suicides** can produce
classic rights of up to 150 m.
However the swell needs to be 6 ft
plus and many sessions ensue at
nearby **Peak Rock**, right off the
main break. The incoming tide is
the best time to hit Leo with tide
variations jacking the swell by 2–3
ft. Offshore is NW.

Shoreham

From Point Leo, the next wave
venue is Shoreham and a break
called **The Pines**. Occasionally this
location can spit some epic pits but
the swell has to be huge. Largely
protected from the SW winds that
often accompany solid localised
swells, it can really turn on when
the elements combine.

Above: Rye Beach
delivers the goodies
on a magic over-
head day.
Photo: Peter Wilson

Another worthwhile surf stop is the nearby and rather quaint township of **Flinders**. Hosting a variety of reef breaks, **Cyrils** is the primo wave. A long, hollow righthander, it's best surfed on the incoming and high tides holding swells up to 9 ft. Aptly named, the other drawcard is **Meanos**, a punchy lefthander that grinds over very shallow reef. Stroke into this wave like you mean it; there's no going over the falls here.

Cape Schanck

Between the town of Flinders and Cape Schanck there are few waves of any consequence. Occasionally though, the lighthouse at **Cape Schanck** provides the backdrop to some serious lefts when the swell hits. Reeling off the kelp beds and rock platform, the grunty lefthanders wind down the line for some intense surfing. It can be surfed from 9–12 ft but don't say we didn't warn you. In contrast, the righthander on the western side of **Bushrangers Bay** is generally very protected. Breaking off **Pulpit Rock**, the swell has to be pretty big before this wave gets a look.

The remainder of the coast that stretches to the heads can offer some of the most rewarding beach and reef surfing you might see, but invariably to the travelling surfer it can be incredibly frustrating. Many times I've sped down the South Eastern Highway with everything on my side; blue skies, offshore winds, 6 ft swell, only to spend my afternoon searching for a wave that wouldn't crush me with continual closeouts.

Top on the surfing check list is **Gunamatta,** which produces some beautiful waves depending on the shifty banks that move constantly with the severe rip action. The nearby ocean outfall can be a little off putting but it doesn't deter the large group of locals who surf the hollow left and right peaks during most conditions. Divided by two distinct carparks, Gunamatta ideally requires a clean 4–6 ft swell and a light NW wind to produce the flawless perfection that people rave about.

Portsea

Just past the St Andrews turn off, **Rye** is the next consistent break that can produce great lefts and rights when the banks are favourable at **Ocean Beach**. Similarly, heading toward **Portsea** there are a multitude of wide open beaches with a combination of quality waves and dangerous reefs. There are even places that work during

Mornington Peninsula

accessed by special buses or walking. Here lies the old ruins of the Army Cadet School that was once equipped with the cannons responsible for firing Australia's first shots of World War I.

Located at the extremity of Point Nepean's headland there's a break known as **Quarantine** or **Corsair.** It's a heavy left that can dish out extremely good thrashings from both the waves and the locals. Best accessed by boat, you can also reach it via a long walk from the boom gates but if you get caught, good luck!

Why is this spot so prized? Well it's just one of those freaks; you walk around the corner after checking 50 spots that are all crap, when suddenly there's this majestic left-hander. Ah yes, Quarantines is an appropriate name because once you arrive you'll want to stay a while.

Perhaps the best way to score good waves on the Mornington Peninsula is to go to one of the local surf shops. Buy something, wax will do, and try to, real casual like, pry into where there might be good banks. If you play it right you might score a solo session but more than likely they'll see through your flimsy façade and pick you for the wave hungry pig you really are**.**

onshore winds, it just takes persistence, local knowledge and time to find these tasty setups. **Spooks** at Portsea back-beach is one such location. Accessed by the London Bride carpark, the reeling right-hand barrels provide spectacular rides and a scary but rewarding double up that pitches ferociously on the inside section.

Below: Josh Palmateer weaves for speed as the curtain falls on a thundering Victorian beach break.
Photo: Peter Wilson

Point Nepean

At the end of the peninsula lies Point Nepean which can only be

The East Coast

Rewards For Those Who Seek

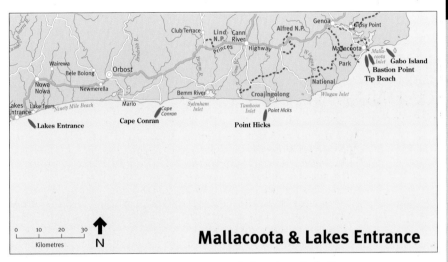

Mallacoota & Lakes Entrance

Mallacoota

My first surfing experience on this coast was a hiking trip (on sand the whole damn way!) to the north of Mallacoota. I have vivid memories of us gorging on a huge crab I had somehow caught before stumbling upon some of the most beautiful beach breaks I have ever seen.

The closest and arguably the best break north of Mallacoota, **Gabo Island** has quality lefts but access is limited to boats. Because Gabo needs a solid swell to really pump, the journey can be a little hellish and generally ideal conditions are enjoyed on a strong S–SW swell accompanied by a NW–W wind. It can also handle northerly swells.

But for quality surf and easy access you can't go past **Bastion Point**. Peeling majestically at the entrance to the Mallacoota Inlet, its long righthanders churn invitingly over a forgiving sand bottom. If you want to push the adrenalin button there are some heavier reef breaks further around the point. The south side is called **Tip Beach** and is probably the best bet for waves along this stretch.

Next stop is the secluded **Point Hicks** where a short but happening righthander works on S–SE swells and NE–NW winds. Best ridden over 6 ft, it's named after Lt. Zachary Hicks, who first sighted the landmark in 1770 as a crew member on Captain Cook's expedition. Although there are camping facilities, they are pretty basic and you'll need to bring the "kitchen sink" to feel comfortable.

Lakes Entrance

Further south along the Princes Highway, you'll find **Cape Conran**, a spectacular region that can provide some excellent waves. I've crashed in the back of my Holden to be woken by clean A-frames

May–August.

Access can be tough with long hikes and bushwalks to empty bays.

Reef and sand.

Good board carry bag, tent and back pack. Mid range boards and 4–5 mm wetsuit.

Unpredictable weather patterns and strong currents.

Reef cuts and wipe-outs in the middle of nowhere.

Uncrowded waves, great scenery.

breaking up and down the coast. Unfortunately camping is illegal in this area and the place is damn fickle! I think I've scored it one in ten trips, but I continue to return.

Keep driving and you'll reach **Lakes Entrance** which can produce reasonable waves, however strong winds usually chew a consistently powerful swell, transforming the place into a washing machine.

In contrast, the classic **Red Bluff** reef break (about 150 km south), is rare, indeed exclusive to this chunk of coastline. A long left-hander which ideally needs an E–SE swell and N–NE winds to start sectioning down the line, it's a popular pitstop but definitely worth a paddle when it's on.

Continuing further south is **Ninety Mile Beach** which has no known or consistent banks. Gaining a reputation for fierce rips and currents, not to mention those playful White Pointers, I'd have to say give it a miss until you reach more fertile surf grounds.

Wilsons Promontory

The Australian mainland's most southerly tip, Wilsons Promontory's rugged national park em-

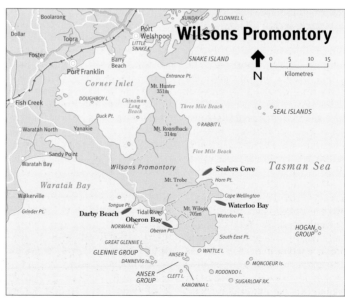

braces some 160 km of awe-inspiring coastline. Surfing here is for the hardy only. Access is extremely tough and the weather patterns very erratic but if you time it right, you could enjoy some of the most rewarding and uncrowded waves of your life.

A short walk from the tidal river camp ground, **Oberon Bay** has some fun beach breaks that wedge nicely when the swell is from W–SW with light winds.

The remainder of the areas are accessed by long, well-planned hikes to isolated swell funnels such as **Sealers Cove**, **Waterloo Bay** and **Darby Beach** which all produce waves in most conditions. The many protected coves offer shelter for travelling yachts and sometimes can pump out classic,

crowd-free waves.

I have hiked around "The Prom" several times, only once with surfing equipment. As Murphy's law would have it, the only time I didn't see waves was when I lugged my precious piece of fibreglass around for five days. The other trips were filled with classic body surfing

Above: Brendan Ryan buries his toes in the deck as he plummets down the face of a monster.
Photo: Steve Ryan

Below: One of The Prom's beaches, Squeaky Beach.
Photo: Courtesy VTC

Above: 200 stiches, one for each barrel. Mark Jepson shows what can happen when you're on the receiving end of a big, angry Victorian reef break.
Photo: Steve Ryan

Opposite: Look closely amongst Gibson's Steps dramatic scenery and you'll find a few surfing surprises.
Photo: Simon de Salis

sessions which included the occasional barrel. It really doesn't matter if you're without a board, as the scenery and experience are quite overwhelming. That said, I've never seen a clean wave peel down the line and been glad not to have my stick!

South Gippsland

Venturing into the South Gippsland

area and west to Melbourne, the next noteworthy surf region is **Inverloch** which can provide some quality waves. On its day, the entrance of the **Anderson Inlet** can have classic left and right barrels. The more consistent areas though are towards **Cape Patterson** where reliable breaks can be found among the cool, clear waters of the **Bunurong Marine Park**.

Many of my childhood years were spent on surfmats, riding the numerous reef and sand breaks that dot this coastline. When we finally upgraded to surfboards we still surfed many of these same waves. The winding road along to **Wonthaggi**, in particular, provides some juicy peaks especially on S–SW swells and N–NE winds. Crowds aren't a problem, except in the peak summer months when grommies begin the surfing cycle all over again.

The last break before you reach Phillip Island is **Kilcunda.** Renowned for its quality lefthanders, "Killers" offers a varied power scale of locations catering for any level of surfing ability.

The advantage with this quiet little town (although I don't know if one pub and a take-away outlet constitutes a town) is that the wind often blows offshore from the NE during autumn and summer. Invariably there's some kind of swell around this area, so it's well worth the time to check the local hotspots. From here it's over to the surf-rich Phillip Island.

—*Chris Rennie*

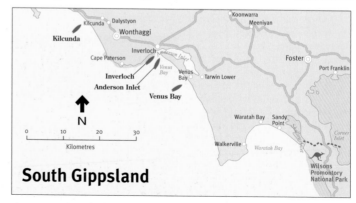

South Gippsland

The Apple Isle

A Surfing Wilderness

Tasmania welcomes surfers with some of the cleanest air and water and the remotest barrels in the world. From Hobart's fickle point breaks backdropped by the spectacular Mt Wellington, to the huge reef breaks and bombies on the wild west coast, the water may be cold but the waves are hot!

Situated between the 40th and 43rd parallel, Australia's southernmost state, "Tassie" is home to some of the world's largest tracts of World Heritage wilderness. An action-sport paradise, this island state offers a pulse-racing mix of surfing, skiing, diving, fishing, whitewater rafting, caving and jet boating in pristine terrain. No matter where you are, you're never more than an hour from the ocean. During winter you can even surf and ski in the one day!

Tasmania's population of 450,000 occupies 63,000 square km (equivalent to the size of Ireland) ranging from sub-alpine forests to untouched sun-bleached beaches. Although Tasmania is the smallest and least populated of the nation's six states, its capital Hobart is actually Australia's second oldest city located a mere 2,700 km from the icy expanse of Antarctica.

Situated in the southeast of the state, Hobart boasts historic Salamanca Place, an icon in itself, where beautifully preserved Georgian warehouses brim with contemporary art galleries, antique caverns and multicultural restaurants. On Saturdays, locals stock up with fresh produce from the famous Salamanca Markets.

The waters off Hobart have a few classic point breaks that occasionally fire, but most of the premier surf locations are found around the Tasman Peninsula. Also, the wild west coast generates plenty of swell. The Bass Strait islands have good surf potential too, but like much of the island's pristine coastline, they remain relatively unexplored.

Separated from mainland Australia by treacherous Bass Strait, the "Apple Isle", as it is commonly known, cops the full fury of the chilly Southern Ocean swells. Some of the biggest waves ever recorded have lashed Tasmania's coastline. Bass Strait alone has claimed over 250 ships to date and commands humble respect from participants in the internationally renowned annual Sydney to Hobart Yacht Race, a 630 nautical mile event beginning at Sydney Harbour before finishing at Hobart's Constitutional Dock.

In 1770, more than a century before James Cook claimed mainland Australia for Great Britain, Captain Abel Tasman sighted the rugged coast of Tasmania and named the area after Anthony Van Dieman, Governor-General of the East Indies and sponsor of his voyage. Soon afterward, the island played host to some of Great Britain's most infamous convicts, and "Van Dieman's Land" forged a reputation as Australia's harshest penal colony. The island was subsequently renamed Tasmania, in 1885, to honour the Captain's pioneering spirit.

From these harsh beginnings, Tasmania has always been a paradoxical balance of beauty and

Above: Clean water, solid waves and empty line-ups have led some surfers to describe Tasmania as "God's own country". Here a deserted West Coast pit steamrolls into another forgotten bay.
Photo: Bill Morris

oppression, its human history as rugged and dramatic as its landscape. It is a place of contradiction, where loggers and conservationists fight over the same area of forest. Where progressive views on self-sufficiency and technology reside alongside racial intolerance and archaic social legislation.

Tasmania's predominantly mountainous terrain provides for some breathtaking scenery from both the air and ground level. The world-famous Overland Track, for example, a 60-km bushwalking pilgrimage through gorges, mountain peaks and moors, will give you an insight into the majestic forces which carved out the unique landscapes. Year round, people scale the 1,617 m Mt Ossa and other popular peaks including Ben Lomond, Mount Wellington and Cradle Mountain. In the north west of the state, Ben Lomond, at 1,300 m above sea level, is considered Tasmania's premier downhill skifield.

Wherever you are, never underestimate the weather. In some regions, clear blue skies can change to debilitating blizzards in a matter of an hour. Summer is warm with long twilight nights often accentuated by nature's spectacular southern lightshow, the Aurora Australis.

The food is pretty good too—you can expect to dine on world-class Atlantic salmon, Pacific oysters, abalone and other marine morsels accompanied by excellent local wines and gourmet cheeses produced from the lush pastures of King Island. Visit Tassie's Cascade Brewery, Australia's oldest operating brewery, or the country's southern-most pub on Bruny Island.

Once you have experienced Tasmania first-hand, the memory of its natural beauty and empty waves will live with you forever. Thanks to the efforts of conservationists all over the world, the state's World Heritage Areas, encompassing 1.4 million hectares of wild terrain, remain an international benchmark in measuring pollution. Furthermore, 40 percent of the island has been set aside as national parks.

Along the coast of Tasmania there are plenty of virgin surfing spots awaiting discovery by generations of adventurers to come. It's pure hardcore surfing and the water is cool, cool, cool—here's to wetsuit technology!

The North and North East Coasts

Fickle Waves and Fast Rides

Tassie's north coast is extremely fickle and doesn't score huge waves. Cape Grim to Cape Portland is generally sheltered from a lot of swell, except when heavy seas buffet the east and west coasts and occasionally penetrate the Bass Strait islands. But you never know your luck.

Devonport

Although the coastline between Devonport and Stanley has hundreds of potential beach, reef and point breaks, swells seldom occur. This coastline once received heaps of swell—NE swells were common and supplied good quality waves—but due to some unknown climactic change, they're now unbelievably rare. Perhaps the north coast region's first real surf location is the **Devonport River**, which relies on large NW–NE swells, particularly during winter, when big NW fronts push through.

This performance lefthander peels up the river over boulders and basalt reef. It is best surfed on a three-quarter tide that helps push the walls towards the top carpark and provides fast rides.

If you follow the beach road west from the Devonport River for about 2 km you will come to **Backbeach** and **Robbo's Point**. A reef break that lies behind the bluff on the eastern end of Back Beach, Robbo's picks up heaps of swell and provides good right-handers at mid tide. SW breezes are offshore and will ensure the best conditions.

Sulphur Creek

Lying 40 km west of Devonport on the Bass Highway, the Sulphur Creek region can also produce a few waves. The new highway bypasses Penguin and Sulphur Creek, and once you've passed these locations, travel down a large hill that offers excellent ocean views. If you notice heaps of swell with NW or NE direction, take a 2-km detour off the Bass Highway to **Midway Beach** which provides waves on all tides when the wind is SW offshore.

Travel 500 m further east and

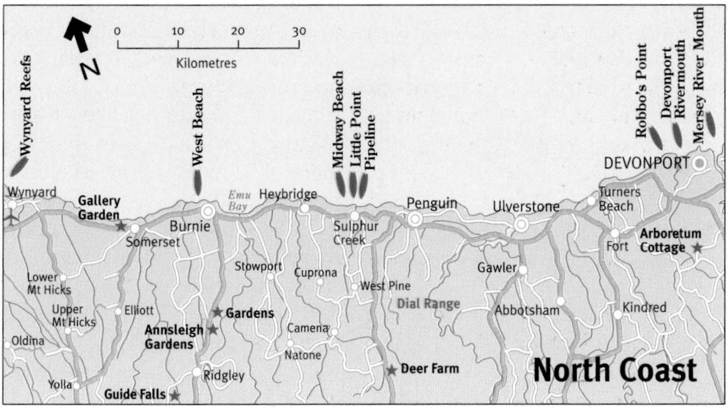

May–August.

Sealed roads to some locations but you'll need to do some trekking.

Basalt reef and sand.

Mid-range board, good backpack and thick wetsuit.

Sharks, snakes and reef.

Hypothermia, cramps and head-planting in the middle of nowhere.

Great scenery. No crowds and quirky surf locations.

North Coast

Above: The Apple Isle's fearsome custodian—the Tasmanian Devil—may be small, even cute, but you don't want to upset them. *Photo: Rick Eaves*

Below: Dress the part and beat the cold. A Tassie local takes on the Devonport rivermouth in full hood, booties and a tailor-made seal skin. *Photo: Rick Eaves*

you may be lucky enough to find **Little Point** converting rare NE swell into long, walling lefthanders over a basalt reef. A popular neighbour, **Pipeline's** intense righthanders break short and sharp with the added advantage of being very sheltered from the wind. Both locations work better on high tides.

Next stop is Burnie. Keeping on the expressway, drive past the centre of town until you strike the lights. Here the road briefly touches the ocean and runs down to a carpark at **West Beach**. On a heavy NW swell and mid tide, the western end of the beach can be a fun option.

Wynyard

Heading west from Burnie, follow the Bass Highway until you see a conspicuous headland called Table Cape. An extinct volcanic plug, it signals the first turnoff to Wynyard along the Old Coast Highway.

In front of the turn off is the first

reef. In fact, the **Wynyard Reefs** are surfable every 100 m for the next five kilometres although most of them aren't great quality. When there are waves (due to groundswell and SW winds) they are usually pretty hard to catch and are best surfed on a low to mid tide.

Boat Harbour is about 20 km west of Wynyard. You can't miss the turnoff on the Bass Highway. If you have time, drive over to Table Cape, where the views are outrageous. Boat Harbour used to be good on NE swells but nowadays that's pretty rare. You have to be lucky to catch it on, however if you're travelling with a friend, there are some nice restaurants here to enjoy, while you wait for the surf to really crank.

Tam O'Shanter Bay

Jammed between George Town and Bridport, Tam O'Shanter Bay at Lulworth picks up more SW–NW swell than most places. From Devonport, head east, take the Exeter Highway, go over the Batman bridge and head north to George Town. The Lulworth, Weymouth turn off is a few kilometres past Pipers River.

Here you will find the **Tam O'Shanter** lefthander peeling down a rocky point. Offering fast and mellow sections, it's a fun wave, especially on a heavy SW swell with a three-quarter to full tide. However, it doesn't handle a maxing NW swell as the rip sweeps down the point.

Located reasonably close to Launceston, Tam O'Shanter is one

of the most consistent breaks on the north coast, so at times it can get a bit crowded. If the traffic looks a bit thick, there are other decent waves in close proximity, so don't be afraid to have a good look around the area.

Thinly populated and not renowned for great surf, the North East is excellent for camping, diving, fishing and can offer good waves with virtually no crowds.

Popular with surfers attracted to its warmer weather and proximity to both Launceston and Hobart, the North East coast enjoys less severe weather patterns than the West Coast regions. Check the synoptic chart for any low- or high-pressure systems that sit between 30° and 50° latitude way out in the Tasman Sea. These produce the most idyllic surfing conditions.

—*Glenn Saltmarsh*

Above: A seriously chilly day at Tam O'Shanter Bay. *Photo: Rick Eaves*

Overleaf: A lone surfer scrambles for safety as the St Helens Barway goes into overdrive with some double-storey lefthanders. *Photo: Simon de Salis*

Gladstone & Binalong Bay

Situated in the far NE of the state, **Great Musselroe Bay** can be found by following the B82 road past Bridport to Gladstone. Just north of here, the **Great Musselroe rivermouth** produces good waves when assisted by a NE swell. There are also decent waves around **Eddystone Point**, which lies at the southern end of the bay, about 30 km due east of Gladstone. A SE swell is best.

Stick on the coast road and head north from St Helens, where you can access a variety of other lineups. The **Bay of Fires**, for example, has some moody beach breaks, although access is pretty difficult. **The Gardens** offers steep beach breaks in a NW swell, while **Binalong Bay** is a scenic area with steep beach breaks, working through a NE and southerly swell.

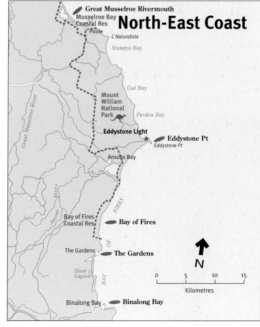

North-East Coast

Great Musselroe Rivermouth
Musselroe Bay
Coastal Res
Poole
C Naturaliste

Stumpys Bay

Cod Bay

Mount William National Park

Purdon Bay

Eddystone Light

★ Eddystone Pt
Eddystone Pt

Ansons Bay

Great Musselroe River

Ansons River

FIRES

Bay of Fires Coastal Res

Bay of Fires

The Gardens

The Gardens

Sleep Lagoon

BAY OF FIRES

Binalong Bay

Binalong Bay

N

0   5   10   15
Kilometres

Text by Veda Dante

Surf FOR THE Earth

SURFERS LEARN HOW TO CARE

PERHAPS SURFERS' AFFINITY WITH THE OCEAN LIES in the simple fact that we evolved from creatures that inhabited the seas in prehistoric times. Indeed, 75 percent of the planet we live on is covered with water. Without our oceans, life would literally lose its cool and the Earth would be just another Mars—hot, barren and inhospitable.

Soothing, nurturing and purifying, the sea regulates the ebb and flow of our everyday lives, supports an incredible variety of sea life and purifies the air we breathe. It's hardly surprising that we refer to our favourite recreational playground as "Mother Ocean".

Over the centuries we have used her waterways to discover new lands, transport goods and ride her majestic waves, but somewhere along the way we have lost an important connection. Nowadays our relationship with the ocean has become, in many ways, one based upon greed and rampant consumerism.

Ironically the very medium which has allowed us to thrive, is now under threat from our careless mismanagement of waste and discarded by-products. Today, disintegrating marine ecosystems and water quality, caused primarily by pollution and large-scale commercial fishing, are considered the most serious coastal environmental issues. Figures compiled by the federal Department of the Environment's Coastcare program reveal that each year as much as three billion litres of sewage effluent are poured into Australia's estuarine and ocean waters.

One of the world's most complex marine ecosystems, Australia's 36,735-km long coastline comprises 7,000 spectacular beaches and approximately 12,000 smaller islands. Rich with marine life, the country's shores—bordered by the Pacific, Indian and Southern Oceans—are highly regarded internationally. However, considering the huge size of the Australian landmass, the task of monitoring our coastal waters is a massive one.

As surfers we spend more time than most enjoying the gifts of the Big Blue. Through our experiences riding one of nature's most powerful forces, we form a unique bond with the ocean and are passionate with our praise.

Therefore, it seems appropriate then that the United Nations (UN) should enlist the support of surfers to preach the marine message. Seasoned surfer Wayne 'Rabbit' Bartholomew and Australian junior indigenous surfing sensation Joshua Slabb were appointed UN Ambassadors for the 1998 International Year of the Ocean. Says Josh: "I think surfers, especially locals, respect the beach a lot. Our tribe, which is part of the Cooejingburra clan, relies on the ocean for food—it's the biggest source of food in my area."

Inspired by events and activities involving the Ocean Charter, Ocean Education and Ocean Awards, the UN hopes The Year of the Ocean will help "focus public attention to the importance of the world's oceans and marine environments as resources for sustainable development."

Traditionally, ocean environmentalism in Australia has been synonymous with its surfing history. The formation of the Bells Beach Surfing Recreation Reserve in 1973—the first reserve of its kind in the world—demonstrated that surfers, environmental groups and the general community could honour a "sacred site" by having it protected under government legislation. Since then, other surfing reserves have been created at Margaret River (WA) and in South Africa.

"Today the Bells Beach Surfing Reserve is a model of environmental management", says John Foss, Chairman of Australia's Surfrider Foundation. Surfrider's State of our Surf (SOS) project provided one of the first comprehensive surveys of our coastline. "Human Impact on Australian Beaches" (Michael Legge Wilkinson, 1996) surveyed over 1600 beaches and identified ocean outfalls and stormwater drains as being key sources of pollution.

Like many contemporary conservationists, Foss believes that both surfing and marine reserves play an important role in coastal preservation and protection. Encouraged by the declaration of the Solitary Islands Marine Reserve off NSW's Coffs Harbour, Surfrider branches are also lobbying for marine reserve status for Queensland's South Stradbroke Island and Mudjimba Island Reserve, as well as NSW's Voodoo Point.

Although plenty of serious issues remain, surfers have found many ways to have fun

Left: Bells Beach owes its conservation status to action by surfers. This magnificent surfing arena is now protected for all to enjoy. Vegetation is being established along the shore edge.
Photo: Peter Wilson

Below: The original soul surfers show how it's really done. You won't score any brownie points with the karma police by shitting in your own backyard. *Photo: Steve Ryan*

while providing some of the answers. Beach culture festivals involving internationally renowned bands such as silverchair, Pearl Jam, Blink 182, Porno for Pyros, and Midnight Oil have harnessed the universal medium of music to raise awareness on pressing environmental issues. The Surfrider Foundation's hugely successful MOM CD (Music for our Mother Ocean) introduced pro-environmental surfing messages to some 15,000 people around Australia.

Recognised as one of the most influential surfers of all time, US surf messiah Tom Curren forged new ground for surfing environmentalism when, as world surfing champion, he became the President of the European chapter of the Surfrider Foundation.

Rallying support to take on reckless developers and heavy industry, he travelled to Australia to record Ocean Surf Aces, a collaborative debut CD with sales benefitting the Surfrider Foundation.

According to four-times world champion Kelly Slater, who has already played a number of benefit gigs with Curren, music is just another way to allow the whole world to go surfing together.

"People are into buying recycled products and the politicians are beginning to align themselves with the environmentally-aware causes.

"The word is out and people want to contribute, so we can never have enough education on the problems. Hopefully one day we'll get to a point where we don't really need it, but we never want to revert back to where we are now," says Slater.

Other talented surf musicians such as Peter King and Rob Machado have picked up their instruments to join Slater and work towards a universal respect of the lifeblood of our planet. The trio recently signed a major American recording deal to release their debut album entitled Songs from the Pipe.

Californian surfing legend and accomplished guitarist, Rob Machado sums it up appropriately: "We're all one, we all use the ocean for our enjoyment, so we should all stick together to protect it."

SANE's (Surfers Appreciating the Natural Environment) Gordon Stammers agrees. "Surfers deal with the sea all the time. They have a knowledge of how the sea works just to be able to surf. Extending that knowledge to those who don't surf is what SANE's all about. It's the only way to educate the public and surfers have to take some sort of responsibility," he said.

As surfers we have an opportunity to act at the forefront of marine environmentalism by helping to provide invaluable, firsthand feedback from our beaches regarding injured wildlife, illegal dumping, chemical spills and water pollution. Surfers can assist many conservation groups, including Australia's Surfrider Foundation and Greenpeace, to effectively target problem areas along our coastlines. One call could save the life of a stranded whale, wipe out ear infections or hepatitis at your local beach, or help prosecute an offender whose blatant coastal abuse is punishable under the Department of Environment's criminal code.

Surfing Australia—the Australian Surfriders Association as it was formerly known—served as critical lobbyers for the Bell's Beach Reserve. Supported by Ecorecycle, Coast Action and Coastcare promotional activities, Surfing Australia has developed surf schools and promotional policy based on the principle that "beach access is a general right of the whole surfing community".

The organisation advocates a few simple guidelines for beach-goers: keep to paths and boardwalks to protect fragile dune vegetation; avoid taking plastic, glass and disposable cans to the beach; and basically, "if you carry it in, carry it out."

So next time you're about to throw some rubbish out of the car window, or leave it behind at your favourite camping site, think again. Do the right thing and you'll be doing everyone a favour—including yourself.

Opposite: The pristine Margaret River coastline. *Photo: Tungsten/Nikon*

Above: Rob Bain faces the challenge at 13th Beach. *Photo: Peter Wilson*

Below: Gaining valuable publicity for the cause of clean water, Greenpeace mounts another publicity exercise. *Photo: Greenpeace*

January–March,
May–August.

Good roads to most
breaks, some
trekking and boat
trips required to get
quality waves com-
pletely to yourself.

Forgiving sand and
reef bottoms.

Mid range board
and favourite tube
riding stick. Tent
and fishing rod.

Kelp and territorial
seals.

Chills and spills in
remote locations.

Powerful, hollow
waves with spectac-
ular camping sites.

The East Coast
Cool Swells Plus Quality Points and Reefs

From **Bicheno** northwards, the waves are generally fun beach breaks with a few points and reefs. They cop a lot of swell but when the surf is really maxing, the south east coast has more to offer.

St Helens

Travelling along the coastal road, you will enter St Helens where occasionally NE swells produce good waves at **Georges Bay**. Right on St Helens point, you will find some great waves at **Beer Barrel Beach**. It is possible to meet up with seals in the surf here—a some-times bonding, sometimes hair-rais-ing experience.

By following the sand tracks around to the southern side of St Helens Point to **Perrons Beach** you will discover 3 km of peaks. When there's either a SE or NE

swell, check out the waves in the northern corner. **Dark Hollow**, just north of Beaumaris, is a peaky beach break that picks up heaps of S–SE swell. The crowds reflect just how good this place gets.

This whole region of the East Coast is beautiful and very quiet with great camping and fishing. Roughly 5 km south of St Helens, the abundance of beach breaks begins and they continue to the Freycinet Peninsula.

Scamander

Nestled between Beaumaris and Scamander, **Shelly Point** is an excellent beach break that can break point fashion over sand. During NE and SE swells, both sides of the point are usually very good with westerly winds being offshore.

Below: When the Scamander Rivermouth lets off some steam, riding it's a gas!.
Photo: Rick Eaves

Easily viewed from the highway, the **Scamander rivermouth** attracts heaps of swell and holds good, peaky sandbanks on a favourable NE and SE swell. Westerly winds are offshore and are also the go for the nearby **Falmouth** beach breaks that can sometimes provide a few surprises near the creek, but a better option is **Four Mile Beach**.

Heading south down the main road you can't miss it. Once you've hit Four Mile, make a beeline for the northern end of the beach where you'll find an awesome left-hander. Like many of Tassie's breaks, **Cattle Grids** offers excellent, fast waves that wind mechanically over a forgiving sand bottom.

Working best on a NE swell, Cattle Grids is complemented by the reef break at **Outside Four Mile** that will send you scrambling for your gun. A heavy, fast righthander on Four Mile's southern outside point, it requires a large SW swell and an offshore westerly wind to hit its straps.

Just south of here, **Iron House** reef and beach can also prove a good option on a large SW swell. Accessed via a bush track at the north end of the bay, occasionally some solid righthanders break majestically along an offshore reef situated in the SW corner. If you're looking for a place to hang, check out the local Cray Drop Inn resort for a bit of Tassie hospitality.

About 10 km further south, **Little Beach** is a picturesque stopover that is ideal for camping. Perfect white sand, a beachbreak and short point break setup; what more could you want except a SE swell?

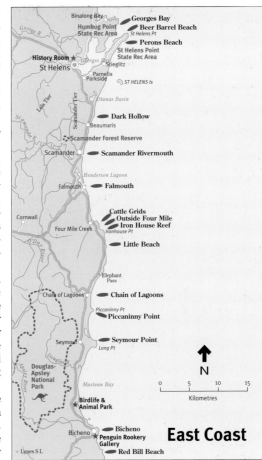

East Coast

Bicheno and the Freycinet Peninsula

A little further south, the road intersects with the bottom of Elephant Pass and the Tasman Highway. There are plenty of beach breaks between here and Bicheno. When there's a NE or SE swell, **Chain of Lagoons, Piccaniny Point, Seymour Point** and **Red Bill Beach**

all have their moments of glory. From Bicheno, the Tasman Highway heads inland, but if you take the turn-off to Freycinet Peninsula you will see another road marked the **Friendly Beaches**. They live up to their name, being great for camping, very scenic and quiet. There are also plenty of peaky beach breaks when there's swell.

If you have a boat and a sense of adventure, **Schouten Island** can be a fun day-trip that usually delivers the goods on a large NE swell. Motor around to the north end where you should find an inside right point break reeling off for a lucky few, maybe just for you.

Swansea

The stretch of coast between **Swansea** and **Orford** is full of quality point breaks in moderate to heavy E–SE swells. Keep your eyes peeled for turn-offs and signposts. It's a quiet area but surfers for miles around will sniff out a large swell and be instantly on the hunt for good waves. So get up early to catch the worm!

Swan River is at the eastern end of **Nine Mile Beach**, just north of Swansea. This is a sandbar set-up which reaches over to the northern fringes of the spectacular Freycinet National Park, with Moulting Lagoon to the north and Great Oyster Bay to the south. Here you'll find plenty of lefts and rights produced on big southerly swells accompanied by NW–NE offshore winds.

Swansea Point is located right in Swansea and offers an excellent righthander in heavy S–SE swell,

with offshore W–NW winds.

To get to **Rubbish Tip Point**, take the Tasman Highway south out of Swansea, cross the bridge, then turn left just past the boat ramp. This area requires heavy S–SE swells and W–NW offshore winds.

Located about 30 kms south of Swansea, **Buxton Point** is another fun righthand point break. Prime conditions are a S–SE swell and W–NW offshore winds.

Further to the south is **Cullaroo Point**, easily visible from the Tasman Highway. You have to park along the road to access the break. This righthander needs heavy S–SE swells and offshore W–NW winds.

Little Swanport

The nearby **Lisdillon** area offers a lefthand reef break that gets pretty good in heavy S–E swells and westerly offshore winds. There's a well-marked track off the highway, so keep your eyes peeled. **Little Swanport** is a favourite for surfers in for the long haul, with good camping facilities right near the highway. To get there, take the Saltworks Rd just north of the Little Swanport township. There's an excellent left that peels off the sandbar into the **Ravensdale rivermouth**, especially during it's heavy S–SE swells. There's also a reef at the southern end of the bay which offers a good righthander in heavy S–SE swells and westerly, offshore winds.

Continuing further south along the Tasman Highway, look out for a track which heads towards the coast about 10 km before the township of Triabunna. Follow it for about 15 km and you should see **Hermitage Reef**. It's a bit of an effort to get there, but the lefts and rights produced by NE–SE swells provide plenty of stoke.

Orford

Just south of Triabunna and across Prosser Bay lies the town of Orford. Situated right near the golf course, the **Orford rivermouth** can pump out long lefts

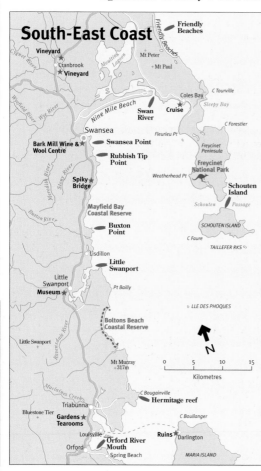

during heavy E–NE swells.

Leave the Tasman Highway at Orford as it goes inland, and turn left at the Orford bridge. Just outside the township is **East Shelley Beach**, where you'll find both an outside and an inside break (the inside being more hollow on a lower tide) at the southern end. Both are excellent righthanders in heavy E–NE swells, and westerly offshore winds.

Perhaps Tassie's best wave, **Boneyard** requires a medium to heavy groundswell and westerly offshore winds. From Orford, take the very scenic Wyelengatha Rd to Bream Creek. Find the southernmost end of **Marion Bay** and about 800 metres offshore you should see Boneyard, a pumping, long and hollow righthander which is best ridden on a low tide.

This majestic wave is the product of a perfect sandbar formed offshore by the water draining out of Blackman Bay. It's a hell of a paddle but you can guarantee you won't be out there on your own— 80 to 120 guys is not uncommon (and that's during the week). Surfers flock to this break like flies to a barbecue!

—*Glenn Saltmarsh*

Above: Tasmanian surfers are a hardy breed, braving low temperatures and icy winds. But when the surf's up you won't find them sitting around the fireplace in their shacks.
Photo: Rick Eaves

Below: Common at many Tassie surf locations, kelp can easily snare your leggie.
Photo: Veda Dante

May–August.

Bitumen and dirt roads to many locations. Some breaks are best reached on foot.

Flat basalt reef covered in kelp and sand bottoms.

Semi gun, favourite barrel threader, fishing rod and standard cold water bear suit.

Sharks, kelp, slippery rocks and inconsistent swells.

Hellish wipeouts. Some places miles from assistance.

Apart from Hobart, minimal crowds and some of Tassie's most consistent waves.

Hobart and the Tasman Peninsula

Plenty of Variety

There's not much surf worthy of mention in the waters off Hobart itself, but the sleepy capital is home to a lot of fanatical wave devotees.

South Arm

The closest surf is across the River Derwent at **South Arm**, which is located on a small peninsula about 20 minutes away.

Take the A3 Highway across the Derwent, then turn off at either Bellerive or Rokeby and follow the B33 (South Arm Rd). First stops are some of Tassie's famous points, many of which you'll find at the south end of **Seven Mile Beach** (located on the eastern side of the peninsula). Notoriously fickle, they can get good on big S–SW swells which produce 5–6 ft waves and perfect righthand point breaks. Peeling over rock and sand, the breaks are offshore during SW–NW winds.

Heading south to Lauderdale is **Lauderdale Point** which is just south east of the town centre, and **Mays Point** which is a little further south along Mays Point Rd. **Inside Mays** is left of the carpark, while **Outside Mays** is just over the hill and a further 15 minute walk. The water's freezing around here but if the waves are on, it's not hard to motivate. Mays is arguably the best break in the area but the crowds usually determine which point you surf. The waves are generally fast with both tube sections and slower sections available for plenty of manoeuvres. Another fun wave is **Cremorne Point** which is easily found near the town.

From here, return to the B33 and head for some of Hobart's more consistent breaks at **Clifton Beach**. A long beach which picks up plenty of swell, Clifton has a variety of peaks to choose from. Prime conditions include a small to medium S–SE swell and NE to westerly offshore winds.

Goats Beach

Goats is about five minutes south of Clifton and is subject to a similar amount of swell. Here you'll find fun, peaky waves all over the beach when the banks are good. Best in small to medium, S–SE swell and NE–NW offshore winds.

At the southern end of Goats lies **Rebounds**, appropriately named after the swells that recoil off the cliffs to create the playful waves. Find yourself a good camping spot and hang around for a while, this is one place where you can really unwind.

Preceding pages:
We can't really say where this place is. What we can tell you is that we've surfed it and it's bloody perfect! This is a pretty good day and that set is about 15 ft.
Photo: Rick Eaves

[Map of Hobart area showing: Loneley Sandfly, Hobart, Rokeby, Kingston, Seven Mile Beach, Nierinna, Gellibrand Pt., Sandford, Margate, Electrona Snug, Oppossum Bay, Ralphs Bay, South Arm, Clifton Beach, Dennes Point, Killora, Sandpits, BETSEY I., Barnes Bay, Betsey Island Wedge, Clifton Beach, Goats Beach, N, 0 2.5 5 7.5 Kilometres, **Hobart**]

HOBART & TASMAN PENINSULA

TASMANIA

Drive up the hill immediately south of Goats before continuing out to the headland. Look south and you'll see a long beach with Betsey Island just offshore and **Betsey Island Wedge** 500 m down the beach. Betsey Island splits the swell in heavy SW–SE conditions, delivering short but intensely powerful left and right beach breaks. Offshore winds are northerly.

RSL or **Sandpits** are some other beach breaks further down South Arm Rd (turn left at the South Arm RSL). Best conditions are small to medium, S–SE swells with NW offshore winds.

Dodges Ferry

Head back up to the A3 Highway, across Pitt Water, past Sorell and onto Carlton Beach. **Park Beach** is located at the western end of the carpark and offers soft, fun beach breaks. The **Carlton rivermouth** is at the eastern end (in front of the Surf Club) and its long wally lefts can get pretty good on solid SW–SE swells with E–NE offshore winds. There's quite a strong surfing community here which can offer you more advice and direction.

Southport

To reach one of Australia's most southern breaks, return to Hobart, then head south along the Huon Highway for about an hour until you reach **Southport.** From here, follow the track as far as it takes you, then prepare yourself for a 90-minute walk (on duck board mostly, so make sure you wear good shoes), until you reach South East Cape Bay.

Lyon Rock is an excellent wave but relies heavily on the sand banks. It's located at the western end of South East Cape Bay and produces both lefts and rights in small, SW swell and NE offshore winds. This wave breaks similarly to Lighthouse up on the West Coast and is a good small swell location.

Eaglehawk Neck

From Sorell, follow the Arthur Highway (A9) across the Forestier Peninsula and down through Eaglehawk Neck which is only a few hundred metres wide. There's some awesome scenery here, like the spectacular natural formations at Tesselated Pavement, The Blowhole and Devils Kitchen. The shapely swells are the icing on the

Above: Hobart's surf may be inconsistent, but a keen surfing population always make the most of the local conditions when the swell finally arrives. *Photo: Rick Eaves*

Above: Tassie offers a multitude of great surfing sites.
Photo: Rick Eaves

cake and there are plenty of good locations.

Now revered as a prime surfing spot, this compact strip of land was once well-known for quite different reasons. Between 1830 and 1877, when the Port Arthur penal settlement was operating, the easily-guarded, narrow neck of land ensured prison escapes were few.

To surf the waters around Eaglehawk Neck requires a reasonable NE–SE groundswell up to

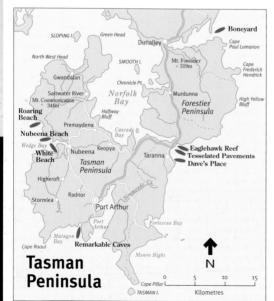

SLOPING I. Green Head **Boneyard**
Dunalley *Cape Paul Lamanon*
North West Head SMOOTH I. Mt. Forester + 319m *Cape Frederick Hendrick*
Gwandalan Chronicle Pt.
Saltwater River *Norfolk Bay* Murdunna *High Yellow Bluff*
Mt. Communication + 344m **Forestier Peninsula**
Roaring Beach Halfway Bluff
Premaydena *Cascade Bay*
Nubeena Beach
Wedge Bay Keopya **Eaglehawk Reef Tesselated Pavements Dave's Place**
White Beach Nubeena Taranna
Tasman Peninsula
Higheroft *Simmonds Ck*
Radnor
Stormlea Port Arthur
Port Arthur *Fortescue Bay*
Maingon Bay
Cape Raoul **Remarkable Caves** *Monro Bight*

Tasman Peninsula **N**
0 5 10 15
Cape Pillar
TASMAN I. Kilometres

6–8 ft. **Tesselated Pavement** or "Tessos" is located at the northern end in Pirates Bay and is a demanding righthander that can double and triple suck making for a challenging first bottom turn. The swell comes out of deep water and jacks on the reef providing excellent tube sections. This area is best in offshore westerly winds with a high tide.

Though **Eaglehawk Reef** is north of Tessos, it's still located in Pirates Bay. This wave is a powerful lefthander that demands a smooth, confident take-off and breaks over very shallow reef. A 3–6 ft swell on a high tide, with light westerly winds, offers the best conditions.

At the extreme southern end of Eaglehawk Beach, **Dave's Place** also provides excellent waves in E–NE swell coupled with SW–SE offshore winds.

Tasman Peninsula

A popular surfing destination, the Tasman Peninsula offers a range of choice breaks. Head down the Arthur Highway, past the convict ruins of Port Arthur, and follow the signs to the picturesque **Remarkable Caves**. Accessed via a walk trail and a sometimes eerie paddle through the caves, Remarkables can provide hollow righthand peaks when the sandbanks are stable during medium S–SW swells. The offshore wind is NE–NW and the break is best on low to medium tides.

Kelpies, located on the western shore of the Peninsula, is a lefthand point break that can be long and wally or sometimes full-on hollow pits. You can access Kelpies from **White Beach** near Wedge Bay. It's a 40-minute walk across private property, so be discreet. Medium to heavy SE swells and offshore SE winds or seabreezes are the best combination.

If the swell is in the small to moderate range, **Nubeena** may also have good waves depending on the breeze. If the winds are S–NE offshore, Nubeena will usually have some great peaks located at the middle and southern ends of the beach.

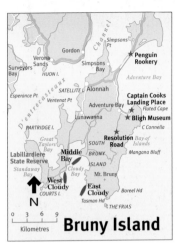

Bruny Island

Though Bruny Island is a popular summer getaway for the city surfers in search of waves, during winter when the bigger swells hit, the definition of 'crowded' here means more than just a couple of people. The north and south islands are joined by a slender isthmus housing a huge penguin rookery. To these cheeky birds, Bruny Island is home—to surfers it's a surfing treasure chest.

To get there, head south out of Hobart towards Kingston, before taking the Channel Highway to Kettering where the car ferry departs for Bruny. About 20 minutes and $20 later, you will have crossed the D'Entrecasteaux Channel and reached the northwest shores of Tassie's southern-most island. Head due south, following the road as it traces the near-meeting of Isthmus Bay (to your right) and Adventure Bay (to your left).

Not far from Captain Cook's landing place, **Coal Point** lies at the southern end of **Adventure Bay**. It's a fast, ledgy, heavy left-hander which breaks over a concoction of rock and kelp. Heavy SE–NE swells and offshore, W–SW winds help funnel a solid swell that will satisfy most adrenalin freaks.

Driving further south you'll find **Cloudy Bay**, a name associated more with elegant wines than excellent beach breaks. It's a beautiful spot to camp, the Southern Ocean and pristine horseshoe bay backdropped with the hills of Mt Bruny, providing for some truly spectacular sights. NE–NW winds are offshore and when combined with a small to moderate swell, you should find yourself some fun righthanders.

Across Cloudy Bay lies the **Labillardiere State Reserve** and Australia's southernmost lighthouse. Further south there are a few peaky breaks that face a slightly easterly direction, so they need a fairly heavy swell to work. W–SW winds are offshore.

Below: Once the gateway to Australia's harshest penal settlement, Eaglehawk Neck is today a place of absolute freedom for many surfers. *Photo: Rick Eaves*

The West Coast

Hard-core Surfing

December–May

Dirt roads and four wheel drive tracks.

Sand-covered reef and some kelp beds.

7-ft plus boards, long leashes and spare boards.

Strong rips, big hold downs and thick lips. Severe weather patterns and watch out for quicksand.

Snapped boards and bones from giant wipeouts.

Big drops and wild waves, just you and your mates.

Wild and treacherous, Tassie's West Coast is consistently bombarded by swell. Well before the English claimed Van Diemens Land, the Dutch sailed down this unpredictable coastline, their compasses spinning wildly in the mineral-rich rock wilderness that stopped them exploring further.

Trial Harbour

Accessed via the Lyell Highway from Hobart or Murchison Highway from the north, the Trial Harbour experience begins with the ride. Both routes travel through rugged, mountainous terrain with a variety of spectacular scenery.

Typically, most of the better surf regions need the swell to settle and form good banks before offshore winds combine to produce isolated perfection. If you like the big juice, there's no better place to begin than **Trial Harbour**. To get there, head west from Zeehan and look out for the Remine turn-off. Situated about 30 km from Zeehan, Trial picks up a lot of swell and can be surfed when it's small or large, although 3–9 ft on a W–SW swell is ideal.

Presenting a jacking A frame take-off, this powerhouse left breaks over kelp and reef. The more west the swell, the longer and suckier the sections. **The Pearl** is a slightly deeper, second A Frame which caters for those with superior ability and slightly larger-sized gonads. Both need NE–SE winds to be offshore. Sitting out the back of the break you could almost be in Hawaii as you look in over mountains and beaches with a waterfall cascading from the cliffs.

There's also a right reef break at the northern end of Trial Harbour close to where the track starts up the hill. Although it's not really in the same class as the left, it's still popular when the swell co-operates.

Granville Harbour and Ahrberg Bay

From Zeehan take the Hydro Road to Granville Harbour where you'll

Below: One of Tassie's premier big wave locations, the West Coast is a wild surfing experience. *Photo: Rick Eaves*

see the **Tasman River** turn-off. The rivermouth beach break can be fun when the swell is small but the choicest location is **Granville Harbour**. Providing shelter from a maxed-out swell, the harbour's shapely lefts and rights can really fire on a NE wind.

If you have a four wheel drive, take the beach foreshore track north from Granville and drive for about 40 minutes until you reach a 5-km long beach. This is the home of the **Cruncher**, a heavy righthander that requires good banks and SE–NE winds to work at the southern end of the beach. **Ahrberg Bay** lies at the opposite (northerly) end of this beach and is a pumping righthander that has long, hollow sections when fanned by favourable NW winds.

You might think it's a hoax, but if the locals warn you of quicksand while driving along some West Coast beaches take heed! Because the area receives a lot of rain and often many creeks can't cut through the foreshore sand dunes, the water travels underneath the beach and flows close to the surface before discharging into the ocean. A few unsuspecting adventurers have watched their vehicles sink without a trace—trust me.

North of Ahrberg Bay, **Pieman**

Heads is accessed via a rough four wheel drive track. There are some good lefts here that break off the southern heads and into the river. It's a beach break point set-up, NE winds are offshore.

—*Glenn Saltmarsh*

Above: Wave after wild wave, the West Coast awaits the best and the bravest.
Photo: Rick Eaves

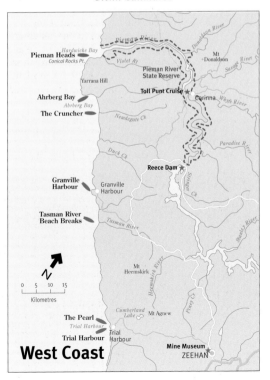

West Coast

December–May

Sealed and dirt roads to most breaks. Some locations accessed by 4WD or on foot.

Sand and flat reef covered in kelp beds.

Mid-range board and high speed big wave gun for down the line waves.

Hungry Tassie Tigers and Great White Sharks.

Strong rips and hypothermia after catching one too many barrels. World class high performance waves, great scenery, clean water and empty line-ups.

The North West Coast

Awesome Scenery, Great Breaks

We're talking some really isolated surf locations here, so pack the necessary provisions and be prepared for some seriously good breaks.

Mt Cameron

From Smithton you can follow the Bass Highway to the popular surf region of **Marrawah** or take the more scenic route by heading west from Smithton's Bridge Hotel to Montague. Here, the scenery over the islands just north of the NW tip of Tassie is simply awesome. This road has 20 km of gravel that leads directly to the rear of Mount Cameron.

If you're lucky and the sandbanks are good, there may be some rights reeling off the point for about 200 m but this is rare. There is also a left that breaks back into the point. NE–SE winds are offshore.

This region has been reclaimed by the descendants of the Tasmanian Aborigines, and the indigenous people call this place **Preminghana**. Now the custodians of this magnificent area, they act as local rangers and are friendly to appreciative surfers who respect their surroundings. **Mount Cameron** is a special place to local surfers and Preminghana is a sacred place to the Aborigines. With a little courtesy, these two tribes will always enjoy a happy co-existence.

The righthander off the mount is a fast, full-faced wave that will either pitch from take-off, or hold back enough for high speed off-the-lip manoeuvres. It starts off fast then backs off into deeper water but if the bank lines up on the inside, it can be linked all the way to the beach. The left tends to be shorter but it's still fast and hollow with plenty of punch.

Thunder Reef is at the back of Mount Cameron, on the outer northern end. Always check with the local Aborigines when surfing this area. They're a friendly mob, so expect a warm welcome. Take the gravel track behind the mount and head north for about 500 m. You'll see a small carpark and if you climb the hill, you'll come across Thunder Reef. Grab your gear and head down for a kilometre walk to the headland.

The swell rises out of deep water and hits the basalt reef about 200 m in front of the cliff. The left peels perfectly and holds a very big swell. You will need a solid board over 7 ft. Be pretty confident with your ability, and prepared to back yourself. It's a fantastic down-the-

Map

North-West Coast

- Flat Topped Bluff
- Bluff Pt.
- Stydland Bay
- Thunder Reef
- Mt. Cameron
- Mt. Cameron West
- Welcome River
- Ann Bay
- **Marrawah**
- Green Pt.
- Greens Beach
- Nettley Bay
- West Pt.
- Redpa
- Marrawah
- BETSEY I.
- **Lighthouse**
- Mawson Bay
- Shersons Hill
- **Bluff Reef**
- Arther Pieman Ped Area
- Bluff Hill Pt.
- N
- 0 2.5 5 7.5
- Kilometres
- Cruise ★ Arthur River
- Gardiner Pt.

line wave that offers big tubes to those who are game to take off near the growling rocks. Best in big swells which require light SE–NE winds, Thunder Reef will break on a minimum 6 ft swell.

Marrawah

The turn-off to **Greens Beach** is only 20 m from the shop at Marrawah. Just drive down the hill—you can't miss it. There are three breaks here, a right in the corner (fast, hollow, high tide, big swell), a fun beachbreak a little further down, and the left directly in front of the carpark; the latter being the more popular. A fast, hollow wave breaking over sandstone reef and kelp, this lefthander is great fun and although it's not as powerful as some of the other quality breaks in the area, it's pretty consistent. The swell needs to wrap around the point and it takes a 10 ft plus open ocean wave to work. Southerly wind is offshore and a half to high tide is really the best for here.

Close to **Greens Beach** is another beautiful spot with amazing views of Mount Cameron and **Studland Bay**. People here are pretty laidback as long as you're not hassling anyone.

The next call is about 2 km away at **Nettley Bay**, where you'll find numerous left and right peaks depending on the condition of the sandbanks. This area is best surfed on SE–NE winds. If you enjoy rock fishing, then try catching some local salmon for dinner.

Lighthouse

Follow the Arthur River Road south out of Marrawah and take the first turn to the right, which is about 3 km into the bumpy gravel road. Drive a further 8 km, then take the first proper turn-off to your left and you'll find yourself within 50 m of **Lighthouse/West Point.**

When this wave is on, it's truly a world class beach break. It's as perfect as the fabled Hossegor beach breaks in France, only it packs more raw power. There are three waves in this small bay that break up to 10 ft, then another peak that breaks perfectly at 10–15 ft way out the back (all dependent on the sandbanks).

A small, hollow left which breaks into the rip near the creek, provides an A-frame take-off that turns into a bowling shoulder. The righthander which breaks from the back of the rip is pretty fast and hollow as it steamrolls right

Above: Unafraid, Pete Townsend runs the gauntlet on a funnelling Lighthouse race-track.
Photo: Simon de Salis

across the bay. There's also a wave which breaks from the southern end, either off the point or the nearby kelp bed. Another A-frame take-off, this powerful and hollow left can also break the whole length of the bay.

E–NE wind is offshore with tides dependent on the sandbanks. The camping's pretty simple out here and if you look around you can even find some old Aboriginal hut sites.

Bluff Beach and Reef

Bluff Reef is one of the most exciting waves in this area. Victorian surf legend Wayne Lynch once described it as not unlike a West Peak at Sunset. A righthander that needs a half to high tide to cover the reef, Bluff also requires at least a 6 ft swell and can hold waves up to 25 ft.

Follow the Arthur River Road south from West Point for about 8 km. Turn right at Bluff Hill light-house and follow the gravel road. **Bluff Reef** and **Bluff Beach** are north of the lighthouse and you can't miss the track. Bluff Reef is about 150 m offshore and is a big A-frame take-off that can be intimidating. Peeling for about 40 m, the wave is fast, hollow and powerful. You'll need a 7 ft plus rhino chaser to really take it on. Some advice: don't try to take-off on the shoulder, as you will probably get pitched. The peak may be bigger but it's a lot safer. Light, SE–S winds mostly offer the best wave conditions.

A long sandy stretch, Bluff Beach lies just north of the reef. There's a right in the corner which can get pretty good, but a left often peels off the righthander as well. Offshore winds are S–SE and the Bluff is generally best surfed on a 6–9 ft swell.

Arthur River is about 14 km south of Marrawah and you really need a 4WD to explore this area.

Below: Wayne Lynch once described surfing at Bluff Reef as similar to West Peak Sunset. Here local Shane Flannagan demonstrates how to tame the beast. *Photo: Simon de Salis*

Offshore winds are E–NE and there are quality beach breaks either side of the rivermouth when the swell is under 6 ft.

Sandy Cape

South of the Arthur River to Sandy Cape you'll need a 4WD. The track hugs the coast and there are numerous breaks to find and name yourself due to a large amount of swell coming in. E–NE swells are best and whether you're surfing, fishing or exploring there are always plenty of surprises.

A few years back, a mate and I were startled from our sleep by a pack of fiesty Tasmanian Devils who were rocking our Landcruiser from side to side after latching on to a wallaby carcass we'd slung off the bullbar. If you're venturing into this area, just remember there are no shops, no fuel and no pubs; only campers like yourself.

The area between **Sandy Cape** and **Cape Grim** was once inhabited by the Tasmanian Aborigines so it's basically one large midden or sacred place. You can still see evidence of Aboriginal rituals in the large piles of shellfish fragments, which are found scattered throughout the surfers' favourite haunts. The area is very fragile so show some respect to the indigenous sites while savouring the uncrowded waves.

—*Glenn Saltmarsh*

Above: Enjoying the sunshine, Tassie Junior champ Jy Johannesen gets ready to duck and cover on a glassy day at Marrawah's Nettley Bay. *Photo: Rick Eaves*

The State of Contrasts

*Deserts, Sharks and
Empty Beaches*

Preceding pages: Guy Walker having too much fun on a perfect Yorke's sandbar.
Photo: Peter Wilson

Opposite: Rough roads, flies and oppressive heat; how easily we forget when we find the liquid gold.
Photo: Peter Wilson

Welcome to the "state of contrasts". From the Simpson, Great Victorian and Strzelecki Deserts in the north to the icy Southern Ocean swells which thrash against the Great Australian Bight, South Australia is a paradoxical challenge for the adventurous surfer.

Renowned for its 50°C temperatures, lush wine producing country and remote surf peninsulas, this diverse state is also home to the mighty Murray River. Australia's longest waterway, the river runs 2,575 km from its source in the Snowy Mountains to Lake Alexandria, before finally emptying into the Southern Ocean.

Flanked by Victoria and New South Wales on the east, Northern Territory to the north and Western Australia to its west, South Australia is also known for its Coober Pedy opals and spectacular dive locations that guarantee adrenalin freaks a face to face experience with the Great White Shark—if you're willing to jump inside a steel cage.

Empty beaches, powerful reef breaks, big sharks and wild desert outposts, including the infamous Cactus, make for a fairly hardcore surfing experience. There's plenty of driving, camping and trekking, and while the flies and heat can drive you mad, the uncrowded beaches are a surfing indulgence. From the gentle Victor Harbor sandbanks to the bone-crunching rock ledges that barrel and spit along the Yorke and Eyre Peninsulas, you'll need a full wetsuit and your wits about you in this cold water wave haven.

Popularly known as the "Crow-eaters", many South Australians are fanatical about Australian Rules Football, perhaps the nation's most popular professional sport. If the waves are flat, it's worth checking out the excellent local competition that has bred many of the country's most famous champions. As well as a good game of football, pink salt lakes, a 9,600 km outback fence, and, if you're in the right place at the right time, you may even experience one of Australia's many UFO sightings. Bearing in mind the latter, you will not be surprised to learn that the state has decriminalised marijuana.

With a population of just over 1.1 million, South Australia's capital of Adelaide—or Tandanya as the Australian Aborigines call it—is one of the country's most graceful cities. Parochially refered to as the "City of Churches", Adelaide is blessed with quality architecture and has a thriving arts community, internationally recognised for its experimental film and music.

Why not time your visit to coincide with one of the state's many festivals, including: the International Tattoo, an Edinburgh-style gala performance featuring over 250 musicians from around the world; Womadelaide, a world music cultural carnival; and the Adelaide Festival which features world film premieres and international performances. Or perhaps the annual Mount Compass Cow Race is more your thing.

If you've got the munchies after a late-night party, call one of the many pie carts who'll deliver a "Pie Floater", a unique Adelaide tradition that's been going strong since

1915. It's a hot meat pie with tomato sauce sitting in a bowl of steaming green pea soup. Oh yeah!

Adelaide's seaside suburb of Glenelg is where you'll find both Magic Mountain, a funfair open every day till late, and a unique shark museum at Rodney Fox Reflections. About 30 km south of Port Adelaide is the Port Noarlunga Underwater Aquatic Reserve's trail for snorkellers and scuba divers. Experience the region's spectacular marine ecosystem by following this fully signposted, 800-m treasure hunt.

To fully appreciate the natural beauty of the state, drive south of Adelaide to where massive sand dunes, limestone cave systems and a 17 m high, four-tonne lobster make for some novel and interesting experiences.

About an hour's drive south of Adelaide, the **Fleurieu Peninsula** is the city's holiday playground. Check out Victor Harbor's Little Penguins or the Urimbirra Wildlife Park, where you'll also see dingoes, crocodiles, wombats, kangaroos, koalas and other native wildlife.

Australia's biggest offshore land mass, **Kangaroo Island** is home to a variety of wildlife including fur seals, sea lions and yes, kangaroos. There are plenty of good point breaks to discover and while you're down south, check out **Maslin Beach**, South Australia's first legalised nude hang. Just make sure you apply sunscreen to all the relevant parts.

If you head for the Great Australian Bight between May and October, you'll probably witness the majestic Southern Right whales on their annual migration. You won't see any surf here, just raw headlands pounded by massive swells so soak up the awesome sights.

Heading to the western edge of the state, you'll find the Nullarbor Plain (which is Latin for 'no trees'), an area rife with contradiction and mystery. Underneath the Nullarbor lies the world's longest cave system, which attracts a variety of international (and highly experienced) adventurers each year.

Surfing the Edge can involve taking a dirt track to uncrowded bliss or a rocky road to the middle of nowhere. Just respect the rights of the locals and don't be afraid to ask some questions; the rest is up to you.

Yorke Peninsula

Isolated Beaches and Sheer Cliffs

May–August.

Unsealed roads, four wheel drive and cliff climbs to some breaks.

Sharp reef, flat reef and forgiving sand bottoms.

Aeroguard, trekking shoes, fast, strong boards that can handle some power.

Sharks, snakes and reef.

If you face plant the reef, you are a long way from help.

Uncrowded barrels, dolphin pods, psychedelic sunsets and camping on the beach.

In 1802, Matthew Flinders likened the Yorke Peninsula to an "ill-shaped leg and boot" but for surfers this weathered appendage is hallowed ground.

In modern times a surf adventure to a rugged coastline of sheer cliffs, isolated tube rides, and an ocean teeming with marine life is a fun way to escape and survive on the simple pleasures of life.

Leaving Adelaide and heading north along the Port Wakefield Road, turn left at the top of St Vincents Gulf before dissecting the peninsula on your four hour journey to the southern tip of Yorkes.

Innes National Park

Accessed by corrugated roads which shake the shit out of your car or the newly sealed road which passes through the spectacular Innes National Park, Yorkes offers all kinds of waves along its 40 km stretch of coastline. Winding tracks and steep cliffs command respect as do the waves—wipeout and the nearest first aid facility could be miles away. Daily encounters with snakes, lizards, flies, bees, dolphins and sharks are common, while whales and seals are also known to make regular appearances.

With many breaks to choose from, Yorkes delivers good surf in most conditions. The larger the swell the more options you have, all within one hour's drive of each other. The first hill at **Stenhouse Bay** marks the entrance of the Innes National Park and brings you out overlooking **Althorpe Island**, **Chinamans Hat** and

Kangaroo Island to the east. Follow the road to the water and **Baby Chinamans**, a little lefthand reef break that is popular with the grommets might be happening. It's shallow but not too powerful and works on a medium to large swell with NW winds. Most crew pass it by, driving an extra kilometre to Chinaman's, an excellent lefthander renowned for its powerful tubes.

Chinamans & Ethel Wreck

For experienced surfers only, **Chi's** has it all. A small compact take-off zone filled with boils for elevator drops which turns into an intense, hollow pocket that surges its way over a sharp, narrow ledge. Northerly winds provide offshore conditions which make each ride much more critical. Entry and exits are tricky across the ledge and once you're out there, the waves only come to the committed.

As in many locations, winter is Yorke's most consistent surf sea-

Below: The Chinamans wedge slingshots for a lucky few, but it's not as easy as it looks.
Photo: Seaview

Above: The last pit-stop this side of the black stump is a welcome sight when you're down to your final muesli bar.
Photo: Peter Wilson

son, with light NW winds, a low to medium tide, and a 4–6 ft swell offering the best mix of ingredients. Venturing deeper into the park, you'll find **Ethel Wreck**, a small beach facing west to catch maximum swell. Best in SE–NE winds and a small swell, the left grinds off the ledge in the corner while a right forms in the rip channel opposite.

A short drive to nearby **Westcape Beach** provides gutsy lefts and rights when the banks are on. Westcape is about 3 kms long and is protected from howling westerlies and northerlies. Like Ethels, the beach is extremely deep out the back and the waves have heaps of push. Any swell over 6 ft is out of bounds for these locations.

Pondalowie Bay

On the way to the next stop at Pondalowie Bay, you'll inevitably see kangaroos, emus and an assortment of native wildlife. One of the more popular breaks, **Pondie** is consistently offshore during the summer months with beach access made easier by a boardwalk and a viewing platform. Occasionally sand dumps on the inshore reefs producing workable lefts around 3 ft, and rights if the swell is any bigger. At low tide with S–SE winds and a medium to large groundswell, Pondie is fun until the axe-like shorebreak tempts you into trying a floater. About 200 m down the beach is **Richards**, named after one of the local park rangers. Predominantly a right, it is best surfed on an easterly and is a good option to avoid the crowds at Pondie.

Baby Lizards

After sampling these breaks, head towards **Marion Bay** and turn left along the Corny Point Rd. About 15 km along the dirt road, turn left into **Formby Bay**, stop on the cliff side carpark and look right for **Baby Lizards** near the start of **Dustbowl Beach**. Walk the track until the cliffs stop and you'll find a variety of reef setups, with the righthander finishing at the base of the headland being the most regularly surfed break in this area. A fairly fat wave, it relies heavily on SE–E winds and swell in the 2–4 ft range. However, it does have a couple of sucky sections allowing some good moves off the top. Directly opposite, the left reef enjoys a few moments of glory when the sand banks take shape.

Trespassers

If the swell jacks, **Lizards** will close out and it might be worth heading over to **Trespassers**. Pack plenty of supplies because the walk is a mission. Across the cliffs you can watch Trespassers break and decide if it's worth trudging on. It works on easterly winds with a medium to large swell but on a high

tide it can be inconsistent. Not really hollow, the big faces are great for full-blooded manoeuvres with the swell approaching the reef from a variety of directions.

If conditions are big and wobbly, **Snails**, the left on the other side of the reef is worth a look.

Corny Point & Dustbowl

As another alternative, trek back to the car and head north towards Corny Point. Turn left down Daly Heads Rd and about 10 km west you'll come to a carpark right above one of South Australia's premier breaks. At 6 ft, **Daly Heads** reels off three major sections, all about 50 m apart. The third reef is serious stuff—not top to bottom—just big moving walls of water. Best at around 4–6 ft, you can take out a bigger board easily with so much water in these waves. Sets don't always line up, so be prepared to scramble wide or cop a mountain of whitewater.

Riding from the outside take-off zone, you race into the first reef with plenty of speed to attack the bowl. Lowish tide and S–SE winds on a strong swell are the ideal conditions. Any bigger and you'll have to check the inside point.

Keep driving past Daly and you'll reach the front of the headland, a good spot to stretch the legs and check your options. Looking left, **Dustbowl Beach** stretches miles back to Baby Lizards. On NW winds and small swells, it usually has a bank or two with strong rips. Aptly named, Dustbowl can produce some torrid conditions during summer, so if it's on, try to plan your surfing expedition for early morning to avoid the wind and blinding glare.

Occasionally **Rockpools**, a powerful righthander located around the rocks at the end of the beach, can deliver some outstanding waves that shape up like Bells. Best surfed at around 4–6 ft when the swell's slightly too big for Dustbowl, Rockpools is largely protected from strong NW winds and breaks into deep water.

Out in front of the headland is **Salmon Hole**, a semi-righthand point break with good quality sections. Up to 6 ft, the hole winds down the rocks with good shape and one brutal suck-rock to contend with. Usually surfed at about 4 ft, Salmon Hole tends to get crowded so check out Rockpools to the left which will probably be a few feet bigger and have less crew out catching the action.

—*Brian "Squizzy" Taylor*

Above: Cool is a tall man in the eye of a storm. A stylish moment for Michael Lowe at Pondalowie Bay.
Photo: Peter Wilson

G'day from WALLABY POINT

The Classic Australian Beach Town

Text by David Miller

No single beach has all the things you'd want. To get the right mix you need to cobble together bits and pieces from all over—a break from here, a view from there, a pub from somewhere else.

It's not perfect of course. If it was perfect it'd drive you mad with boredom and you'd wind up running amok in a fast food joint or moving to Canberra (Australia's political capital), or something.

Wallaby Point is a good name. Simple. Down to earth. It doesn't set up high expectations like a Tranquil Waters or Sunny Haven or Surfer's Paradise. It would be hard to live up to a name like that. If things didn't work out you'd feel as if you'd let the side down and you should go apologise to the local tourism board.

At the same time you don't want to go too far the other way—White Pointer Bay, Coffin Point, Cape Catastrophe or the like. This sort of thing has got a grim "we're all doomed" feel about it which is off putting, though to be fair it probably keeps the crowds down.

Wallaby Point is not a city beach—too crowded, too ugly. And it can't be a lonely beach in the middle of nowhere; a bloke needs more than surf to sustain life. He needs pubs and bars and friends and girls—or to be realistic the sweet possibility of girls, the sweet hope of girls.

So Wallaby Point is a compromise. It has a bit of both. There's a small township that runs back from the beach towards the hills. There are farms on one side and a national park on the other. It's a long way off the highway on a road that goes nowhere in particular.

The beach is about 2 km long and has prominent headlands at either end. It's short enough so that you can walk to the far, protected corner; long enough that you can find a break to yourself. It won't take long before you feel free to let it all hang out, so to speak, without frightening the children.

Wallaby Point is not a legendary surf spot, yet there always seems to be a wave. There's beach breaks that grab any swell running.

Protected corners for windy days. Unpredictable reef breaks that will lure you into sight unseen. And for big swells there's a point break with long rides that thins the crowds and has a tricky jump off the rocks spot that puts few victims through the mincer each session and gives everyone a good laugh.

The beach is often bypassed by travelling surfers. More often than not they speed past the turn off en-route to somewhere more glamorous up the coast. It does not have the reputation of other spots but on its day, Wallaby Point gets as good as anywhere.

It's not tropical, not even sub tropical. Which is fine. If it was it'd be full of resorts called Palm Village or Coconut Grove and the locals would be working as cabana boys at Club Med. Or worse there'd be a backpackers full of rich hippies wearing G-Strings and trying to buy drugs.

Wallaby Point is further from the equator. Houses have open fires. The winds are light. There are plenty of still, slate-grey days where the sky is low, the water's cold and the surf is good. It's the type of place that separates the men from the boys and the hardcore from the pretenders and the…well you probably get the drift. It's a bloke thing.

It's a pretty town. Most of it lies sleeping in the sun opposite the south end of the beach. Modern development has passed it by. The buildings are classically Australian—weatherboard cottages, iron roofs and wide verandahs. Solid, handsome, old public buildings.

There is no architecture in the modern Neo-Brutalist style. No concrete boxes. The popular "F– – k You" school of architecture is not represented, where governments or corporations put up big, ugly buildings totally at odds with the looks and history of their surrounds.

Wallaby Point has no high-rise apartments luxury resorts, time share condominiums or treeless quarter acre block housing subdivisions. Every now and then a developer unveils big plans for a colossal resort, but somehow it never happens. In a strange coincidence each and every one of them seems to meet some kind of grisly fate—helicopter crash, shark attack, spontaneous human combustion and the whole thing gets shelved.

Still, the tourist is not ignored at Wallaby Point. No sir. There's the Lagoon View Caravan Park, home to misfits, drifters, drunks, savage dogs and old age pensioners through the year and bursting at the seams with disfunctional families during the school holidays.

The Wallaby Point Hotel—a once grand old pub now slightly faded—sits opposite the beach. It's got big musty rooms that open

onto timber verandahs with pretty iron lacework, an old ballroom where bands play, and best of all, a rambling beer garden that overlooks the surf.

At the beach is an old art deco surf club built in the 1920's. The clubbies are about as up to date as the clubhouse. These are not your "with it" surf club members reaching out for today's youth. No. They're more your old style bum faced clubbies. The kind that purposely move the flags to snuff your favourite peak, confiscate your board and laughingly run you over in the surf boat. The kind that turn on kegs and gang bangs behind the clubhouse. They don't like surfers. Surfers don't like them. The two groups are sworn enemies and wage constant guerilla warfare, which is exactly the way it should be. There is nothing worse than hip modern clubbies who know what the decent thing is, do it and spoil everyone's fun.

Life on the beachfront follows predictable patterns. People sit under pine trees on the grass bank above the beach scoffing fish and chips and ice-creams. Kids play on the swings. Blokes ride bicycles or skateboards. Dogs catch frisbees and old people sleep in the sun.

You are unlikely to see rollerblading, beach volleyball, musclemen, FM radio programs, homeboys, busking mime artists or government-funded street theatre encouraging you to say no to drugs.

There is, though, a carnival at Christmas time. It has a ghost train, a ferris wheel, a

Above: Wallaby Point—where men are men and common sense is a foreign currency!
Photo: Peter Wilson

Left: What's the use of catching a good one when the audience has its eyes on some hunk on another wave! *Photo: Mick McCormack*

freakshow, a tatooed lady and a guy with a pit full of poisonous snakes.

You can get pretty well anything you want to eat in Wallaby Point. For the traditionalists there's a meat pie shop and of course an especially greasy takeaway place specialising in Chiko Rolls and buckets of fat. But perhaps the cherry on the cake is the Retired Servicemen's League dining room or the great Aussie Food Hall, that does authentic Australian food ie: really bad Chinese. Surprisingly, Wallaby also has some good restaurants run by wealthy city refugees who are recruited specifically for this purpose, though of course their numbers are strictly controlled.

On the headland is the Wallaby Point Country Club—a nine hole golf course. It's not your businessmen-entertaining-clients type of course. It's more your thongs and board shorts, six pack in the golf bag type of deal. Nearby is the town footy oval. It has a cricket pitch and a rickety pavilion. Here rival factions play social matches in the style common to social matches everywhere. Which is of course to the death.

Further along there is an old cemetery that sits on a rise above the beach. There's a couple of old stone memorials visible from the surf and looking at them does three things for you: it puts you in touch with your heritage; it serves as a timely reminder of the empty folly of human vanity and it gives you a perfect marker to lineup the right takeoff spot.

Beginning there and running the length of the beach is a long stretch of sand dunes. They are pretty much your standard sand dunes and provide cover for all traditional dodgy sand activities—indecent exposure, drunken fornication, sacrifices to the Prince of Darkness, etc.

Wallaby Point gets a few sharks but no more or less than the national average. The shark alarm goes off a few times each summer which is enough to give you the chance to stay in the water and try to impress chicks with your couldn't give a damn fatalistic cool though it's not enough to make you think about taking up tennis.

Wallaby Point has no organised boardriders club. There's a shortage of the officious types you need to get these kind of things to work. Guys who dream of surf stardom tend to drift away to somewhere else. Instead there are bunch of loose tribes based around a shared world view.

There's soul surfers. There's animals. There's hippies. There's petrol heads. Smokers. Drinkers. Grommets. Bikies. There's old bastards. There's old, fat bastards. There's older, fatter bastards. One weekend a year though, everyone comes together. There's a huge contest/expression session/ anarchic cock up, followed by a glittering black tie presentation evening at the Wallaby Point Hotel.

And then there's the girls. Typically the Wallaby Point chick is great looking though she doesn't flaunt it. She is not big headed. She may even seem a bit modest and standoffish. But this is deceptive and merely serves to cloak the hot-blooded passion and almost uncontrollable primal urges that throb wildly within her nubile form.

She is not though without faults. In fact she has a tragic flaw. A hopeless weakness for lazy, aimless, unambitious surf bums, coincidentally a type commonly found in Wallaby Point.

Lawyers, doctors and rich businessmen pursue her but sadly leave her cold, especially

when they throw their money around and try to buy her affections. Actually she prefers a night at the pub and is more than happy to buy a few rounds. It's strange but she just can't seem to help herself.

The people of Wallaby Point are patriotic but in a low key kind of way. Not in the cornball slowmo weeping at the Olympics, hand over the heart, kind of way. Or in the wogs go home, bail the master race, white man's burden way either. They don't wear Chicago Bulls outfits and back to front baseball caps and have a proud sense of their own traditions.

In Wallaby Point all the sacred Australian religious and cultural festivals are observed— Christmas, Easter and Anzac Day. The Melbourne Cup, the AFL Footy final, the State of Origin Rugby and World Series Cricket. There's also a particular local oddity known as "Cracker Night" that remains a highlight of the social calendar. Local authorities turn a blind eye to misguided national 'laws' and there is a brisk trade in contraband fireworks, bungers,

skyrockets, jumping jacks...you name it.

There's a couple of huge bonfires down near the beach and everyone gathers around. The night is a spectacular success which is hardly surprising. After all you've got leaping flames, heavy drinking, large explosions and semi permanent injuries, what more could you ask for?

That's the good thing about the Wallaby Point authorities. They can keep things in perspective. They are flexible on petty things like renegade dogs, nudity, beach parties and pub closing times. Yet they come down hard on the serious offenders like jetski riders, litterbugs, board thieves, community toilet pervos or anyone caught playing techno music in a public space.

Above: Surfin' Kulture.
Illustration: Mark McBride

Below: When the surf's up, Wallaby Point is the place to be.
Photo: Andrew Buckley

June–August.
(Winter)

Drive to most of the
primo breaks with
ease.

Flat reef and sand
bottoms.

Hotdog boards for
small to medium
waves.

Crowds and rips.

Dirty water near riv-
er mouths after rain.

Fun waves that are
easily accessed.

Preceding pages:
Newcastle petrol
head and surfing
powerhouse Luke
Egan rips the guts
out of a Mid Coast
wave face.
Photo: Peter Wilson

Below: South
Australian state
champion Jeff
Hardick about to
detonate a helpless
Mid Coast lip.
Photo: Peter Wilson

The Mid Coast

Hotdog Swells and Remarkable Tides

Gazing over the lazy waters of St Vincent's Gulf on the Mid Coast on a scorching summers day, it's hard to imagine this stretch of water producing any rideable waves.

Around 40 minutes drive from the heart of the city along the Main South Road, the "magic" Mid Coast is located along Adelaide's southern suburbs. Follow the signs to Noarlunga, then head west to meet the 10 km stretch of coastline that is magical, not for the quality of its surf, but for the fact that it keeps thousands of city surfers regular.

Facing west, the Mid Coast is perfectly positioned to receive any swells travelling through the narrow swell window of Investigator Strait. Only swells with SW and W directions squeeze between Kangaroo Island and Yorke Peninsula to reach this tiny section of coast scattered with superb reef formations.

Situated inside a gulf, the Mid Coast tends to be plagued by lengthy flat spells due to southerly swell directions during the summer.

St Vincent's Gulf also has remarkable tides—dodge tides too. Weaker, smaller waves are quickly diminished in a matter of hours on an outgoing tide. The incoming tides bring consistently bigger sets to most of the breaks. The closest surfing destination to Adelaide, the Mid Coast handles the large crowds relatively well. Arrive at midday during a swell and you can expect to surf with a dozen or more crew; pick your times better and you can get it all to yourself.

The Esplanade runs parallel to the Mid Coast for its entire length with carpark access to all breaks for relatively easy surf checking. Most surf is around the 2–4 ft range with SE–NE winds offshore at all locations.

194

SOUTH AUSTRALIA

THE MID COAST

Seaford

Seaford is the most popular area. The righthand reef break is probably the longest wave on the coast and comprises an outside, middle and inside section. Depending on the tide, Seaford can also handle stormy conditions, so if there's swell it's always worth a look. An excellent lefthander best suited to clean conditions and larger swells, **Seaford Reef**, situated 200 m offshore, has great length, shape and usually less crowds. Right next door is **Frednerks**, another reef break with lefts and rights. Too shallow at low to mid tide, it fires on a high tide with a large swell.

Another 200 m south is **The Trough**. A lefthand reef break popular with the goofies, it has a good first section that flattens off as it winds into the channel. Jump in the car and travel north two kilometres then pull into the large carpark of **Triggs** (named after the nearby navigational tower). Triggs 1 and 2 are fun, hotdog waves with good shape but not a lot of power. **U turns** is a left reef break and, like Triggs, works best on larger swells.

Southport

From here, head north to Southport. At the southern end of the beach is the fabled **Onkaparinga** rivermouth which through the 1980s had unreal sandbars imitating Mundaca's mechanical lefthanders, only on a smaller scale. Greg Webb, Danny Higgins, and Chappy Jennings were around to score the best of it. Now the river holds back a lot of water needed to create the ruler-edged bank. It has its moments, but only in the middle of winter.

Follow the esplanade over the footbridge that crosses the river, through the sandhills and onto Southport main beach where you will find one of the Mid Coast's favourite summer hangouts, **The Hump**. From mid morning to midday, when an outgoing tide meets a decent groundswell, the long lefts march in behind the Port Noarlunga Reef. On smaller swells, Southport usually picks up the most swell on the coast and is used as an indicator for other locations by local surfers.

Above: To hordes of keen Adelaide surfers, the Mid Coast is a launching pad to develop their skills for the heavier Southern Ocean swells.
Photo: Peter Wilson

Above: Old jungle saying: "Do what you love and you will love what you do".
Photo: Twiggy

Adelaide

↑
N

0   5   10   15
Kilometres

Largs Bay
Gepps Cross
● Adelaide
Uraidla
Glenelg Jetty
Stirling
O'Halloran Hill
Hahndorf
Morphett Vale
The Hump
Y Steps
Kangarilla
Onkaparinga Rivermouth
Seaford Reef
Frednerks
Prospect Hill
The Trough
McLaren Vale
Port Willunga

Gulf St. Vincent

Aldinga Bay

Mount Compass

Myponga
Carrickalinga Head
Myponga
Normanville
Yankalilla Bay
Hindmarsh Valley
Rapid Bay
Port Elliot
Goolwa
Fleurieu Peninsula
Victor Harbor
Cape Jervis
Waitpinga
Rosetta Head
Goolwa Beach
Cape Jervis
Tunk Head
Newland Head

Dumpers and Y-steps

Leaving Southport, cruise further into the township of Port Noarlunga. The road leads you to the jetty where you can occasionally shoot the pier during winter when NW winds reach 30–40 knots. Across the top of Witton Bluff and onto the southern end of **Christies Beach**, you will find **Dumpers** which works during raging SW storms all year round. A punchy beachbreak with lefts and rights semi-protected from the wild weather, it's probably the heaviest break on the coast.

About 100 m further north is **Y-steps**. The Mid-Coast's equivalent of Queensland's Duranbah, a horse-shoe reef 300 m offshore refracts the swell 45 degrees towards shore. Once you fight your way through the lid riders, you can score some sucky rights and lefts amongst the 'roaders' who surf Y-steps regularly and rip the place to shreds. Glassy conditions and a medium swell are the key factors.

The Mid Coast has seen a large slice of South Oz surfing history and it has developed some great surfing talents. While it is neither up there on the power side, nor does it offer over-challenging conditions, its clean, well-shaped waves keep every suburban surfer happy while they wait for their next serious surfing safari.

—*Brian "Squizzy" Taylor*

Victor Harbor

Antarctic Swells and Unique Landscapes

The Victor Harbor region on the south coast of the Fleurieu Peninsula offers an incredible variety of waves. The ocean rarely sleeps here as low pressure systems dominating the southern half of the continent produce Antarctic swells that roll in to the coastline to forge many truly unique landscapes.

South Australia's most popular summer holiday destination, only 90 km from Adelaide, the south coast provides welcome relief from the heat, with cool Southern Ocean sea breezes.

A relatively short drive over the Mt. Lofty range and then along South Rd, brings you to **Encounter Bay**, known historically as the meeting place for Matthew Flinders and Nicholas Baudin in 1802, when England and France were at war. Victor Harbor and the south coast are also rich in Aboriginal history and were once home to seal and whale hunters.

Goolwa Beach

Goolwa, situated on the eastern end of the region, has miles of coastal dunes and is on the doorstep of the beautiful **Coorong National Park**. The Murray River, Australia's largest river, runs beside the town before entering the sea a few kilometres east at Goolwa Beach. Occasionally the river mouth is surfable, but beware of sharks. Accessed via Goolwa Beach, these beach breaks are best suited to smaller swells with NE winds. Anything bigger and you're in for a duck-diving marathon.

Middleton

Travelling west, the main road out of Goolwa follows the coast to

May–August.

Good roads to most of the popular breaks. Some beachwalks to more isolated waves.

Sand covered reef and flat reef or sand bottoms.

Warm wetsuit, booties, hotdog board and big wave guns.

Strong currents, sharks and powerful waves.

Reef cuts.

Relatively uncrowded beach breaks, powerful big wave locations and scenic national parks.

Below: Driving that diagonal line. Nomadic surf trip specialist Neal Purchase Jnr pulls a hefty backhand re-entry on an inviting Middleton section. *Photo: Peter Wilson*

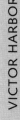

Middleton. A kilometre prior to your destination, you'll find Chapman Road and a place known to surfers as **Day Street**. Along the esplanade there are several carparks to check the options. This stretch of beach sometimes gets reasonable banks and is worth a look on a small to medium swell with NE to N winds. However, most surfers drive along Middleton's main road before turning off at the tavern to check the main beach or **Middleton Point**. Both are best in medium-size swells.

It's a long way to paddle out the back—any session in a 4-ft strong swell requires an ironman-like performance. Wait and select the better ones; lefts, rights, you can get a real shake happening on 200 m rides as the wave closes out and reforms several times. Known as "magic carpet rides", even on crowded days you can always find an acre of room to yourself. Northerly winds are offshore, however some of the best days are during light onshores. Just 200 m west from the point, **Middleton Bay** is popular with the better surfers as the inside rip usually ensures shapely waves if the sandbanks are good.

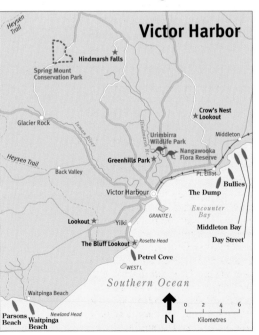

Port Elliot

When the swell reaches 4–6 ft head towards Victor Harbor along the Main Goolwa Rd to Victor Rd and then into Port Elliot. Turn off the main road opposite the drive-in to check **Bullies**, a big wave location that will test your fitness and equipment. Heaving out of deep water, the righthanders burst on the reef just beyond a thumping shorebreak that claims a few victims each session. The odd tube and 6–8 ft slabs of water rearing up in a variety of ugly ways makes for some spectacular moments. In the eastern corner, the beach meets giant granite boulders which refract the swell forming sick, powerful wedges. With this in mind, **Knights Beach** is only worth checking when the swell is smaller. Facing south, this stretch of coast cleans up with any hint of NE–NW winds.

The Dump

Most of the crew will head a further 2 km west towards Victor until arriving at Investigator carpark on First Avenue, overlooking the rights and lefts of **The Dump**. This reef setup works best around 4 ft and closes out if bigger on a low tide. The right has the most to offer and you can score a classic if you wait for a lined-up wall from out the back. Not real heavy or hollow, there's plenty of wave face to whack before clubbing the close-out shorey. Clean 4 ft lines with a strong offshore are best for the left which connects with the rights.

From The Dump you get a side-on view of **Bullies**, **Chiton** and **Knights**, so checking one out gives you a rough idea of the rest. Winter months are more consistent for this stretch of coast as in summer the swells are usually too small. Like anywhere, Victor has its flat spells.

When it's small, head towards the centre of Victor Harbor and follow the signs to Waitpinga (Aboriginal for 'windy place')—which sure lives up to its name.

Petrel Cove

Before heading the 11 km out to **Waits Beach**, check out Petrel Cove next to the Bluff on **Encounter Bay**. One of the few protected spots during the southerly summer trade winds, Petrel's is a short, rock-lined cove that can develop a good bank with sucky righthanders in the 2–4 ft range. To get there, follow the Waitpinga signs and turn left at the South Coast Hospital, which takes you down to the Esplanade. After reaching the foreshore, head west to the huge granite bluff and follow the scenic drive to the other side. The carpark gives you easy access to waves that are quite punchy.

Above: Simon Robinson makes chop suey out of a beautiful Parsons' wall.
Photo: Peter Wilson

SOUTH AUSTRALIA

VICTOR HARBOR

Above: Brett Herring tucks into a shady shack. Victor is one harbour that really does have a lot of waves.
Photo: Peter Wilson

Opposite: South Australia's large variety of powerful waves gives rise to many radical surfing styles.
Photo: Andrew Buckley

Overleaf: Victor's beach breaks can dish out some real power on a decent swell.
Photo: Andrew Buckley

Peering west, you'll see **Kings Headland**. A short right over reef with one very shallow sucky section, it requires a northerly wind, medium size swell and a ten minute walk from the carpark. Both Petrels and Kings are fickle options and most surfers opt to head for Waits.

Waits Point

The trip out to Waits is as easy as following the signs from Victor to a classic Southern Ocean surf beach. Fully exposed to powerful swell and unforgiving to the inexperienced, Waits can deliver balmy, glassy, surreal days or howling offshore can't-see-for-the-spray days. This translates to grinding V-shaped banks or 3-ft shitty closeouts.

Rips? Even on small days, you won't find many beaches with the relentless power of **Waits**. It has claimed a number of lives over the years, both surfers and fishing folk, so before you jump off that sand be sure you can read the water conditions. Exposed to continuous swell, the sandbanks move regularly, with winter and spring usually offering the best conditions. Waits is a popular spot when the swell is small, and its new bitumised road and carpark eliminate

the past hassles of negotiating a bog pit when it rains.

In the central part of the beach, the rivermouth is normally worth a check, or motor on back to the entrance before heading across to the **Waits Point** and **Parsons Beach** turnoff. Waits Point handles windy days, sheltered from the westerlies and strong offshores.

Parsons Beach

Located nearby, Parsons is clean in any easterly winds. Clear, sparkling water draws you to walk down the headland to the rights and lefts at the point, or maybe a nice bank further down the beach. Usually the rip that runs along the point forms rights, with a sucky bowl on the end, or lefts if it's over 4 ft and freight-training out the back.

Quantity not quality describes these two beaches that struggle to cope with the volume of swell. Surf 6 ft and over just isn't in the equation here with thunderous closeouts brutally destroying any banks formed during another brief halt in groundswell. To score good waves here, keep a keen eye on the place and take plenty of supplies for the trekking mission.

—*Brian "Squizzy" Taylor*

May–August.

Sealed roads and four wheel drive tracks to most breaks.

Reef and sand bottoms.

Warm wetsuit due to cold currents and winds.

Sharks, inconsistent swell.

Some dirty water near rivermouths.

Empty waves if you get lucky, good fishing, scenic national parks, great wine-making region.

The South East Coast

Wilderness, Wine and Waves

Huge pine forests, thick swampy scrub and sensational red wine are all special characteristics of the south east coast. As it receives more rainfall than most South Oz regions, it is considerably more fertile. The continental shelf also dips in a lot closer here compared to the rest of the surrounding coastline, making the water temperature a little cooler.

Nelson & Port MacDonnell

Situated near the Glenelg river-mouth, **Nelson** is a small town offering some nice beach breaks on northerly winds and small swells. Travelling west, you come to the turn-off for Port MacDonnell. Like many of the pit stops in the south east, Port Mac is a major crayfishing town. A coastal road takes you to the lighthouse where an average left is usually surfed during storms. Moving further west you'll find a decent righthander (reliant on northerly winds) called **Posties,** which is located near the controversial sewerage outfall. Here you'll find a maze of dirt tracks to some reasonable lefts like **Pebbles,** but make sure you get some reliable directions from one of the locals or you could find yourself on a road to nowhere.

Southend

Snaking through Mount Gambier, the Princess Highway then veers towards the coast. Chuck a lefty to **Millicent** and head on towards Southend, a small town on Rivoli Bay, and **Beachport**. Nearby is the **Canunda National Park**, with one reasonable short hollow left called **Cullens** that needs SE–NE winds and a largish swell. There are a few beaches further into the park that get good at times, but it's all 4WD access.

Beachport

The left off **Southend Point** and around past the jetty also has potential during larger swells and SE winds but is generally pretty fickle. Beachport at the north-west end of **Rivoli Bay** delivers surf right on the town's doorstep. Before arriving in the centre of town, park your car at the front beach carpark. This

South East Coast

Map showing:
Langhome Creek, Finnis, Lake Alexandrina, Narrung, Ashville, Goolwa, Port Eillot, Encounter Bay, Victor Harbor, Younghusband Peninsula, Maningle, Coonalpyn, Caramia Conservation Park, Mexmi Rescue Conservation Park, Tinlinara, Messoni Conservation Park, Keith, The Coorong, Salt Creek, Gun Lagoon Conservation Park, Bordertown, Deson Camp, Southern Ocean, Lacepede Bay, Kingston SE, Guichen Bay, Robe, Stony Rises, Clay Wells, Beachport, Halhorleigh, Rivoli Bay, Millicent, South End, Cullens, Snuggery, Mount Gambier, Posties, Cape Banks, Port MacDonnell, Cape Northumberland

0 20 40 60 Kilometres N

area is surfed when the swell's too big for the back beach and can provide some fun. The scenic drive along the opposite side of town also has a few powerful reef setups that are worth checking. Northerly winds or calm conditions with a small swell are essential to crack these breaks.

Robe

Following the Princess Highway west brings you to the popular holiday town of Robe. Like Beachport, the surf is located near Robe's town centre. **Long Beach** (it goes on for miles) doesn't have great quality surf but offers an easy alternative if you can't find a decent break nearby.

Little Dip National Park

Little Dip National Park just south of Robe has better quality surf. Tracks weave in and out of the scrub before a short trek across the sand hills brings you to the beach of **Stony Rises**. Northerlies are offshore and at times the banks are

unreal. Steve's Place, the local surf shop, will point you in the right direction if you need it.

Coorong National Park

From Robe, travel north past **Kingston** and the sand hills of the Coorong National Park. Access to the beach is limited to a few 4WD tracks, often used by fishermen rather than those seeking quality surf, but nothing ventured nothing gained!

The Coorong is located south of the Murray River mouth and is a series of lagoons separated from the sea by the Younghusband Peninsula (which is on average 2 km wide). A major breeding ground for pelicans, wild duck, swans and ibis, the Coorong was declared a national park about 30 years ago.

Throw your line out anywhere along Coorong's beautiful beaches, or head north with your boat to its tranquil lagoons. The best entry points for boats are from Goolwah and Hindmarsh Islands.

—Brian "Squizzy" Taylor

Above: Hot South Oz local, Nat Hozier makes the most of a typical South East Coast shorebreak. *Photo: Peter Wilson*

Kangaroo Island

Crystal Waters and Open Ocean Surf

May–August.

Car ferry, boat charter.

Reef and sand bottoms.

Warm wetsuit, definitely need a car, big wave gun and mid-size board.

Sharks, strong rips, unfavourable winds and reef.

Reef cuts.

Empty barrels, spectacular wildlife and scenery.

South Australia has more than 20 islands located off its coastline and Kangaroo Island is the largest. At 100 km long and 30 km wide, the island is world-renowned for its natural beauty. Years ago, policies were established to protect wildlife from introduced species such as foxes and rabbits. The native animals and their spectacular surroundings make this place very special.

At the southern tip of the **Fleurieu Peninsula**, the view from Cape Jervis across the 11-km stretch of water, known as **Backstairs**, showcases Kangaroo Island. The popular choice of transport is aboard the ferry *Phillandrer,* which takes about an hour to reach the coastal town of **Penneshaw**. It's fairly expensive to transport you and the car, but the cost is well worth it as there's plenty of ground to cover in order to find the breaks that will give you the best joy.

Once on Kangaroo Island, take the bitumen road to a turn-off at American River, a holiday spot at the entrance of Pelican Lagoon. From here, it's a short drive down a dirt road to check the surf at **Penington Bay**. The colour and clarity of the water is remarkable when the swells are small and the wind is offshore. Northerly winds and a small swell of around 2–4 ft are ideal for the lefts and rights depending on the sandbanks.

From here the main bitumen road continues north to **Kingscote**, the island's largest town which faces back into the calmer waters of St Vincents Gulf.

Stokes Bay

Take the Playford Highway west and follow the signs which head to the north coast. Adjacent to farmland, the beaches, bays and cliffs offer some stunning scenery. **Stokes Bay** is surfable during strong SW winds when most places are blown out. A reasonable lefthander, the wave breaks in front of the carpark during large storms and big seas.

Follow the South Coast Road, parallel to the coast, and take the turn to D'Estrees Bay. This road leads into the national park before continuing

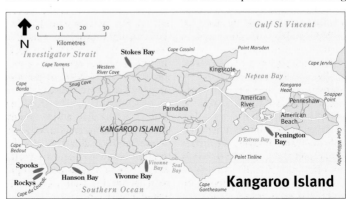

Kangaroo Island

to the coast and **The Sewer**, a good righthand rocky point set-up that works best with N–NW winds and a moderate swell. It doesn't barrel but packs plenty of power at 4 ft, reeling off plenty of workable wall.

Vivonne Bay

Travelling further west along South Coast Road, you'll reach Vivonne Bay. There's a general store to replenish supplies plus a camping area above the rivermouth. As the bay sweeps east, the wave size increases and so does the quality. Better sandbanks form with larger swells, forging deeper channels. NE to NW winds are offshore while a medium size swell is ideal.

Continuing westward, you eventually arrive at the turn-off to **Hanson Bay**. The reef on the small headland opposite the shacks is the go when it's 4 ft and bigger. The next bay along is open to all available swell and is surfed only when it's around 2–4 ft. Northerly winds are offshore and tend to straighten up the swell lines helping the beach and reef operate at their best.

Flinders Chase NP

This national park occupies the entire western end of the island from Cape Borda on the north coast, to Sanderson Bay on the south. After passing the ranger's office and camping area at Rocky River, the road leads to **Remarkable Rocks** and **Cape du Couedic**. A 30-minute walk brings you to a cliff overlooking two lefthanders, **Rockys** and **Spooks**. Winding along a small point, Rockys doesn't really barrel and tends to wall up so you can carve all over it.

Easterly winds are offshore and a large 4–6 ft swell is best. Looking across the bay, Spooks breaks on a reef 300 m off the cliffs before crashing into them. The waves are generally a couple of feet bigger and more powerful than Rockys.

Around the cape, a large ocean food chain exists—a seal colony calls this area home—so beware. During small swells, a trip out to the western beaches can prove worthwhile. **Sandy Creek** can also get pretty good with E–NE winds but is a long trek on foot.

Above: With crystal waters, empty barrels and picturesque bays, Kangaroo Island makes an exotic stopover after roughing it on the desert fringe. *Photo: South Australian Tourist Commission*

March–August.

Sealed and gravel roads. Some four wheel drive access to good waves.

Sharp reef, mellow reef and sand.

Big wave gun, warm wetsuit, bring your own basic supplies and a medical kit.

Great White Sharks, sharp reef, strong currents, Australia's heaviest locals.

You are a long way from medical facilities—be careful.

Dramatic surfing backdrops, un-crowded hollow perfection, and great fishing.

Eyre Peninsula

Wild Coastline, Wild Surfers and Untamed Waves

Stretching 469 km from Port Augusta in the east to the isolated outpost of **Ceduna** in the west, the Eyre Peninsula's wild coastline offers some dramatic surfing experiences.

Famed for its pink lakes, the desolate Nullarbor Plain and notorious shark breeding grounds, "The Eyre" may be a solid 8 to 10-hour drive from Adelaide, but it's well worth the surfari. Near the southern tip of the Peninsula you'll find **Port Lincoln**, where the underwater scenes of the Hollywood blockbuster *Jaws* were filmed at Dangerous Reef.

Sleaford

A 15-minute drive down to Sleaford or Fishery Bays is the closest surf from here. **Sleaford Bay** has mainly beach breaks with a small rocky cove producing a few wedges in the western corner. **Fishery Bay** has

mellow waves with the odd suck-rock off the left and right points along each headland. S–SW swell and northerly winds provide the best conditions.

Coffin Bay

Heading west from Port Lincoln, the coastline is pretty severe and inaccessible before opening into the calm waters of Coffin Bay. The only surf here is in the nearby national park or you can chance the sharky waters of **Almonta Beach**.

Sheringa Beach

Continuing to the north along the Flinders Highway, there's usually some decent swell around **Coles Point** and **Greenly Beach**. When the wind is SE or NE, Greenly develops good beach breaks and provides plenty of options. High vertical cliffs dominate from here until you reach **Sheringa Beach**. The local store is great for supplies with petrol, beer, food and camping permits all available. The turn-off next to the shop heads 10 km to the spread of beaches. Sheringa works well in small swells and northerly winds. A mixture of reef and sand weave along the beach producing some excellent, crystal-clear waves. Tracks and carparks run along the beach for easy access.

Elliston

The next port of call is the township of Elliston where you'll see Flinders Island surrounded by the waters of the Great Australian

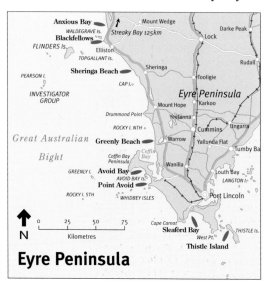

Eyre Peninsula

Bight. Just north of the town a road leads to the southern end of **Waterloo Bay** and out to **Black-fellows Reef**. Blackfellows' left-hander gets thick, gnarly and dangerous even at 4–6 ft—this place is only for the experienced rider. Solid walls rise quickly out of extremely deep water, heaving Southern Ocean power violently onto the reef. Take-offs are impossible on some waves and low-tide surfs are risky. Some waves barrel, while others bottom out keeping everyone honest with some horrendous wipeouts. Stand-out locals say easterly winds with 3–6 ft swells provide the best surfing conditions. Treat the place with respect and you should emerge unscathed.

Anxious Bay

At the northern end of Anxious Bay, you can either turn off to the town centre, or head further west about 30 minutes to access the magnificent **Streaky Bay**. A short drive west takes you to **Back Beach** where you'll find playful reef and sandbanks that work on small swells and northerly winds. For larger waves, head south out towards **Granites** and **Smooth-**pool especially when the swells are big and the winds are SE. Both are long lefts that work from 3–9 ft, with Granites producing a better quality option.

Smoothpool is powerful but not quite as shapely as the waves at Granites where the take-off gets heavy around 6 ft. The big walls then speed along the reef tending to bend, twist and section along the inside. A little further out from Granites is **Indicators**. These waves are similar, only shorter and more intense due to their proximity to the nearby rocks. **Sceales Bay** further south also has some waves, although you'll need to tap into some of the local knowledge to successfully find them.

Cactus

Pass **Ceduna**—the last full-service town before the Nullarbor Plain—then **Penong** and travel a further 20 kms to **Point Sinclair**. Here you'll find the fabled **Cactus**, a break with a colourful surfing history. It's a great place, but be warned the surf takes no shit and nor do the locals! A small shop near the camping ground can help you with daily supplies and provides shelter from the midday sun.

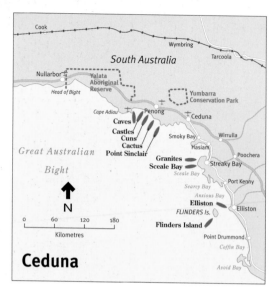

South Australia

Cook
Wymbring
Tarcoola
Nullarbor
Yalata Aboriginal Reserve
Head of Bight
Yumbarra Conservation Park
Cape Adiau
Penong
Ceduna
Caves
Castles
Cuns
Smoky Bay
Wirrulla
Cactus
Hasiam
Point Sinclair
Great Australian
Poochera
Granites
Streaky Bay
Bight
Sceale Bay
Sceale Bay
Port Kenny
Searcy Bay
Anxious Bay
N
Elliston
FLINDERS Is.
Elliston
0   60   120   180
Flinders Island
Kilometres
Point Drummond
Coffin Bay

Ceduna

Avoid Bay

Cuns

The southern end of the bay has a wave running below the cliff called Cuns. Although not as popular as nearby breaks it handles stronger southerly winds and prefers 3–6 ft swells. Wrapping around the cliffs, Cuns speeds up, sectioning across the reef and closes out as it approaches the break of Cactus. A mellow, lefthand reef break surfed around 3–5 ft and best on S–SE winds, Cactus closes out around 4 ft at low tide and handles a little bigger on full tide. A hotdog wave, it offers nice walls to explore your full range of manoeuvres.

Mouse plagues, snakes and relentless flies are sometimes part of the deal. However, sliding out into the clean, cool waters to escape the dry desert heat, then kicking back under the stars next to the campfire, full of bush tucker, are a couple of life's real pleasures.

Below: Sometimes the best way round a section is over it via a roof ride.
Photo: Peter Wilson

Castles

In the centre of the bay lies Castles, which is predominantly surfed through the inside section. Although the outside section begins well, it fades into deep water. Inside Castles, around 4 ft is best, with well-shaped, racy barrels shooting along the shallow reef. With any bigger surf, the

paddle out is mighty back-breaking.

Across the channel is **Caves'** righthander. Easily the best wave in the bay, it's where you'll find most of the locals. It works in 3–8 ft swells with northerly winds and gets crowded when conditions are good. Barreling on take-off, Caves walls up nicely to the inside before crunching onto sharp, shallow reef.

A variety of waves exist around the bay and headland of Point Sinclair, although they are rarely surfed because these are such wild, unpredictable seas. Self preservation and common sense are required when surfing these remote edges of Australia.

From Cactus stretch vast expanses of nothingness interrupted only by handfuls of scrub. It's still 480 km to the Western Australian border, so step off the Eyre Highway and have a look at the Great Australian Bight—an impressive stretch of rugged coastline connecting South Australia with Western Australia. It really does look like some cosmic giant bit off more than it could chew. Before this part of the highway was bituminised in the late '60s, the journey was a hazardous, hellish experience.

—*Brian "Squizzy" Taylor*

Above: The Eyre is honeycombed with wave-riding bliss for the determined explorer. *Photo: Peter Wilson*

The Wild West

The Ultimate Surfari

Preceding pages:
If you have the guts, The Bluff has the power. But you'll have to fight your way through a heavy crowd to score waves like this.
Photo: Twiggy

Opposite:
Injidup sandhill attracts avid sand-boarders whenever the waves are small.
Photo: Peter Wilson

Home to the most powerful waves outside of Hawaii, the 'Wild West', as it is known to many travelling surfers, has forged an enviable reputation for its remote Indian Ocean and Southern Ocean swells. One of surfing's last great frontiers, Western Australia is the land of the long road trip; a place where the desert meets the ocean and the careless meet their maker. With mile after mile of deserted beaches, overgrown tracks, sand dunes and occasionally towering forest you'll have to do plenty of four wheel driving, get bogged and down right dirty—but the rewards are well worth it.

Australia's largest state has pristine coastline, hollow waves and spectacular marine life, and produces some of the largest high performance waves in the world. From the intense barrels and beach breaks of the south west, to the long and hollow point breaks of the inhospitable north, WA offers surfing purists the ultimate surfari.

One of the oldest land masses on earth, WA's northwest interior is home to the renowned Bungle Bungle rock formations and the famous Aboriginal Wandjina figures—arguably the oldest sophisticated rock art/cave paintings on earth. Rich in natural resources, inland WA is the site of intensive mining operations for iron ore, bauxite, uranium and gold. The Sand-gropers, as they are affectionately known, also boast the world's largest cultured pearling industry located at Broome, while WA corporate giant Argyle Diamonds supplies more than a third of the world's most precious stones, including the rare pink diamond.

Fringed by some of the remotest surfing locations on the planet, the north west's string of offshore islands (which include the Muriens, Monte Bello, Cocos, Barrow, Dirk Hartog and Abrolhos Islands) are all capable of producing amazing waves at certain times of the year, usually April–July. But limited access rules, uncharted waters and huge tiger sharks usually keep the crowds to a minimum. Local crayfishermen often score 6-8 ft perfection to themselves. During March and April, scuba divers from all over the world flock to WA's breathtaking Ningaloo Reef, to swim with the biggest fish in the sea, the Whale Shark. The reef is an ideal place to view these mysterious creatures that grow up to 15 m long.

Set on the picturesque Swan River, Perth residents enjoy a mild Mediterranean climate. The city offers locals a relative sense of space, while average house plots are huge and reasonably priced. Surrounded by flat plainland, which bursts into a riot of colour when the wildflowers bloom, the metropolis sprawls casually before fading into long country drives to coastal towns both north and south.

Fremantle, the site of Australia's historic America's Cup sailing win in 1987, has been hailed by many maritime experts as one of the world's best preserved 19th-century seaports, with over 150 buildings gaining classification by the National Trust. It is also a focal point for the state's thriving rock lobster industry that supplies much of the live lobster market

Above: A typical south west WA reef break unloads over a shallow rock platform much to the delight of a solitary surfer.
Photo: Peter Wilson

Opposite: WA's offshore islands are home to some long point breaks.
Photo: Peter Wilson

throughout Japan and the USA.

Producing some of the largest pro surfing competition waves outside of Hawaii, Surfers Point at Margaret River has hosted many national and international events. Set near spectacular Karri forest, Surfers Point is renowned for its ridiculously powerful lefthanders that barrel over a shallow reef. One particular section of the wave known as the "Surgeon's Table" has claimed several surfer's lives and should be treated with respect by travelling adventurers.

In 1991 the world's leading male and female pro surfers gathered to battle huge, 15–18 ft waves in one of the most spectacular surfing contests in competitive history. Chewing through 24 surfboards in a cou-

ple of days, the thick-lipped Surfers Point waves were relentless, almost drowning top Australian female competitor Pauline Menczer who suffered a horrendous wipeout on a large setwave during her heat. Meanwhile, established pros such as Tom Curren, Simon Law, Nick Wood and Tom Carroll revelled in the conditions scoring huge tube rides, while surfing waves from Surfers Point through to the Margaret River mouth about a kilometre further north from the take-off zone.

Having some of the best wine-growing conditions in the world, WA's Margaret River and Rainbow Coast regions are also near the top of the list for many surfing safaris.

—Mark Thornley

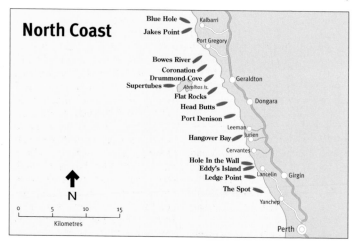

The North West Coast

*Remote Coastline and
Plenty of Drama*

This huge stretch of WA's coast includes The Batavia Coast in the north, which was named for one of the many 18th-century Dutch sailing ships that lie shipwrecked along this extremely windy and treacherous coastline. To appreciate its full surfing potential you will need a 4WD to tackle rugged desert tracks and shifting sandunes. In many locations you'll also need to take everything with you—food, water, shelter, shower, a sense of humour and an appetite for adventure. After all that's why they call it the Wild West. Yeehah!

Dongara

Approximately three hours' drive north of Perth (300 km), Dongarra marks the beginning of the Batavia Coast. The breakwater at **Port Denison**, a small home port to part of WA's extensive crayfishing fleet, is where surfers can catch a long left hander that breaks over a limestone reef beyond the safety of the breakwater. This wave involves a fair paddle out (approx 200 m) and, given the right conditions (easterly wind and clean swell), can produce excellent surf. North of here there are also a few small and shapely beach breaks on a moderate SW swell and light easterly winds.

Headbutts

Accessible only by 4WD vehicle and even then, depending on the tide, it's still a fair walk along the beach. This stretch of finely silted sand is one of the best beach break regions along the Batavia Coast.

Consistent gutters and channels with shifting sandbars often combine to produce crystal clean beach breaks. The turn-off is along the gravel road to Flat Rocks but you'd be lucky to find it if you went alone so take a local. Watch for other 4WD vehicles with surfboards. Works best in SE or NE winds and small to moderate W–SW swells.

Flat Rocks

Producing one of the most consistent, popular and shapely waves on the Batavia Coast, Flat Rocks has hosted many state surfing contests. Easily accessed via the sign-posted turn-off on the Brand Highway just south of the S-Bends Roadhouse, it's approximately 30 km south of Geraldton. A gravel road lined with wheat paddocks takes you all the way to the Flat Rocks carpark where you can watch the surf without having to get out of your vehicle. The wave, a left hand reef break, travels hundreds of metres along a submerged reef.

April–July.

 Rough gravel roads and kms of dunes. A 4WD and zodiac will give best access to the breaks.

 Mostly shallow reef and point breaks with lots of power.

 Bring a mid-ranger and your fastest tube guns. Spring suit and booties.

Cyclones (May–June), plenty of heavy locals, sharks. Vertical take-offs.

Sharp, shallow reef and urchins ensure cuts. Long way from medical care.

 Warm, clean water and long, super hollow barrels.

Undoubtedly the best part of the wave, the inside section offers some great carving and off-the-top sections, as well as the odd tube for those game or talented enough to negotiate the reef. A deep water channel that runs alongside the break makes it a fairly easy paddle out and, like most of the waves around the Geraldton region, Flat Rocks is best surfed in an easterly wind with a moderate SW swell (3–5 ft). Aside from being a long ride, the added bonus is that the inside section remains relatively clean, even during a howling onshore.

Geraldton

Approximately four hours' drive north of Perth (400 km), Geraldton is WA's fourth largest city. Many of the resident crayfishermen are keen surfers who catch their wave quota during the off season. With numerous beach and reef breaks working on different wind and swell patterns, some of the more popular waves include the **Backbeach**, **Hell's Gate** and **Sunset**.

Drummonds Cove, just north of Geraldton, is one of the better spots in the region. It's a mixture of reef and sand, and given the right conditions (easterly winds and favourable sand flow), can produce good-shaped peaks with a bit of punch.

Abrolhos Islands

As the summer home to much of Geraldton's crayfishing fleet, the Abrolhos contain several good surfing locations. Littered with fickle reef breaks, the Wallaby and Easter groups work in a variety of wind and swell conditions. Located nearly 80 km west of Geraldton, the Abrolhos are inaccessible to most surfers unless you can afford a charter boat or are good friends with a crayfisherman. Prone to tidal influences and sudden changes in the weather, not to mention the numerous sharks which prowl the reefs, the hollow waves at **Super Tubes** and other choice locations make for a memorable trip.

Bowes River

Located near Northampton (approximately 60 km north of Geraldton), Bowes River has several good lefthand reef breaks within close proximity of each other. The actual river mouth, just south of the main reef breaks, can also produce good beach break surf, given the right conditions. Bowes works best in small to moderate W–SW swells with an easterly wind. There are no shops or toilet facilities so, if you're planning to checkout this stretch of coastline, it's best to call into Northampton for some food and drinks before taking the Bowes turn-off.

Kalbarri

Home to Jake's Point, one of the best lefthanders in WA, this is a surfing pit stop where the experienced and courageous can push themselves in truly testing surf.

Located on the Murchison River (about 180 km north of Geraldton), there are two main breaks at Kalbarri—**Jakes Point** and **Blue Holes**. Both are frequented by a pack of wave-hungry locals that have probably caught more barrels than most readers have had roast dinners. At first glance Jake's can look deceivingly inviting but once you reach the take-off zone you begin to appreciate just how radical and challenging the waves really are.

One of the most intimidating free-fall takeoffs in Australia, the wave transforms very quickly and

Below: Kalbarri's spectacular coastal gorges.
Photo: Tungsten/Nikon

suddenly into a fearsome barrel. It also breaks hard and fast onto a very shallow reef only metres away from dry rock that marks the tip of the point. Who knows? If you make the takeoff you just might pull into one of the best barrels of your life. Then again, you might get splattered all over the reef!

Jake's works best in moderate size W–SW swells (4–8 ft), though it can handle bigger surf for those competent enough to tackle the exhilarating 250 m long walls.

The most favourable winds are easterly and southerly. When the swell drops and the wind turns NE you can check out **Blue Holes**, a ledgy righthander located between Jake's and the Murchison river. Blue Holes is more of a fun wave than Jake's and holds swells up to 6 ft. Once again, the local surfers dominate, though the vibe at Blue Holes is a bit more mellow.

Shark Bay

No prizes for guessing how this stretch of coastline received its name. Home to numerous large Tiger Sharks, the islands off Shark Bay, (Dorre and Dirk Hartog Islands), have good quality surf though getting there is the biggest problem. Charter boats are expen-

sive to hire and accommodation is extremely limited on these sparsely inhabited islands. Shark Bay is also home to one of Australia's most popular tourist destinations, Monkey Mia. Here, many busloads of tourists arrive daily to feed a pack of playful dolphins that enjoy close contact with humans along the shoreline. There are also waves worth exploring around the **Steep Point** region, but it's a long way off the main highway if it's flat. Still, if you've got plenty of time, petrol and plan well, you can score big time.

Carnarvon

Famous for its Apollo moon mission and space tracking station built during the 1960s, Carnarvon could best be described as a desert oasis. Many surfers from the Bluff (about 150 km north) call into Carnarvon for supplies each week. The town, with a population of more than 8000, has numerous facilities including supermarkets, banks, restaurants and a choice of five pubs.

Bernier and Dorre Islands block most of the swell from getting into Carnarvon, though you can ride tiny beach breaks north of the Fascine when there's a big swell running. **Blowholes** (about 60 km north of Carnarvon) is where most of the

Above: Clubbing the Flat Rocks end section on a windy day can be heaps of fun.
Photo: Tungsten/Nikon

Overleaf: A guy called "Motor" enjoying one of those magic days at an Exmouth beach break.
Photo: Peter Wilson

local kids get their first taste of real surf. There are a couple of rideable waves at the Blowholes, including one particular righthander which breaks off a little island and works well in a NE wind.

The Bluff

When the surf's up, The Bluff is truly one of Australia's most spectacular surfing locations. To find it, just keep heading north past the Blowholes along the sand and gravel tracks. The Bluff's radioactive-red cliffs, a large finger of limestone jutting hundreds of metres out of the desert coastline and into the Indian Ocean, are home to some of Australia's fastest and most perfect left-hand tubes. Unfortunately it usually only works during the winter months (June to September) and, even then, the good swells are inconsistent.

Although mostly accessible by 2WD vehicles, a 4WD is a better option, in fact an absolute necessity if you want to discover new breaks. Watch out for rocks, potholes and corrugations when it's dry. Kangaroos, emus, goats, cattle, sheep and salt trucks are other traffic hazards. There's no electricity or running water so bring all your supplies, including food, shelter and fresh water with you. If you're lucky you might be able to camp in one of several "Gilligan's Island" style palm frond humpies which the local surfers sometimes leave unattended. Make sure you check in with camp rangers Phil and Sue Ogden, who

have been living a surfing lifestyle at the Bluff for quite a few years.

Working on a southerly wind, although southeast is perfect offshore, The Bluff's paddle out involves jumping off from the keyhole (a small gap in the reef 100 m inside of where the wave finishes breaking). Watch out for the numerous urchins which infest the reef. Depending on the tide, there are about three different take-off zones, the top of the point, the cove or the wide area. But nearly every wave at the Bluff shares one thing in common—speed. Cutbacks and vertical top turns are pretty rare here. Usually it's a case of pumping your board as fast as you can to negotiate an express tube while being very wary of the razor sharp coral reef below. Cuts from the reef are inevitable so make sure you bring a first aid kit with you.

Although the Bluff is located in a desert environment, bring plenty of warm clothing and blankets as the temperature can plummet to near freezing at night.

Turtles

The Bluff and Gnaraloo depend on big storms in the Southern Ocean to generate swells that march north along this coast towards Indonesia. Turtles, however, is where you can usually tap into smaller, more localised swells. About 10 km north of the Bluff you can recognise Turtles by the 2WD vehicles parked at the bottom of the large sand dunes. Those with 4WD vehicles can enjoy the luxury of driving over the dunes (along the appropriate track of course) right down to the water's edge. A good quality left and righthander that both break into the channel for about 200 m, Turtles handles anything up to about 6 or 7 ft. Tubes, lip bashing, floaters, slashing cutbacks and general hotdogging is the norm. Camping isn't permitted here so bring water and food with you for the day. There are other rideable waves north and south of Turtles for those who have the time to explore.

Below: Dolphin Point surf check.
Photo: Peter Wilson

Dolphin Point

Dolphin Point (about 10 km north of Turtles) marks the starting point of the entire Gnaraloo headland that stretches for a couple of kilometres. Naturally picking up a lot of swell, it's only really surfed in small to moderate seas. E–SE winds are best. There are three rideable sections, the outside bubbles, the middle and a freight train inside suck section. Getting out at **"Dolly" Point**, even in a small to moderate swell, can be an interesting challenge. It's best to try and paddle south alongside the cliff face for a 100 m or so until you come to a bit of a channel. Then paddle about 200 m out to the farthrest bubbles, keeping inside the channel and south of the breakers the whole time. If you fail to do this, you will have to try to push through the impact zone of the middle or inside sections which can be very taxing.

Once out there, Dolly Point offers some majestic take-offs with long, carving sections perfect for extended bottom turns, fades and full rail cutbacks, not to mention the odd barrel on the inside. It is surprising more people don't surf Dolly Point. Maybe the challenge of getting out there puts them off. Oh yeah, don't be fooled when looking down at Dolly Point from the limestone cliff top. The waves are always much bigger when you get out there.

Gnaraloo

Undoubtedly Australia's premier lefthand tube, Gnaraloo's twisted, shallow, double and triple suck sections that bend and warp make it easily one of the most dangerous waves on the continent. There are really three main sections at Gnaraloo: **Midgies**, **Centre Peak** and **Tombstones**. Midgies, named after the swarms of carnivorous sand-flies which inhabit the area, is where Gnaraloo starts to break for about 2 km down the point, peeling perfectly for nearly 400 m before closing out next to Centre Peak. Not very many people surf Midgies. You can easily lose your bearings, because you're such a long way out to sea, and it's a vast wave arena. However, more and more surfers are venturing up there as Gnaraloo becomes increasingly more crowded.

Centre Peak appears to be a fast-moving peak that suddenly hits a shallow ledge just as you're jumping to your feet. By the time you're doing a bottom turn, the wave has jacked considerably in size and is walling steep, way out in front of you. Big, perfect tubes with fast and clean carving sections are on offer if you make the take-off, but be very cautious 200 m down the line when the wave approaches Tombstones. If you don't make a clean exit at the right time, you run the risk of getting pulverised on extremely shallow coral reef by the rest of the set. And that means getting washed down with the sweep all the way to the end of Tombstones—about 1 km from the take-off.

Tombstones

For experienced surfers only, a series of ledges in the reef produce steps in the wave which make the take-off extremely difficult. They also contort the tubes into hideous chambers. Hawaii's Johnny-Boy Gomes compared Tombstones, foot-for-foot, with Pipeline in power, intensity and danger. A 200-m paddle over dead water before you hit the impact zone, time it so you're pushing through the shallowest

section of reef between sets, otherwise you are certain to cop a beating. Just ask former world champion Martin Potter who dislocated a shoulder while paddling out, before even catching a wave. Gnaraloo works best in swells ranging from 4–10 ft, with E–SE winds.

The Bombie, immediately north of where Tombstones concludes, is a huge Sunset Beach-like right-hander. Though it's a perfect big wave, there have only ever been a few people game enough to paddle out and have a go. Other sections, some that appear rideable, break further to the north along the reef. Camping at Gnaraloo is similar to Bluff in that you have to bring everything with you—food, water, gas, generators, and tents etc. But there are running water, toilets and showers as well as a shop which sells the very basics. However, it's about a two-hour drive back to Carnarvon so stock up on supplies before you leave town. **Fencies** (named after a fence line that runs to the ocean edge) is a sand and

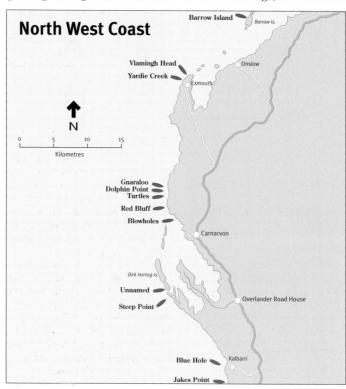

reef break peak located right on the edge of Three Mile camp. It works best in small swells and can provide surfers with a lot of fun when the surf is too small for the main breaks.

Warroora

To get to the next station north of Gnaraloo, you have to drive all the way back to the Blowholes and onto the highway before travelling north for 100 km or so, then take the signposted road back towards the ocean. The gravel road takes you to the Warroora homestead where you can camp. Mostly fishermen frequent this stretch of coastline although surfers have been known to score some fantastic waves here.

There are a variety of waves at Warroora and like the Bluff and Gnaraloo, you have to bring everything you need with you. There are a couple of breaks which work close to shore but most of the reef line at **Warroora** is about 1 km or so out to sea. At certain points along this long reef system, which stretches for about 200 km all the way north past **Coral Bay**, **Maud's Landing** and **Ningaloo**, there are gaps where good shaped waves peel through. But you will need a boat to sample the best juice.

Yardie Creek

Perhaps the best gap in the outside barrier reef system. **Yardie Creek** is an excellent left that peels for hundreds of metres with a bowling, tubular inside section. This wave breaks about 1 km out to sea so once again you need a boat for easy access. Getting to Yardie Creek, a spectacular freshwater gorge that's ideal for camping, involves driving on the sealed highway north to Exmouth then taking the unsealed road south for about 65 km. Until recently this road was only accessible by 4WD vehicle.

Exmouth

A popular destination for those chasing the winter sun during April to July, Exmouth enjoys some of the best gamefishing in the world. As for surf, there are several locations, such as the **Lighthouse Bombie** and a range of quality beach breaks around **North West Cape**.

The islands off Exmouth, such as the **Murion Group**, all have good surf when there's a solid swell running. In fact, most of the islands north of Exmouth to Broome have surf. **Barrow Island**, **Monte Bello** and the **Cocos Islands** all have some great left and right reef setups but getting there isn't easy.

—*Wayne Murphy*

SURFBOARD ART

Text by Mark Thornley

THE SILVER SURFERS

of the endless summer, these colourful nomads epitomised the flower children's yearning for freedom, new horizons and self discovery.

Fearless artists carving abstract arcs on a liquid canvas, they inspired a kaleidoscope of imagery reflecting synchronicity and soul, magic and surrealism. And unlike many others, come the dawn of the last day in the Age of Aquarius, surfers were still "riding the waves", enjoying the buzz of the world's greatest high.

Following in the wake of Hawaiian individualists like Gerry Lopez and Micky Dora, Australian surf guru Mark Richards returned from Hawaii in 1974 with an Al Dove inspired flame design on his Ben Aipa stinger. The first of its kind in Australia, he made it famous with a barnstorming victory at Bells Beach and then in the Coke Surfabout at Narrabeen where he finished second to Wayne Lynch in 1975.

"It was a board that people gravitated to because it was so different and when I returned to Australia, people just flipped out over the unbelievable spray job. It was the first flame design anyone here had ever seen," Richards recalls.

The Al Dove Story

A talented Honolulu scene painter and part time shaper for Brewer Surfboards in Hawaii, Al Dove was the artist behind the pandemonium. In fact he actually invented MR's trademark Warner Bros style shield before adding murals of King Kong, the Water Wiggle and Superman to the twin fin quiver of Australia's legendary four time world champ.

"I used to watch Superman movies religiously during the afternoons. I loved the fact

TO MANY SURFERS A DISTINCTIVE BOARD SPRAY IS as much a part of the surfing experience as riding the wave itself. Dolphins, Harley Davidsons, Bart Simpson, mermaids, flames, Superman, skulls and naked girlfriends—like surfing, everyone has their own style and unique way of expressing themselves.

Spawned in the '60s, airbrush art quickly became synonymous with surfing's flamboyant characters. Traveling the world in search that he was invincible, and I also dug the King Kong movie with Jessica Lang in it so I got Al to paint that scene when Kong's crushing the helicopter on top of the building with the girl in his arm," laughs MR.

To many surfers, Dove re-ignited beach culture iconism where the Silver Surfer cartoon character left off. Using airbrushes and often hand painting scenes to capture surfing's magical powers, his last collaboration with MR depicted the Aussie surf star surrounded by planets and flying through outer space.

Emblazoned across magazine covers and promotional photos around Australia, the super hero theme inspired an entire generation of impressionable young surfers whose daily dreamscape was eat, surf, The Banana Splits and Lost In Space.

Now running the Richard's Surf Shop in Newcastle, MR sees a fair cross section of current surf fashion trends and believes surfers may be neglecting their right to represent themselves. "During the '60s and '70's, I think surfers were a bit more individual than they are now. I mean for such a radical group of free-thinking, spirited individuals, surfers have become pretty boring in their choice of colours for surfboards and wetsuits," he said.

Fitzy and a guy called MW

Another colourful Australian surfing character not afraid to splash some paint around was Terry Fitzgerald. The introduction of his Hot Buttered label soon drew national cult status thanks to his legendary big wave antics and Martin Worthington's radical surfboard art.

A freelance public artist currently working from Insight Surfboard's Mona Vale factory in NSW, Martin has painted everything from restaurants to surfboards and special effects for advertising productions. To him, self-expression is a very personal thing and is about representing a point of view rather than following parameters of cool.

"Quite often a lot of guys will come to me and want to do a piece of artwork themselves but they're not quite sure, and so, if I can bring their idea to life on their board that gives me a bit of a buzz," he said.

Charging between $35 for a rail band to $300 for a mural, Martin has sprayed boards for a talented swag of surfers ranging from cosmic underground Californian legend Owl Chapman, to some of today's leading pros. "I've been doing a lot of boards for Richie Lovett and Mike Rommelse who are pretty specific with their designs. I think it might be a psychological thing for some surfers, the fact that their boards stand out and attract the judges' attention to help score the points," Martin concluded.

Veg enters the Funzone

Resident artist at Funzone (QLD glassing/ shaping factory), David Vretchkoff or 'Veg' as local surfers know him has forged an enviable reputation as a surfboard artist. Terrorising the local beaches on his personalized Rasta Man spray, his art has been in hot demand from celebrity surfers such as Pearl Jam's Eddie Vedder, Midnight Oil and the Manly Football team. Veg currently does sprays for Byrning Spears, Bad Company, Osmosis, Goodtime, plus Aloha and Mambo Mals. He finds a lot of surfers quite conservative with their tastes and likes nothing more than a creative challenge.

"Once I did a Harley Davidson that I charged about $400 for. This guy just gave me a photo of his bike and told me he wanted a

"Oz surfboard art...."

"Well the weirdest one... I guess (laughs) is these people having sex (laughs) I did a close-up of people having sex...very close...like pornographic." —**Paul McNeil**

life-like depiction in front of a beach scene. It was a good challenge and they're the ones that I enjoy the most" Veg said.

A Piscean who has been in the industry for over ten years, Veg reckons he's getting more '70s style mural requests than ever before, believing surfboard art is turning full circle and coming back into vogue. Charging an average $100 for a cartoon or basic dolphin scene, Veg uses a variety of techniques to achieve different effects with each spray taking him roughly two hours to complete.

"Sometimes I use hand painting for detail but I mainly use airbrushes. I've got spray guns of every size that can throw a huge fan like you'd use to paint a car, right down to a fine airbrush that can spray 0.30 ml.

Mambo Jambo

Like many surfboard artists, Mambo's Paul McNeil graduated from scribbles on his skateboard to full blown sprays purely by trying his hand. Following in the auspicious brush strokes of Reg Mombassa and David McKay, he is a dedicated designer who is not scared to experiment.

"Well the weirdest one... I guess (laughs) is these people having sex (laughs) I did a close-up of people having sex...very close... like pornographic. "I never intended for it to ever be used really—it was supposed to be a joke—but somehow it's ended up in this surfboard book called 'Board'. There's this full page of...penetration basically. So it's like,

God I can't show my mum!"

"Personally, I think surfboards are very desirable objects. Like guitars for instance. You can do something with them; make a beautiful noise. Surfboards, I guess, are kinda the same. They're like a shiny bike—very desirable—surfboards have that quality."

Over the years there have been many great surfboard artists who have ridden their creativity with the style and soul of a worthy world champion. In recent years, even current world champion Kelly Slater has been taking to his own competitive quiver with colour pens. A surfing Jesus, maybe his doodlings will seed a new generation of devoted surfboard art followers.

Whatever the case, the sprays of underground artists survive. Capturing the imagination of local surf communities they live on Art as legend, putting colour into our lineups, magazines, or hung pride of place in a forgotten beach house. Long live the Silver Surfers!

Preceding pages: From left to right, board designs by Paul McNeil.

Opposite: From left to right, board designs by Mambo artists.
Photo: Courtesy of Wayne Golding

Below: Veg, surfboard artist extraordinaire, with one of his creations.
Photo: Peter Wilson

Perth and Metro
Surfin' the Sunset Coast

Preceding pages:
A Kalbarri local shows positional finesse on a solid day at the fabled Jakes Point.
Photo: Tungsten/Nikon

Below: Tripping the light fantastic—sunset over Perth's beaches.
Photo: Peter Wilson

April–September.

Most breaks reached via bitumen roads and convenient carparks. Others via sandy tracks.

Sand and reef set-ups ranging from deep to shallow.

Small to mid-range hot dog boards. A boat for outer reefs.

Swell-starved crowds; easily blown out by a strong southwester. Very windy.

Reef cuts and stingrays.

Clean water, board-shorts in summer.

Perth is one of Australia's most laid-back capitals with a beautiful Mediterranean climate. From a surfers point of view, however, there is not a great deal to rave about. Aside from a couple of great waves at Rottnest Island, which is a 20-minute ferry ride off the nearby port town of Fremantle (see the feature in this chapter), the fringing barrier of off-shore reefs ravage most of the Indian Ocean groundswell before it hits the local beaches.

The southern-most boundary of the Perth metro surfing area, Man-durah has a variety of beaches that can occasionally produce reasonable-quality waves. **Tim's Thicket**, **Melros Beach**, **Singleton Beach**, **Golden Bay** and the reef/sand setups at **Avalon Beach** are all worth a look if there's any southerly swell around and it's offshore, but don't expect anything epic from December to March. Perhaps **Surf Beach** which is accessed via the

Secret Harbour turn off, has the best setups on the rare occasion the waves do turn on.

City Waves

Australia's first major artificial surfing reef project, **Cables Station Reef** catches more swell than the surrounding beaches thanks to its alignment with a hole in the fringing outside reef. Occasionally on a heavy groundswell, Cables can break reasonably well offering a short tube section followed by a righthand wall that waddles into deeper water. But this is rare and surfers eagerly await the man-made reef's completion that could see a perfect left and right peak rattling off 150 m rides by 2000.

In 1997, Cottesloe Beach was the site of a freak shark attack. Two people were lucky to escape death after a Great White Shark bit their waveski in half. Normally a sedate beach with fun winter waves, **Cottesloe Beach**

occasionally offers a good left off the groyne during April to September. Similarly, the neighbouring reef breaks at **Cove** and particularly at **Seconds**, a sometimes hollow left-hander, can deliver some fun waves, but don't hold your breath!

Making the most of Perth's meagre swells, the **City Beach Groyne's** shapely lefthander offers a bit more consistency and the added bonus of being sheltered from the prevailing south westerly that howls in the afternoon during summer. With the aid of the full moon and a hot summer night, you can score some fun midnight sessions on a reasonable SW swell. Similarly, neighbouring **Floreat Groyne** can also produce some quality, hollow righthanders when a heavy swell and light easterly winds prevail.

Perhaps the most consistent wave close to the city is at **Trigg Point**, a good righthander that can produce hollow 3–5 ft waves when the larger SW and NW groundswells hit during May to September. Usually insanely crowded, it reels for about 50–100 m over a sandy reef bottom directly in front of the Trigg Surf Lifesaving Club and is best surfed on a light NE wind and low tide. You can check a variety of locations along this beach by pulling off

West Coast Highway into a series of carparks. Look out for the best rips and banks that quite often churn out better and longer waves than the Point. Generally the No 1–2 carparks produce the best and largest peaks but often **Scarborough Beach**, about 1 km further south, has some solid left and right barrels directly in front of the Observation City high-rise development. In fact most of the beaches around this area including **Brighton** and **Hale Road** can occasionally produce fun 3–4 ft beachies, but suffer from fragile sandbanks that are often destroyed when the larger swells arrive during winter.

If you have access to a dinghy or zodiac, check out **Seal Island**, a 15-minute boat ride from **Mindarie Keys** where you may find a fun left and right if there are light winds and a solid SW swell. Keep motoring north for about 20 minutes and you may find a semi secret, hollow lefthander that works on a moderate southerly swell and is supposedly haunted by Henry, the resident ghost of a nearby shipwreck.

Yanchep/Two Rocks

Back on the road, head for Yanchep/Two Rocks, about a 40-minute drive north of the city along Wanneroo Rd.

Perth

N

0   5   10   15

Kilometres

Burns Beach
3 Mile Reef
Wanneroo
Marmion Reef
Seal Island
Whiteman Park
Trigg Point
Scarborough Beach
Midland
Brighton Beach
Floreat Beach
Perth
City Beach
Perth Airport
Cottesloe Beach
Cable Station Reef
Fremantle
Stragglers Reefs
Jandakot Airport
CARNAC I.
Woodman Pt.
Armadale
Cliff Head
GARDEN I.
Byford
Rockingham Jetty
Palm Beach Jetty
Kwinana
SEAL I.
Rockingham
SHAG IS.
Penguin Island
PENGUIN I.
Mundijong
FIRST ROCK
Shoalwater Islands
Marine Park
Serpentine
Murray Reefs
Peelhurst
Singleton
Keysbro
Serpentine River
Halls Head
Mandurah

lies **Deurs**, a shapely right that can spew some great barrels and re-entry sections on a moderate to heavy swell. Shifting peaks help spread the pack when it's crackin'. E–NE breezes are best.

Lancelin

Regarded as one of the best wave-sailing locations in the world, Lancelin also has its share of decent waves. From the shifty, well-formed sand bottom peaks of **Back Beach**, to the Indian Ocean power of the Lagoon's outer reef breaks such as the South Passage, there are plenty of options when the swell hits.

A powerhouse left with some great top turn sections, **Hole In The Wall** can be accessed by boat or a long paddle as can the quality righthander at **South Passage** that works best on large S–SW swells and light NE winds. Don't bump into any of the resident Bronze Whaler and Tiger Sharks. Directly in front of the main beachfront shops, **Lancelin Island** also poses a long, sharky paddle if you don't have a boat, but it does offer a variety of reef breaks that attract swell on the west side of the island. Situated in the southwest corner of Lancelin lagoon, **Eddy's Island's** wally left and rights are a popular choice for surfers who would rather go surfing than paddle a marathon. Pitching deep water swells over a shallow reef platform, the take-offs can be challenging on the bigger days making for some fun tubes and rippable walls, but generally it's best surfed at around 3–5 ft. SW swells and E–SE winds are ideal.

If you're in a 4WD, motor past the infamous Endeavour Tavern and out of the main townsite. Here you'll find a huge sand-dune system that provides sandboarders with an adrenalin rush whenever there's a flat spell.

From here you can drive north to **Cervantes** along a rough coastal road where you will find the world-famous **Pinnacles**, a series of sand monoliths, and, if you're lucky, a righthand reef break at the prophetically-named **Hangover Bay**.

—*Mark Thornley*

Once you find the Two Rocks turn off, follow the road until it finishes, then turn right. Watch for the first major sand turn off on your left and you will see the entrance to **The Spot**. If you don't have a 4WD, the sand track can get a bit rugged during winter, so look before you leap. Usually catching more swell than the city beaches, The Spot is a fickle left-hander that occasionally cranks down-the-line 4–5 ft lefts for up to 200 m over a shallow and irregular reef. Working best on a moderate to heavy SW–W swell it is extremely popular with Perth daytrippers and locals, making for some heavy crowds whenever it fires. **Nails**, a shallow left just south of the main peak, and a couple of beach breaks further north, can help to spread the crowd when the banks are happening.

About 10 minutes drive north

Rottnest Island

An Island "Mecca" With Top Surf

April–September.

Boat ferry from the mainland. Bitumen roads and bike tracks to the breaks.

All reef breaks over sharp coral or weedy rock shelves.

Mid-range boards. Bicycle with a board holder or a board bag with a strap.

Better breaks can get crowded and blown out by SW trades.

Sharp coral, dugites and tiger snakes, sea urchins. Limited medical facilities.

Quality, hollow waves. Surf on any wind direction when there's a swell.

A 30-minute ferry ride from mainland Perth, Rottnest Island is a pristine recreational playground for local surfers, divers, fishermen and holidaymakers seeking a slice of island paradise. Copping the full force of raw Indian Ocean swells, a variety of exceptional reef breaks are complemented by relaxed villa accommodation, crystal clear water and sheltered bays offering some of the best diving in Australia.

Named in 1696 by the early Dutch explorer Willem de Vlamingh, who mistook the island's resident Quokkas for large rats, Rottnest literally translates from Dutch as "rats' nest". Unfortunately, de Vlamingh's name for the island denigrates its beauty. However, you should be careful not to leave any food lying around your villa at night or you will be swamped by a furry posse of crafty Quokka's.

Strickland Bay

Located on the southern side of the island, "Rotto's" biggest crowd pleaser, Strickland Bay, picks up all available S–SW swells with high performance left and rights handling up to 6–8 ft waves. Offering fast hollow barrels or a steep workable wall, the right is a fairly short, intense wave and can get very good. But when the swell gets over 3–4 ft, the left steals the show, offering a long, tight barrel before unravelling some smooth chunks of workable wall prior to shutting down over the inside rock ledge. Don't get carried away and pull in here or you might find yourself at the island hospital.

On moderate to large SW swells, **Mary Cove's** offshore reef, a bit further south, can also produce some good lefts and rights.

Below: Rottnest's main mode of transport, the trusty bicycle, gives you a good pre-surf warm-up.
Photo: Peter Wilson

Chicken Reef

To the east lies another hollow left-hander that can dish out even worse wipeouts than Stricklands. Breaking over a sharp coral reef, Chicken Reef drags the southerly swells back in towards the point at Salmon Bay before pitching a smooth, sucking take-off over a super shallow ledge. It can shotgun you straight into the barrel or send you roller-skating over the brightly coloured, razor sharp coral that makes the Pocillopora Reef system so attractive to international divers.

Distinguished by a huge Osprey (sea eagle) nest that sits on top of a large rock island right in front of the break, "Chickens" is best surfed on a mid tide and a moderate to heavy swell when the take-off zone links up to the fast inside reform. Working well on N–NE winds, Chicken Reef is a bit of a gamble, especially when your only means of transport is by bicycle and most of the breaks are located along the south west wing of the island. Fringed by some breath-taking lagoons it's a great place to get away from the day-tripping crowds of Thomson's Bay. It can sometimes really deliver the goods along with some fairly mellow right and left hand reef breaks at nearby **Salmon Point** that occasionally line up on the west side of the point.

If you have access to a boat or zodiac then take advantage of it. Without question it's the best way to explore Rotto's main reef breaks and outer bombies but beware, these waters are treacherous and have claimed many ships. When heading south west of Strickland's,

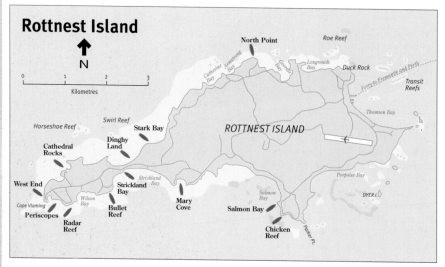

Rottnest Island

N

0   1   2   3
Kilometres

North Point   Roe Reef

Catherine Bay   Armstrong Bay

Geordie Bay

Longreach Bay   Duck Rock

Ferry to Fremantle and Perth

Transit Reefs

Thomson Bay

Horseshoe Reef   Swirl Reef   Stark Bay   ROTTNEST ISLAND

Cathedral Rocks   Dinghy Land

West End   Strickland Bay   Porpoise Bay

Wilson Bay   Strickland Bay   DYER I.

Cape Vlaming   Mary Cove   Salmon Bay

Periscopes   Bullet Reef   Salmon Bay

Radar Reef   Chicken Reef

Parker Pt.

particular care should be taken when scouting swell magnet reefs such as **Radars** and **Bullets** which can unload some hideous righthand barrels on a mid tide and a moderate to heavy S–SW swell. If the surf is going off and you want to park your boat in a nearby channel, make sure you overestimate a safe distance from the take-off zone and that your anchor is going to hold. There's nothing worse than paddling in from a great session to find your boat swamped on the rocks.

West End/Cathedral Rocks
Copping the full brunt of the SW–W swells and winds, **West End** offers an unpredictable wave that can hold some mammoth size when the winds are light and N–NE on a heavy swell. Similarly, the neighbouring **Cathedral Rocks** which still houses the rusty wreck of a luckless tuna boat on its shoreline, can offer a solid, usually hollow left-

hander up to 6 ft when a moderate to heavy SW swell is running. Partly sheltered from the predominant SW winds, it's a good bet when Stricklands turns onshore on a decent swell. And just around the corner at **Narrowneck**, a fun righthander can occasionally work at **Dinghy Land** on light SE–NE winds and a moderate SW swell.

Above: WA's world title prospect, Yallingup's Taj Burrow, charges through some Rotto juice.
Photo: Peter Wilson

Below: Dave Macaulay at Rotto.
Photo: Tungsten/Nikon

Above: Tip-toeing through the urchin minefield after a sunset session at Cathedral Rocks. *Photo: Peter Wilson*

Opposite: Josh Palmateer buys a ticket on the Strickland Bay express. *Photo: Peter Wilson*

Overleaf: Touring West Oz pro, Jake "The Snake" Paterson charges through the bowels of a Pea Break barrel. *Photo: Twiggy*

Stark Bay

If you have an appetite for big waves, you'll want to check out **Stark Bay**, but don't bite off more than you can chew. Rotto's premier big wave location, this place rivals Banzai Pipeline for the power and shape of its perfect barrels when a moderate to heavy SW–NW swell and light SE–NE winds combine. Best accessed by boat, the 800 m warm-up paddle from the shore is not such a bad idea when it's huge, as there is not much room for error when negotiating the elevator drop into a dredging pit. Best surfed on a mid to high tide, Stark Bay is definitely not for surfers who need a few waves to blow the cobwebs out.

Further east, you will come to **Armstrong Bay**. Here you will find **North Point**, a sometimes hollow righthander at the east end. Breaking close to the reef, it walls up over a series of rock ledges and looks easier to surf than it really is. Requiring a moderate to heavy SW swell, it is generally an average wave.

Occasionally on a huge SW–NW swell, one of the island's most popular swimming beaches known as **The Basin** can offer a few waves when everywhere else is out of control. A sandbar known as **Transit** can also line-up just west of the ferry jetty in Thompson's Bay. Often seen feathering out the back even on small to moderate swells, this can be a fun wave for malibus and shortboards but it needs a monster swell to start working. It's a long paddle without a boat and usually best left to beginners or those who aren't scared of sharks.

After a solid days surfing and mountain biking, check out Rotto's famous Quokka Arms Pub. Fire up the barbies, hang in the beachside beer garden or get stuck into a game of pool.

If you're still amped, and you know someone with a boat, try a spot of fishing or diving in the crystal-clear lagoons. If you have a fishing permit, drop in a few craypots and hopefully you'll catch a feed of the delicious rock lobster that thrive amongst the island's maze of reefs.

—*Mark Thornley*

The South West
One of Surfing's Sacred Sites

Opposite:
Hot Yallingup local
Marty Chandler
wails through a
high speed cuttie on
home turf.
Photo: Twiggy

April–October.

Bitumen roads,
carparks to most
breaks; 4WD tracks
and beach access to
good waves.

Short, intense reef
and beach breaks,
sometimes very
shallow.

Bring your full
quiver, you'll need
them all. A helmet's
a good thing also.

Heavy hold downs,
best breaks some-
times crowded.
Strong currents.

Reef cuts.

Big, perfect, hollow
swells that can be
uncrowded. Some
of Australia's best
waves.

When the Australian National Surfing Titles were held at Margaret River in 1969, news of the region's powerful waves and breathtaking scenery spread quickly, giving rise to a thriving tourism industry that has never looked back. An unspoilt wave haven that Tom Carroll, Tom Curren and other contemporary surf legends have declared a sacred site, the south west has changed dramatically from the maze of pot-holed roads and dilapidated farms that once eked out a meagre existence from dairy cows and potatoes. Now home to surfing super stars such as Taj Burrow, the region has grown rapidly, gaining international acclaim for its wineries, towering Karri forest and spectacular coastal scenery. Stretching from Cape Naturaliste to Cape Leeuwin, WA's south west can be divided into four distinct surf regions.

Dunsborough

The most northerly and developed of these wave havens, "Dunny" as it is affectionately known, is a surfing retirement village and home-away-from-home for many Perth millionaires who made their fortunes during the 1980s boomtime. With pristine beaches and a pub famous for its colourful crowd and Sunday sessions, there are a few quality waves to be had south of Geographe Bay in this popular surfing suburb.

Located on the sheltered side of the prevailing south westerly, **Rocky Point**, a hotdog lefthander, requires a large SW–W swell to be worth a look, while two lefts known as **The**

Other Side Of The Moon and **Lighthouse**, can be worth the trek to **Sugarloaf Rock** when a light easterly wind combines with a small clean S–SW swell. Similarly, **Windmills** is a relatively short but hollow righthander which, depending on the condition of the reef or sandbank, works on a light to moderate southerly swell and is a fun warm-up for the heavier stuff to come.

Yallingup

Point your gas guzzler south along the main highway and watch out for a road sign on your right labelled Biddles Road. Once accessed by a torrid 4WD track, **Three Bears** or "Bears", comprises three breaks; Papa, Momma and Baby Bears with the names reflecting the skill level required to tackle them. A top to bottom freight train with a solid tube section, **Papa** throws out the challenge to the experienced surfer, providing a knee-buckling, high performance wave, while **Momma** and **Baby Bears** tend to serve up father's leftovers. Working best on a light NE breeze with a moderate to heavy SW–W swell, Bears rates highly with the locals and deserves the homage.

If you've bagged a few barrels at Papas, get back onto the main road (Caves) and treat yourself to a beer at Yallingup's historic watering hole, Caves House. Renowned for its hospitality, diehard locals and the eerie ghost trail that winds down to the beach, there's nothing better than kicking back and enjoying the view in the grassy beer garden after a great day's surfing.

From here you're five minutes from Yallingup's **Main Break** carpark, the best swell indicator in the area. Depending on Main Break's form, which can hold 8–10 ft swells and occasionally produces some fantastic hollow rights and long, loping lefts, check out the banks at **Rabbit Hill** where a righthander may be bowling into the shore, courtesy of a seething rip. If the swell is scarce, **Shallows**, a nearby rock ledge, may provide a bit of fun with right and left zippers that peel over a forgiving reef.

If there's no joy here, head back up the hill that descends into the bay and you'll see an observation point and dirt turn-off to your right. From here you can spot **Supertubes**, a super shallow righthander that spits an intense barrel on light winds and a moderate to heavy swell. On a mid tide, don't waste any time and get out there. Otherwise take a glance further south up the beach (with binoculars if you have a pair), and look for a wave wedging off a sand/reef bottom. That's **Smiths** and if there's a pack sitting out the back, it's usually worth a bash for the short, hollow right and a slower lefthander that occasionally enjoys some size. Subject to overcrowding, Smiths works best on a moderate to heavy SW swell and provides shelter from southerly sea breezes.

Injidup

When you're surfed out, head directly for the Caves Park Store where Andy and the crew will whip you up the best banana smoothie and tempe burger you're likely to taste this side of the Nullarbor. If you're into fishing, pull out the rods and stock the esky with some coldies because Smiths offers some of the best beach angling on the coast.

Another ten minutes further south lies one of Tom Curren's favourite spots, Injidup. Like many south west locations Injidup derives its name from Aboriginal words: "Inji" refering to the stem of the Inji flower used in indigenous corroborees and "up" being the aborigi-

nal term for water that is standard in most of the coastal town names.

To access Injidup turn right at Wyadup Rd, then left at the bottom of the sealed road and you'll arrive at **Carpark**, a hollow right that pumps on a moderate to heavy south west swell. From here you can look straight into the bowels of **Pea Break**, a thick-lipped, hollow righthander with a critical drop (and a nasty habit of eating surfboards) that is very popular on a moderate SW swell.

If you're a goofy and the backside barrels are proving a bit of a handful, don't stress; just follow the dirt track from the beginning of the carpark out to the headland a little further south and you'll find **Injidup Point**, a long winding lefthander that can really line up on a heavy SW swell. Protected from the predominant onshores that ravage the south west during summer and sometimes throughout

the year, Injidup is affected only by a NW wind and can be surfed all day depending on the swell.

The next stop is Juniper Road where the track gradually deteriorates into a tyre-munching maze of jagged rocks and water-forged drop-aways. Take it easy and you'll make it to a sandy junction. To the left you'll find **Guillotines**, a wally righthander with some brief hollow sections. And to the right an even worse track that leads to **Gallows**, a wedgey left that's best surfed on a mid tide and a light to moderate swell. North of Gallows lies **Hangmans**, a short, hollow right breaking over a shallow reef that can occasionally produce some fun barrels on a small to moderate SW swell. All these breaks are best surfed on a light NE wind and provide a good option when the swell is down. If the surf looks unenticing, break out the diving gear and check some of the ledges and caves in the nearby lagoons for some big resident rock lobsters.

Cowaramup

Centrally located between Yallingup and Margaret River, Cowaramup Bay is one of the south west's prime surfing pit stops. As you drive down the hill and into the quiet surf township, check out the headland on your right. That's **North Point** and when the southerly swell's up and the breeze is easterly, it's one of the most intense barrels in the area, throwing out the challenge with grinding, thick-lipped chambers and down-the-line walls that provide plenty of fun in between the break's notorious sneaker sets.

If you're smart or just plain lazy and like a rush, walk to the extremity of the headland and jump off the big barnacle rock. From here you can paddle through the keyhole and

Above: When Margaret River pumps, surfers really go for it. Just steer clear of the ten-storey whitewater. *Photo: Seaview*

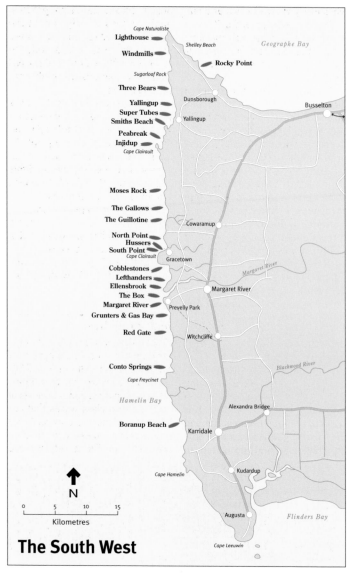

Cape Naturaliste

Lighthouse

Shelley Beach

Geographe Bay

Windmills

Rocky Point

Sugarloaf Rock

Three Bears

Dunsborough

Yallingup
Super Tubes
Smiths Beach

Busselton

Yallingup

Peabreak
Injidup

Cape Clairault

Moses Rock

The Gallows

The Guillotine

Cowaramup

North Point
Hussers
South Point

Cape Clairault

Gracetown

Margaret River

Cobblestones
Lefthanders
Ellensbrook
The Box
Margaret River

Margaret River

Prevelly Park

Grunters & Gas Bay

Red Gate

Witchcliffe

Blackwood River

Conto Springs

Cape Freycinet

Hamelin Bay

Alexandra Bridge

Boranup Beach

Karridale

N

0   5   10   15
Kilometres

Cape Hamelin

Kudardup

Augusta

Flinders Bay

The South West

Cape Leeuwin

straight out the back, but watch your timing or you'll be put through the mincer. Attracting the hordes when it's 3–4 ft during summer, the crowd soon thins out when it jacks to 6–8 ft and surfers have to negotiate sledge hammer lips, gaping barrels and serious hold downs. Although still rideable on the prevailing SW breeze like many of the region's premier locations, a strong north westerly will ruin it.

If the swell's up and you have a hankering for some lefthanders, head over to the other side of the bay where **South Point** will be reeling off some long walls. A smooth, peaky wave with heaps of room for roundhouse cutbacks, it jacks off a sucky bubble section right in front of a shallow rock shelf, so pick the larger sets that push a little wider to avoid bungy jumping into a face full of rock. Protected from the sea breeze, the howling SW wind is actually a blessing for South Point, feeding it with wind-assisted swells. The smooth take-offs and long rides (up to 200 m) attract the surf-hungry masses when everywhere else is blown out.

Best surfed at around 5–8 ft on a low to mid tide in the early morning or late afternoon, it can get insanely crowded so get up early or surf till it's dark.

Having sampled the fruits of the points, follow the bitumen road that leads south out of the townsite. When it turns to gravel take the second turn on your right and head for **Big Rock**. A powerhouse right and lefthander capturing the same swell as Margaret River, this place turns big groundswells into cavernous cylinders and long, workable walls. Offering two to three defined take-off zones at **Cobblestones** and **Noiseys**, the Rock is renowned for its hollow righthanders and freight train lefts that will push the buttons of any experienced surfer when the swell is really up.

The next bay south is home to **Lefthanders**, Cowaramup's most consistent high performance left. Subject to overcrowding, "Lefties" is a long hot dog wave breaking over a flat reef bottom. Peaking off two bubble sections, the take-off is smooth, the tube sections fun and the lips very whackable. On the right tide and swell, the adjacent

beach breaks can also produce quality waves to help spread the pack. A popular spot for local shredders, it is best surfed on a moderate to heavy SW swell with light NE winds but handles the seabreeze reasonably well.

After heading back onto Caves Road, a 15-minute drive further south will bring you to **Ellensbrook**. On a moderate to heavy SW–W swell, this place really cranks offering a variety of short, intense rights and some mindblowing lefthanders. Catching the larger swells, the **Bombie** packs heaps of punch, converting raw power into double storey lefts, while a smorgasbord of reef breaks including a near perfect lefthand barrel, prefer a moderate SW swell and E–NE winds to hold their form.

Margaret River

From Ellensbrook it's just 20 minutes to the vibrant epicentre of Margaret River. The site of WA's most famous wave, **Surfers Point** offers sweeping panoramic views of several world class waves that are international surfing drawcards for travellers and professionals. Holding waves of up to 15 ft, the lefthander at

Below: The boys check out the Cobblestones' floor show at Cowaramup Bay.
Photo: Paul Sargeant

Margaret River main break is legendary for its elevator drops, chunky barrels and the wide open walls that make for some spectacular bottom turns and off-the-top combinations.

Margaret River hosts the majority of WA's premier surfing events. When "Margarets" reaches 8 ft, insanely powerful whitewater sections and an absurdly shallow inside ledge, ominously known as the "Surgeon's Table", will keep you on your toes with some heavy hold-downs.

Best surfed on light SE or NE winds, (although it can handle light to moderate sea breezes fairly well), the rights can also offer some nice tubes. However, the lefts are the showpiece, spitting double tube rides and long walls, before unravelling a series of cutback sections to end off 200 m of surfing body stone. Paddle out through the keyhole channel on the shore and let the rip give you a free ride out the back. Show some respect for the thick lips and you'll enjoy a good session.

About 500 m south is **Suicides**, a big jacking wedge that can really start firing when the swell is heavy and clean. Best surfed on a mid to high tide, the take-off zone is pretty shallow with the right fading into a deepwater channel while the left reels down the line before closing out on a shallow rock ledge.

If you have access to a zodiac check out **The Bombie**, an awesome lefthander that breaks further south off **Prevelly Park**. A wave for the experienced surfer only, this bone-crunching left spits out some mindless barrels on large SW–W swells and also offers some powerhouse rights when a favourable SE or NE wind is blowing.

One of Tom Carroll's favourite waves, if the 500-m paddle from the shore doesn't faze you, the heavy hold-downs will sort you out. **Boat Ramps**, another offshore reef that's located directly out from nearby **Gnarabup Beach**, also offers a big left with a nice wall when the swell moves from moderate to heavy, and is best surfed on higher tides.

Further south of Prevelly along a bumpy dirt track, you will find a series of quality left and righthanders. The pick of these is **Grunters**, a long, powerful right that as its name suggests, has plenty of grunt. Holding up to 10 ft of swell, the double suck take-offs and shallow reef ensure plenty of thrills and spills. Just down the road **Gas Bay** is a good small to mid swell location that churns out a consistent and highly workable righthand barrel over a sand-covered reef. **Boodjidup** also is a good option on smaller swells when it crafts perfect A-frame beach breaks.

Talk about heavy, the notorious **Box** sucks almost square over a dry reef ledge bombie about a kilometre north of the main break. Featuring prominently in many surfing magazines, the Box right-hand barrel machine needs a decent W–SW swell to push the takeoff zone out from a psycho reef and requires some deft tube sense to emerge unscathed from its short, spinning pits. Freefall take-offs and mutated wave faces can make this place a nightmare and reserves it for the super confident and sometimes downright crazy.

If by chance the elements aren't co-operating then there's plenty of action to be found in the local wineries, craft shops and pubs, or continue further south along Caves Road and check out the towering Karri forest and the surfing potential of **Conto Springs**. Accessed via the Leeuwin Naturaliste National Park, this wedgey lefthander can hold waves up to 6 ft and breaks off some boulders in front of an idyllic, grassed camping ground.

Further south along Caves Rd, turn off into Boranup Drive and battle a series of tracks to the northern corner of Hamelin Bay. Here you'll find **Boranup Beach**, a pristine stretch of shifting sandbars that can produce perfect A-frame peaks on the larger S–W swells. Catching about half the swell of Margaret River, Boranup is a good bet when Margarets and Grunters are out of control or too crowded.

—*Mark Thornley*

Opposite page:
Aboriginal powerhouse Andrew Ferguson rips the bag at Ellensbrook.
Photos: Peter Wilson

WESTERN AUSTRALIA

The Rainbow Coast
Virgin Waves and Tall Timbers

Below: Shelley Beach—a typically picturesque Rainbow Coast bay. *Photo: Veda Dante*

Walpole/Nornalup

Heading towards Australia's south west extremity at Cape Leeuwin, the warm Indian Ocean starts to mix with the cold torquoise hues of the wild Southern Ocean. With virtually no surf south of Augusta, the best option is to head east towards the scenic Walpole Nornalup National Park. Turn off the South Western Highway at Crystal Springs where you will find a winding track leading to **Mandalay Beach**. Home to some epic beach breaks that can barrel perfectly up to 6–8 ft, this long beach is best surfed in NE–NW winds and moderate to heavy SW–SE swells but beware of strong rips.

A relatively unexplored area littered with some fickle beach and reef breaks, check out **Hush Hush Beach**, **Circus Beach** and **Lost Beach** where you might just score a perfect, uncrowded peak to yourself on large southerly swells and northerly winds. Continuing east along South Coast Highway you will find **Conspicuous Beach** where

strong currents and moody sandbanks occasionally produce great waves up to 6 ft.

There are also a few quality reef breaks at **Peaceful Bay** including one particular righthander, that can be accessed via Conspicuous Beach Rd.

Denmark

Continue on your deep south pilgrimage and turn off the South Coast Highway. About 30 minutes north of Denmark you will reach a turn-off for **Parrys Beach**. A long stretch of shifting left and right sandbar peaks offer hollow 3–5 ft waves on a moderate to heavy SW swell and northerly winds. Kick back in the sheltered camping grounds and enjoy the fishing and scenery until the surf delivers the goods.

A little further south, **William Bay** comprises a series of sheltered and spectacular swimming pools including Madfish Bay, Elephant Rock, Waterfall Bay and Greens Pool. South of here, **Lights Beach**

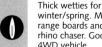
April–September.

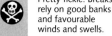
Sealed and gravel roads, 4WD tracks and beach access to some breaks.

Reef and sand bottoms.

Thick wetties for winter/spring. Mid-range boards and rhino chaser. Good 4WD vehicle.

Pretty fickle. Breaks rely on good banks and favourable winds and swells.

Strong currents and big sharks. Reef cuts and blue-ringed octopus.

Uncrowded, sometimes perfect, clean beach breaks. Great, big wave reefs.

can hold some nice beach breaks on a solid S–SW swell and light N–NE winds.

A sleepy little town with superb beaches, perhaps Denmark's most famous wave is a long righthander that occasionally reels off the point at **Ocean Beach**, whenever the Wilson Inlet breaks through and dumps sand onto the nearby headland. Relatively protected from the elements, Ocean Beach needs a hefty SW swell to really turn on and usually offers average left and right beachies as does its popular easterly neighbour, **Goat Boat Beach**.

From here, take the Lower Denmark Road where you can access **Lowlands** and **Mutton Bird Beach**. A fair trek, or short drive along the shoreline, Muttonbird Beach picks up some solid swell and is held in high regard by locals for its long, hollow beach breaks that crave northerly winds and southerly swells.

Above: Another day, another barrel. Life is good at the end of the rainbow. *Photo: Tungsten/Nikon*

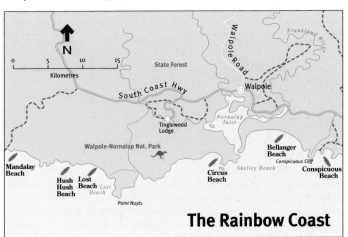

The Rainbow Coast

Albany, Hopetoun and Esperance

Clean Lines and Solitude

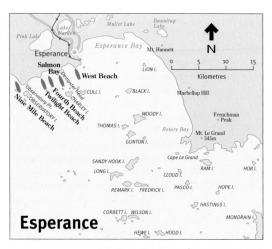

Esperance

April–September.

Bitumen roads, 4WD tracks and beach access.

Mainly beach breaks over sand-covered reef. Some reef breaks over flat rock.

Mid-range board–big wave gun. Need a good steamer and booties for winter.

Can be fickle and easily blown out during summer and winter.

Watch out for Great White Sharks and strong rip currents.

Crystal green water. Sometimes big, perfect waves and no one out there.

Albany

At Albany, king waves, jutting headlands and cold water make for some hardcore surfing experiences. Prior to reaching the town, take a detour at Frenchman's Road before turning off at Sand Patch Road which will take you to **Sand Patch**. If the wind is NE and the swell SW–S, waste no time in climbing down the cliffs as you'll probably get barrelled off your head on a few of the beach breaks here.

Mostly protected from the large islands in King George Sound, Albany's **Middleton Beach** can occasionally get some good waves on a big SE swell but is often a reasonable place to learn. Nearby **Nanarup Beach** can also be worth a look when a moderate to heavy south swell is running. From here you need to return to the South Coast Highway to access some of Albany's best waves at **Cheyne Beach**. Offshore in westerly rather than northerly breezes, it can turn on some filthy righthand barrels when a clean SE swell is running. If you want to roll the dice and feel lucky, there are some fickle but sometimes awesome righthand barrels to be had at **Point Anne** and **Point Charles** on a large southerly swell. Turn off South Coast Highway and follow Devils Creek Road to see if you won.

Hopetoun

Heading towards Esperance, the next stop is Hopetoun where there are a variety of good surfing locations including a solid lefthander that

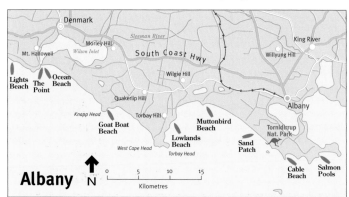

breaks directly out from the port's breakwall. Affectionately known as **Sharkies**, an adrenaline-charged paddle out over a deep shark gutter keeps you on your toes as do the powerful 6–8 ft lefts that mechanically churn on a solid southerly swell. On the smaller swells there are also some moody beach breaks to be found at the **Culham Inlet, Myles Beach** and **Two Mile** when the wind is from the north.

Esperance

Situated 721 kilometres south east of Perth, Esperance enjoys brilliant blue water that is a few degrees cooler than the rest of the state due to the absence of the warm Leeuwin Current that tapers away from WA's southern-most coastline. A chain of offshore islands shelter much of the swell from the town's beaches. However around to the west, the torquoise water and spectacular granite headlands hide some surfing jewels. Check out **West Beach, Salmon Bay, Fourth Beach, Nine Mile Beach, Twilight Beach** and **Free Beach** which all work on southerly swells and northerly winds. The fishing, from either the beach, rocks or boat is fantastic (and so is the diving) but beware of the notorious Great White Shark that frequents these waters.

—*Mark Thornley*

Above: A punchy beach and reef set-up. From Walpole to Esperance there are hundreds of bays with hidden treasures.
Photo: Peter Wilson

Overleaf: Southern ocean solitude. A committed surfer drives off the bottom at a maxing righthand bombie.
Photo: Twiggy

Pages 256-7: Mambo Surfing History Tapestries.
Photo: Courtesy of Mambo Graphics

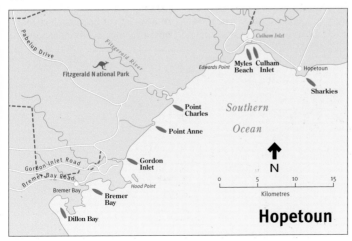

Hopetoun

pic: hoole

kauai doublezip
backpack

pic: cavallo

equipment
to travel
the world

horn cord leash

repair kit

detatchable tour bag

heavyweight coffin travel cover (up to 4 boards, inc. guns)

OCEAN EARTH
AUSTRALIA

TODD PRESTAGE

RIDE YA LIFE AWAY

KING WAVES KILL

Mobil

M bil
Super

Land of the long weekend

BEACH CREW

AUSTRALIA

T-Ray

the path less travelled

SURF DIVE 'N' SKI

N.E. Swell 3 to 5 ft
N. Winds @ 5 Knots
MiD + High Tide @ 7am

GEORGE ST SYDNEY

CHATSWOOD CHASE

WESTFIELD PARRAMATTA
BONDI JUNCTION
WESTFIELD MIRANDA
WARRINGAH MALL

DARLING HARBOUR

WESTFIELD TUGGERAH
ARGYLE CENTRE THE ROCKS

WESTFIELD EASTGARDENS   CROWN C

RAL PLAZA WOLLONGONG

SURFGOD
IT TAKES
ONE
TO KNOW
ONE

Life lesson #13c......Chapter 4

KUTA LINES
AUSTRALIA

MARCUS STOCKER - SURFER, BOARDER, TUNER

PHOTOS WAYNE RYAN & ANDREW CHRISTIE

Wetsuits for the Chosen Crew

DOOLAGAHS

PROTECT RESPECT

DOOLAGAHS SURF PRODUCTS

BLACK ROCK HAS A REPUTATION AS ONE OF THE MOST HOLLOWEST LEFT HANDED REEF BREAKS IN AUSTRALIA. AS YOU WALK DOWN THE TRACK THROUGH THE TREES TOWARDS BLACK ROCK, YOU GET A FEELING DIFFERENT FROM ANY OTHER SURF BREAK IN AUSTRALIA. THERE IS A CULTURE HERE THAT HAS EXISTED FOR THOUSANDS OF YEARS. A CULTURE THAT HAS HUNTED, FISHED, GATHERED, BORN,LIVED AND DIED HERE, HAD CEREMONIES, KEPT RECORDS OF THIS AREA BY WAY OF STORY TELLING AND ROCK ART, AND EXPERIENCED CHANGES IN CLIMATE AND CULTURE. DOOLAGAHS HAS COME FROM THIS STORY TELLING. THE DOOLAGAH IS THE PROTECTOR OF THE ENVIRONMENT. WE CAN LEARN A LOT ON HOW TO PROTECT THE ENVIRONMENT FROM THE WAY THE ABORIGINAL CULTURE VIEW THE LAND AND THE SEA. IF YOU VISIT THE AREA, RESPECT THE AREA AND THE COMMUNITY, TALK TO SOME LOCALS, EXPERIENCE THE CULTURE AND SURF ONE OF AUSTRALIAS' FINEST BREAKS. ALSO, KEEP AN EYE OUT FOR THE DOOLAGAH.

Experience the Culture

DOOLAGAHS
PROTECT·RESPECT
AUSTRALIA

Australian Distributor: Doolagahs Surf Products Australia. Ph: 61 2 9317 5521 Fax: 61 2 9317 5711
www.doolagahs.com.au
Doolagahs Indigenous Design Pty. Ltd. Born in Black Rock, South East Coast Australia

CONTENTS
PRACTICALITIES

The following Practicalities sections contain most of the practical information you need for your journey to Australia. **Travel Advisory** *provides background information about Australia. The* **Area Practicalities** *sections focus on each destination and contain details on transport, accommodation, surf shops and surf schools. These sections are organized by state and correspond to the first part of the guide.*

PRACTICALITIES

CONTENTS

Australia at a Glance

An island continent unparalleled in natural resources, cultural diversity, indigenous history and geographic isolation, Australia is indeed the "Lucky Country". Relatively immune from natural disasters, political instability and poverty, the nation enjoys a strong coastal culture accompanied by an environment of opportunity. Hosts of the Sydney 2000 Olympic Games, at the dawn of a new millennium, the Australian people have much to celebrate.

As a continental island, Australia covers an area of 7,682,300 sq km and is the world's sixth largest country. The great majority of its 17 million population live in the capital cities, or along the 36,735 km of coastline. Bound by the waters of the Pacific Ocean to the east, the Arafura Sea to the north, the Indian Ocean to the west and the Southern Ocean of the south, Australia is without doubt the most surfable coastline in the world.

Last century, Australia was largely a group of penal colonies governed by England, but in 1901, the country celebrated its independence with Federation. Almost 100 years on, Australia's call for autonomy via republicanism continues to be debated in public and political arenas. Today, there are six states and two territories with their own governments, as well as a Federal Government, whose parliamentary systems are based on those of the UK. There is also a local government system which predominantly concerns itself with community issues. All governments in Australia are elected for three year or four year term, and voting is compulsory. The nation's capital is Canberra in the Australian Capital Territory, which is home to the Federal Parliament.

Historical Overview

Australia, once part of the super-continent Gondwanaland, has been occupied by people for more than 50,000 years. According to archaeological records go, Australia's indigenous Aborigines possess the oldest continuous culture on earth. Their complex spiritual and physical philosophies remain largely misunderstood, not only by the majority of the Australian population but by international travellers. Passed down through milleniums of story telling, their approach to the environment, community, law, ancestry and their connection to the land (known as the Dreamtime), is derived from an intricate knowledge of natural relationships. While there was much Asian contact in the north of the country, Europeans didn't discover the Great Southern Land until the 17th century. In 1606, Portugese explorers sailed through the Torres Strait, and in the years that followed, many Dutch mariners landed or found themselves shipwrecked on the unsympathetic west coast.

Abel Tasman came aross Tasmania, which he called Van Dieman's Land, in 1642. The country was often described as being unfit for human habitation, even though the Aboriginal people thrived. It was not until Captain James Cook charted the east coast in 1770 that the perception or perhaps priorities of the land changed. The English, keen to solve the problems of overcrowded prisons, sent a fleet out to establish a penal colony in 1788. From Port Jackson at Sydney Cove, the colony of New South Wales grew slowly with limited supplies. The surrounding country was explored, settlers arrived and farming land was cultivated. Sadly, the original inhabitants were displaced and disposessed in the rush for new found wealth. In the mid-nineteenth century gold was discovered, more colonies were established and thousands of migrants arrived to begin a new chapter of their lives.

After Federation in 1901, Australia maintained its close ties to England, helping to fight three wars, including World War II, when, after the threat of Japanese invasion, links to the USA were formed. The American and Australian troops defeated the Japanese in the Pacific and became allies in the Korean and Vietnamese wars. After WWII, Europeans and, more recently, Asian refugees and migrants have been the major newcomers. Australia is now one of the most multi-cultural societies on the planet, but despite this integration, the process of reconciliation still continues with the Aboriginal population.

Travel Advisory
WHAT YOU SHOULD KNOW BEFORE YOU GO

What to Bring Along

This varies greatly depending on your destination and time of the year. If heading to the Great Barrier Reef over summer, bring light clothes. If you choose Tasmania as your destination, be prepared for cool weather whatever the season. Where ever you choose to be in Australia during the summer period, you should be able to get away with mainly light clothes, but the further south you head, the more you should incorporate warm clothing. Although day temperatures can be pleasant throughout Australia's southern states, cold winds and overnight winter temperatures will have you wrapping up.

The following advisories are meant for surfers (and perhaps any surf enthusiasts like boogey boarders, knee boarders and windsurfers). Before leaving home, consider this practical check list:

Surfboards you bring on an Australian surf safari will depend on what type of surfer you are (or intend to be once here). Some waveriders arrive with entire quiver ensembles, but most limit themselves to two or three boards at the most. Three is ideal for Australia, say beginning with a 6'4" stick for smaller waves (1-3 foot swell), a 6'8" for mid-range waves (4-7 foot), and a 7'4" and up board for bigger waves (like the 8 foot plus howlers that regularly grace Western Australia and Victoria). The key here is to get boards which are relative to your weight. If you can only bring two boards, a 6'3" to 6'8" works well as an all-round short board while a 6'10" to 7'4" should suffice for when the waves get bigger. If you're limited to one board, the 6'8" is a versatile board which will perform in conditions ranging from 3-6 foot, but any bigger than that and you'll be under-gunned.

Generally speaking, narrower boards with less rocker are the best shape for Australia's larger surf, while wider boards will give you more speed in smaller waves. A stronger glass job and thicker stringer will give you greater durability; qualities you'll need if you plan to keep a favourite board in one piece while travelling across the continent. Speaking of travelling, the improved fin systems now available on the global market, should be included on at least one of your boards in order to avoid breakages. Compared to past experiences, you'll hardly notice any performance disadvantages that may be incurred.

Most surfers like to travel with their own gear, but for those who can't be bothered trekking boards half way around the world and plan to stay for a while, there are plenty of surf shops and some of the world's best surfboard shapers to satisfy your aquatic needs. After all, the world's leading surf brands like Quiksilver, Billabong and Ripcurl were all founded in Australia, so why not update your beach wardrobe with a local purchase.

Board Bags are also very important. The most convenient types are the double or triple capacity which are not too bulky and are easy to pack away (yet strong enough to protect your board).

Wax is another constant necessity in Australia's warm waters because here it melts and comes off boards fairly easily. So the harder the board wax the better. Using a full adhesive, back deck grip plus wax for your front foot is probably the best combination in Australia where you'll have the opportunity of surfing in both wet suits and boardshorts.

Leg Ropes/Leashes have become an invaluable surfing tool. Use the thicker, heavy duty type, and a few spare leashes will inevitably come in handy. With that in mind, thinner beach-break type leashes are also good for smaller days when a big leash creates too much drag. Nose guards for your board are another suggested precaution - whether it's for your board, to protect your fragile scone or to avoid spearing anybody else in the line up.

Ding Repair Kits are only worth bringing if you plan to surf the more remote areas, or are on a super tight budget. There are plenty of surf shops (who do repairs) and sell the kits if required. There are also a host of shaping factories to fix your injured board.

Wet Suits: A Short John or even a thin spring suit is suitable for the Australian summer, however, a steamer with a rash vest underneath is essential in the colder regions. If you don't want to turn into an ice block (particularly if you're surfing Tasmania or Victoria in winter), make sure you have a good 3-4 mm wet suit with double seams, booties and a surf cap. Wet suits also offer great protection against reef rash, board wax and the sting of jellyfish.

Booties, particularly reef booties, are useful for walking on the reefs at low tide and to get in and out of the surf. They're great for fishing as well.

Fishing Gear: Australia is surrounded by some of the world's cleanest oceans and offers a huge variety of beach, rock, reef, deep sea and game fishing. It's heaps of fun when the surf is flat, and in the more remote areas, people actually rely on it for their daily meals. OZ is one of the few remaining places on earth where you can enjoy fantastic waves while living off the land and sea.

Diving Gear: According to leading diving personalities, including the late Jacques Cousteau, Australia's Great Barrier Reef (Qld) and Ningaloo Reef (WA), are amongst diving's seven wonders of the world. Swim with the Whale Shark, the largest fish in the sea, hand feed Moray Eels and giant Potato Cod, or simply check out the seasonal coral polyp spawn on the reefs. Just get out there, as there are heaps of snorkelling and scuba diving charters around.

Surf Helmets Great protection from sun, wind, reefs and boards.

Duct Tape comes in handy for temporary ding repairs to common household needs, you're bound to utilise a few of its many uses. The silver kind is the best.

Additional Items

Toiletries, slide and print film, contact lenses, condoms, clothing, sea sickness medication and other items needed in emergencies are readily available in all cities and towns throughout Australia. The following is an additional check list of items you should consider bringing with you or obtaining when you first arrive in Australia:

Rash Guards (rashies) are also useful, especially the long-sleeved types. Surf hats help shield the sun even if they can be annoying to wear. The best types are the ones that quick dry and are thin and flexible with strong velcro straps (so they won't be ripped off when you duck-dive under a wave).

Sun Protection: You will be surfing in a part of the world known for its high skin cancer rates, so sun protection is extremely important. Always use a sun screen with a minimum SPF rating of 15+ and regularly re-apply throughout the day, even when it's cloudy. Remember to cover places like the backs of your legs, neck, lips and ears when applying sunblock. Zinc cream, which is available in weird and wonderful designer colours, is also a very effective sunblock.

Sunglasses should be worn as much as possible, as prolonged exposure to the sun can cause eye damage. There are some great designs which combine fashion with function, like the wrap-around styles.

Mosquito Nets These are great to have whenever dozing or sleeping outdoors. Mosquitoes and bush flies can make sleeping feel like an eternal nightmare, and in some parts help to prevent serious health problems (see Ross River Virus, under 'Health'). Mossie nets can be found in most camping shops and army disposal outlets.

Mosquito Repellant This is also a must. In the late afternoon be sure to put this liberally around your ankles, legs and other exposed places. Supermarkets and camping shops sell such repellent (popular brands like Rid and Aerogard), but you might prefer to use a non-chemical/environmentally friendly version. Basically, insects don't like citrus, and citronella oil is well known for its powerfully repellent qualities.

Vinegar works wonders for jellyfish stings, so try and have a small bottle with you especially when surfing remote areas. It's also a tasty accessory if you happen to catch any seafood.

Flashlight: A flashlight or 'torch' as we call them Down Under, is a useful travel companion if you are staying in a remote region or camping out. A small, powerful and even waterproof version would be the best. Be careful to choose one which uses a common battery (C size or AAA) which can be readily found in any supermarket.

Climate

Being in the Southern Hemisphere, Australia's seasons are the reverse of those in Europe and North America. Summer is from December to February, Autumn from March to May, Winter from June to August and Spring from September to November.

In the north, the seasons seem to have a life of their own, especially around Darwin, as there are basically two seasons, the Wet from September to April and the Dry from May to August. The top half of Australia lies north of the Tropic of Capricorn and enjoys a tropical climate for much of the year. However, temperatures and humidity can sometimes prove unbearably high in summer, so visits to the north are generally best undertaken during winter.

Southern Queensland, northern New South Wales and north Western Australia experience sub-tropical climates, with pleasant days year-round. Even though winter nights may be cool, winter days are generally sunny and warm. The southern states are at their best during summer, with hot days and calm weather. Autumn and spring can also offer beautiful weather, especially in Victoria and Tasmania, however the low temperatures can be uncomfortable. Although the temperature rarely gets below zero, the strong winds from Antarctica are particularly chilly but winter days can be pleasant when there is no wind. Spring and Autumn are considered Australia's best surf seasons, highlighted by offshore winds and generally more groundswell.

Temperatures in the tropical north are 25–34° (78–94°F) year-round, with night time temperatures varying from 20–25°C (70–78°F). In the sub-tropical regions, the day time temperatures vary from 20–30°C (70–87°F), to lows of 10–15°C (50–60°F). Temperatures in the south average 15–25°C (60–78°F) over summer, but days of 30–40°C (87–105°F) are not uncommon, while night time temperatures vary from 5–15°C (42–60°F). with lows of zero over winter.

Time Zones

Due to such a vast land mass, Australia is split into three time zones. The eastern states, Qld, NSW, ACT, Vic and Tas are all 10 hours ahead of Greenwich Mean Time (GMT), while SA and NT are 9.5 hours ahead of GMT. WA, however is 8 hours ahead of GMT. The only problems arise over summer when a number of states introduce daylight saving time. From October to March the country can have five different time zones with NSW, Vic, ACT, Tas and SA all putting their clocks forward one hour.

Money and Banking

All prices in this book are listed in Australian dollars and are only intended as a guide. The Australian dollar is widely traded and equal to roughly US60 cents (as at June 1998). Denominations are $100, $50, $20, $10, $5, while coins are $2, $1, 50c, 20c, 10, and 5c.

There are many banks and building societies in Australia where visitors can cash travelers' checks or exchange foreign currency. These are open 9 am–4 pm Monday to Thursday, 9 am–5 pm Friday with some also open Thursday night until 8 pm and Saturday morning from 9am–12 noon. In all capital cities, large towns and airports there are also currency and travelers' exchange centers. All popular brands of traveler's cheques are accepted in Australia, and transaction fees can vary, so it may be wise to shop around.

Credit cards are widely used and accepted in Australia, the most popular cards being Visa, Mastercard, American Express, Diners Club and Bankcard, while EFTPOS is widely available.

Tax, Service and Tipping

There are no VAT, GST or service charges on Australian goods and services, so the price shown or quoted is the price you pay.

Tipping is not expected in Australia, except in restaurants and some of the larger hotels. In restaurants it's a courtesy, but only if you're pleased with the food and service, to leave a small tip; about 5–10 per cent of the bill is sufficient. In some of the larger hotels, tips may be given to staff, but no one in Australia feels obligated to tip.

Office Hours

Most government business is conducted between 9 am–5 pm, Monday to Friday. Shops are open 8 am–5.30 pm Monday to Friday (until 9 pm Thursday), and 8 am-12 noon on Saturdays, while those in capital cities are open 10 am-5 pm on weekends.

Supermarket late night shopping days vary from state to state. Some chemists are open 24 hours, as are large petrol stations. Convenience stores vary in hours. Some of the small family-operated stores are open 6 am-6 pm daily, while a number of the larger chains often stay open 24 hours such as Ezy Plus and 711's.

Mail

To mail a standard letter or postcard within Australia costs 45c and prices vary from 70c to $1.20, depending on the distance to send a postcard or letter overseas. Post offices or their agents are found in all towns throughout the country and are generally open from 9 am-5 pm, Monday to Friday. Stamps can also be purchased from convenience stores and newsagencies.

Telephone and Fax

Australia has an excellent telephone system which has recently been deregulated. The major phone companies are Telstra and Optus. Public phone boxes are located throughout Australia and they allow local STD (Subscriber Trunk Dialing) and International Dialer Direct calls to be made (all the numbers listed in this book have the STD code first). Local calls attract a flat fee of 40c, irrespective of the duration, while STD call rates vary with distance and time of day (STD calls are cheaper on weekends and at night). Pre-paid phone cards can be purchased at shops and newsagents and mean you're not always having to carry the exact amount of change.

To get operator assistance on trunk calls, or to reverse the charges, dial 12550, and to make an operator assisted call on national or international numbers, dial 1234. For direct access, call the international code 0011, your country code (consult a telephone directory for a complete listing), the city code and then the phone number. The same applies if you're trying to call Australia. To obtain directory assistance anywhere in the country, dial 013.

Telstra has introduced a variety of telephone options which make it easier and cheaper for you to contact businesses around the country. Where possible, utilise the FREECALL 1800 services which mean precisely that—a free call. Also, regardless of where you are in Australia, dialing Telstra's Priority 1300 Service means you only pay the cost of a local call (mobile phone users are charged at mobile rates). So whenever you see "13 ** **" go for your life knowing you'll only be paying the standard 40 cents per call.

Visitors to Australia will find a wealth of useful information in both the white and yellow pages of the telephone books that cover each city and country area. In addition to lists of helpful phone numbers and community services, there is information on shopping, markets, history, transport, entertainment, tourist services, attractions. events and even maps.

Australia also has one of the most advanced mobile phone networks in the world, with over 90 percent of the population covered by digital and analog services. Calls to mobile phones are around the same price as STD calls.

Be wary of '0055' numbers, most of which are used to access local surf reports. They cost at least 70c per minute, or higher if you're calling from a mobile or public phone.

All the phone and fax numbers in Australia recently changed to provide greater uniformity between country and city areas and also to cater for the extra demand. So if you find difficulty in reaching your Australian contacts, just get operator assistance to help you update the number.

Electricity

Australia runs on 220-240 Volts, so currency converters will be required for 110 V products from North America. The standard connection is a three pin, which is different from the British three pin. Adaptors can be purchased from hardware, luggage and airport stores.

Tourist Information

Tourist information offices are found in each state capital. These include:

Queensland Government Travel Centre, Cnr Adelaide & Edward St, Brisbane, QLD, 4000. Tel: 13 18 01.

Sydney Visitors' Centre, 106 George St, The Rocks, NSW, 2000. Tel: 02-9255 1788. For information on regional areas, contact the nearest Harvey World Travel or your travel agent.

Victorian Tourist Information, Melbourne Town Hall, Collins St. Vic, 3000. Tel: 132 842.

Tasmanian Travel and Information Centre, Cnr Davey & Elizabeth Streets, Hobart, Tas. 7000. Tel: 03-6230 8383.

South Australian Travel Centre, 1 King William St, Adelaide, SA, 5000. Tel: 1300 366 770.

Western Australian Tourist Centre, Cnr Wellington St & Forrest Place, Perth, WA, 6000. Tel: 1300 361 351.

Northern Territory Holiday Centre, Regional Tourist Association, Cnr Gregory Tce & Hartley St, Alice Springs, NT, 0870, or Cnr Knuckey & Mitchell St, Darwin, NT, 0100. Tel: 1800 621 336.

Canberra Visitor Information Centre, 330 Northbourne Ave, Dickson, ACT, 2602. Tel: 1800 026 166.

Travel Information brochures are available in some airports. Local and regional tourist offices in most towns will provide invaluable advice on accommodation, places to eat and entertainment attractions.

Before coming to Australia you may wish to contact the Australian Tourism Commission (ATC) in your country for information which will help you plan your holiday. Offices include:

Japan, (Australian Business Centre) New Otani Garden Court Bldg 28F, 4-1 Kioi-cho, Chiyoda-ku, Tokyo 102. Tel: 52140720, Fax: 52140719.

Japan, (Osaka City Air Terminal) OCAT Bldg 4F, 1-4-1 Minato-machi, Naniwa-ku, Osaka 556. Tel: 6353291, Fax: 6353297.

New Zealand, Level 13, 44-48 Emily Place, Auckland. Tel: 3799594, Fax: 3073117.

Singapore, # 17-03 United Square, 101 Thomson Rd, Singapore 307591. Tel: 2554555, Fax: 2538431.

UK, Gemini House, 10-18 Putney Hill, London SW15 6AA. Tel: 7802229, Fax: 7801496.

USA, 2049 Century Park East, Suite 1920, Los Angeles, CA 90067. Tel: 229 870, Fax: 5521215.

Security

Australia is a safe country to travel if you use common sense. Hitch hiking is not recommended, but is said to be as safe as hitch hiking in most other Western countries. Car theft is a problem throughout Australia, so don't leave any valuables in your car before you lock it and utilise the car alarm if you have one. The cities are generally safe and well policed, but don't walk the back streets at night by yourself. Just take the simple precautions that you would normally observe at home. Lock motel doors, take advantage of safety deposit boxes to store your valuables, photocopy all your tickets and vital documents. Don't carry around vast amounts of cash or travellers' cheques, and don't flash your money around. A few basic safety steps can make for a truly memorable journey.

Health

All travelers should purchase travel insurance, not only to cover for cancellations and loss of luggage, but for medical emergencies. Australia offers exceptional public and private health services, with hospitals and medical centres located in most towns throughout the country. So it's safe to say, that in any medical emergency you will be adequately cared for. In case of minor health problems, a visit to a doctor is inexpensive and chemists (drug stores) can be found in most towns. In any emergency, whether it be fire, police or ambulance, dial 000 and ask for the service you require.

Medicare, Australia's government funded health care body, offers cover to travelers who come from reciprocal health care countries. These include: the UK, Northern Ireland, New Zealand, Finland, the Netherlands, Sweden, Italy and Malta. To apply for Medicare, you will need both a passport and another form of identification. Further enquiries can be directed to 13 20 11.

There are no vaccinations required for entry into Australia, unless you have visited an infected country in the previous 14 days. AIDS and sexually transmitted diseases are under control in Australia, however condoms are recommended and intravenous needles should never be shared. While Malaria is not a problem, Ross River Fever is carried by some of the mosquitoes of tropical and subtropical Australia, so always wear insect repellent and cover up at night.

One health issue which should concern you, is skin cancer. Considering Australia has the highest rate of skin cancer in the world, with NSW recording the highest figures, here's a few simple facts and prevention tips we think you should be aware of:

1. It only takes one bad sunburn for skin to be irreversibly damaged.
2. 66% of the day's UV radiation occurs between 11 am - 3 pm (daylight saving time).
3. Two-thirds of skin damage due to exposure to the sun occurs before age 20.
4. There's no such thing as wind burn. The last time you thought you were wind burnt, you were actually sunburnt from UV radiation. Wind mainly dries the skin - it does not burn the skin.
5. Temperatures can be misleading—a cool or cloudy day may have the same UV radiation levels as a hot day.

Sunscreens absorb or reflect the dangerous UV rays of the sun that damage the skin, and Australia's Skin Cancer Council advise you apply a minimum SPF15+.

The Cancer Council are quick to emphasize that no sun screen can provide 100% protection, and their Slip, Slop, Slap & Wrap campaign offers a simple reminders: SLIP on a shirt with collar and sleeves, SLOP on a SPF15+sunscreen, broad spectrum and water resistant, SLAP on a hat with a wide brim or a cap with flaps to shade your face, neck and ears, and WRAP on sunglasses with Australian Standard AS1067 that fit the face well.

Australian Water Hazards

The various oceans which surround Australia are home to many unusual sea creatures, and while most aquatic activities encourage interaction with marine creatures, a few of them should be either treated with extreme caution or avoided like the plague.

The Biters

The chance of being bitten by any animal when surfing is remote; the general rule is to leave sea creatures alone and they will do the same.

Sharks

Australia has a reputation for shark attacks, but with only one or two such events taking place each year, there is more chance of being struck by lightning. Two jet-skiers playing 200 m off a Perth suburban beach last October were reminded to expect the unexpected regardless of these low statistics.

More interested in their jet ski, the 5 m-long long shark forced the evacuation of a variety of beaches until it disappeared into the depths of the Indian Ocean. You can reduce your chances of being attacked by avoiding surfing in murky water, rivermouths and after dusk. You should also try to avoid close contact with the following species. The Great White Shark (*Carcharodon carcharias*) is very rare, but most likely to be encountered around seal colonies.

Tiger sharks (*Galeocerdo cuvieri*) are more common in tropical seas, especially around turtle breeding areas such as northern Australia. Although considered a generally shy species, it may be best to leave the water if a Tiger is seen cruising along the reef. The whaler shark family, which includes the grey reef shark (*Carcharhinus amblyrhynchos*), silvertip (*Carcharhinus albimarginatus*), bull shark (*Carcharhinus leucas*) and bronze whaler (*Carcharhinus brachyurus*) are fast moving, territorial and have bitten divers and surfers in the past. The great hammerhead (*Sphyrna mokarran*) grows to 6 m in length and has a reputation for being aggressive to surfers and divers. Avoid annoying wobbegong sharks (*Orectolobus sp.*) Although they look docile and lazy, they have a nasty set of jaws and have latched onto many legs and curious arms in the past. Angel sharks (*Squatina australis*) also have a nasty set of teeth, but generally prefer to flee than use them. Always face any approaching shark, and though this may seem bizarre and perhaps impossible, try not to panic.

Fish

The most aggressive fish encountered in Australia is the damsel fish. When guarding eggs they will fearlessly attack other fish and divers, giving repeated bites to hands, head and other body parts. Gropers can be quite aggressive when being fed, especially the potato cod (*Epinephelus tukula*).

Spiders

Australia has several varieties of venomous spiders including Redbacks and Funnel Webs.

Other animals

Saltwater crocodiles (*Crocodylus porosus*), found throughout northern Australia should be given a wide berth. Stay away from mangroves, creeks and murky water in Australia. Territorial Seals, especially large bulls, can also give a nasty bite if they feel threatened.

Venomous Creatures

Australia has an abundance of venomous creatures on the land and underwater, but most are shy and retiring, and are quite harmless if left alone.

Venomous Fish

All species of stingray, stingaree and eagle ray have one or more spines on their tail that should be avoided. Though the venom is not fatal, a number of people have been killed by the spine cutting an artery, so take care around rays that often bury themselves in sandy gutters found around beachbreaks. A number of deaths have occurred from contact with stonefish. A grotesque looking fish, they have a row of spines along their back and with their cryptic camouflage are hard to see. Keep an eye out for these nasties or other stonefish relatives such as (scorpionfish, lionfish and firefish) when diving or reef walking around live coral. If stung by a ray or stonefish, immerse the wound in hot water, treat for shock and get immediate medical attention. Any fish with spines, such as catfish, cobbler, gurnards and flathead should be avoided.

Sea Snakes

Quite a few species of sea snakes live in tropical Australian waters. Although highly venomous, sea snakes are generally quite docile and easy to avoid. If bitten, restrict circulation and seek medical attention from the nearest hospital or flying doctor service that should have the appropriate anti venom.

Molluscs

Australia is home of the deadly blue-ringed octopus (Hapolochlaena sp.), of which there are several species in tropical and temperate seas. Although small (around 100-200 mm), their bite is deadly, so don't touch any small octopus with blue bands or blue rings. There are also numerous species of cone shells (Conus sp.) that shouldn't be handled. Living in beautifully patterned shells, Cones inject a venomous dart to immobilise their prey, that can also be highly toxic to humans.

Sea Jellies, Corals & Anemones

Avoid all contact with sea jellies as most give a nasty sting. Try not to swim in murky water in tropical Australia from October to May as this is when box jellies are most common. Hundreds of people have died from the sting of box jellies, so cover up to protect yourself.

Bluebottles and Jellyfish cause intense pain. If you're unlucky enough to be stung, remove any of the remaining tentacles with your fingers or tweezers. Apply cold packs or crushed ice wrapped in a thick towel to the area. **Do not rub!** Seek immediate medical assistance. Flooding the area with vinegar can often temporarily relieve the pain. Most anemones are quite harmless, but a number can cause quite bad reactions upon contact with bare skin. Corals should generally be avoided, not only because a number of species can cut and sting, but also to reduce damage to the coral.

Poisonous creatures

Seafood is very popular in Australia, but there are a few simple rules to remember. Don't eat box fish (fish with a hard outer casing), pufferfish or porcupine fish (fish with a number of spines over their bodies), moray eels or reef crabs with black nippers. These animals are poisonous. Don't eat shellfish from areas with heavy industry, pollution or sewerage discharge. Many of these areas are signposted to stop people collecting such organisms.

While it is possible to get food poisoning from almost any seafood if it hasn't been refrigerated, the major danger is ciguatera poisoning. Created by toxic chemicals from algae being passed down the food chain, the poison is concentrated in larger reef fish. Not all fish carry the poison, but avoid eating the following tropical reef fish: any gropers, large rock cods, triggerfish, the humpback snapper (*Lutjanus gibbus*), chinaman (*Symphorus nematophorus*), longnose unicornfish (Naso unicornis) and the bohar snapper (*Lujanus bohar*).

Food and Drink

Australia has one of the most ethnically diverse populations in the world and they have all contributed their culinary treasures to this multicultured continent. While the range can be limited in smaller towns, most large towns usually have Chinese, Vietnamese, Thai, Indian, French, Italian, Greek, Lebanese, Mexican and Japanese restaurants. Seafood and steak venues are very popular, while vegetarian and vegan alternatives are continually growing. Restaurant prices vary greatly and since some of the cheapest places have the best food, it is sometimes best to follow your taste buds. Most restaurants in Australia are BYO (bring your own alcohol), while tipping is acceptable if you enjoyed the meal and service.

Australian produce is globally recognised for its quantity, quality and diversity. Australian wines, seafood, red meat, fruit and vegetables are available at a variety of large supermarket chains, local fresh market enterprises and roadside stalls. Australia is also one of the world's major wine exporters, and inexpensive and good quality wines are easily found.

Due to Australia's relatively dry, hot climate, most Aussies enjoy a drink of cold beer. There are numerous home-grown brands like Victoria Bitter (VB), Fosters, XXXX, Melbourne Bitter, Emu Export and Tasmania's Cascade, and most popular international brands are available (except in remote or extremely patriotic areas). Fast foods are quite popular in Australia and there are snack bars, pizza places, fish and chip shops, hamburger joints, chicken shops and Chinese take-away in most towns. All the major fast food companies are represented in Australia.

Calendar

Australians enjoy a number of public holidays each year. The fixed national holidays are New Year's Day (Jan 1), Australia Day (Jan 26), Easter (Good Friday and Easter Monday varies), Anzac Day (April 25), Queen's Birthday (2nd Monday in June, except WA), Christmas Day (Dec 25) and Boxing Day (Dec 26). Each state also celebrates bank holidays, cup days (such as the Melbourne Cup), show days and labor days, which are usually held on a Monday to give everyone a long weekend.

Australian schools generally have four terms a year, except Tasmania which has three terms. School holidays are held at roughly the same time in each state, but overlap and vary by a week or two. Summer holidays are mid December to the end of January, while the other holidays fall in April, late June to early July and late September to early October. It may be best to consult a calendar or diary before planning your travel itinerary, or else check with your travel agent.

Shopping

Unless buying items duty free, clothing, photographic equipment and electrical goods are generally more expensive than in Europe and North America. But some goods are definitely worth buying in Australia, such as opals, Australian wines, bush wear (Akubra Hats and Blundstone Boots) and sheep skin products.

Souvenirs naturally will depend on your personal taste, but there are the usual outlets filled with tea towels, fluffy kangaroos, t-shirts, posters and postcards. Probably the best souvenirs of your trip to Australia will be Aboriginal artworks, carvings and other items. Don't be seduced by imitations. Ask questions about the artist and perhaps the community that he or she comes from in order to determine a better sense of its authenticity.

Photography

All brands, sizes, speeds and types of films are available in Australia. Although prices are reasonable, film is best bought duty free or in bulk. Both slide and print film can be purchased throughout the country, but slide film can be harder to find in small towns. Print film can be processed just about anywhere, with prices comparable to most other countries. E6 slide film can be processed in all the capitals, and quite a few other cities. Most professional laboratories offer one and two hour services. Kodachrome films are all sent to Melbourne for development, and the turn around time may take up to two weeks.

Accommodation

Enticing travelers from all over the world, Australia offers the visitor a wide range of accommodation to suit every budget. There are hotels, motels, holiday units, caravan parks, backpacker lodges, youth hostels, bed & breakfast places, beach resorts and camping facilities. Prices can vary dramatically and are not always based on style and comfort, but availability, popularity and location. The comprehensive accommodation listings provided for each state are provided as just a guide, however, prices and facilities may alter, so enquire before making bookings. Also, peak holiday times such as Christmas, Easter and school holidays often require you to make an advance booking ranging from a few days prior to even a week or month ahead, so again, enquire before you commit.

If you're traveling with a dog, you'll need to phone ahead and see if the venue permits pets. Accommodation sites located in National Parks comply with park rules which prohibit pets, but in general, it really is up to the discretion of the service provider.

The various motoring organisations have published accommodation guides which provide comprehensive, up-to-date information in both regions, states and nationally. For example, RACV (Victoria) manual entitled Accommodation, is published each year and lists information ranging from lodges and houseboats, to hotels and resorts. It costs $5 for members, and retails for $10.

NRMA (NSW) publishes smaller booklets called Holiday Guides dedicated to regions such as the Mid-Coast and South Coast. The Guides are free for members and cost $10 for non-member.

The Youth Hostel Association of Australia (YHA) also produce a compact publication called the Accommodation and Discounts Guide. Released annually, it not only provides listings on each hostel around the country, but also offers invaluable travel information on transport, local activities, entertainment and attractions.

Lower Priced Accommodation, Budgeting

Most backpacker bunkhouses are basic and share-style, with a communal kitchen, toilet, and showers. The Youth Hostels Association (YHA) have a comprehensive network of hostels around the country. Hostels offer a great opportunity to meet both international and local travelers, many of whom have flexible schedules and may be interested in sharing parts of your journey. Hostels vary in price from $10 to $20 a night. While some caravan parks also have bunkhouses, most have fully self-contained vans and cabins, which can vary in price from $20 to $60 a night (a figure which can be shared depending on the maximum amount of people allowed). Some basic motels also offer cheap accommodation, with rooms starting at $30 a night.

Medium Priced Accommodation, Cruising

Holiday units, which are generally self-contained, vary in price from $30 to over $100 a day, but are generally cheaper by the week. Most motels would be in the medium price range, costing $40 to $90 a night. Bed & breakfast places and guesthouses are quite popular in the southern states and vary from $45 to $90 a night, which often includes breakfast.

High-Priced Accommodation, Splurging

Large hotels, which are generally 4 or 5-star and offer room service and a number of other facilities, range in price from $100 to $250 a room, and $200 to $1,000 for a suite. Island and beach resorts usually have a variety of different rooms. These can vary in cost from $100 to over $1,000 a night, but many of the island establishments include all meals and activities.

In the Practicalities sections a number of accommodation places are listed as a guide. Remember, prices and availability are subject to change, so make the necessary enquiries before booking and paying deposits.

Transportation

This comprehensive run-down of the wide range of travel services available will enable you to plan and budget your trip. More specific details for each area are found in the relevant Practicalities section. Again, prices are in Australian dollars. Prices and schedules are given as an indication only, so check with local operators or your travel agent for the most up-to-date information prior to departure.

Getting to Australia

Australia is a popular destination serviced by most international airlines. Flights from Europe generally come through Singapore, Hong Kong or Bangkok; flights from Asia are generally direct, and flights from North America are via Hawaii or direct from Los Angeles. Services also run from New Zealand, Africa and South America.

Sydney International Airport is the busiest airport in the country, and is also where you are likely to experience the most delays. Most flights start or terminate in Sydney after sometimes visiting other airports around the country. Brisbane and Melbourne International Airports are the next most popular and generally experience less delays. Placing visitors on the doorstep of the Great Barrier Reef, Cairns International Airport, is also quite busy. There are also international airports in Adelaide, Darwin and Perth. Canberra is only serviced by domestic flights, while Hobart is serviced by international flights from New Zealand. Australia's two major airlines, Ansett and Qantas, offer both domestic and international flights.

Prices for flights naturally vary, with the most popular routes being the cheapest, such as London/Sydney and Los Angeles/Sydney. It is generally cheaper to land on one side of the country or the other. From Europe and Asia it is cheaper to land in Perth or Darwin, while from North America and New Zealand it is cheaper to land in Sydney, Brisbane or Melbourne. Always shop around for prices, go through a travel agent rather than direct to the airline and keep an eye out for discount fares or special deals.

Visas

Everyone visiting Australia, except New Zealanders, requires a visa for entry. Visas are issued by the Australian Consular Office (listed below) in your country. Tourist visas are free and available either for a stay of less than 3 months, or for more than 3 months. The tourist cannot work in Australia (Class 676 & 686). Working holiday visas are available for those aged 18 to 26 (there are some exceptions for older people), from the countries of the United Kingdom, Republic of Ireland, the Netherlands, Canada, Japan and Korea (Class 417).

Visa extensions are possible once (and prior to the expiry of your current visa) in Australia through the Department of Immigration, which have offices throughout Australia. Extensions cost A$145, and expect to battle through a lot of red tape. This does not guarantee your application will be approved, as the fee is for administrative purposes and is not refundable. For more information, Australian Consular Offices include the following:

Canada, (Australian High Commission) Suite 710, 50 O'Connor St, Ottawa, Ontario, K1P 6L2. Tel: 2360841, Fax: 2364376.

Denmark, (Australian Embassy) Kristiania-gade 21, DK 2100 Copenhagen. Tel: 35262244, Fax: 35432218.

Germany, (Australian Embassy) Godes-berger Allee 105-107, 53175 Bonn. Tel: 81030, Fax: 8103130.

Greece, (Australian Embassy) 37 Dimitriou Soutsou St, Ambelokipi, Athens 11521. Tel: 6447303, Fax: 6466595.

Hong Kong, (Australian Consulate General) 23/F Harbour Centre, 25 Harbour Rd, Wanchai. Tel: 28278881, Fax: 28276583.

India, (Australian High Commission) No. 1/50 G Shantipath, Chanakyapuri, New Delhi 110-021. Tel: 6888223, Fax: 6887536.

Indonesia, (Australian Embassy) Jalan HR Rasuna Said Kav C 15-16, Jakarta, Selatan, 12940. Tel: 5227111, Fax: 5261690.

Ireland, (Australian Embassy) Fitzwilton House, Wilton Tce, Dublin 2. Tel: 6761517, Fax: 6785185.

Italy, (Australian Embassy) Via Alessandria, 215, 00198, Rome. Tel: 852721, Fax: 85272300.

Japan, (Australian Embassy) 2-1-14 Mita, Minato-Ku, Tokyo, 108. Tel: 5232411, Fax: 52324149.

Malaysia, (Australian High Commission) 6 Jalan Yap Kwan Seng, 50450, Kuala Lumpur. Tel: 2423122, Fax: 2415773.

Netherlands, (Australian Embassy) Carnegielaan 4, 2517 KH The Hague. Tel: 3108200, Fax: 3107863.

New Zealand, (Australian High Commission) 72-78 Hobson St, Thorndon, Wellington. Tel: 4736411, Fax: 4987135.

Philippines, (Australian Embassy) 1st - 5th Flrs, Dona Salustiana Ty Tower, 104 Paseo De Roxas, Makati, Metro Manila. Tel: 7502850, Fax: 7546268.

Singapore, (Australian High Commission) 25 Napier Rd, Singapore, 258507. Tel: 7379311, Fax: 7375481.

Sweden, (Australian Embassy) Sergels Torg 12, Stockholm. Tel: 6132900, Fax: 247414.

Switzerland, as of July 1st, 1997, the Australian Embassy in Bonn, Germany, assumed responsibility for all visa matters. See listing for Germany.

Thailand, (Australian Embassy) 37 South Sathorn Rd, Bangkok, 10120. Tel: 2872680, Fax: 2872029.

UK, (Australian High Commission) Australia House, The Strand, London, WC 2B 4LA. Tel: 171 3794334, Fax: 171 4658210.

USA, (Australian Embassy) 1601 Massachusetts Ave, NW, Washington DC, 20036-2273. Tel: 7973000, Fax: 7973414.

There are also smaller offices in most countries, so consult your phone book for addresses, phone and fax numbers.

Foreign Embassies

Most countries have embassies in Australia, which are located in Canberra. There are also consulate's offices in most state capitals. Obtain the yellow pages phone book for a complete listing (see Consulates & Legations).

Customs

Visitors to Australia can bring with them 1.25 litres of alcohol, 250 g of tobacco, perfumes (although men are limited to carrying $400 worth), and must declare amounts A$10,000 and over. There are natural restrictions on drugs, firearms and ammunitions, but also plant and animal products. Food, furs, and any other animal or wood products may have to be quarantined, while pets will have to be isolated for several months in both countries. Australia has some of the toughest quarantine regulations in the world, which has kept it free of many of the diseases and pests that affect other nations, so please declare all goods.

Travelling in Australia

The two domestic airlines operating in Australia, Ansett and Qantas, both operate fleets of wide body jets and offer many daily flights to all cities around the country. Prices for flights can vary greatly, but are generally cheaper if booked ahead (at least 21 days), or picked up on stand-by. Avoid travel during peak periods (like school holidays, Easter and Christmas) as the fares can be more expensive and bookings difficult. Airfares can be cheaper if booked outside Australia and there are student discounts available, but check with your travel agent for the best deal possible. Domestic flights in Australia do not have to be reconfirmed. For more information or bookings contact Ansett (Tel: 13 13 00) or Qantas (Tel: 13 13 13). Both these numbers can be called from anywhere in Australia for the cost of a local call.

There are many smaller airlines that offer regional flights within Australia (several owned by Ansett and Qantas). These airlines run flights to large towns and islands, generally on small planes. By themselves, these airfares can be expensive, but many can be combined with a package deal on accommodation which includes the cost of the airfare. Again, you should check with your travel agent for the best deal on regional flights.

The Open Road

Though public transport is adequate in the cities, Australia has an automobile culture, and it can be one of the best ways to travel within a state. Australians drive on the left hand side of the road, and most road rules are quite straight-forward. Speed limit signs (in kilometres) are posted everywhere; 60 km/h is typical in built-up areas, with 100-110 km/h standard on highways and freeways. The use of seat belts is compulsory. Police use radar and speed cameras to catch speeding motorists, red light cameras to catch those running the lights, and random breath tests to catch drink drivers. Each state has its own roadside service organization (NRMA in New South Wales, RACQ in Queensland, RAC in Western Australia), which are cheap to join and provide free roadside assistance and many other services. To drive a car in Australia you should obtain an International Driving Permit from your motoring organization.

Car Rental

If staying for any length of time it may be cheaper to buy a car and sell it before you leave the country, giving you the freedom to explore things at your own pace. But if you're only on a limited stay, then car rental is a viable option. Car rentals are available from airports and most towns throughout Australia. The largest companies are Avis, Budget, Hertz and Thrifty. The smaller companies are quite competitive and some offer older cars at very cheap rates. Prices for car hire vary depending on the size of the car, the length of time required and the usage: $45 to $80 a day is average, but then you must add insurance (about $15 a day), country rates and excess kilometres. Always shop around, make sure you understand the terms and conditions, and look out for special deals with airfares that offer free car hire for a certain number of days. When parking around city areas, read the street signs carefully as infringements can be costly (in Sydney expect to be hit for $60). Many areas require meter parking (costing $1-$2 per hour), or simply allow you to park free for a number of hours.

Buses

One of the cheapest ways to get around Australia is by bus. Although it can be cramped and uncomfortable on very long hauls, for example from Sydney to Perth, or Melbourne to Cairns, it can be an excellent option for shorter trips. There are two national bus lines, Greyhound-Pioneer and McCafferty's, offering services right around the country, but many smaller companies service regional areas. Most buses are airconditioned, and have toilets and videos. They make regular stops for meals, at very odd hours sometimes, and most offer a number of different routes. Make sure you tell them about how many surfboards you have as there are tight restrictions on the maximum allowed on each trip (and they'll cost you about $20 extra per board).

McCafferty's Travel Australia Passes are flexible and affordable, allowing unlimited stops along a predetermined route. Passes are valid from 3-12 months. For example, departing from Adelaide, Melbourne, Sydney or Brisbane, their Follow the Sun Pass allows passengers unlimited stops between their point of departure and Cairns. Call McCafferty's for more information and bookings on 13 14 99.

Greyhound-Pioneer's Kilometre Pass, allows you from 2,000 km ($176, $159 concession) to 20,000 km ($1344, $1210 concession) of travel anywhere across the country, to be used within a 12-month period. Their Aussie Pass allows unlimited travel for a certain number of days, these include: 7 days of travel within a one month period ($499); 10 days within one month ($640); 15 days within one month ($745) and 21 days within two months ($982). For information and bookings contact Greyhound-Pioneer on 13 20 30.

Trains

Railways link all capital cities and most major country areas, but the services are pretty limited along the coastline. There are a number of different classes available on most country trains, with first class and economy class sleeping berths, and first class and economy class seats only.

Countrylink's East Coast Discovery Pass offers Sydney to Brisbane to Cairns by rail for $199. It's available to international visitors only and provides unlimited stops, one way travel in economy conditions. For this offer, and other information or bookings, phone Countrylink on 13 22 32.

Aussie Surf Language

A coldie - A beer.

BBQ (Barbie or barbecue) - A ritualistic feast where friends and family gather around an outdoor cooking device ranging from a cut-off 44 gallon drum to a state of the art gas cooker. Ideal for post surf feasts, barbies are a big part of Aussie beach culture.

Beachie – Beachbreak.

Beast – A large car, usually a four wheel drive.

Bender/Out On The Piss – A big night out partying.

Bewdy – Great, good.

Billy – A cone used for smoking *Cannabis sativa*, or a handled tin used to brew tea over an open fire.

Blue – fight.

Bluey – Blue Heeler dog.

Blundies – Tasmanian-made, Blundstone work boots.

Boardies – Boardshorts.

Bong – A smoking device.

Brickie – A building site worker.

Bush – Australia's wilderness areas. Also referred to as "The Sticks".

Bushpig – An unattractive woman.

Chicks/Sheilas - Girls.

Clubbie – Lifesaver.

Combi – A Volkswagon Combi van. Great for transporting people, boards and other surf paraphenalia. Sleeping in a combi is bliss, particularly when you can't be bothered setting up the tent, or bad weather prevents you from doing so.

Cop Shop – Police station.

Corker – Used to describe something that is really good.

Crikey/Strewth – Wow, Really?

Damper – A kind of bush bread baked in an open fire or camp oven.

Dart – A cigarette.

Deckie – A worker on a fishing boat, many of whom surf the OZ coastline.

Deli – A general store or delicatessen with a wide range of convenience products.

Dunny – Toilet. Usually separate from the house, devoid of toilet paper and sometimes home to interesting creatures like the deadly Redback Spider.

Esky – A cooling or refrigeration device usually housing beer, steak and sausages. A standard item for every Australian home and holiday.

Esky Lid – A Bodyboarder.

Filth – Really good.

Fishos – Fishermen.

Foily – A $25–50 wrap of Cannavis Sativa.

Footy – Australian Rules Football or Rugby Union or Rugby League.

Gidday – Hello.

Goin' Off/Off Its Nut – When something is extremely good or radical in nature.

Grub – Food; the quality & quantity of which is irrelevant.

Have a Captain Cook – Have a look.

HQ – A Holden station wagon car used to commute, root and toot.

Keg/Bazza/Chewy/Dredging – Barreling or tubing wave.

King Brown – A large long necked bottle of beer.

Kook/Gumby/Woody – A novice surfer.

Landie – Landrover 4WD.

Mate – Used to acknowledge friends, acquaintances, strangers or enemies. Used in many situations.

Mincer – Someone who minces their words and is extremely social.

Missus/Ball and Chain – Wife or girlfriend.

Mongrel – A person who has irritated another.

Mull/Cooch/Pot – *Cannabis Sativa*

Nags – Horse Racing.

Pig – A low grade surfboard or particularly nasty members of the Australian Police Force.

Pub – Bar or Hotel.

Puss (pronounced like 'us') – Very bad on-shore surf.

Rashy – Rash Vest.

Roo – A Kangaroo. Most active at sunrise and sunset; take extra care when driving during these times.

RSL/(RR'EE) – Retired Servicemen's League sports-style bar which offer cheap meals.

Servos – A roadside petrol station found in regional areas.

Shacker/Bogan – A person who doesn't like the ocean and drives around in hotted up cars.

She'll Be Right – A 'don't worry be happy' kind of expression that is used to dismiss stressful situations or work related matters.

Shreddin'/Shralpin'/Blazin – Surfing very well, performing radical manoeuvres.

Six Pack – Six stubbies or cans of beer.

Smoko – A break earned from the routine of hard work. Usually consists of a shared packet of darts (see above), fast food, cold drink and bottom humour.

Snag – Sausage.

Stick/Gun/Weapon – Surfboard.

Stinker – A very hot day.

Stubbie – A small glass beer bottle.

Swag – A mobile camping bed that can be rolled up when finished.

The Box – Television.

Toon/Case or Slab – A carton of beer.

Unit – A wild or unstable individual, usually very drunk.

Ute – A car with an open back tray used to transport people and dogs.

Wetty – Wetsuit.

Queensland

Home to the Great Barrier Reef, the Daintree rainforests and Australia's largest entertainment theme parks, tropical Queensland, is Australia's most popular tourist destination. The nation's equivalent of Hawaii's north shore, Queensland is truly an international surfing playground with world-class point breaks such as Kirra and Burleigh Heads.

Getting There

International and domestic flights regularly service Brisbane, Cairns and Coolangatta airports. Freedom Air flies direct between New Zealand and Coolangatta, while Japan Airlines, Ansett and Qantas represent the major international carriers. For information on airlines in the area, contact the following: Ansett, Tel: 13 1300; Flight West, 13 2392; and Qantas, 13 1313.

Local Transport

Queensland's long distance railways are run by TravelTrain (Tel: 13 2235). Coachtrans, McCafferty's and Greyhound-Pioneer travel regularly throughout the Queensland area. For all public transport information (train, bus and ferry) in the Brisbane area, call TransInfo or Brisbane Transport on Tel: 13 1230. The major taxi companies are Black & White Cabs, Brisbane Cabs and Yellow Cabs. The state's 24-hour road service assistance company is the RACQ (Royal Automobile Club Queensland).

Medical and Emergencies

Hospitals and medical centres are located in most of the larger towns in Queensland. For an emergency dial 000 and ask for the service you require, be it fire, police or ambulance.

General Surf Info

Surfrider Foundation, Central Queensland. Tel: 07–3936 1899. North Stradbroke Island. Tel: 07–3409 8334.

Flames and Surf Systems, 17 Braun St, Deagon. Tel: 041 474 4442. Mobile surf shop repairs.

The following telephone information services are available in the Brisbane area and cost roughly 75 cents per minute.

Surf and Snow Report, Tel: 1900 912 177. Tide Times, Tel: 1900 914 477 or 07–3224 2616.

Local Weather, Tel: 1900 155 360. Weather Forecasts SE Qld, Tel: 1196. Marine Reports and Forecasts, Tel: 1182. Coast Guard, Brisbane Base, Tel: 07–3396 5911.

Surf Schools

Gold Coast Surf School, PO Box 233, Burleigh Heads, 4220. Tel: 07–5520 1501.

Sunshine Coast Surfschool, 13 Durham Crescent, Buderim. Tel: 07–5445 4870.

Surf Charter Operators

The Brazil Surf Connection, Unit 2, 39 Arthur St, Mermaid Beach. Tel: 07–5526 0792.

TOS Ferry 2, 29 Stanhill Drive, Chevron Island. Tel: 014 668 747. The Spit to Straddy Island and other locations for private surf groups.

Tropical North Coast

Far North Queensland or the Tropical North, is home to the World Heritage-listed Daintree rainforest, and the Great Barrier Reef, which spans 2000 km from the tip of Cape York to Gladstone in the south. With over 2900 individual reefs, 71 coral islands, 350 species of coral and over 1500 species of fish—the Barrier Reef is a truly awesome recreational adventure ground.

Capricorn and Bunker Groups, and the Swain Reefs

The southern-most extremity of Australia's Great Barrier Reef, the Capricorn, Bunker, and the Swains Groups. The Swains can only be navigated by a few experienced skippers. A relatively unexplored surfing destination, The Swains offer a variety of excellent surfing with up to 50 surfable reef breaks depending on tide and swell conditions, fishing and diving destinations. Surf trips are best undertaken from January to June (cyclone season). A 12-hour boat trip from the mainland, the reefs are accessed by charter boats departing from Gladstone, Bundaberg and Hervey Bay. Although you can walk on some of the outer islands, the only form of accommodation is live-aboard on the charter boats, so make sure you score a comfortable cabin.

Surf Shop

Bundie Skeggs Hardcore Surf Shop, 16–18 Bourbong St. Bundaberg. Tel: 07–4152 6111.

Accommodation

1170 Charter, Captain Cook Dve. Tel: 07–4974 9422, Fax: 07–4974 9616. Fish, surf and snorkel your way around the outer Great Barrier Reef. Charter your own course from $140 per person, per day. Sleeps 9 on board (min 7).

Agnes Water

Queensland's most northern surfing beach, Agnes Water has some great beach breaks and is close to the Eurimbula and Round Hill National Parks.

Mango Tree, Via Miriam Vale. Tel: 07–9749 132. Rooms from $49–$59 per night.

Hobans Hideaway, 17 Round Hill Rd. Tel: 07–9749 144. B&B rates from $70 per night.

Agnes Water Caravan Park, Jeffery Crescent. Tel: 07–9749 193. Camp sites from $10–$14. Cabins from $40–$50 per night or $170–$250 per week, sleep up to 6 people.

Bundaberg

Bougainvillea International Motor Inn, 73 Takalvan St. Tel: 071–527 255. Daily room rates from $66–$97 (standard) and $107–$165 (suite).

Alexandra Park Motor Inn, 66 Quay St. Tel: 071–527 255. Park and river frontage units. Rates from $59–$96 per night.

Cane Village Holiday Park, Twyford. Tel: 071–551 022. All 84 sites are powered. Daily rates for sites from $12–$16. Park cabins sleep 2–6 from $35–$50, while cabins sleep 2–6 from $35 per night.

Turtle Sands Caravan Park, Mon Repos Beach. Tel: 071–592 340. All 84 sites are powered. Camping rates from $16 (daily) and $85 (weekly). Villas sleep 2–7 from $57 (daily) and $399–$455 (weekly), while units sleep 2–6 from $50 (daily) and $350–$399 (weekly).

Fraser Island

This offshore island is World Heritage listed, and most of it is national park or state forest. Renowned for its fishing, surfing and diversity of flora and fauna, Fraser is home to many native dingoes that roam wild on the beach. Coach and ferry services are available from Rainbow Beach to Fraser Island. Camping permits should be obtained in advance at Deptartment of Environment and Heritage, Rainbow Beach. Tel: 07–5486 3160.

Fraser Island Retreat, Happy Valley. Tel: 071–279 144. Self-contained units sleep 2–4 from $140 per night.

Eurong Beach Resort, Eurong. Tel: 071–279 122. Self-contained units sleep 2–8 from $70–$160 (daily) and $380–$1000 (weekly).

Yidney Rocks Cabins, Yidney Rocks. Tel: 071–279 167. Cottages sleep 2–8 from $80–$90 (daily) and $540–$600 (weekly).

Cathedral Beach Resort and Camping Park, Cathedral Beach. Tel: 071–279 177. 68 camp sites (no power). Daily camping rates from $14 per person. Park cabins sleep 4–6 from $75–$100 (daily) and $350–$600 (weekly), while on-site vans sleep 2 from $50 (daily) and $350 (weekly).

Sunshine Coast

Just an hour's drive north of Brisbane, the Sunshine Coast provides water sports enthusiasts with year-round activity. Offering a lifestyle which revolves around the sun, sand and surf, miles of surfable coastline will keep you occupied. For info contact Tourism Sunshine Coast. Tel: 07–5443 6400.

Surf Shops

The Bribie Island Beach Hut, 1 North St, Wrim. Tel: 07–3408 1074.

Main Beach Surf, Bay Village Complex, Hasting St, Noosa Heads. Tel: 07–5449 2933.

Surf Cargo, Shops 5 and 6, Sommers Arcade, Coolum Beach. Tel: 07–5446 5444.

TOS Surf Shop, 357A Main Beach Parade, Main Beach. Tel: 07–5531 4211.

XL Pro Surf Shop, 144 Alexandra Pde, Alexandra Headlands. Tel: 07–5479 4966.

Accommodation
Noosa Heads
Chez Noosa Resort, 263 David Low Way. Tel: 07–5447 2027. Self–contained units (sleep 2–4). Daily rates from $45.

The Hastings, Hastings St. Tel: 07–5447 5100. Self-contained units sleep 2–5 from $120–$200 (daily) and $805–$1365 (weekly).

Sunrise Holiday Park, David Low Way, Sunrise Beach. Tel: 07–5447 3294. Camp sites from $12–$20 per night. Cabins from $30–$60 per night.

Koala Backpackers, 44 Noosa Dve. Tel: 07–5447 3355. Daily rates include $14 (dorm), $34 (twin share) and $50–$70 (motel room).

Halse Lodge Guest House, 2 Halse Lane, Noosa Heads. Tel: 07–5447 3377. Located on

2 acres of lawn and rainforest. Room rates from $15 per night.

Peregian Beach
Surf Edge, 38 Lorikeet Dve. Tel: 07–5448 1511. Absolute beach frontage. Rates from $70–$100 (daily) and $210–$600 (weekly).

Hideaway, 386 David Low Way. Tel: 07–5448 1006. Self-contained units. Rates from $40–$70 (daily) and $240 (weekly).

Peregian Motor Inn, cnr Heron St and David Low Way. Tel: 07–5448 1110. Beachside units. Room rates: $35–$70 (s) and $40–$90 (dble).

Peregian Beach Caravan Park, David Low Way. Tel: 07–5448 1223. Most of the 75 sites are powered. Camping rates from $12–$18 (daily) and $60–$95 (weekly). Park cabins from $38–$60 (daily) and $200–$350 (weekly), while on-site vans are $25–$35 (daily) and $125–$215 (weekly).

Coolum Beach
Surf Dance, 29 Coolum Tce. Tel: 07–5446 1039. Self-contained units with Pacific Ocean views to Noosa. Rates from $60–$120 (daily) and $260–$825 (weekly).

Coolum Dreams Bed & Breakfast, 28 Warran Rd. Tel: 07–5446 3868. B&B rates from $50–$90 per night.

Stewarts Coolum Beach, cnr Birtwill St and David Low Way. Tel: 07–5446 1899. Daily room rates from $35–$50.

Maroochy Beach Park, Coolum Beach, David Low Way. Tel: 07–5446 1474. Beach frontage location with 175 powered sites. Camping rates from $12–$19 per night.

Coolum Gardens Caravan Park, cnr Elizabeth St and Beach Esplanade. Tel: 07–5544 6177. Daily rates for camp sites from $14–$19. Cabins from $27–$35 (daily) and $125–$190 (weekly). On–site vans from $23–$35 (daily) and $110–$190 per week.

Maroochy Beach Park, David Low Way. Tel: 07–5446 1474. Daily rates for sites from $13–$20.

Mudjimba Beach
Maroochy Beach Park Mudjimba, Cottonwood St. Tel: 07–5448 7157. Beach access. Camping rates from $12–$20 (daily) and $62–$97 (weekly).

Mudjimba Caravan Park, Cottonwood St, Mudjimba. Tel: 07–5448 7157. Unpowered sites from $13–$18 per night. Powered sites from $15–$22 per night.

Maroochydore
Beach Houses, cnr Sixth Ave and Beach Pde. Tel: 07–5443 3049. Self–contained units sleep 4–6, from $100–$200 (daily) and $350–$950 (weekly).

Maroochy River Cabin Village Caravan Park, cnr Bradman Ave and Diura St. Tel: 07–5443 3033 or freecall 1800 802 737. Daily rates from $34–$49 (villa vans), $45–$60 (ensuite cabins) and $53–$68 (holiday ensuites).

Maroochy Beach Park Cotton Tree, The Esplanade. Tel: 07–5443 1253. All 319 camping sites are powered. Rates from $12–$20 (daily) and $62–$97 (weekly).

Maroochy Beach Park Seabreeze, cnr Melrose Pde and Sixth Ave. Tel: 07–5443 1167. Patrolled beachfront location where all 100 sites are powered. Camping rates from $15–$20 (daily) and $77–$97 (weekly).

Maroochydore YHA Backpackers, 24 Schirrmann Drive. Tel: 07–5443 3151. Minutes walk to shops and beaches. Room rates from $15–$17 per person. Free use of boogie boards, bikes and fishing gear.

Alexandra Headland
Headland Tropicana, 274 Alexandra Pde. Tel: 07–5444 2888. Self-contained units 500 m from beach. Rates from $90–$115 (daily) and $470–$665 (weekly).

Northpoint Apartments, cnr Alexandra Pde and Pacific Tce. Tel: 07–5444 4451. Self-contained units from $70–$100 (daily) and $250–$450 (weekly).

Club Boolarong, cnr Alexandra Pde and Mary St. Tel: 07–5444 3099. Self-contained units sleep 2–6; from $55–$165 per night.

Headland Gardens, 7 Juan St. Tel: 07–5444 4655. Self-contained units 70 m from beach. Rates from $55–$135 (daily) and $275–$845 (weekly).

Mooloolaba
Beachside Mooloolaba, 35 Brisbane Rd. Tel: 07–5478 3911. Self-contained units located on beachfront. Rates from $90–$150 (daily) and $395–$825 (weekly).

The Peninsula Apartments, cnr The Esplanade and Brisbane Rd. Tel: 07–5444 4477. Self-contained units sleep 2–6 opposite beach. Rates from $90–$100 (daily) and $585–$1760 (weekly).

Motel Mediterranean, 197 Brisbane Rd. Tel: 07–5444 4499. Daily room rates from $40–$80.

Maroochy Beach Park Mooloolaba, Parkyn Pde. Tel: 07–5444 1201. Most of the 96 sites are powered. Camping rates from $12–$20 (daily) and $62–$97 (weekly).

Kawana Waters
Surfside on the Beach, 143 Lowanna Dve. Tel: 07–5444 0044. Self-contained unit rates from $120–$180 (daily) and $550–$1320 (weekly).

Stewarts Kawana Waters, Nicklin Way. Tel: 07–5444 6699. B&B rates from $49–$60 (single) and $68–$80 (double).

Sun Surf, 56 Nicklin Way. Tel: 07–5493 3377. Units with cooking facilities. Daily rates from $40–$70.

Kawana International Motor Inn, 18 Nicklin Way. Tel: 07–5444 6900. Facilities include restaurant and salt water pool. Daily unit rates from $40–$85.

Caloundra
Shearwater, 79 Edmund St, Kings Beach. Tel: 07–5491 1744. Adjacent to beachfront. Studio apartments from $65 (daily) and $220–$550 (weekly).

Rolling Surf Resort, 10 Levuka Ave, Kings Beach. Tel: 07–5491 1300. Overlooking main surf beach. Daily B&B rates from $50–$65 (single) and $60–$70 (double).

Caloundra Holiday Resort, Beerburrum St, Dicky Beach. Tel: 07–5491 3342. Beachfront camping. Rates from $14–$25 (daily) and $70–$125 (weekly). Park units from $35–$80 (daily) and $210–$480 (weekly).

Golden Beach Caravan Park, 75 Esplanade, Golden Beach. Tel: 07–5492 1296. Powered camping rates from $15 (daily) and $70–$95 (weekly). Units are $40–$55 (daily) and $200–$400 (weekly), while on-site vans are $24–$36 (daily) and $125–$190 (weekly).

Brisbane

The capital of the Sunshine State, this pretty city has evolved from a sleepy, large country town to become a vibrant and cosmopolitan metropolis. For info. call the Brisbane Visitors Accommodation and Tourist Information Service. Tel: 07–3236 2020.

Surf Shops

Brothers Neilsen, Carindale Shopping Centre, Creek Rd. Tel: 07–3843 1314.

Goodtime Surf and Sail, 29 Ipswich Rd, Wollongabba. Tel: 07–3391 8588.

Primitive Surf, 97 Braun St, Deagon. Tel: 07–3869 2922.

Straddie Shapes and Surfwear, Mooloomba Rd, Pt. Lookout, Stradbroke Island. Tel: 07–3409 8334.

Surf City, Shop 3, Level A, The Myer Centre, Queen St Mall, Brisbane. Tel: 07–3229 1098.

Accommodation

Moreton Island

Boasting the world's highest sandhills, Moreton Island is 89 per cent National Park and offers spectacular surfing beaches. You'll need a 4WD to access the island, and a vehicular ferry service departs from Whyte Island (bookings Tel: 07–3895 1000) or travelers can take the passenger launch from Holt St Wharf Pinkemba (bookings Tel: 07–3268 6333). There are also high speed catamaran transfers to the island. Valid camping and vehicle permits are essential so find out the necessary info when booking your transport.

Tangalooma Moreton Island. Tel: 07–3268 6333. Usual resort facilities with an extra bonus of nightly hand-feeding of wild dolphins. Holiday units from $140–$220 (single) and $160–$240 (double). Villas from $240–$280 (daily) and $1400–$1680 (weekly).

Bulwer Holiday Flats. Tel: 07–3408 2202. Standard units from $65–$80 per night.

Yaldeenie Apartments, The Esplanade, Kooringal. Tel: 07–3409 0120. Beachfront location accessed by 4WD only. Self-contained units from $50–$100 (daily) and $300–$550 (weekly).

North Stradbroke Island

A large road network and several small towns make Stradbroke's breathtaking surf beaches more accessible. Access to the island is either by vehicular ferry (bookings Tel: 07–3286 2666) or by passenger taxis (bookings Tel: 07–3286 2666) from Cleveland. There are numerous caravan parks and motels around Amity Point and Dunwich, so for further info, call the North Stradbroke Island Visitor Information Centre on Tel: 07–3409 9555.

North Stradbroke Island Guesthouse, 1 Eastcoast Rd, Point Lookout. Tel: 07–3409 8888. Located on Home Beach. Room rates from $16 per person (dorm) and $38 (twin share).

Stradbroke Island Tourist Park, North Stradbroke. Tel: 07–3409 8127. Daily rates include $10–$14 (camping), $46 (cabins), $65 (deluxe cabin with spa) and $75 (villas).

Cylinder Beach Camping Ground, Mooloomba Rd. Tel: 07–3409 9025. Camp sites from $10–$18. Located right on the legendary Cylinder's righthanders.

North Stradbroke Island Redland Shire Camping Grounds. Bookings Tel: 07–3409 9555.

South Stradbroke Island

South Stradbroke Island Resort, South Stradbroke Island via the Goldcoast. Tel: 07–5577 3311. Facilities include tennis court, sauna, shared spa and private jetty. Dinner, B&B rates from $120–$160.

To preserve the simple pleasures offered on South Stradbroke, the following campgrounds provide the site, drinking water and hot water for your showers—and basically you'll have to provide the rest.

North Currigee. Tel: 07–5577 2577.

South Curriggee. Tel: 07–5577 3932. These guys actually have a few permanent canvas tents on site.

The Gold Coast

This 10-km stretch of Queensland coastline is not referred to as a Surfers Paradise for nothing. The area combines world class point breaks like Kirra and Burleigh Heads with a pumping nightlife district. So if you've had enough of the isolation and you like a bit of an audience, you've come to the right place! The Gold Coast Tourism Bureau, Tel: 07–5592 2699.

Surf Shops

Aleeda Wetsuits, 29 Taree St, Burleigh Heads. Tel: 07–5593 4927.

City Beach Surf Shops, 25 Cavill Ave, Surfers Paradise. Tel: 07–5592 6199. Thirteen other stores throughout Brisbane, Carindale, Broadbeach, Indooroopily, Toombul, Chermside, Aitkenvale, Mt. Ommaney, and Browns Plains Shopping Center.

Chapman Surfboards, 3/28 Kortum Dve, Burleigh Heads. Tel: 0411 870 356.

Double Keg, Shop 3, 86-90 Musgrove St, Kirra. Tel: 07–5599 3404. Surf lessons available.

Feral Surfboards, P0 Box 1012, Coolangatta 4225. Tel: 0419 246 595 or 07–5598 3760.

Hot Stuff Surfboards, 1969 Gold Coast Hwy. Burleigh Heads. Tel: 07–5535 6899.

Kirra Surf, Gold Coast Hwy, Kirra. Tel: 07–5536 3922.

Mt Woodgee, 122 Griffith St, Coolangatta. Tel: 07–5536 5937.

Nev Surfboards, 2586 Gold Coast Hwy, Mermaid Beach. Tel: 07–5592 4010.

Osmosis Surfboards, Shop 2, 30 Hastings St, Noosa Heads. Tel: 07–5447 3300.

Paradise Surf World, Shop 164, Beachend Paradise Centre, Surfers Paradise. Tel: 07–5538 4825.

Phantom Surfboards, 79 Lower West Burleigh Rd, Burleigh Heads. Tel: 07–5535 9956.

Pipedream Surfboards, Shop 1, Showcase On The Beach, Griffith, Coolangatta. Tel: 07–5599 1164.

Spider Surf-Shop, 1/778 Pacific Parade, Currumbin. Tel: 07–5525 0115. Surf lessons available.

Stuart Surfboards, 2576 Gold Coast Hwy,

Mermaid Beach. Tel: 07–5572 0098.

Town and Country Surf Centre, 2438 Gold Coast Hwy, Mermaid Beach. Tel: 07–5572 9866.

Accommodation

Main Beach

Aloha Lane, 11 Breaker St. Tel: 07–5591 5944. Self-contained units sleep 2–4. Rates from $80–$120 (daily) and $470–$900 (weekly).

Chidori Court, 1 Cronin Ave. Tel: 07–5591 6544. Self-contained units sleep 2–6 from $65–$199 per night.

Main Beach Tourist Park, Main Beach Pde. Tel: 07–5581 7722. Located on the Spit at the northern end of the Gold Coast. Camping rates from $13–$20 (daily) and $78–$140 (weekly). Ensuite sites from $21–$25 (daily) and $126–$175 (weekly).

Surfers Paradise

Surfers Tropique, 27 Wharf Rd. Tel: 07–5592 1575. Located 250 m from beach. Self-contained units sleep 2–6 from $75–$132 (daily) and $515–$920 (weekly).

Warringa Surf, 219 Surf Pde. Tel: 07–5570 2466. 100 m from beach. Self-contained units sleep 2–5 from $462–$720 per week.

Paradise Sands, 42 Old Burleigh Rd. Tel: 07–5539 9793. Absolute beach frontage. Self-contained units from $295–$850 per week.

Club Surfers, 2877 Gold Coast Hwy. Tel: 07–5531 5244. Self-contained units sleep 3-4 from $57–$86 (daily) and $359–$617 (weekly).

The British Arms International Backpackers Resort, Mariners Cove, 70 Seaworld Drive. Tel: 07–5571 1776. Rooms from $14–$22 per night.

Surf & Sun Backpackers, 3323 Gold Coast Highway. Tel: 07–5592 2363. Dorm-style accommodation from $16 per person. Facilities include free boogie board use, plus there are pop-out surfboards for hire ($25 daily) which includes your own wettie.

Broadbeach

Boulevard Towers, 45 Broadbeach Ave. Tel: 07–5538 8555. Beachfront location. Self-contained units sleep 2–5 from $82–$127 (daily) and $575–$875 (weekly).

Surfers Fairways Resort, 1 Fairway Dve, Clear Island Waters. Tel: 07-5575 2533. Self-contained units sleep 2-4 from $80–$100 (daily) and $450–$550 (weekly).

Barbados Holiday Apartments, 12 Queensland Ave. Tel: 07-5570 1166. Self-contained units sleep 2–5 from $67–$125 (daily) and $469–$963 (weekly).

Ocean Beach Tourist Park, Hythe St, Miami. Tel: 07-5581 7711. Daily camping site rates from $17–$20.

Mermaid Beach

Spindrift Oceanfront Apartments, 37 Albatross Ave. Tel: 07-5572 5188. Facilities include heated pool and shared spa. Self-contained units sleep 2–6 from $360–$995 per week.

Mermaid Park Flats Motor Inn, 2525 Gold Coast Hwy, cnr Ventura Rd. Tel: 07-5575 2090. Self-contained units from $40–$140 per night.

Dorchester Lodge, 2367 Gold Coast Hwy. Tel: 07-5575 2799. Self-contained units sleep 2-6 from $40–$90 per night.

Mermaid Beach, 2395 Gold Coast Hwy. Tel: 07-5575 1577. Motel units offering basic cooking facilities. Daily room rates from $25–$65.

Nobby Beach

Magic Mountain Quest Resort, Great Hall Dve. Tel: 07-5572 8088. Self-contained units sleep 2-6 from $115–$235 (daily) and $699–$1400 (weekly).

Sandrift Apartments, 98 Marine Pde. Tel: 07-5575 3677. Self-contained units sleep 2–4 from $85–$100 (daily) and $365–$900 (weekly).

Burleigh Heads

Burleigh Beach Tower, 52 Goodwin Tce. Tel: 07-5535 9222. Self-contained units sleep 2–4 from $128–$219 (daily) and $665–$1183 (weekly).

Hillhaven Holiday Apartments, 2 Goodwin Tce. Tel: 07-5535 1055. Beachfront location adjacent to National Park. Self-contained units from $95–$150 (daily) and $350–$800 (weekly).

Burleigh Point, 300 The Esplanade. Tel: 07-5576 2233. Self-contained units 100 m from North Burleigh SLSC. Rates from $70–$120 (daily) and $320–$780 (weekly).

Aussie Resort, 1917 Gold Coast Hwy. Tel: 07-5576 2877. Self-contained units sleep 2–4 from $95 (daily) and $410 (weekly).

Burleigh Beach Tourist Park, Goodwin Tce. Tel: 07-5581 7755. Most of the 119 sites are powered. Camping rates from $13–$19 (daily) and $78–$140 (weekly).

Palm Beach

Surfers Horizons, 2, 17th Ave. Tel: 07-5535 5222. Beach frontage location. Self-contained units sleep 2–6 from $490–$790 per week. Facilities include saltwater pool and shared spa.

Tropical Sands on the Beach, 1295 Gold Coast Hwy. Tel: 07-5535 1044. Room rates from $75–$150 (single) and $75–$150 (double).

Surfside Court, 1495 Gold Coast Hwy. Tel: 07-5535 5912. Highrise located on beach. Units sleep up to 6 from $65–$150 (daily) and $295–$950 (weekly).

Tally Ho, 1500 Gold Coast Hwy, cnr Tallebudgera Dve. Tel: 07-5535 2955. Motel units offering basic amenities. Daily room rates from $25—35 (standard) and $35–$55 (suite).

Palm Beach Caravan Park, 1336 Gold Coast Hwy. Tel: 07-5535 3359. Camping sites from $16–$20 (daily) and $85–$155 (weekly). Park cabins sleep 2–6 from $29–$90 (daily) and $175–$600 (weekly), while on-site vans sleep 2–6 from $25 (daily) and $125 (weekly).

Currumbin

Sanctuary Beach Resort, 47 Teemangum St. Tel: 07-5598 2524. Facilities include shared spa, tennis court and salt water pool. Unit rates from $90–$110 (daily) and $490–$1200 (weekly).

The Hill Apartments, 38 Duringan St. Tel: 07-5534 4466. Self-contained units sleep 2–6 from $90–$110 (daily) and $490–$1200 (weekly).

Sanctuary Lake Apartments, 40 Teemangum St. Tel: 07-5534 3344. Self-contained units sleep 2-6 from $80–$140 (daily) and $490–$1800 (weekly).

Sand Castles on Currumbin Beach, 31 Teemangum St. Tel: 07-5598 2999. Self-contained units sleep 2–6 from $70–$165 (daily) and $490–$900 (weekly). Min booking 3 nights.

Tugun

Pacific Surf Absolute Beachfront, 373 Golden Four Dve. Tel: 07–5534 6599. Self-contained units sleep 2–6 from $85–$125 (daily) and $390–$950 (weekly).

Crystal Beach Apartments, 329 Golden Four Dve. Tel: 07–5534 6560. Beachfront location. Rates from $55–$120 (daily) and $340–$1050 (weekly).

Surfside, 351 Golden Four Dve. Tel: 07–5534 2561. Daily room rates from $35–$70 (single) and $45–$75 (double).

Kirra

San Chelsea, 146 Pacific Pde. Tel: 07–5536 3377. Facilities include shared spa, solar heated pool and half court tennis. Rates from $360–$900 per week. Min booking 3 nights.

Kirra Vista Holiday Units, 12 Musgrave St. Tel: 07–5536 7375. Self-contained units sleep 2-4 from $65 (daily) and $240–$480 (weekly).

At the Beach Motel and Holiday Units, Gold Coast Hwy. Tel: 07–5536 3599. Standard motel facilities. Daily rates from $45–$70.

Kirra Beach Tourist Park, Charlotte St, off Coolangatta Rd. Tel: 07–5581 7744. Camping rates from $15–$19 (daily) and $78–$133 (weekly). Cabins sleep 6 from $65 (daily) and $450 (weekly).

Coolangatta

Beach House Seaside Resort, 58 Marine Pde, cnr McLean St. Tel: 07–5574 2800 or 07–5536 7466. Self-contained units sleep 2–6 from $125–$150 (daily) and $735–$945 (weekly).

Beachcomber International Resort, 122 Griffith St. Tel: 07–5574 2800 or 07–5536 9555. Facilities include half court tennis, gym pool and shared spa. Self-contained units from $120–$155 (daily) and $665–$945 (weekly).

Columbia Beachfront Apartments, 184 Marine Pde, Rainbow Pde. Tel: 07–5599 0666. Self-contained units sleep 2–6 from $420–$995 per week. Min booking 3 nights.

Antonios Rex Motel and Ritz Flats Holiday Apartments, 104 Marine Pde. Tel: 07–5536 1655. Beachfront units from $65–$80 (daily) and $350–$495 (weekly).

Coolangatta YHA, 230 Coolangatta Rd, Bilinga. Tel: 07–5536 7644. Daily room rates from $10–$24 per person.

New South Wales

Australian surfing was born in Sydney, the host city of the 2000 Olympics. Blessed with the most consistent city line-ups in the country, it continues to be a focal point of contemporary surfing. A competitive breeding ground for legendary Australian world surfing champions such as Tom Carroll, the nation's premier state has some classic set-ups. From the perfect points off the north to the hollow beach breaks and rock ledges of the south, there are no shortages of waves, or indeed surfers, along the state's long and varied coastline.

Getting There

Sydney International Airport is a bustling gateway for travelers departing and arriving on Australia's east coast. National Ansett and Qantas flights regularly service Sydney's Domestic Airport from all other state and territory capitals.

Local Transport

The NSW coastline is covered by a decent network of bus and coach companies, with McCaffertys and Greyhound-Pioneer being the major providers. Country and interstate rail enquiries can be made on 13 2232, while the Sydney Ferries Info Line is Tel: 02-9207 3170. With over 2000 services a day, CityRail can get you around greater Sydney and the southcoast (Tel: 13 1500 or freecall 1800 637 500 for enquiries). Hire cars are available in most towns and airports, with Avis, Budget, Thrifty and Hertz being popular choices. NSW's roadside service is provided by NRMA (National Roads & Motorists Association).

Medical and Emergencies

Hospitals and medical centres are located in most of the larger towns in New South Wales. For an emergency dial 000 and ask for the service you require, be it fire, police or ambulance.

National Parks

It will cost you around $7.50 for a day ticket in any of the NSW National Parks, and you can buy an annual permit for $50, or $60 which includes Kosciusko National park. The permits provide access to all parks in the state, any time of the year. (NSW National Parks & Wildlife Service Info Centre, Tel: 02-9585 6333).

General Surf Info

Davo's Ding Kings, 77 Bassett St, Mona Vale. Tel: 02-9979 1115.

Surfrider Foundation, Head Office. Tel: 02-9265 2688.

Northern Beaches. Tel: 02-4577 0664.

South Coast Regions. Tel: 02-6494 1072.

The following telephone information services are available in the Sydney area and cost roughly 75 cents per minute.

Surf and Snow Report, Tel: 1900 912 177. Tide Times, Tel: 1900 914 477 or 07-3224 2616.

Local Weather, Tel: 1900 155 361

Surf Schools

Central Coast, 170 Avoca Drive, Avoca Beach. Tel: 02-4382 1020.

East Coast Surf School, 14 Johnson St, Byron Bay. Tel: 02-6685 5989.

Learn to Surf, 170 Avoca Drive, Avoca Beach. Tel: 02-4382 1020.

Manly Surf School, 42 Pittwater Rd, Manly. Tel: 02-9976 3566.

Palawan Surf Coaching, Avalon Pde, Avalon. Tel: 02–9918 3870.

Sydney Safe Surf Schools/Sydney Safe Safaris, 102 Austral St, Maloubar. Tel: 02–9311 2834.

ABC Sydney Surfschools, Tel: 02–9314 0290.

Byron Bay Surfboard Coaching Company, Tel: 02–6680 8818.

Surfing Byron Bay, Tel: 02–6680 8101.

Central Coast Surf School, Tel: 02–4382 1541.

Dave Zeman Surf Coaching, Newcastle. Tel: 02–4984 3316.

Endless Summer Surf Academy, Tel: 02–6654 2622.

Manly & Warringah Surf School, Tel: 02–9971 7133.

Pines Surfriders School, Illawarra. Tel: 02–4297 8011.

Let's Go Surfing, Bondi. Tel: 02–9665 4473 or 018 404 605.

Far North Coast

Far northern NSW has magnificent World Heritage rainforests and some of the best beaches in the state.

Surf Shops
All Above Board, 68 Ballina St, Lennox Head. Tel: 02–6687 7522.

Bay Action Surf Shop, 14 Johnson St, Byron Bay. Tel: 02–6685 7819.

Country Style Surf, Shop 6, 4 Yamba St, Yamba. Tel: 02–6646 1330.

Dahlberg Surfboards, Unit 4, 6 Angourie Rd, Yamba. Tel: 02–6646 1040.

Maddog Surfboards, The Industrial Estate, Byron Bay. Tel: 02–6685 6022.

Wavelite Surfboards, Unit 6/84-86, Centennial Circuit Byron Arts and Industry Estate. Tel: 02–6685 8008.

Webber Surfboards, Angourie Rd, Yamba. Tel: 02–6646 3350.

Accommodation
Tweed Heads
Sea Drift, 32 Boundary St. Tel: 07–5536 8855. Units from $240–$600 per week. 200 m from the beach.

Tweed Pacific, cnr Agnes St and Pacific Hwy. Tel: 07–5524 3405. Rooms from $32–$65 per night.

Banora Point Caravan Park, Pacific Hwy. Tweed Heads South. Tel: 07–5523 4100. Camping rates from $14 per night.

Byron Bay
Australia's most easterly town, Byron is famous for its surf, music festivals and eclectic residents that include many Australian celebrities.

Byron Bayside Holiday Accommodation, 14 Middleton St. Tel: 02–6685 6004. Units from $55–$105 per night or $390–$800 per week, sleep up to 6 people.

J's Bay Hostel, 7 Carlyle St. Tel: 02–6685 8853 or freecall 1800 678 195 (reservations only). Hostel is located 400 m from the main beach. Rates from $14–$17 per person & $20–$24 twin share. Includes free use of bikes, boogie boards and malibu surfboards.

Cape Byron Hostel, cnr Middleton & Byron Streets. Tel: 02–6685 8788 or freecall 1800 652 627 (reservations only). Daily rates from $13–$18 per person and $50–$60 twin share.

Angourie
Nat's Apartments, The Crescent, Angourie. Tel: 02 6646 1622. Apartments from $75–$105 per night or $450–$630 per week, sleep up to four people.

Run by aussie surfing legend Nat Young, the accommoodation overlooks the famous righthander at Angourie Point.

Mid North Coast

Popular during the school holiday period, the mid north coast can be real gem when the conditions are right.

Surf Shops

Coopers Surf, 380 High St, Coffs Harbour. Tel: 02–6652 5466. Also another store located at The Plaza.

Crescent Head Surf Co, Shop 1 Main St, Crescent Head. Tel: 02–6566 0550.

Hydro Surf, Shop 4/53 Pacific Drive Port Macquarie. Tel: 02–6584 1477. Opposite Flynns Beach.

Inner Vision, 80 Williams St, Port Macquarie. Tel: 02–6583 7790.

Low Pressure Surf, Shop 10, Beach St Tuncurry. Tel: 02–6555 8556.

Paradise Surf Centre, Shop 1, 49 Horton St, Port Macquarie. Tel: 02–6583 6062.

Rip Curl Surf Shop, cnr Gordon and High St, Coffs Harbour. Tel: 02–6652 6369.

Saltwater Wine, 5 Wharf St, Forster. Tel: 02–6554 7979.

Accommodation

There are plenty of holiday letting agents in this area if you plan on staying for a while, so enquire at local real estate outlets or tourism centres. The NSW Tourism Commission have an extensive network of Visitor Information Centres which cover specific regions. These include the following:

Great Lakes Tourism, Little St, Forster. Tel: 02–6554 8799 or tollfree 1800 802 692.

Port Macquarie & the Hastings, Clarence St, Port Macquarie. Tel: 02–6583 1293 or tollfree 1800 025 935.

Coffs Harbour
Hawaiian Sands Motor Inn, cnr Park Beach Rd & Ocean Pde, opposite Park Beach. Tel: 02–6652 2666. Daily room rates from $44–$80.

Park Beach Caravan Park, Ocean Pde.

Tel: 02–6652 3204. Adjacent to the surf beach. Camping rates from $14 (daily), or $18 with ensuite; park cabins from $38–$70 (daily) and $228–$490 (weekly).

Split Solitary Caravan Park, Pacific Hwy. Tel: 02–6653 6212. Beach frontage accommodation. Camping rates are $12–$16 (daily) and $60–$98 (weekly).

Coffs Harbour YHA Hostel, 110 Albany St. Tel: 02–6652 6462. Facilities include regular beach buses from the hostel, plus access to boogie boards, surfboards, bikes and a ski boat. Rates from $15 per person.

Scotts Head
Kooringal, 18 Matthew St. Tel: 02–6568 1082 or 018 652 419. Self contained cottage sleeps 6–12. Weekly rate is $560–$1120. Min booking of 4 days.

Tombolo Bay Holiday Apartments, 64 Waratah St. Tel: 02–6569 8086. 4 units (each sleep 5) which offer standard facilities. Rates are $70–$125 (daily) and $350–$750 (weekly). Min booking 2 nights.

Scotts Head Holiday Units, 4 Wallace St. Tel: 02–6569 8160. Each unit sleeps 6. Rates from $50–$90 (daily) & $250–$630 (weekly).

Scotts Head Reserve, Scotts Head Rd, adjacent to surf beach. Tel: 02–6569 8122. Camping rates from $14, while park cabins are $28 (daily) or $165 (weekly).

South West Rocks
Boomerang, 2 Memorial Avenue. Tel: 02–6566 6278. Units from $40–$50 per night or $180–$630 per week.

Trial Bay Lodges, 24 Cardwell St, Arakoon. Tel: 02–6566 6116. Units from $135–$445 per week.

Lagoon View Caravan Park, Phillip Drive. Tel: 02–6566 6142. Camp sites from $9–$16. Vans from $24–$40 or $130–$280 per week, sleep up to 6 people. Cottages from $45–$60 per night or $250–$500 per week.

Arakoon State Recreation Area, Trial Bay Gaol, Laggers Point. Tel: 02–6566 6168. Camp sites from $10–$20 per night.

Hat Head
Hat Head Beach Cottage, Enquiries & bookings to 28 Tindara Dve, Sawtell. Tel:

02–6653 1411. Cottage sleeps 4 and costs $45 (daily) and $185 + $15 cleaning fee (weekly).

Hat Head Holiday Park, Reserve Rd. Tel: 02–6567 7501. Half of the 299 sites are powered. Access to kiosk, public telephone and boat launching ramp. Rates from $14 per night.

Corra Lynn, 31 Creek St. Tel: 02–6653 1411. One cottage (sleeps 4) offers standard cooking and laundry facilities. Rates are $40–$45 (daily) and $185–$210 (weekly). Min booking 2 nights. Rates from $14 per night.

Crescent Head
Wombat Beach Resort, Pacific St. Tel: 02–6566 0121. Unit rates from $60–$85 (single) and $65–$110 (double) per night.

Bush 'n' Beach Retreat, 353 Loftus Rd. Tel: 02–6566 0235. B&B rates from $27–$67 (single) and $50–$75 (double), while a budget section offers rooms at $20 per person, per night.

Crescent Head Holiday Park, Pacific St. Tel: 02–6566 0261. Camping sites are $14–$21 daily. Park cabins are $40–$80 (daily) and $238–$532 (weekly).

Port Macquarie
Mercure Inn Sandcastle, 16-24 William St. Tel: 02–6583 3999. Facilities include cocktail bar, babysitting and licensed room service. Daily room rates are $120–$137.

Lighthouse Beach Caravan Park, Matthew Flinders Ave. Tel: 02–6582 0581. Most of the 115 sites are powered. Rates are $15–$19 (daily) and $90–$133 (weekly). Park cabins are $30–$55 (daily) and $210–$385 (weekly), while on-site vans are $29 per night.

Limeburners Lodge Motel, 139 Shoreline Dve via Settlement Point. Tel: 02–6583 3381. Owned by Nat Young's sister, Limeburners provides weary surfers with all the required facilities. Room rates are $16 (single) and $32 (double).

Port Macquarie Beachside Backpackers, 40 Church St. Tel: 02–6583 5512. Rates are $13 per person and include free use of bikes, boogie boards and surfboards.

Lindel Port Macquarie Backpackers, Tel: 02–6583 1791. Dorm, twin and doubles from $15 per person.

Lord Howe Island
Situated in the Pacific Ocean 500 km due east of Port Macquarie, World Heritage listed Lord Howe Island is home to vast colonies of sea birds, rare native birds and fish so tame you can hand feed them.

Pinetrees Resort, Units and cottages. Rates from $95–$145 (twin share).

Blue Lagoon, Tel: 02–6563 2006. Self-contained rooms from $80 per night.

Mary Challis Cottages, Tel: 02–6563 2076. Self-contained. Daily rates $65–$110.

Laurieton
Laurieton Gardens Caravan Resort, 478 Ocean Dve. Tel: 02–6559 9256. All of the 75 sites are powered, with daily rates around $12. Holiday units from $30–$40 and $145–$160 (weekly), while on-site vans are $22 (daily) and $110 (weekly).

The Haven Caravan Park, Arnott St. Tel: 02–6559 9584. Site rates from $11–$15 (daily) and $56–$70 (weekly).

Crowdy Head
Crowdy Head, 7 Geoffrey St. Tel: 02–6556 1206. Units from $50–$65 per night.

Old Bar Beach
Chiltern Lodge Country Retreat, 139 Metz Rd. Tel: 02–6553 3190. Cabins from $115 per night, sleep 4 people.

Old Bar Beach Caravan Park, Old Bar Beach. Tel: 02–6553 7274. Camp sites from $10–$14. Vans from $25–$38 or $125–$230 per week.

Diamond Beach
Albana Beach Resort, Lot 14 Diamond Beach Rd. Tel: 02–6559 2664. Units from $50 per night or $350–$980 per week.

Coastal Resort Caravan Park, Diamond Beach Rd. Tel: 02–6559 2719. Camp sites from $13–$16 per night. Cottages from $40–$82 per night or $270–$560 per week; cabins are $30–$72 per night or $200–$480 per week.

Diamond Beach Holiday Park, Jubilee Parade. Tel: 02–6559 2910. Camp sites from $12–$15 per night. Vans from $35–$55 per night.

Tuncurry

Tuncurry Motor Lodge, 132 Manning St. Tel: 02–6554 8885. Unit rates from $40–$60 (single) and $50–$70 (double) per night.

Shangri-La Caravan Park, South St. Tel: 02–6554 8522. Camping sites are $12–$19 (double, daily). The lodge section provides 20 rooms from $35–$60 (daily) and $192–$420 (weekly). On-site vans are $23 (daily) and $138–$266 (weekly); park cabins are $35–$60 daily.

Tuncurry Beach Caravan Park, Beach St. Tel: 02–6554 6440. Most of the 360 sites are powered and offer the usual camp facilities. Rates are $12–$18 (daily) and $70–$122 (weekly); park cabins are $25–$73 (daily) and $132–$260 (weekly).

Forster

Boronia Apartments, 105 Boomerang Drive, Boomerang Beach. Tel: 02–6554 2165. Apartments from $80 per night or $320–$360 per week.

Pacific Palms Resort, 2 Lakeside Cres, Pacific Palms. Tel: 02–6554 0300. Situated on the fringe of Booti Booti National Park and nestled between Wallis Lake and Elizabeth Beach. Pacific Palms offers 2 and 3 bedroom fully self contained villas. Offpeak rates are $99 (daily) and $594 (weekly).

Dolphin Lodge, 43 Head St, Forster. Tel: 02–6555 8155 or freecall 1800 807 766 (reservations only). Hostel is only 3 minutes from the main beach, bus terminal, shops and clubs. From $14 per person. Rates include free use of surfboards, bikes and fishing gear.

Tiona Park Caravan Park, The Lakes Way, Pacific Palms. Tel: 02–6554 0291. Rates per night are $14 (powered camping sites) and $32 (park cabins).

Forster Beach Caravan Park, Reserve Rd, Forster. Tel: 02–6554 6269. Most of the 283 sites are powered. Sites $12–$18 (daily) and $72–$126 (weekly); park cabins are $24–$58 (daily) and $144–$406 (weekly).

First National property hire have private beach holiday homes. Tel: 02–6554 0540.

Seal Rocks

Treachery Camp, Treachery Head. Tel: 02–4997 6138. Take your pick of cabins, $35 (double) or simple unpowered bush camping, $5 per person, per night.

Seal Rocks Camping Reserve, Kinka Rd. Tel: 02–4997 6164. Camping sites are $10–$12 while park cabins are around $30–$40 per night.

The Central Coast

Holiday mecca for jaded Sydney folks and home to a sizable local surf-mad population, the Central Coast offers heaps of great surfing locations.

Surf Shops

Anna Bay Surf and Sound, Shop 1, 150 Gan Gan Rd, Anna Bay. Tel: 02–4982 1790.

Heatwave Surfboards, 78 Del Mar Drive, Copacabana. Tel: 02–4382 3461.

Kaos Surf, Shop 40, Salamander Centre, Salamander Bay. Tel: 02–4982 0200.

Littles Surf Centre, Shop 266, Erina Fair, Erina. Tel: 02–4365 2944.

Mark Richards Surf Shop, 755 Hunter St Newcastle. Tel: 02–4961 3088.

Pacific Dreams, Shop 3, 17 Stockton St, Nelson Bay. Tel: 02–4984 2144. Also Darby St, Newcastle.

Shark Tower Surf Centre, Avoca Beach. Tel: 02–4382 1541.

Wave Signature Surfboards, Copacabana. Tel: 015 786 544.

Wizstix, 100B, The Esplanade, Terrigal. Tel: 02–4385 2087.

Accommodation

Anna Bay

The Retreat Port Stephens, 266 Nelson Bay Rd. Tel: 02–4982 1244. Cabin rates from $45–$65 (daily) and $150–$350 (weekly), while the lodge section sleeps up to 24, and is $10–$20 (daily) and $350–$700 (weekly).

One Mile Beach Caravan Park, Gan Gan Rd. Tel: 02–4982 1112. Situated on One Mile Beach. Camping rates from $14–$22 per night.

Park cabins are $40–$100 (double) and $240–$700 (weekly); on-site vans are $28–$45 (daily per person) and $168–$320 (weekly for a double).

Birubi Beach Caravan Park, James Patterson Rd. Tel: 02–4982 1263. Most of the 138 sites are powered, with daily rates around $15. The park's cabins cost $35–$45 (daily) and $170–$300 (weekly).

Island Caravan Park, Fenningam's Island. Tel: 02–4982 1207. Most of the 234 sites are powered. Sites are $14–$17 (daily) and $98–$119 (weekly).

Nelson Bay

Dutchies Motor Lodge, Dutchman's Beach. Tel: 02–4981 1644. Units from $50–$85 per night or weekly by negotiation.

Aloha Villa, 30 Shoal Bay Rd. Tel: 02–4981 2523. 11 units offering room service (breakfast), heated saltwater pool and shared spa. Rooms $45–$95 (single) and $50–$150 (double).

Newcastle

Merewether Beach B&B, 60 Hickson St, Merewether. Tel: 02–4963 3526. 300 m south of Merewether Beach. Daily B&B rates from $80 (single) and $95 (double) per night.

Beach Hotel, 99 Frederick St, Merewether. Tel: 02–4963 1574. Rooms serviced by on-site restaurant. Bed and light breakfast $35 (single) and $45 (double).

Stockton

Stockton Beach is a 4WD drive heaven, with over 30 km of beach and sand dunes to explore. Simply find an A-Frame peak and park the car. There's even the wreck of a Japanese trawler to surf off.

Stockton Beach Caravan Park, Pitt St. Tel: 02–4928 1393. Most of the 250 sites are powered and facilities include camp kitchen and kiosk. Site rates are $13–$15 (daily). Park cabins sleep 6 and cost $35–$70 (daily) and $330–$490 (weekly).

Swansea

Black Swan Waterfront, 137 Bowman St. Tel: 02–4971 1392. Water frontage motel units with private jetty. Rooms $45–$60 (single) and $50–$75 (double).

Swansea Gardens Tourist Park, Wallarah St. Tel: 02–4971 2869. Camping rates are $12–$16 (daily) and $69–$85 (weekly). On-site vans are $28–$42 (daily) and $145–$245 (weekly).

Sunset Strip Caravan Park, 68 Pacific Hwy. Tel: 02–4971 1165. Only 10 out of the 127 sites are powered. Daily rates are $12–$15 (camping), $40–$50 (park cabins), and $30–$38 (on-site vans).

Norah Head

Norah Head Tourist Park, Victoria St. Tel: 02–4396 3935. Camp sites from $12–$15 (daily) and $90–$125 (weekly). Cabins from $50–$80 per night or $300–$550 per week.

Forresters

Forresters Resort, 960 The Entrance Rd. Tel: 02–4384 1222. Units serviced by restaurant and room service (inc. liquor). Rooms $65–$125.

Terrigal

Clan Lakeside Lodge, 1 Ocean View Dve. Tel: 02–4384 1566. Beach frontage units offering cooking facilities and restaurant Monday to Saturday. Rooms $80–$135 and $110–$155 (suite).

Terrigal Beach, 1 Painter Lane. Tel: 02–4384 1423. Room rates from $40–$60 (single), $50–$70 (double) and $55–$75 (three people) per night.

Bellbird Caravan Park, 61-69 Terrigal Drive. Tel: 02–4384 1883. Camp sites from $16–$20 per night. Cabins from $60–$90 per night or $300–$630 per week; on-site vans from $45–$65 per night or $225–$455 per week.

Terrigal Beach Lodge, 12 Campbell Crescent. Tel: 02–4385 3330. Rooms from $16–$35 per night.

Avoca Beach

Avoca Beach Motor Inn, 360 Avoca Dve. Tel: 02–4382 2322. 36 air-conditioned units with room service, pool and tennis court facilities. Rooms $75–$95 (single), $80–$95 (double) and $570–$630 (weekly).

Avoca Lake Side, 9 Cape Three Points Rd. Tel: 02–4382 1693. 5 rooms with fireplace and tea-making facilities. Daily Bed and Breakfast rates are $50 (single) and $70 (double).

The Palms Avoca Village, Carolina Park Rd. Tel: 02–4382 1227. Camp sites from $15–$20 per night. Facilities include shared spa, pool, camp kitchen, and sauna. Camping rates from $15–$20 (daily) and $105–$140 (weekly). Park cabins are $70–$80 (daily) and $385–$770 (weekly).

Sydney's Northern Beaches

Home to a series of excellent beaches, the waves north of Sydney have been a breeding ground for two generations of devotees.

Surf Shops

Aloha Surf, 44 Pittwater Rd, Manly. Tel: 02–9977 3777. Greg Clough custom-shaped Aloha Surfboards and top brand surf gear.

Australian Surfer HQ, 221 Manly Wharf. Tel: 02–9976 2370. Also at Terrigal Beach.

Avalon Surf & Sports, 17 Avalon Pde, Avalon Beach. Tel: 02–9918 2820.

Beach Without Sand Surfshop, 1a North Avalon Rd, North Avalon. Tel: 02–9918 2763.

Cascade Surfboards, 10 Boondah Rd, Wariewood. Tel: 02–9997 2085.

CHP Surfboards, 79 Bassett Rd, Mona Vale. Tel: 02–9997 3352.

Division Surf, 8 Bungan Rd, Mona Vale. Tel: 02–9979 5334. Custom surfboards and top clothing range.

Dripping Wet Surf Co, 93 North Steyne Rd, Manly. Tel: 02–9977 3549.

Energy Surfboards, 4 Harkeith Rd, Mona Vale. Tel: 02–9997 2084.

Force 9 Surfboards, 43 Captain Cook Drive, Carringbah. Tel: 02–9526 1007.

Hot Buttered, 3 Vuko Place, Wariewood. Tel: 02–9970 8000.

Insight Surfboards, 4/76 Darley St, Mona Vale. Tel: 02–9997 8266.

Jackson Surfboards, 57 Captain Cook Drive, Carringbah. Tel: 02–9524 2700.

Justice Surfboards, 77 Basset Rd, Mona

Vale. Tel: 02–9999 1501.

Luke Howarth Surfboards, Unit 3, 63 Old Barrenjoy Rd, Avalon. Tel: 02–9918 0475.

Midget Farrelly Surfboards, 11 West St Bourkeville. Tel: 02–9938 3300.

Powerlinez Surf Shop, 16a Waterloo St, Narrabeen. Tel: 02–9913 2128.

Quiksilver Boardriders Surfshop, 303 Barrenjoy Rd, Newport Beach. Tel: 02–9997 8833.

Simon Anderson Surfboards, 76 Darley St, Mona Vale. Tel: 02–9979 7414. Custom surfboards from Simon Anderson, the Oz Surf Legend that invented the thruster.

Sunshine Surfing, 89 Pittwater Rd, Manly. Tel: 02–9977 4399. Top range of surfboards, hire and repairs. Run by former Oz Pro Surfer Kingsley Looker.

Surf Dive'n'Ski, Several outlets. Tel: 02 9387 2912.

Surfection, 651 Pittwater Rd, Dee Why. Tel: 02–9971 8144. Three stores located in Manly and Bondi Junction.

The Surf Company, 21 Warriewood Square, Warriewood. Tel: 02–9913 3956.

Vicious Circle Surfboards, 3c The Strand, Dee Why Beach. Tel: 018 868 500.

Wilderness Sea 'N' Ski, 868 Pittwater Rd, Dee Why. Tel: 02–9971 1100.

Universal Surfboards, 25 Suzanne Rd, Mona Vale. Tel: 02–9999 4385.

Accommodation

Palm Beach
Barrenjoey House, 1108 Barrenjoey Rd. Tel: 02–9974 4001. Rooms from $70–$130 per night.

Avalon
Avalon Beach B&B, 51 Riviera Avenue. Tel: 02–9918 7002. Rates from $80–$100 per night.

Newport
Newport Arms, Kalinya St. Tel: 02–9997 4900. Rooms from $65–$80 per night.

Mona Vale

Reef Resort, 8-12 Terrol Crescent. Tel: 02–9979 5764. Units from $450–$700 per week. Min booking 3 nights.

Narrabeen

Narrabeen Sands Hotel. 1260 Pittwater Rd. Tel: 02–9913 1166. Rooms from $70–$80 per night.

Lakeside Caravan Park, Lake Park Rd, North Narrabeen. Tel: 02–9913 7845. Camp sites from $19–$21 per night. Cabins from $67 per night or $368 per week, while villas are $77–$87 per night or $432–$532 per week.

Manly

Manly Surfside Holiday Apartments, 96 North Steyne. Tel: 02–9977 2299. 22 units (each sleep 6). Rates are $90–$300 (daily) and $220–$2000 (weekly).

The Sands, 114 North Steyne. Tel: 02–9977 5213. Beach frontage, self-contained units from $110–$189 (daily) and $660–$1323 (weekly). Min booking of 3 nights.

Manly Paradise, 54 North Steyne, cnr Raglan St. Tel: 02–9977 5799. Rooms from $79–$110 per night. Opposite the break at North Steyne.

Manly Seaview Motel, cnr Pacific St and Malvern Ave. Tel: 02–9977 1774. Only 100 m from Manly Beach and 500 m from North Steyne Surf Club. Room rates from $75–$99.

Steyne, 75 The Corso. Tel: 02–9977 4977. 37 rooms offering basic tea-making facilities. B&B rates $49–$90 (single), $74–$95 (double), and $280–$560 (weekly).

Sydney's Southern Beaches

Here you will find world-famous Bondi Beach and a few other gems to try your luck whilst having a bit of R&R in Australia's most vibrant city.

Surf Shops

Bondi Surf Co, Shop 2, 72-76 Campbell Parade, Bondi Beach. Tel: 02–9365 0870.

Cronulla Surf Design, 8 Cronulla. Tel: 02–9544 0433.

Emerald Surf City, 130 Cronulla Rd,

Cronulla. Tel: 02–9527 4149.

Gordon & Smith Surfboards, 155 Ewos Parade, Cronulla. Tel: 02–9523 0149.

Maroubra Underground Energy Surf, Shop 36 McKeon St, Maroubra. Tel: 02–9344 8022.

Pure Sea Surf Shop,108 Cronulla Rd, Cronulla. Tel: 02–9523 8664.

Surf Dive 'N' Ski, Level 3, 393 George St, Sydney. Tel: 02–9299 4920 (Head Office). Six stores located throughout the city and Bondi Junction.

Surfworld, 180 Campbell Parade, Bondi Beach. Tel: 02–9300 0055. Two other stores located in Coogee and Maroubra Junction.

Triple Bull Surf & Snowboards, 57 Elouera Rd, Cronulla. Tel: 02–9544 0354. Run by touring Oz Pro Surfer Richard Marsh.

Accommodation

Bondi, Bronte and Tamarama

Bondi Lodge Boutique Hotel, 63 Fletcher St, Tamarama Beach. Tel: 02–9365 2088. Rooms from $60–$90 per night.

Lamroch Hostel, 7 Lamroch Ave. Tel: 02–9365 0221. Dorm beds are $20 per night or $120 a week. Twin share rooms (2 single beds plus ensuite bathroom) are $60 a night and $360 per week.

Bondi, 178 Campbell Pde. Tel: 02–9130 3271. Rooms from $50 (single) and $75–$85 (double), while suites are $95–$130 (double) per night.

Thelellen Beach Inn, 2 Campbell Parade. Tel: 02–9597 7111. Rooms from $35–$57 per night.

Thelellen Lodge, 11a Consett Ave. Tel: 02–9130 5333. Room rates per night from $35–$37 (single) and $45–$49 (double).

Coogee

Coogee Sands Motor Inn, 161 Dolphin St. Tel: 02–9665 8588. Rooms from $85–$120 per night.

Coogee Bay, cnr Coogee Bay Rd and Arden St. Tel: 02–9665 0000. Rooms from $68–$125 per night.

Surfside Backpackers, 186 Arden St, Coogee. Tel: 02 9315 7888. Rooms from $18 per night.

Maroubra

Trade Winds Travel Inn, 200 Maroubra Rd. Tel: 02-9344 5555. Rooms from $99–$142 per night.

Sands, 32 Curtin Crescent. Tel: 02-9661 5953. Rooms from $65–$85 per night or $315–$450 per week.

Cronulla

Cronulla, cnr Kingsway and Elouera Rd. Tel: 02-9523 6866. Rooms from $45–$100 per night.

Karingal, 7 Elizabeth Place. Tel: 02-9322 1234. Units from $220–$800.

Cronulla Carapark, cnr Kingsway and Gannons Rd. Tel: 02-9523 4099. Vans from $50 per night or $250–$350 per week.

Royal National Park

Situated 50 km south of Sydney's city centre, the Royal National Park is said to be the second oldest national park in the world. Gateway to the many bays which meander towards Wollongong, the park's 20 km of coastline, stretching from Bundeena to Stanwell Park, offers a wide variety of beach, reef and point breaks. Choice locations such as Garies and Era Beach offer surfing seclusion and quality waves in a spectacular backdrop where coastal rainforest meets the sea.

Surf Shop

Magic Island Surfboards, 796 Lawrence Hargrave Drive, Coledale. Tel: 02-9548 2987.

Accommodation

Bundeena Caravan Park, 74 Scarborough St. Tel: 02-9523 9520. Most of the 34 sites are powered, with rates starting per night at $15–$17 (double) and weekly from $85–$119. Park cabins are $40–$55 per night (double) or weekly $190-350.

Garie Beach YA Hostel, Royal National Park. Booking enquiries, key payment and exchange to be made at YHA Central Reservations, 422 Kent St, Sydney. Tel: 02-9261 1111. The hostel is in a remote sheltered setting and therefore offers simple pleasures such as sink with pumped water and small gas rings - BYO everything else. There's no electricity, telephone or refrigeration, and showers are only available at Garie Beach carpark in the next valley. Rates around $7 per person, per night.

The South Coast

Miles and miles of wild surf-beaten beaches make the South Coast popular for those who wish to "get away from it all".

Surf Shops

Beach Scene Surf Shop, 1/136 Terralong St, Kiama. Tel: 02-4233 1189.

Bush Surf Co, Ulladulla. Tel: 02-4455 3155. Batemans Bay. Tel: 02-4472 6389.

Byrne Surfboards, 115 Princes Hwy, Fairy Meadow. Tel: 02-4226 1122.

Merimbula Surf Shop, Tel: 02-6495 1841.

Natural Necessities Surf Shop, 115 Fern St, Gerringong. Tel: 02-4234 1636.

Puckos Surf Shop, 98 Terralong St, Kiama. Tel: 02-4233 1177.

Richo Surfboards, Shop B, 6 Princess Hwy, Wollongong. Tel: 02-4283 7196.

Skipp Surfboards, 24 Flinders St, North Wollongong. Tel: 02-4228 8878.

Southern Man Surf Shop, Ulladulla. Tel: 02-4454 0343.

Wave Creation Surfboards, 31 Rowlinds Rd, Gerringong. Tel: 02-4234 1931.

Accommodation

Wollongong

Boat Harbour, 7 Campbell St. Tel: 02-4228 9166. Units from $84 per night.

Piccadily Motor Inn, 341 Crown St. Tel: 02-4226 4555. Rooms from $55 per night.

Bulli Beach Tourist Park, 1 Farrell Rd, Bulli. Tel: 02-4285 5677, Fax: 02-4285 5062. Cabins from $52 per night.

Shellharbour

Windradene Seaside Guest House, 29 Addison St. Tel: 02–4295 1317. Rooms from $50–$80 per night.

Ocean Beach, 2 Addison St. Tel: 02–4296 1399. Rooms from $35 per night.

Shellharbour Beachside Tourist Park, John St. Tel: 02–4295 1123. Beach frontage accommodation. Rates are $14–$25 (daily) and $80–$125 (weekly). Park cabins are $48–$105 (daily) and $330–$630 (weekly).

Kiama

Kiama Ocean View, 9 Bong Bong St. Tel: 02–4232 1966. Room rates from $40–$100 per night.

Kiama Beachfront, 87 Manning St. Tel: 02–4232 1533. Facilities include room service and restaurant. Room rates $42–$74.

Surfside Caravan Park, Bourrool St. Tel: 02–4232 1791. Camping rates are $14–$17 (daily) and $84–$119 (weekly), while park cabins are $48–$75 (daily) and $300–$525 (weekly).

Easts Van Park, Easts Beach, off South Kiama Dve. Tel: 02–4232 2124. Rates are $17–$21 (daily) and $102–$147 (weekly). Holiday units are $59–$121 (daily) and $295–$750 (weekly), while park cabins are $39–$109 (daily) and $220–$650 (weekly).

Kendalls Beach Caravan Park, Bonaira St. Tel: 02–4232 1790. Adjacent to beach. Site rates are $14–$17 (daily) and $72–$119 (weekly); On-site vans are $36–$60 (daily) and $220–$420 (weekly).

Gerringong

Beachview Resort Motel, Fern St. Tel: 02–4234 1359. Unit rates from $68–$128 per night.

Nesta House, Fern St, Gerringong. Tel: 02–4234 1249. Rooms from $13 per night.

Seven Mile Beach Caravan Park, Seven Mile Beach Rd. Tel: 02–4234 1340. Site rates $14–$17 (daily) and $72–$119 (weekly). On-site vans are $36–$60 (daily) and $220–$420 (weekly).

Ourie Park Caravan Park, Bridges Rd. Tel: 02–4234 1285. Most of the 310 sites are powered. Rates from $14–$17 (daily) and $72–$119 (weekly).

Sussex Inlet

Bentley Waterfront Motel and Restaurant, 164 River Rd. Tel: 02–4441 2052. Unit rates $50–$65 per night. Cottage section from $60–$100 (daily) and $295–$525 (weekly).

Alonga Waterfront, 166 River Rd. Tel: 02–4441 2046. Each cottage sleeps 4–8 and comes with cooking facilities. Boats also for hire. Rates $45–$80 (daily) and $240–$550 (weekly).

Badgee Caravan Park, 148 River Rd. Tel: 02–4441 2146. Water frontage accommodation. Site rates $16–$22 (daily) and $96–$154 (weekly). On-site vans from $30–$60 (daily) and $165–$385 (weekly).

Inlet Anchorage Caravan Park, 200 River Rd. Tel: 02–4441 2598. Camping sites are $12 (daily) and $60 (weekly), cottages are $40–$50, and on-site vans are $30–$50 per night.

Seacrest Caravan Park, Sussex Rd. Tel: 02–4441 2333. All 96 sites are powered, with facilities including private jetty. Rates from $10–$20 per night.

Bendalong

Berringer Lake Holiday, Berringer Rd. Tel: 02–6772 9691. Cabin rates are $50–$60 (daily) and $320–$450 (weekly).

Bendalong Tourist Park, Bendalong Rd. Tel: 02–4456 1167. Camping sites are $17–$25 (daily) and $102–$175 (weekly). Park cabins are $55–$120 (daily) and $370–$840 (weekly), while the cottage is $90–$160 (daily) and $550–$1120 (weekly).

Mollymook

Beachhouse Mollymook, 3 Golf Ave. Tel: 02–4455 1966. Beach frontage accommodation opposite golf course. A bed and light breakfast set-up is $58–$128 (single and double) per night.

Mollymook Surfbeach, 2 Shepherd St. Tel: 02–4455 3222. Unit rates from $60–$120 (single), $65–$130 (double), and $350–$1100 (weekly).

Mollymook Caravan Park, Princes Hwy. Tel: 02–4455 1939. Camping rates are $13–$18 per night and weekly $78–$126. Park cabins are daily $40–$80, and weekly $240–$560, while on-site vans are daily $30–$45 and weekly $180–$315.

Ulladulla
Beach Haven Holiday Resort, Princes Hwy. Tel: 02–4455 2110. All 243 sites of this beach frontage resort are powered. Camping sites are $14–$23 (daily) and $85–$158 (weekly). Park cabins are $32–$82 (daily) and $190–$573 (weekly), while on-site vans are $25–$78 (daily) and $151–$544 (weekly).

Ulludulla Tourist Park, South St. Tel: 02–4455 2457. Camping rates from $16–$24 (daily) and $96–$168 (weekly). Park cabins are $35–$120 (daily) and $190–$840 (weekly).

Seabreeze Tourist Village, cnr Campden and Princess Hwy. Tel: 02–4455 2348. Camp sites from $14–$18 per night and $80–$120 per week.

Lake Tabourie
Lake Tabourie Tourist Park, Princes Hwy. Tel: 02–4457 3011. Camping rates from $9–$24 (daily) and $54–$133 (weekly). Park cabins are $28–$110 (daily) and $168–$770 (weekly).

Wairo Beach Tourist Park, 425 Princes Hwy, Lake Tabourie. Tel: 02–4457 3035. Most of the 320 sites are powered and have access to camp kitchen, pool, tennis court and mini golf. Sites are $16–$22 (double); park cabins are $40–$120 (double) per night.

Bawley Point
Mimosa Hill Wildflowers, 96 Bawley Point Rd. Tel: 02–4457 1421. 2 cottages (each sleep 4). Cottage rates are $75–$110 per night.

Racecourse Beach Tourist Caravan Park, Murramarang Rd. Tel: 02–4457 1078. Most of the 305 sites are powered with facilities including mini golf, pool, tennis court and kiosk. Daily rates are $12–$23, park cabins are $33–$90.

Batemans Bay
The Beach House, 22 Myamba Pde. Tel: 02–4472 4086. Cottage rates from $70–$150 (daily) and $400–$950 (weekly). Min booking 2 nights.

Breakaway Lodge, 647 Beach Rd, Surf Beach. 12 beach frontage flats. Rates are $40–$90 (daily) and $240–$1200 (weekly).

Taliva Holiday Lodge, 236 Beach Rd, Batehaven. Tel: 02–4472 4904. Situated opposite beach with restaurant and solar heated pool. Rates from $30–$70 (daily) and $160–$560 (weekly).

Bay Surfside, 662 Beach Rd, Surf Beach. Tel: 02–4471 1275. Beach frontage flats from $39–$105 (daily) and $220–$715 (weekly).

Pleasurelea Caravan Park, 438 Beach Rd, Batehaven. Tel: 02–4472 4258. Camping rates are $15–$22 (daily) and $110–$150 (weekly); park cabins are $35–$100 (daily) and $200–$700 (weekly).

Clyde View Caravan Park, 107 Beach Rd. Tel: 02–4472 4224. Beach frontage accommodation. Rates are 13–$22 (daily) and $78–$154 (weekly); park cabins are $38–$90 (daily) and $220–$580 (weekly).

Broulee
Broulee Holiday Inn, 18 Imlay St. Tel: 02–4471 6266. Unit rates from $40–$80 (daily) and $250–$525 (weekly).

Caraluki, 8 Clarke St. Tel: 02–4471 6441. Flats from $38–$48 (daily) and $189–$510 (weekly).

Broulee Beach Caravan Park, Lyttle St. Tel: 02–4471 6247. Camping rates are $15 (daily) and $105 (weekly); park cabins are $47–$60 (daily) and $280–$350 (weekly).

Narooma
Narooma is located at the mouth of the Agonga Inlet. Local attractions include Montague Island where seals, penguins and whales can be seen during peak holiday times. Contact the Montague Island Visitor Information Centre on 02–4476 2881 for further info.

Island View Beach Resort, Princes Hwy. Tel: 02–4476 2600. Beach frontage accommodation. Camping sites are $14–$24 (daily) and $65–$168 (weekly); park cabins are $34–$135 (daily) and $120–$945 (weekly).

Bluewater Lodge YHA, 11-13 Riverside Dve. Tel: 02–4476 4440. Situated on the edge of the Wagonga Inlet and only minutes from the surf beach. Hostel rates are $15, plus a $2 surcharge per person.

Merimbula
Merimbula Park Cabins, Short Point Beach. Tel: 02–6495 1216. Beach frontage cabins from $175–$900 per week.

South Haven Caravan Park, Elizabeth St. Tel: 02–6495 1304. Adjacent to lake and beach, facilities include steam room, indoor heated pool and squash court. Camping sites are $16–$35 (daily) and $90–$215 (weekly); park cabins are $30–$85 (daily) and $150–$625 (weekly).

Wandarrah YHA Lodge, 8 Marine Pde. Tel: 02–6495 3503. Located 150 m from the surf beach, this hostel has 44 beds and 14 separate rooms. Daily rates are $15 per person.

Pambula Beach

Idlewilde Motor Inn, Princes Hwy. Tel: 02–6495 6844. 16 rooms with access to indoor heated pool. Rates are $39–$85 (single) and $49–$105 (double).

Royal Willows Hotel Motel, Princes Hwy. Tel: 02–6495 6005. B&B rates from $30–$50 per night.

Holiday Hub, Pambula Beach Rd. Tel: 02–6495 6363. Camping rates are $15–$30 (daily) and $96–$198 (weekly). Park cabins are $44–$88 (daily) and $264–$528 (weekly); on-site vans are $26–$66 (daily) and $156–$396 (weekly).

Eden

Great Southern, 158 Imlay St. Tel: 02–6496 1515. Hotel rooms from $20–$30 (single) and $40–$60 (double) per night.

Garden of Eden Caravan Park, Princes Hwy. Tel: 02–6496 1172. Camping rates are $14–$19 (daily) and $98–$133 (weekly), while park cabins are $26–$80 and $130–$560 (weekly).

Shadrack Resort Caravan Park, Princes Hwy. Tel: 02–6496 1651. Beach frontage accommodation where all 126 sites are powered. Camping sites from $15–$28 (daily) and $89–$96 (weekly), while park cabins are $40–$60 (daily) and $243–$660 (weekly).

Twofold Beach Caravan Park, Princes Hwy. Tel: 02–6496 1572 or 02–6496 1572. Camping rates are $13–$18 (daily) and $84–$126 (weekly). Park cabins are $31–$110 (daily) and $200–$750 (weekly); on-site vans are $26–$38 (daily) and $165–$266 weekly.

Saltwater

Check out the local camping grounds

Victoria

From Melbourne's vibrant nightlife to the cold and relentless swells of the Southern Ocean, Victoria is truly a hardcore surfing experience. Home to some of Australia's largest rideable waves, you'll have to brave cold water and some hair-raising shark stories before you even attempt to takeoff. But with world famous line-ups such as Bells Beach and Winkipop to choose from, it's not hard to motivate. As many hardy travellers will tell you, just the drive down Great Ocean Road can be the ride of a lifetime.

Getting There

Many overseas carriers provide regular flights into Melbourne International Airport. Dozens of daily Ansett and Qantas domestic flights from other state capitals also arrive at Melbourne Airport, which is located at Tullamarine, 22 km from the city centre.

Local Transport

The Met is Melbourne's public transport system, with trams, buses and suburban trains. Tickets are valid for all three transport modes, with a wide variety of passes available from stations and on trams and buses. Most services start around 5 am and finish about midnight. The burgundy and gold free City Circle trams pass many of the city's sites so take advantage of the tour (they run every 10 minutes from 10 am to 6 pm daily). For more information, phone the Met Information Centre on 13 16 38. Avis, Budget and Atlas are the main taxi providers who service metropolitan Melbourne.

Medical and Emergencies

Hospitals and medical centres are located in most of the larger towns in Victoria. For an emergency dial 000 and ask for the service you require, be it fire, police or ambulance.

General Surf Info

Surfrider Foundation Victoria. Tel: 03–9287 1475. Mornington Peninsula, Tel: 03–5986 3846. Phillip Island, Tel: 03–5952 2148.

Wave Rider, 10 Mohr St, Tullamarine. Tel: 03–9335 4950.

The following telephone information services are available when in the Melbourne area and cost roughly 75 cents per minute.

Local Weather, Tel: 1900 155 363

Surf Schools

Island Surfboard Surfschool, Phillip Island. Tel: 03–5952 3443.

Southern Juice Surfschool, South West districts. Tel: 03–5593 3190.

Surf Shack Surf School, East Gippsland. Tel: 03–5153 1330.

East Coast Surf School. Tel: 03–5989 2198.

Go Ride A Wave Surf School, Ocean Rd, Anglesea. Tel: 03–5263 2111. Lessons at Lorne and Torquay from November to Easter.

West Coast Surf School, Torquay. Tel: 03–5261 2241. Lessons at Ocean Grove and Torquay.

Melbourne Metro

"Grid City" has its surf enthusiasts who can be found at many near-city locations testing the waves at any time of the year.

Surf Shops

Bacbeech Surf Shop, Blackburn Square, Berwick. Tel: 03–9796 1634.

Box Hill Skate, Ski and Surf, 693 Station St, Box Hill. Tel: 03–9897 4200.

Bumps Ski and Surf, 465 Glenhuntly Rd, Elsternwick. Tel: 03–9528 2701.

Chirnside Park Sea 'n' Snow, Shop 620, Chirnside Shopping Center, Chirnside Park. Tel: 03–9726 7999.

City Surf and Snow, 30 Bridge Rd, Richmond. Tel: 03–9428 5603.

GenX Surfing Australia, Shop 24 Dandenong Plaza, Dandenong. Tel: 03–9792 0955.

Invert Surf 'n' Skate, 61 Church St, Bentleigh. Tel: 03–9593 1765.

The Jetty Surf Shop, Chadstone. Tel: 03–9569 0267. Seven stores throughout Fountain Gate, Glen Waverley, Greensborough, Maribyrnong, Ringwood and Broadmeadows.

Ozmosis Surf, Quayside Shopping Centre, Frankston. Tel: 03–9781 2930.

Pro Ski and Surf, 656 Glenferrie Rd, Hawthorn. Tel: 03–9818 0257.

Repeat Performance Surf, 87 Ormond Rd, Elwood. Tel: 03–9525 6475.

Ringwood Surf and Sail, 134 Maroondah Hwy, Ringwood. Tel: 03–9870 6378.

Rip Curl, Shop 11, Melbourne Airport, Sky Plaza. Tel: 03–9330 3591.

Sea Level, 411 Hampton Rd, Hampton. Tel: 03–9598 0716.

Snapper Head Surf Shop, Shop 21, Karingal Hub Shopping Centre, Frankston. Tel: 03–9776 7501.

Surf Dive 'n' Ski, 213 Bourke St, Melbourne. Tel: 03–9650 1039. Other stores in South Yarra, Knox City, Southland and Doncaster.

Surf Headquarters, Shop 47, Waverley Gardens Shopping Centre, Mulgrave. Tel: 03–9546 4422.

Surfworks, Shop D3, Northlands Shopping Centre, Northlands. Tel: 03–9471 0199.

Tsunami Surf, 16a Werribee Plaza Shopping Centre, Werribee. Tel: 03–9748 0048.

Victoria Surf, 115 Victoria St, West Melbourne. Tel: 03–9329 8787.

Wooz Surf and Street Wear, Shop 96 Epping Plaza, Epping. Tel: 03–9408 9388.

Accommodation

Melbourne International Hostel, 78 Horward St, Nth. Melbourne. Tel: 03–9329 8599. Rooms from $13–$55 per night.

Chapman Gardens YHA, 76 Chapman St, North Melbourne. Tel: 03–9328 3595. Rooms from $15–$44 per night.

East Coast

Surf Shops

Red Bluff Surf Shop, 5/31 Esplanade Lakes Entrance. Tel: 03–5155 2788. Repairs available.

Surf Shack Surf Shop, 503 The Esplanade, Lakes Entrance. Tel: 03–5155 4933.

Accommodation

Mallacoota
Silver Bream Motel Suites and Flats, 32 Maurice Avenue. Tel: 03–5158 0455. Rooms from $38–$85 per night. Holiday flats from $40–$100 per night or $300–$600 per week. Sleep up to 5 people.

Mallacoota's Shady Gully Caravan Park, Lot 5 Genoa Rd. Tel: 03–5158 0362. Camp sites $10–$16 per night. Cabins from $40–$50 per night. On-site vans from $25–$36 per night.

Beachcomber Caravan Park, 85 Betka Rd. Tel: 03–5158 0233. Camp sites from $10–$17. Cabins $30–$55. On-site vans from $22–$45.

Wilderness Lodge, Maurice Ave. Tel: 03–5158 0455. Daily room rates from $13–$15 per person.

Lakes Entrance
George Bass Motor Inn, 607 Esplanade, Princess Hwy. Tel: 03–5155 1611. Rooms from

$56–$120 per night.

Hybiscus Lodge, 132 Marine Pde. Tel: 03–5155 1768. Flats from $35–$95 per night or $220–$580 per week, sleep up to 5 people.

Echo Beach Caravan Park, 33 Roadknight St. Tel: 03–5155 2238.

Camp sites from $13–$23. Holiday flats from $38–$85, sleep up to 5 people. Cabins from $28–$75, sleep up to 6 people.

Koonwarra Caravan Park, 687 Esplanade, Princess Hwy. Tel: 03–5155 1222. Camp sites from $14–$25. Cabins from $40–$75, sleep up to 4 people. Holiday Flats from $43–$95, sleep up to 8 people.

Surfside Park, 38 Roadknight St. Tel: 03–5155 1792. Camp sites from $15–$25.

Fraser Island Resort Lodge, PO Box 202, Lakes Entrance. Tel: 03–5156 3256. Rooms from $25–$69 (daily) or $196–$414 (weekly).

Riviera Backpackers, 3 Clarkes Rd. Tel: 03–5155 2444. Daily room rates from $13 per person.

Wilsons Promontory

A bushwalkers paradise, Wilsons Promontory National Park boasts superb bushland scenery, with great surfing and diving. Located 140 km from Melbourne, The Prom was declared a National Park as early as 1908 and remains a marine wonder. Charter boats which run from Port Albert, Port Welshpool and Port Franklin will help you get there. Wilsons Promontory National Park Daily Visitor Fees: Motorcycles, $2; Cars, $6; Small Bus, $24.

Accommodation

Yanakie Caravan Park, Foley Rd. Tel: 03–5687 1295. Camping sites have access to boat ramp and parking. Daily rates are $14 (double). Park cabins that sleep 6 are $40–$70 per night.

Shallow Inlet Caravan Park, Lester Rd, via Foster. Tel: 03–5687 1385. All 60 sites are powered and offer standard facilities. Camp sites daily are $13 (double). Park Cabins (8, which each sleep 6) are $40–$50 daily per double.

Tidal River Area, Tidal River. Tel: 03–5680 9555. Camp sites from $13 per night. Cabins that sleep 6, from $90–$100 (daily) and $540–$600 (weekly). Holiday Flats that sleep 4 are from $45–$71 to $70–$102, while motor huts cost from $36–$58 (daily) and $252–$378 (weekly). Lighthouse Cottage rates from $15–$30 per night in bunkhouses sleeping up to 12.

The Little Mud Hut Foster, 17 Pioneer St, Foster. Tel: 03–5682 2614. Rooms from $15 per night.

Inverloch

The Reefs Apartments, 20 William St. Tel: 03–5674 3514. $110–$130 per night or $550–$750 per week; sleep up to 6 people.

South Kolora, Kongwak Rd. Tel: 03–5674 1305. $60–$70 per night or $300–$350 per week; sleep up to 8 people.

Broadbeach Caravan Park, cnr The Esplanade and Cuttriss St. Tel: 03–5674 1447. Camp sites $14–$18. Cabins from $40; sleep up to 5.

Sand Castle Cabin Park, 14 Cuttriss St. Tel: 03–5674 2203. Cabins from $30–$38 per night; sleep up to 5.

Inverloch Foreshore Reserve, cnr The Esplanade and Ramsay Boulevard. Tel: 03–5674 1236. Camp sites from $14–$17 per night.

Sandy Point

Iluka Holiday Cottages, cnr Manuka and Anderson Sts. Tel: 03–5684 1318. Cottages sleep up to 6, from $75 per night or $315–$560 per week.

Telopea Caravan Park, Beach Pde. Tel: 03–5684 1312. Powered sites from $14. Cabins from $32, sleep up to 4 people. On-site vans from $32, sleep up to 7 people.

Kilcundra

Kilcunda Caravan Park, Bass Hwy. Tel: 03–5678 7260. Camp sites from $10–$15. Cabins from $40–$45, sleep up to 6 people. On-site vans from $30–$35, sleep up to 4 people.

Powlett River Caravan Park, Powlett River Rd North. Tel: 03–5678 7520. Camping sites from $10–$13. On-site vans from $25–$35, sleep up to 2.

Phillip Island

Popular with surfers, not to mention the ubiquitous penguins, Phillip Island attracts surfers out for some top waves.

Surf Shops

Full Circle, 4 Vista Place, Cape Woolamai. Tel: 03–5956 7453.

Island Surfboards, 147 Thomson Avenue, Cowes. Tel: 03–5952 2578. Also at 65 Smiths Beach Rd, Smiths Beach. Tel: 03–5952 3443.

Islantis Surfer Supplies, 12 Phillip Island Rd, Newhaven. Tel: 03–5956 7553.

Accommodation

First Class Bed and Breakfast, Ventnor/Nobbies Rd, Ventnor. Tel: 03–5956 8329 or 018 389 284. Daily B&B rates from $60–$100. Close to the waves at Cat Bay and Flynn's Reef.

Sea Breeze, 40 Forest Avenue. Tel: 03–5956 7387. Holiday flats sleep up to 5, from $60–$90 (daily) and $280–$630 (weekly). Close to the waves at Woolamai Beach and Express Point.

Newhaven Caravan Park, Phillip Island Rd. Tel: 03–5956 7227. Daily camp site rates from $11–$16. Cabins from $35–$60, sleep up to 5 people. On-site vans from $27–$42, sleep up to 4.

St Pauls Discovery Centre, Forrest Avenue, Newhaven. Tel: 03–5956 7202. Daily room rates from $16–$31 per person.

Amaroo Park YHA, 97 Church St, Cowes. Tel: 03–5952 2548. Room rates from $10–$16 per night.

Mornington Peninsula

Surf Shops

Balin Surfboards, 2197 Point Nepean Rd. Tel : 03–5985 5676.

Impact Zone Surf Centre, 168 Main St, Mornington. Tel: 03–5976 2430.

Mordy Surf and Sail, cnr Nepean Hwy and Beach Rd, Mordialloc. Tel: 03–9580 1716.

Peninsula Surf Centre, 835 Nepean Hwy, Mornington. Tel: 03–5975 1800. Two other stores at Rye and Frankston.

Trigger Brothers Surf, 3297 Nepean Hwy, Sorrento. Tel: 03–5984 4401.

Accommodation

Portsea
Clifton Lodge, Great Ocean Rd. Tel: 03–5598 8128. Cottages from $50–$85 per night or $250–$540 per week.

The Portsea Camp, 3704 Nepean Rd. Tel: 03–5984 2333. Shared rooms from $30–$70.

Portsea Caravan Park, 70 Back Beach Rd. Tel: 03–5984 2725. Camp sites from $18–$25. On-site vans from $35–$50, sleep up to 4 people.

Sorrento
Rose Caravan Park, Melbourne Rd. Tel: 03–5984 2745. Camp sites from $15–$25 per night. Cabins from $40–$60, sleep up to 5 people. On-site vans from $35–$50, sleep up to 4 people.

Sorrento Foreshore Reserve, Tel: 03–5984 2797. Daily site rates from $10–$15. Contact the ranger.

Bells Environmental Youth Hostel, 3 Miranda St. Tel: 03–5984 4323. Daily room rates from $12 per person.

Rye
Kanasta Caravan Park, 9 Sinclair Avenue. Tel: 03–5985 2638. Camp sites from $15–$25. On-site vans from $28–$55, sleep up to 6 people.

Rye Foreshore Reserve, Tel: 03–5985 2405. Camp sites from $10–$15.

Moonlight Bay Resort, 4 Napier St. Tel: 03–5985 7499. One studio and seven, 1-2 bedroom apartments (sleep 6) $60–$165 daily and $550–$1120 weekly. Includes access to shared spa, solar heated pool and BBQ.

Torquay Coast

Surf Shops

Anglesea Surf Centre, 111 Great Ocean Rd. Tel: 03–5263 1530. Repairs and hire available.

Full Bore, Factory 6, Baines Crescent, Torquay. Tel: 03–5261 3312.

Lorne Surf Shop, 130 Mountjoy Parade, Lorne. Tel: 03–5289 1673.

Mocean Surf Shop, 55 Mountjoy Parade, Lorne. Tel: 03–5289 1011.

Quiksilver Retail Shop, Surfcoast Plaza, Torquay. Tel: 03–5261 4768.

Surf Report Available:
Sharkies Surf Shop, Shop 12, The Cumberland Resort, Lorne. Tel: 03–5289 2421.

Strapper, 106 Surf Coast Hwy Torquay,Tel: 03–5261 2312.

Surf and Fish, 73 Great Ocean Rd, Apollo Bay. Tel: 03–5237 6426.

Accommodation

Torquay
Bernell Caravan Park, Surfcoast Hwy. Tel: 03–5261 2493. Daily rates include $15–$27 (camp sites) and $39–$83 (cabins).

Jan Juc Park, Sunset Strip. Tel: 03–5261 2932. Camp sites from $14–$18 per night. Cabins from $45–$55 per night, sleep up to 6 people.

Torquay Public Reserve, Bell St. Tel: 03–5261 2496. Camp sites from $17–$26 per night. Cabins range from $46–$85 per night and sleep up to 4 people.

Surfcoast Retreat, RMB 1053 Aquarius Ave. Tel: 03–5261 3025. One, 2-bedroom unit (sleeps 6) costs $50–$60 daily for a double, or $240–$360 weekly. Min bookings required at peak times.

Anglesea
Surfcoast Resort Anglesea, 105 Great Ocean Rd. Tel: 03–5263 3363. Apartments from $110–$145; cabins from $80–$105; each sleeps up to 8 people.

Roadknight Cottages, 26 Great Ocean Rd. Tel: 03–5263 1820. Cottages from $85–$130 per night or $520–$880 per week, sleep up to 6 people.

Driftwood Park, 45 Murray St. Tel: 03–5263 1640. Camp sites from $13–$17 per night. Cabins from $40–$57 per night, sleep to 6 people.

Anglesea Family Caravan Park, Cameron Rd. Tel: 03–5263 1583. Camping sites from $15–$23. Cabins from $45–$75 per night, sleep up to 5 people.

Lorne
Lorne Main Beach Motor Inn, 3 Bay St. Tel: 03–5289 1199. Daily unit rates from $110–$200.

Lorne Chalet, 4 Smith St. Tel: 03–5289 1241. 36 rooms serviced by restaurant (BYO). Daily rates including all meals are $77–$98 (single) and $343–$686 (weekly).

Kalimna, Mountjoy Parade, Tel: 03–5289 1407. 25 units offering standard amenities including fax, pool and tennis court. Rooms per night $64–$80 (single), and $74–$120 (double).

Great Ocean Road Backpackers YHA, 10 Erskine Avenue, Lorne. Tel: 03–5289 1809. Rooms from $15–$23 per night.

Apollo Bay
Seafarers Motel Lodge, Great Ocean Rd. Tel: 03–5237 6507. Units from $90–$115 per night or $600–$930 per week, sleep up to 5 people.

Pisces Caravan Park, Great Ocean Rd. Tel: 03–5237 6749. All 105 sites are powered and include access to TV room, sheltered BBQ and restaurant. Site rates from $15–$28 per night. 13 ensuite park cabins (sleep 5) $48–$75 per night, and standard park cabins (sleep 4) $38–$65 per night.

Recreation Reserve Caravan Park, Great Ocean Rd. Tel: 03–5237 6577. Most of the 160 sites are powered and cost from $12–$20 per night.

Waratah Caravan Park, 7 Noel St. Tel: 03–5237 6562. Camping sites from $14–$26. Cabins from $36–$75 per night, sleep up to 6 people.

Surfside Backpackers, cnr Great Ocean Rd and Gambier Streets. Tel: 03–5237 7263. Rooms from $15 per night.

West Coast

Surf Shops

Port Campbell Trading Co, 27 Lord St, Port Campbell. Tel: 03–5598 6444.

Southern Guns Surf Shop, 174-176 Liebig St, Warrnambool. Tel: 03–5562 0928.

Southern Juice Surf Shop, Port Campbell. Tel: 03–5593 3190 or 041 756 4709.

Warrnambool Surf Centre, 100 Liebig St, Warrnambool. Tel: 03–5562 1981.

Accommodation

Cape Otway
Bimbi Park, Otway Lighthouse Rd. Tel: 03–5237 9246. Daily site rates from $10–$17. Cabins sleep 4 from $65–$75, and units sleep 4 from $65–$75.

Cape Otway Cottages, 615 Hordern Vale Rd. Tel: 03–5237 9256. This 58 ha property has self-contained studio and apartment. Rates per double are $75–$115 (daily), or $595–$770 (weekly). Min booking 2 nights.

Lavers Hill
Lavers Hill Roadhouse, Great Ocean Rd. Tel: 03–5237 3251. Limited facilites with these 7 powered sites. Includes restaurant and access to servo facilities. Rates per double are $12 (daily), on-site vans from $34 per night, while the bunkhouse (sleeps 13) costs $20 per person.

Princeton
Apostles View Motel and Country Retreat, RMB 1435 Booringa Rd, off Great Ocean Rd (turnoff opp. Twelve Apostles). Tel: 03–5598 8277. 10 units offering fax facilities, heated indoor pool, and dinner delivered to unit. Daily rates from $50–$90 (single) and $60–$90 (double).

Clifton Lodge, Great Ocean Rd. Tel: 03–5598 8128. Self-contained cottages sleep 6. Breakfast by arrangement. Rates from $50–$85 (daily) and $250–$540 (weekly) .

Kangaroobie, Old Ocean Rd. Tel: 03–5598 8151. Farm lodge accommodation offering 14 bunk rooms (BYO linen) with recreation room and shared cooking facilities. Rates per person include all meals and assorted farm activites. Rates from $35 (daily) and $140 (weekly).

Port Campbell
Port Campbell Motor Inn, 12 Great Ocean Rd. Tel: 03–5598 6222. 16 units with standard facilities. Daily rates $65–$95 (single) and $75–$95 (double).

Port Campbell Bed and Breakfast, Timboon, Port Campbell Rd. Tel: 03–5598 6260. A 35 ha cattle grazing, non-smoking property offering cooking facilities, TV and CD player. B&B $40–$60 (single) and $80–$100 (double).

Port Campbell YHA Hostel, 18 Tregea St, Port Campbell. Tel: 03–5598 6305. Daily room rates from $10–$12 per person.

Portsea
The Portsea Camp, 3704 Nepean Hwy. Tel: 03–5984 2333. Self-contained bunk rooms sleep 6 from $30–$70 (4 person rate) per night.

Peterborough
Peterborough Motel, 9 Irvine St. Tel: 03–5598 5251. 12 units serviced by restaurant, heated pool and shared spa. Rooms $50–$70 (single) and $55–$80 (double).

Great Ocean Rd Tourist Park, Great Ocean Rd. Tel: 03–5598 5477. All 86 sites are powered. Daily sites per double are $12–$16. On-site cabins sleep 6, from $40–$70 per night.

Peterborough Coastal Caravan Park, MacGillivray Rd, off Great Ocean Rd. Tel: 03–5598 5294. All 36 sites are powered and cost $12–$16 daily per double.

Port Fairy
Eastern Beach, cnr Griffith St and Bourne Avenue. Tel: 03–5568 1117. Flats from $45–$85 per night or $280–$620 per week, sleep up to 4 people.

Royal Oak Hotel Port Fairy, 9 Bank St. Tel: 03–5568 1018. Rooms from $20–$65.

Port Fairy Gardens Caravan Park, 111 Griffith St. Tel: 03–5568 1060, Fax: 03–5568 2576. Situated 200 m from East Beach and on the historic Moyne Rive. Most of the 130 sites are powered. Facilities include tennis court, mini golf, kiosk, TV for hire and pool. Daily double rates for sites are $16–$22, 16 park cabins (sleep 7) are $37–$80, and 5 on-site vans (sleep 6) are $30–$48.

Port Fairy Youth Hostel YHA, 8 Cox St. Tel: 03–5568 2468. Rooms from $12–$15 per night. Shared units also available from $12–$15.

Tasmania

Australia's smallest state, The Apple Isle has some impressive credentials including the nation's deepest natural freshwater lake (Lake St Clair); Australia's oldest brewery (Cascade) and lays enviable claim to the world's cleanest air. Last stop before the icey wastelands of Antarctica, Tasmania is blessed with large tracts of World Heritage wilderness and empty lineups in forgotten bays. Don't be deceived by this small land mass; the surfing and adventure activities are as diverse as the spectacular topography.

Getting There

Visitors flying to Tasmania can arrive via one of four airports, be it Hobart in the south, or Launceston, Devonport or Wynyard in the north. Qantas and Ansett fly regularly to Tasmania from all major Australian cities, anddirect flights are available from New Zealand as well.

Local Transport

Tasair provides regular passenger services between Hobart and Devonport. For flight details phone 03-6248 5577. AusAir specialises in the North coast, Bass Strait and Moorabbin (freecall: 1800 331 256). TigerLINE is Tasmania's statewide coach service which offers day and half day tours from Hobart (Tel: 03-6234 4077). Tasmanian Redline Coaches (Tel: 03-6231 3233) and Ace Coaches (Tel: 03-6272 4833) also provide charter services and tours throughout the region. Metro Hobart manages all local transport services. For timetable enquiries call 13 2202. Travelling around Tasmania is easiest by car. If you haven't brought your own car on the ferry, AutoRent Hertz, Avis Car Rentals, Budget Rent-A-Car and Thrifty Car Rentals are available at the airport and in most towns. RACT (Royal Automobile Club Tasmania) is the state's roadside service provider.

Medical and Emergencies

Hospitals and medical centres are located in most of the larger towns in Tasmania. For an emergency dial 000 and ask for the service you require, be it fire, police or ambulance.

National Parks

Some of the world's last remaining ancient wilderness lies protected within Tasmania's National Park areas, including the state's World Heritage Area which encompasses 1.4 million hectares of wild rivers, mountains, forests and plateaus. A variety of passes are available which give you access to these wilderness areas, such as the annual pass which covers all 14 of Tasmania's national parks. The cost is roughly $42. For further info contact the Tasmania Parks & Wildlife Service on 03-6233 6191.

General Surf Info

Surfrider Foundation Tasmania, Tel: 03-6435 2414 or 03-6229 8398.

In Tasmania you can camp just about anywhere free of charge, so if the weather is accommodating take advantage of some truly spectacular camping locations in some of the most pristine national parks to be found anywhere in Australia. However, the general rule of thumb in Tassie is whatever the season, always be prepared for unexpected changes in weather. If you like keeping on the move and having a mobile home, an ideal way to explore Tasmania's surf hotspots is by Campervan; some operators are listed below:

Tasmanian Campervans, 139 Cremorne Avenue, Cremorne. Tel: 03-6248 9623.

Tasmanian Campervans, 122 Harrington St, Hobart. Tel: 03-6237 1111.

Koala Campers, 115 Kennedy Drive, Cambridge. Tel: 03–6248 5155.

Freedom Touring, Hobart. Tel: 03–6248 1024.

Bargain Car Rentals, 173 Harrington St, Hobart. Tel: 03–6234 6161.

Local Weather, Tel: 1900 155 364

Surf School

Surfing Tasmania Surfschools, Hobart and regional. Tel: 03–6431 1422.

The North Coast

Surf Shops

Beach Beat Surf Shop, 34 King Edward St, Ulverstone. Tel: 03–6425 4438.

Canoe and Surf, 144 William St, Devonport. Tel: 03–6424 4314.

Accommodation

Ulverstone
The Lighthouse, 33 Victoria St. Tel: 03–6425 1197. Hotel with 29 rooms serviced by restaurant and facilities including shared spa, sauna and gym. $47–$80 for bed and light breakfast.

Willaway Apartments, 2 Tucker St. Tel: 03–6425 2018. Self-contained, 2 bedroom units. Rates from $45–$70 (daily) and $315–$380 (weekly).

Apex Caravan Park, Queen St, West Ulverstone. Tel: 03–6425 2935. Water frontage accommodation offering camp kitchen and boat parking. Rates from $12 (daily) and $60 (weekly).

Ulverstone Caravan Park, Water St. Tel: 03–6425 2624. Water frontage. Camping site rates are $11 (daily) and $70 (weekly). Holiday units are $54 (daily) and $243 (weekly), while park cabins are $43 (daily) and $216 (weekly).

Devonport
The largest town on the northern coastline, Devonport is nestled between the Mersey and Forth Rivers.

Mersey Bluff Lodge, 247 William St. Tel: 03–6424 5289. Self-contained units. Daily room rates are $60–$70.

Mersey Bluff Caravan Park, Mersey Bluff. Tel: 03–6424 8655. Water frontage accommodation where most of the 126 sites are powered. Rates are $15 (daily) and $80 (weekly). Cabins sleep 6 from $48 (daily) and $60 (weekly), while on-site vans are $38 (daily) and $220 (weekly).

MacWright House Youth Hostel, 155 Middle Rd. Tel: 03–6424 5696. Room rates from $9–$11 per night.

Tasman House Backpackers, 169 Steele St. Tel: 03–6423 2335. Daily room rates from $8–$10.

Launceston
Windmill Hill Tourist Lodge, 22 High St. Tel: 03–6331 9337. Heritage building offering standard facilities. Rates from $60 per room. Holiday units (sleep 4) from $65 per night.

Treasure Island Caravan Park, 94 Glen Dhu St, South Launceston. Tel: 03–6344 2600. Most of the 155 sites are powered. Camping sites from $13–$15 (daily) and $84–$105 (weekly); park cabins are $48–$52 (daily) and $303–$328 (weekly); on-site vans (sleep 6) from $32 (daily) and $224 (weekly).

Launceston City Youth Hostel, 36 Thistle St, South Launceston. Tel: 03–6344 9779. 14 dorm rooms with tea-making facilities. Rates from $12 per night.

Launceston City Backpackers, 173 George St. Tel: 03–6334 2327. Rates from $14 per night.

Hawley Beach
Hawley House, Esplanade. Tel: 03–6428 6221. Heritage building offering cooking facilities. B&B rates from $90–$130 per night.

Hawley Beach Court Villas, 16 Dumbleton St. Tel: 03–6428 6744. Self-contained units. Rates $27–$55.

Green Beach
Greens Beach Caravan Park, Tel: 03–6383 9222. Water frontage accommodation where most of the 55 sites are powered. Rates are $6–$11 (daily) and $55–$65 (weekly).

The East Coast

Surf Shops

Redbill Surf Shop, 41a Foster St, Bicheno. Tel: 03– 6375 1717.

Scamander Beach Surf Shop, 6 Lagoon Esplanade, Scamander. Tel: 03–6372 5529.

Accommodation

Binalong Bay

Binalong Bay Character Cottages, Main Rd, St Helens. Tel: 03–6376 8262. Units sleep 6–8 for $50–$60 per night.

St Helens

Bayside Inn, 2 Cecilia St. Tel: 03–6376 1466. 27 rooms serviced by restaurant. Room rates from $65–$105 per night.

Cockle Cove Beachfront, 234 St Helens Point. Tel: 03–6376 3036. Apartments sleep 3–4 from $45–$60 per night.

Kellraine, 72 Tully St. Tel: 03–6376 1169. Units sleep 2-6 for $30-35 per night, $180–$220 per week.

St Helens Caravan Park, Penelope St. Tel: 03–6376 1290. Most of the 100 sites are powered. Daily rates are $14–$18 for camping, while on-site vans are $35.

St Helens YHA Lodge, 5 Cameron St. Tel: 03–6376 1661. Room rates from $11–$13 per night.

Scamander Beach

Blue Seas Holiday Villas, Wattle Drive. Tel: 03–6372 5211. Units sleep 2–6 from $45–$85 per night.

Surfside, Tasman Hwy. Beach frontage. Tel: 03–6372 5177. Rooms from $42–$58 per night.

Kookaburra Caravan Park, 70-78 Scamander Avenue. Tel: 03–6372 5121. Camp sites from $8–$10 or $70 per week. Vans from $25 for 2 people per night or $175 per week.

Falmouth

Cray Drop-In, Iron House Point. Tel: 03–6372 2228. Self-contained units (sleep 10) with access to fully licensed restaurant and bar, swimming pool, shared spa and golf course. Rates are $50–$60 (daily) and $300–$360 (weekly).

Bicheno

The Silver Sands Resort, Burgess St, Safety Beach. Tel: 03–6375 1266. Rooms from $45–$70 per night.

Diamond Island Resort, Tasman Hwy, Red Bill Beach. Tel: 03–6375 1161. Rooms from $60–$120 per night.

Camp Seaview, 29 Banksia St. Tel: 03–6375 1247. Cabins sleep 4–8 from $25–$45 per night. Bunkhouse with shared cooking facilities, $13 per night.

Bicheno Caravan Park, 52 Burgess St, Bicheno. Tel: 03–6375 1117. Camp sites from $10 (daily) and $70 (weekly). Vans from $25–$30 per night or $150–$200 per week, sleep up to 4 people.

Redbill Point Caravan Park, West Arm Rd, Beauty Point. Tel: 03–6383 4536. Camp Sites from $11–$14 for 2 people. Cabins from $50 per night. Ensuite vans from $40 per night and regular caravans from $30 per night. All rates for 2 people.

Bicheno Youth Hostel, Tasman Hwy. Tel: 03–6375 1293. Sleeps 8-10 from $10–$12 per person, per night.

Coles Bay/Freycinet National Park

Freycinet Lodge, Tel: 03–6257 0101. 60 cabins (sleep 2-6) serviced by restaurant. Daily room rates $130–$160.

Churinga Farm Cottages, Coles Bay Rd, Coles Bay. Tel: 03–6257 0190. 55 ha farm and bushland property with self-contained cottages (sleep 2–5). Rates $55 (single), $70 (double) and $420 (weekly).

Iluka Holiday Centre, Esplanade, Coles Bay. Tel: 03–6257 0115. Half of the 60 sites are powered. Daily rates are $12, while on-site vans are $30. Holiday units (sleep 6) from $80.

Freycinet National Park, Tel: 03–6257 0107. Water frontage camping ground. Sites from $12 (daily) and $84 (weekly).

Freycinet Backpackers, Tel: 03–6257 0100. Beach frontage lodge with shared cooking facilities. Room rates $14 per person per night.

Swansea

Swansea Cottages, 43 Franklin St. Tel: 03–6257 8328 or 018 137 499. Self-contained cottages which sleep 7–9. Rates $95–$140 (daily) and $480–$840 (weekly).

Kabuki by the Sea, 'Rocky Hills' Tasman Hwy. Tel: 03–6257 8588. Self-contained cottages (sleep 3). Rates are $95–$120.

Swansea Caravan Park and Holiday Village, Shaw St, Swansea. Tel: 03–6257 8177. Most of the 125 sites are powered. Rates are $12 (daily) and $84 (weekly), while their cabin section (sleep 5) rate is $40–$55.

Swansea Kenmore Cabin and Tourist Park, 2 Bridge St. Tel: 03–6257 8148. Water frontage location where all 100 camping sites are powered. Rates from $13–$15 per night; the cabin section rate is $45–$58 per night.

Swansea YHA Hostel, 5 Franklin St. Tel: 03–6257 8367. Situated near the beach with uninterrupted views of Great Oyster Bay and Freycinet Peninsula. Rates from $12 per person.

Little Swanport

Gumleaves, Swanston Rd. Tel: 036244 4167. Self-contained cabins situated on 166 ha of bushland, sleep 7. Daily rates are $59–$75. The bunkhouse section rate is $49–$59, while backpacker cabins cost $15 per person.

Orford

Spring Beach Holiday Villas, Rheban Rd, Spring Beach. Tel: 03–6257 1440. Self-contained units. Daily rates are $85–$100.

Blue Waters, Tasman Hwy. Tel: 03–6257 1102. Motel with 18 rooms, from $38–$50 per night.

Sea Breeze, cnr Rudd Ave and Walpole St. Tel: 03–6257 1375. Rates from $35 per night.

Maria Island National Park

No cars are allowed on the island, and you'll also find an absence of electricity, showers, hot water and shops.

Maria Island Camp Ground, Darlington campsite, Tel: 03–6257 1420. Water available at campsite. Rates are $3 per person, while bunkhouse rates are $8–$16 (daily) and $20–$40 (weekly).

Tasman Peninsula

Dominated by the archaic legacy of Port Arthur, the Tasman Peninsula is surrounded by breathtaking coastline and isolated surfing beaches. Connected tenuously to the mainland by Eaglehawk Neck, some 80 km southeast of Hobart, the Peninsula offers a uniquely southern experience.

Surf Shops

Coastal Connection, Shop 1, 31 Cole St, Sorell. Tel: 03–6265 3350.
Also on the Tasman Peninsula.

Accommodation

Dunalley

Fulham Cottages, 'Fulham'. Tel: 03–6253 5247. Self-contained cottages which sleep 5–10. Rates from $80–$94 per night.

Potters Croft, 'Brynfield', Arthur Hwy. Tel: 03–6253 5469. Water frontage B&B accommodation. Rates from $65 per night. Cottage section (sleeps 5) from $60–$80 (daily) and $380–$450 (weekly).

Taranna

Norfolk Bay Convict Station, Arthur Hwy. Tel: 03–6250 3487. B&B rates from $50–$100 per night.

Eaglehawk Neck

Wunnamurra Waterfront B&B, 21 Osprey Rd. Tel: 03–6250 3145. Water frontage accommodation. Rates from $55–$85 per night. Non-smoking property.

Lufra Country Hotel, Pirates Bay Drive. Tel: 03–6250 3262. Rooms from $60–$70 per night.

Penzances Pirate Bay Motel, Blowhole Rd. Tel: 03–6250 3272. Rooms from $25–$65 per night.

The Neck Beach House, 423 Pirates Bay Dve. Tel: 03–6250 3541. Self-contained units accommodate up to 6 people; $60–$110 (daily) or $420–$560 (weekly).

Eaglehawk Neck Backpackers, 687 Old Jetty Rd. Tel: 03–6250 3248. Lodge set-up with shared cooking facilities. Rates are $12 per night.

Nubeena
Fairway Lodge Country Club, Main Rd. Tel: 03–6250 2171. Self-contained units with facilities including indoor heated pool, shared spa, sauna and golf course. Rates from $80–$90 per night. Motel section rooms from $80–$90. Near the turn-off for the breaks at Roaring Beach.

White Beach Holiday Villas, White Beach Rd. Tel: 03–6250 2152. Self-contained units (sleep 6). Rates from $55–$80 per night.

Parkers, Main Rd. Tel: 03–6250 2138. Self-contained units sleep up to 5. Rates from $30–$55 per night.

White Beach Caravan and Cabin Park, White Beach Rd. Tel: 03–6250 2142. Beach frontage sites from $12 per night. Park cabins sleep 6 are $45–$50 (daily) and $280 (weekly), while on-site vans are $30 (daily) and $196 (weekly).

Treasure Island Caravan Park, White Beach Rd, Nubeena. Tel: 03–6250 2142. Camping sites vary depending on the amount of people, but on-site vans (sleep 2) are $30 per night.

Port Arthur
Fox and Hounds Motor Inn, Arthur Hwy. Tel: 03–6250 2217. Room rates $65–$85, while holiday units are $110–$125.

Andertons Accommodation, Remarkable Cave Rd. Tel: 03–6250 2378. Rooms (sleep 8) with shared cooking facilities. Rates from $45–$60 per night.

Port Arthur Caravan and Cabin Park, Garden Point, Port Arthur. Tel: 03–6250 2340. Most of the 62 sites are powered. Daily rates are $13. Self-contained park cabins sleep 6 from $45–$65 (daily), while a backpackers section starts at $13 per person.

Roseview YHA Hostel, Champ St. Tel: 03–6250 2311. Email: ajenniso@tassie.net.au Overlooking the Port Arthur Historic Site. Rates from $12 per person, per night.

Hobart/South Arm Penin.

Surf Shops
Dodges Ferry Surf and Leisure, 56 Carlton Beach Rd, Dodges Ferry. Tel: 03–6265 9347.

Pure Surf, 55 South Arm Rd, Rockeby. Tel: 03–6247 7165.

Red Herring Surf, cnr 29 Elizabeth St Mall and Collins St, Hobart. Tel: 03–6231 2707. Two other stores at Eastlands and Northgate Shopping Centres.

Seaworld, 103 Elizabeth St, Hobart. Tel: 03–6234 1805.

Skigia & Surf, 217 Elizabeth St, Hobart. Tel: 03–6234 6688.

South Arm Surf Shop, 530 South Arm Rd, Lauderdale. Tel: 03–6248 1383.

Accommodation
Carlton
Steeles Island, River St, Carlton Beach. Tel: 03–6265 8077 or 018 120 341. Cabins situated on 4 ha private property, sleep 2–5. Rates $150–$175. A separate cabin section costs $65 (daily).

Hobart
Australia's second oldest city (after Sydney), Hobart is backdropped by the spectacular Mt Wellington and is close to some supprisingly good point and beach breaks.

The Islington, 321 Davey St. Tel: 03–6223 3900. Luxury Rooms from $75–$160 per night. National trust property.

Globe, 178 Davey St. Tel: 03–6223 5800. Rooms from $22–$32 per night.

Sandy Bay Caravan Park, 1 Peel St, Sandy Bay. Tel: 03–6225 1264. Half of the 181 sites are powered. Rates are $14 (daily) and $84 (weekly). Self-contained park cabins sleep 7 from $55 (daily), while on-site vans are $32 (daily) and $192 (weekly).

Ocean Child Hotel Lodge, 86 Argyle St. Tel: 03–6234 6730 Rooms from $12 per night.

Adelphi Court YHA Hostel, 17 Stoke St, Newtown. Tel: 03–6228 4829. Facilities include limited camping gear for hire. Rates are $13 per person.

Transit Centre Backpackers, 199 Collins St. Tel: 03–6231 2400. Rooms from $12 per night.

Huon Waterways

The Huon is a peaceful region known for wilderness areas such as the Hartz Mountains National park, and world renowned cuisine such as atlantic salmon. The Huon's Waterways and Wilderness will leave you breathless.

Accommodation

Driftwood Holiday Cottages, Bay View Rd, Dover. Tel: 03–6298 1441. Self-contained cottages with beautiful views of Port Esperance. Rates from $90 (single) and $110 (double).

3 Island Holiday Apartments, Station Rd, Dover. Tel: 03–6298 1396. Self-contained units. Rates from $45–$65 per night.

Balfes Hill YHA, RSD 340 Cradoc Rd, Cradoc. Tel: 03–6295 1551. Located in the centre of the Huon Valley, Balfes Hill is positioned on 6 ha. Weekly rates and transport to orchard work (during the seasons Nov–May). Rates from $12 per person.

Lune River YHA Hostel, Main Rd, Lune River. Tel: 03–6298 3163. Noted as Australia's most southern hostel, Lune River YHA has access to both remote beaches and wilderness areas. Rates are $10 per person.

Bruny Island

A 15–20 minute ferry ride from the mainland, Bruny Island is a haven for Hobart surfers in search of bigger, uncrowded waves. A vehicular ferry, the Mirambeena, operates frequently throughout the day, linking Kettering with Roberts Point, North Bruny. Timetable and fares are listed in the Hobart Mercury each Friday, or contact Transport Tasmania (Tel: 03–6233 5313) or the Bruny D'Entrecasteaux Visitors Center (Tel: 03–6267 4494). You can also hire cars, caravans and motor homes, so check out the local papers to see what's on offer.

Accommodation

Kellys Lookout, Bull Bay Rd. Tel: 03–6267 4494. Self-contained unit (sleeps 8). Rates are $90 (daily) and $420 (weekly).

Mavista Cottages, Adventure Bay. Tel: 03–6293 1347 and 015 875 052. One and two storey units sleep 2–8. Rates from $68–$100 (daily) and $408–$600 (weekly).

Rosebud Cottage, Adventure Bay. Tel: 03–6293 1325. Cottage sleeps up to 7. Rates from $60 per night. $360 per week.

Inala Country Accommodation, Cloudy Bay Rd. Tel: 03–6293 1217. Self-contained unit (sleeps 6) situated on a 250 ha property. Rates are $60–$70 (daily) and $360–$420 (weekly).

Captain James Cook Memorial Caravan Park, Adventure Bay. Tel: 03–6293 1128. Daily rates for camping sites are $7 per night, while on-site vans are $32.

Adventure Bay Caravan Park, Adventure Bay. Tel: 03–6293 1270. All 52 sites are powered. Site rates are $13 (daily) and $78 (weekly). On-site vans are $30–$40 (daily) and $180–$240 (weekly). Self-contained cabins are $40–$55 (daily) and $240–$300.

Captain James Cook Memorial Caravan Park, Adventure Bay. Tel: 03–6293 1128. All 48 sites are powered. Site rates from $7–$10 per night; on-site van (sleep 6) are $32.

Lumeah YHA, Quiet Corner, Main Rd, Adventure Bay. Tel: 03–6293 1265. Lodge accommodation providing cooking facilities. Room rates from $13–$15 per night.

West Coast

Accommodation

Strahan

Sailors Rest, Harvey St. Tel: 03–6471 7237. Units (sleep 8) are $60–$75 per night.

Cape Horn Accommodation, Frazer St. Tel: 03–6471 7488 or 03–6471 7169. Rates from $40 per night.

Strahan Lodge, Ocean Beach Rd. Tel: 03–6471 7142. B&B rates from $30 per night.

Strahan Cabin Park, cnr Jones and Innes St. Tel: 03–6471 7442. 100 m to beach, park cabins sleep 5 from $45–$70 (daily) and $180–$400 (weekly).

Strahan YHA, Harvey St. Tel: 03–6471 7255. 10 rooms (sleep 2–10) offer shared cooking facilities. Rates from $13–$15 per night.

Stanley

West Inlet Farm Holiday Villa, The Neck. Tel: 03–6458 1350. Private beach frontage. Self-contained units (sleep 3) from $90–$120 (daily) and $550–$600 (weekly).

Stanley Caravan Park, Wharf Rd. Tel: 03–6458 1266. Beach frontage location where most of the 101 sites are powered. Rates from $12 (daily) and $66 (weekly). Park cabins (sleep 2–8) are $40–$50 (daily) and $240–$300 (weekly); on-site vans are $30 (daily) and $180 (weekly). A backpackers section offers rooms from $12 per night.

Smithton

Milfarm Cottage, West Rd, Roger River. Tel: 03–6456 5118. Self-contained unit (sleeps 7). Rates from $70–$100 per night.

Tall Timbers, Scotchtown Rd. Tel: 03–6452 2755. 59 rooms offering standard motel facilities. Room rates from $65–$90. Spa and self-contained units also available.

Bridge Hotel Motel, Montagu Rd. Tel: 03–6452 1389. Room rates $25–$60; B&B rates from $32–$74 per night.

Burnie

Emu, 12 Main Rd, Wivenhoe. Tel: 03–6431 2466. 30 room motel serviced by restaurant. Room rates from $60.

Ocean View Motel, 253 Bass Hwy, Cooee. Tel: 03–6431 1925. Beach frontage location. Rates from $50–$60.

Treasure Island Caravan Park, 253 Bass Hwy, Cooee. Tel: 03–6431 1925. Beach frontage location where most of the 73 sites are powered. Facilities include indoor heated pool, camp kitchen and kiosk. Camping rates are $10–$13 (daily) and $78 (weekly). Park cabins (sleep 6) are from $50, while on-site vans are from $35 (daily) and $210 (weekly).

South Australia

From the southern fertile vineyards to the harsh Simpson Desert in the north, South Australia is a land of unique contrast. To experience the rugged arc of the Australian Bight is to gain an insight into the energies which have sculpted this vast land. When you surf the many gulfs and remote peninsulas of this state, you encounter the Southern Ocean's huge variety of quality reef and beach breaks; you are truly surfing the Edge.

Getting There

A number of international carriers fly regularly into Adelaide Airport, which is located less than 10 km from the city centre at West Beach. Domestic flights link Adelaide with all other capital cities across Australia, with Ansett and Qantas providing the major services.

Local Transport

Local buses servicing Adelaide are run by TransAdelaide, so for timetable enquiries, call 08-8210 1000. Regular buses and coaches service most towns throughout the state; the major companies being Greyhound Pioneer and McCafferty's. The railways in South Australia don't link much of the coastline, and considering this is where you'll be heading, alternative choices will have to be made. So if you want to get around at your own pace and pleasure, Avis, Budget and Hertz offer a wide range of hire cars to service your needs, and they can be found in most towns and airports. If you're likely to be doing alot of remote travelling, it's a good idea to join the local roadside service, the RAA (Royal Automobile Association of South Australia).

Medical and Emergencies

Hospitals and medical centres are located in most of the larger towns in South Australia. For an emergency dial 000 and ask for the service you require, be it fire, police or ambulance.

General Surf Info

Gone Surfing Australia Enterprises, 20 Pontoon St, Seaford. Tel: 08-8386 3662.

Surfrider Foundation, South Australia. Tel: 08–8296 6776.

Kangaroo Island Surf Charters, Kangaroo Island. Tel: 08–8553 2882. Provides ferry ride, 4WD and guided tour of some of SA's most hardcore waves. Run by Paul Pratt.

Local Weather, Tel: 1900 155 365

Surf School

Surf Culture Australia, 69A Nashwauk Crs, Moana. Tel: 08–8327 2802. Surfboard and bodyboard tuition. Surf camps to the Yorke Peninsula.

South East Coast

Accommodation

Port MacDonnell
Seaview Motel & Hotel Units, 77 Sea Pde. Tel: 08–8738 2243. Daily unit rates from $30 per person, while holiday units (sleep up to 4) cost from $35–$40.

Port MacDonnell Harbour View Caravan Park, 59 Sea Pde. Tel: 08–8738 2085. Beachfront location with 25 camping sites. Daily rates from $12 per person. Park cabins (sleep up to 5) from $45 per night; on-site vans (sleep

2–6) cost from $28–$32 per night.

Southend

Southend on Sea Tourist Park, Eyre St. Tel: 08–8735 6035. Camping sites from $12 per night. On-site vans sleep 2–6 from $28.

Launceston

Windmill Hill Tourist Lodge, 22 High St. Tel: 03-6331 9337. Heritage building offering standard facilities. Rates from $60 per room. Holiday units (sleep 4) from $65 per night.

Treasure Island Caravan Park, 94 Glen Dhu St, South Launceston. Tel: 03-6344 2600. Most of the 155 sites are powered. Camping sites from $13–$15 (daily) and $84–$105 (weekly), while park cabins are $48–$52 (daily) and $303–$328 (weekly). On-site vans (sleep 6) cost from $32 (daily) and $224 (weekly).

Launceston City Youth Hostel, 36 Thistle St, South Launceston. Tel: 03-6344 9779. 14 dorm rooms with tea-making facilities. Rates from $12 per night.

Launceston City Backpackers, 173 George St. Tel: 03-6334 2327. Rates from $14 per night.

Robe

Robe Garden Motel, Main St. Tel: 08–8768 2185. Room rates from $54–$70 per night.

Melaleuca Motel, 20 Smillie St. Tel: 08–8768 2599. Daily unit rates from $50–$70.

Nampara Cottage, 30 Laurel Tce. Tel: 08–8768 2264. Self-contained cottage located near Long Beach. Rates from $45–$80 (daily) and $300–$560 (weekly).

Robe Long Beach Tourist Park, The Esplanade, Long Beach. Tel: 08–8768 2237. Camping sites from $11–$14 per night. Park cabins (sleep 6) from $34–$75, while park cabins sleep up to 6, rates from $28–$35 per night.

Lake George Wilderness Holiday, Bog La. Tel: 08–8735 7260. Located near Lake George. Camping sites from $15 per night; cottage (sleeps 6) from $85 per night.

Salt Creek

Gemini Downs Holiday Units, Highway One. Tel: 08–8575 7013. Unit rates from $35–$45 per night. Plus they have camping sites from $12 per night.

The Mid Coast

Surf Shops

Big Surf Australia, Main Rd, Middleton. Tel: 08–8554 2399. Open 7 days a week. Broadcast a surf report (0055 31543). Andy Inks owner/shaper and Shane Ellis surfer/shaper.

Club Surfboards, PO Box 108, Old Noarlunga 5168. Tel: 08–8386 1939.

Cutloose Surfboards, 778 Anzac Hwy, Glenelg. Tel: 08–8294 3866.
4 Piping Lane, Lonsdale 08–8326 0939. Stocking some of SA's leading custom surfboards.

Extreme Surf, Street & Snow, 144 Jetty Rd, Glenelg. Tel: 08–8295 1219. Stock all major brands.

Frost Surfboards, 242 Esplanade, Seaford. Tel: 08–8386 3006.

Island Surf & Sail, cnr Brighton and Sturt Rds. Tel: 08–8296 9776. Longboard specialists, sole agent for McTavish.

Jetty Surf Shop, 112 Rundle Mall, Adelaide. Tel: 08–8232 2280.

JR's Surf & Ski, 121 Grenfell St, Adelaide. Tel: 08–8223 5505. Six stores throughout SA.

Mid Coast Surf, Lot 6 and 8, 200 Dyson Rd, Christies Beach. Tel: 08–8384 5522.

Ocean Graffix, 21 Saltfleet St, Port Noarlunga. Tel: 08–8382 6729. Large range of leading label surfboards and surfboard hire available.

On & In Surf Shop, 134 Wakefield St, Adelaide. Tel: 08–8223 2974. Repair and custom make wetsuits, and provide second-hand and hire facilities.

Point Break Surf & Street, Castle Plaza, Edwardstown. Tel: 08–8357 4400.

Power Plug, Main Rd, Middleton. Tel: 08–8555 1239. Custom Surfboards and repairs.

Rapid Surf & Ski, 180 Main North Rd, Prospect. Tel: 08–8344 1166.

Southport Surf & Skate, 159 The Esplanade, Port Noarlunga South. Tel: 08–8386 0404, Fax: 08–8327 0011. Stock all brands including locally made surfboards. Broadcast the SA Surf Report (0055 83266).

Accommodation

West Beach
Seavista Holiday Units, 52 Seaview Rd. Tel: 08–8356 3975. Beach frontage location. Self-contained units from $30–$60 (daily) and $200–$600 (weekly).

Cootura Holiday Units, 8 West Beach Rd. Tel: 08–8271 2415. Self-contained units from $35–$50 (daily) and $245 (weekly).

West Beach Caravan Park, Military Rd. Tel: 08–8356 7654. Beachfront location. 601 sites featuring camp kitchen, pool and shop. Daily camping rates from $13–$18. Self-contained park cabins sleep 2-6 from $51–$67 per night, while on-site vans sleep 2-6 from $35–$45 per night. A bunkhouse section sleeps up to 52, from $10 per person, per night.

Glenelg
Colley Motel, 22 Colley Tce. Tel: 08–8295 7535. Self-contained units from $48–$95 per night.

Alkoomi Holiday Units, 7 North Esplanade. Tel: 08–8294 6624. Self-contained units sleep 2-6 from $45–$94 per night.

Glenelg Backpackers Seaside Resort, 1 Moseley St. Tel: 08–8376 0007. Self-contained lodge 100m from beach. Bed and light breakfast rates from $28 per night.

Christies Beach
Christies Beach Hotel Motel, Gulf View Rd. Tel: 08–8382 1166. Daily room rates from $45–$50.

Christies Beach Tourist Park, Sydney Crescent. Tel: 08–8326 0311. Beach frontage location. Daily rates from $14 (powered camping sites) and $45 (park cabins).

Port Noarlunga
Port Noarlunga Motel, 39 Saltfleet St. Tel: 08–8382 1267. Daily unit rates from $50–$55.

Port Noarlunga Tourist Park, Esplanade. Tel: 08–8326 0311. All 50 sites are powered. Daily camping rates from $12–$14.

Moana Beach
Moana Beach Tourist Park, 44 Nashwauk Crescent, Moana. Tel: 08–8327 0677. Most of the 141 sites are powered. Camping rates from $13–$15 (daily) and $72–$105 (weekly). Self-contained cottages (sleep 4), cost from $60–$70 per night, while park cabins sleep 4–6, from $40–$50 (daily) and $240–$350 (weekly). A bunkhouse section (sleeps 12) from $10–$13 per night.

Kangaroo Island

Australia's third-largest offshore island, Kangaroo Island is a haven for many species, from seals and sea eagles to relaxing mainlanders craving relaxation. The wrecks of 40 ships are a testament to the deep attraction people have always had toward the island's rugged cliffs and pristine beaches. The Kangaroo Island Sealink carries both cars and passengers, and operates between Cape Jervis in Adelaide, and the island's Penneshaw. (The journey takes about an hour). Passenger-only ferries are also operated by Kangaroo Island Ferry Connections and Kangaroo Island Fast Ferry. Further enquiries can be directed to the Kangaroo Island Gateway Visitor Information Centre. Tel: 08–8553 1185.

Accommodation

American River
Riverview Cottage, Government Rd. Tel: 08–8553 7169 or 08–8553 7151. Self-contained cottages sleep up to 8, rates from $70 (double) per night.

Casuarina Coastal Units, 9 Ryberg Rd. Tel: 08–8553 7020. Cabins sleep up to 5, cost from $45 per night.

Linnetts Island Club Caravan Park, The Esplanade. Tel: 08–8553 7053. Most of the 27 sites are powered. Facilities include shared spa, sauna and pool. Daily camping rates from $15–$20; holiday flats (sleep up to 5), from $49–$70 per night. There's also a motel section, with daily room rates from $28–$153 (single).

Emu Bay
Emu Bay Holiday Homes, Lot 7 Bayview Rd. Tel: 08–8553 5241. Self-contained units 700 m from beach. Daily unit rates from $68–$75. Self-contained cabins (sleep up to 6), cost from $35–$45 per night.

Emu Bay Caravan Park, Esplanade. Tel: 08–8553 2325. Cabins sleep 2–6 cost rom $60 per night.

Karatta
Wingara Farm House, Church Rd. Tel: 08–8559 7222. Cottage sleeps up to 12 from $50–$70 (double) per night.

Attarak Holiday Farm Bed & Breakfast, Mt Taylor Rd. Tel: 08–8559 7202. B&B rates from $35 per person, per night.

Western KI Caravan Park, South Coast Rd. Tel: 08–8559 7201. Half of the 30 sites are powered. Daily camping rates from $15. On-site vans (sleep 2–6) from $35 per night. The park cabin, which is actually a double-decker bus that sleeps 7, costs from $45 per night.

Fleurieu Peninsula

Surf Shop
Southern Surf, 36 North Tce, Port Elliot. Tel: 08–8554 2375.

Accommodation
Goolwa
Narnu pioneer Holiday Farm, Monument Rd, Hindmarsh Island. Tel: 08–8555 2002. Each cottage sleeps up to 12. Daily rates from $68–$80.

Goolayyahlee Cottage, 13 Eaton Ave. Tel: 08–8431 1120. Self-contained cottage (sleeps 2-10). Daily rates from $35–$65.

Goolwas Hindmarsh Island Caravan Park, Madsen St. Hindmarsh Island. Tel: 08–8555 2234. Half of the 104 sites are powered with facilities including solar heated pool, tennis court and launching ramp. Daily camping rates from $10–$12.

Goolwa Caravan Park, Noble Ave. Tel: 08–8555 2737. Most of the 248 sites are powered, with facilities including putting green, pool and shared spa. Daily rates for camping sites from $14. Park cabins (sleep 2-6) are $46–$58, while on-site vans (sleep 2-6) are $32–$48.

Middleton
Mindacowie Guest House, 48 Goolwa Rd. Tel: 08–8554 3243 or 014 955 139. B&B rates from $95–$185. The Magpie Studio Apart-ment (sleeps 4) from $95–$150.

Middleton Caravan Park, 23 Goolwa Rd. Tel: 08–8554 2383. Most of the 70 sites are powered. Daily camping rates from $14 per night. Cabins (sleep 2–5) are $40–$50 per night, and on-site vans cost from $35.

Port Elliot
Cavalier Inn Motel, 7 The Strand. Tel: 08–8554 2067. Situated on the headland between Horseshoe Bay and Boomer Beach. Facilities include licensed restaurant and swimming pool. Daily room rates from $68 per night.

Royal Family Hotel, 32 North Tce. Tel: 08–8554 2219. Room rates from $25 (single) and $35 (double).

Port Elliot Caravan Park, Horseshoe Bay. Tel: 08–8554 2134. All 258 sites are powered. Daily rates include $14 (camping), $48–$68 (park cabins), $63–$78 (cottages) and $33–$38 (on-site vans).

Victor Harbor
City Motel, 51 Ocean St. Tel: 08–8552 2455. 15 units offering standard motel facilities. Room rates from $55–$80.

Anchorage Seafront Music Cafe, cnr Flinders Pde and Coral St. Tel: 08–8552 5970. Heritage guest house with 21 rooms. Rates from $55–$135. Also, a 60 bed backpacker's facilities from $17.50 per person, per night.

Bayview Victor Motel, 11 Hindmarsh Rd. Tel: 08–8552 1755. Units from $49–$59.

Ocean Crest Motel, 117 Mentone Rd. Tel: 08–8552 3233. 10 units offering shared cooking facilities. Daily room rates from $45–$60.

Victor Harbor Caravan Park, 114 Victoria St. Tel: 08–8552 1111. All 265 sites are powered. Daily rates include $14 (powered camping sites), $60 (villas) and $40–$55 (cabins).

Victor Harbor Holiday Centre, Bay Rd. Tel: 08–8552 1949. 312 sites (224 powered) from $14 per night. Holiday units (sleep 8) from $60–$68, park cabins (sleep2–4) from $56, while on-site vans start at $38 per night.

Yorke Peninsula

You can buy some surfing basics like leg ropes and board wax from the Innes Park and Marion Bay general stores. Both offer great advice on local conditions.

Accommodation

Marion Bay
Marion Bay Seaside Apartments, Lot 98 Stenhouse Bay Rd. Tel: 08–8339 1909. Self-contained holiday apartments with ocean views. Daily rates from $70–$80.

Marion Bay Caravan Park, Willyama Dve. Tel: 08–8854 4094. Most of the 100 sites are powered. Daily camping rates from $10. Park cabins (sleep 7) from $40–$45, and on-site vans (sleep 2–4) from $25.

Stenhouse Bay
Stenhouse Bay Lodge, Tel: 08–8339 1909. Ocean views with jetty 200 m away. Self-contained dormitory (34 beds). Rates from $15 (per person, per night) or $180 per night for the entire dorm.

Port Victoria Hotel Motel, Main St, Port Victoria. Tel: 08–8834 2069. Bed and light breakfast rates from $40–$55 per night.

Daly Head
Hillocks Drive Bush Camping Area, Hillocks Dve, Butlers Beach (16 km E of Marion Bay). Situated on 7 km of excellent surfing coastline. Limited facilities mean the 200 sites are unpowered. Camping rates from $5 per night. On-site vans (sleep 2–6) from $18–$25 daily.

Corny Point Caravan Park, Main Rd. Tel: 08–8855 3368. Most of the 52 sites are powered. Daily rates from $12. On-site vans (sleep 2–8) from $25.

Parsons Beach/Port Rickaby
Port Rickaby, Main St. Tel: 08–8853 1177. Most of the 80 sites are powered. Daily camping rates from $10 per person. On-site vans (sleep 4–6) from $22 per night.

Port Victoria
Gulfhaven Caravan Park, Davies Tce, Port Victoria. Tel: 08–8834 2012. Seafront location where most of the 76 sites are powered. Daily site rates from $11; park cabins are $28–$48.

Eyre Peninsula

Surf Shops

Gravelle Surfboards, Main St, Penong. Tel: 08–8625 1094.

Hot Spot Surf, Shop 1, 16–18 Hallet Place, Port Lincoln. Tel: 08–8683 3144.

Accommodation

Penong
Penong Hotel, Eyre Hwy. Tel: 08–8625 1050. Daily room rates from $30–$40.

Camping Grounds can also be found at Fisheries Bay, Cactus Beach, Point Sinclair and Greenly Beach.

Streaky Bay
Streaky Bay Community Hotel Motel, 35 Alfred Terrace. Units (sleep 3) from $48–$73 per night, while hotel rooms range from $25–$69 per night.

Koolangatta Cottage, Piednippie Calca Rd. Tel: 08–8626 1174. Cottages from $30 per night, sleep up to 4 people.

Labatt House, Alfred Tce. Tel: 08–8626 1126. Waterfront location. Daily room rates from $10 per person.

Streaky Bay Caravan Park, Government Rd, Sceale Bay. Tel: 08–8626 5099. Half of the 30 sites are powered. Site rates from $9 per person. On-site vans (sleep 6) from $25 per person.

Streaky Bay Foreshore Tourist Park, Wells St. Tel: 08–8626 1666. Half of the 210 sites are powered. Camping rates from $11–$14 (daily) and $67–$87 (weekly). Park cabins are $30–$45 (daily) and $180–$267 (weekly).

Venus Bay
Venus Bay General Store Accommodation, Main St. Tel: 08–8625 5075 or a/h 08–8625 5102. Cottages (sleep 2–10) from $30 per night.

Venus Bay Caravan Park, Matson Tce. Tel: 08–8625 5073. Most of the 72 sites are powered and facilities also offer hire boats. Daily rates for camping from $10–$12. Park cabins that sleep up to 6, from $31, and on-site vans that sleep 2–6 from $21.

Tumby Bay
Tumby Bay Motel, 4 Berryman St. Tel: 08–8688 2311. Room rates from $40–$65 per night.

Tumby Bayside Holiday Units, Yaringa Ave. Tel: 08–8688 2087. Daily unit rates from $25–$60 (daily) and $150–$360 (weekly).

Seabreeze Hotel, Tumby Bay Tce. Tel: 08–8688 2362. Daily room rates from $19–$46.

Tumby Bay Caravan Park, Tumby Tce. Tel: 08–8688 2208. Most of the 94 sites are powered. Daily camping rates from $12–$14. Park cabins that sleep up to 5, cost from $40 per night; on-site vans (sleep 4–6) from $28 per night.

Elliston
Ellenliston Motel, Beach Tce. Tel: 08–8687 9028. Units with standard cooking facilities. Rates from $45 per night.

Rocket Site Cottage, Esplanade. Tel: 08–8277 6716. Cottage sleeps 2–7 from $40 per night.

Elliston Hotel Motel, Fifth St, Town centre. Tel: 08–8687 9009. Unit rooms from $35–$50 per night.

Elliston Caravan Park, Flinders Hwy. Tel: 08–8687 9061. Located opposite jetty, most of the 80 sites are powered. Daily camping rates from $8–$12. Park cabins (sleep 2–5) from $35, and on-site vans (sleep 4–6) from $20.

Coffin Bay
Coffin Bay Motel, Shepherd Ave. Tel: 08–8685 4111. Bed and light breakfast rates from $50 per night.

Alpine Cottage, 337 Esplanade. Tel: 08–8685 4068. Units (sleep up to 5) from $40–$60 (daily) and $250–$385 (weekly).

Siesta Lodge Holiday Units, Esplanade. Tel: 08–8685 4001. Beachfront location. Units (sleep 2-8) from $35–$45 per night.

Casuarina Cabins, The Esplanade. Tel: 08–8685 4173. Cabins (sleep 4) from $28–$32 (daily) and $175–$210 (weekly).

Coffin Bay Caravan and Camping Park, The Esplanade. Tel: 08–8685 4170. Most of the 148 sites are powered. Daily camping rates from

$10–$13. Park cabin (sleeps up to 6) from $35; on-site vans (sleep 4–6) from $25 per night.

Port Lincoln
Boston Island Homestead, on Boston Island. Tel: 08–8682 1741. Homestead cottage (sleeps up to 12). Weekly rates $200 per person.

Hilton Motel, 13 King St. Tel: 08–8682 1144. Beachfront location. Daily room rates from $60–$90 (single) and $65–$150 (double).

Blue Seas Motel, 7 Gloucester Tce. Tel: 08–8682 3022. Overlooking Boston Bay. Daily room rates from $45–$55.

Sleaford Bay Holiday Park, Sleaford Bay Rd. Tel: 08–8685 6002. Each cabin sleeps 5. Rates from $30–$40 (daily) and $170–$240 (weekly).

McKechnie Springs Farmstay, Tel: 08–8684 5057. Self-contained cottage or woolshed accommodation. Daily room rates from $15 per person.

Kirton Point Caravan Park, Hindmarsh St. Tel: 08–8682 2537. Most of the 210 sites are powered. Camping rates from $10 (daily) and $60 (weekly). Park cabins are $37–$58 (daily) and $222–$406 (weekly). Separate cabins are $27–$37 (daily) and $138–$259 (weekly).

Port Lincoln Caravan Park, Lincoln Hwy, North Shields. Tel: 08–8684 3512. Most of the 176 sites are powered. Daily camping rates from $13. Cabin section rates from $34, while on-site vans are $30 (double).

Elliston Caravan Park, Elliston. Tel: 08–8687 9061. Camping rates from $12, cabins (sleep 6) from $25–$35, while on-site vans (sleep 2) cost from $20 per night.

Western Australia

The largest state in the country with the smallest population per square kilometre, Western Australia's beauty lies in its diverse landscape and wide open spaces. You'll have to do plenty of driving from Perth, the capital of WA, to the fertile south west and the inhospitable north, but the empty lineups, pristine coastline, big surfs and isolated beaches stretching as far as the eye can see, are well worth it. WA is truly one of surfing's last frontier lands.

Getting There

Perth International Airport is the first port of call for many international airlines entering Australia, particularly from Asia and Europe and offers some of the cheapest airport duty-free shopping in the world. Perth is also regularly serviced by domestic flights from the other state capitals of Australia, with Ansett and Qantas being the major carriers. For rail buffs there is the famous Indian-Pacific train (operating between Sydney and Perth via Adelaide) which offers a unique opportunity to cross the Nullarbor Plain on the straightest section of rail line in the world. Departs twice a week from both Sydney and Perth.

Local Transport

Since Western Australia is such a large state, often with hundreds of kilometres separating the various towns, the easiest way to get around is on regional flights. Airlines include Ansett, Qantas, Skywest, Airlink and National Jet Systems. Those who want to explore the coastline will find hire cars available at airports and most towns. The major hire car companies are Avis, Bayswater, Budget, Hertz and Thrifty. Four wheel drive vehicles can also be hired through South Perth 4WD. Roadside service is provided by the RAC (Royal Automobile Club of WA).

Buses provide services to all major towns along the coastline, but expect to be in for a long haul on many of the trips. The main bus companies are Greyhound-Pioneer, McCafferty's and South West Coach Lines. While the rail lines link many areas in the southwest corner of the state, areas north of Geraldton are not accessible. Transperth is Perth's metropolitan public transport system, and a Transperth ticket is valid on all three modes of transport (bus, train and ferry).

Medical and Emergencies

There are hospitals and medical centres located in most of the larger towns in Western Australia. For an emergency dial 000 and ask for the service you require, be it fire, police or ambulance. A Flying Doctor service is also available for remote geographic areas in WA's north and south west.

General Surf Info

Surfrider Foundation, Western Australia. Tel: 08–9256 8056.

Force Five Abrolhos Adventures, 3 Trigg St, Geraldton. Tel: 08–9921 6416.

If you want a "do it yourself" surf adventure, and wish to explore WA's more remote surfing regions, check out South Perth Four Wheel Drive Centre, 80 Canning Hwy, Victoria Park, Perth. Tel: 08–9362 5444. These guys have a huge range of overland surfari vehicles and cater specifically for surfers.

Surf and Snow Report, Tel: 1900 912 177. Tide Times, Tel: 1900 914 477 or 07-3224 2616.

Local Weather, Tel: 1900 155 366

Surf Schools

Batavia Coast Surf Academy, Geraldton. Tel: 08–9921 3127 or 041 890 3379.

Main Break Surf School, Margaret River. Tel: 08–9757 2888.

Mitch Thorson Professional Training. Tel: 08–9757 1058.

Surfrider Surfschools, 360 West Coast Drive, Trigg, 6029. Tel: 08–9448 0004, Fax: 08–9447 0309. For private/individual surf coaching. All equipment is provided (by appointment only) and includes wetsuit, surfboard, helmet and sunscreen. Cost is $30 per person, per hour, or $20 per hour for 2 or more people. Private lessons can be arranged at a time and location to suit your needs.

The North West

Surf Shops

Cape Hideaway Surf, 08–9949 2224. Shop 3C, Kennedy St. Exmouth.

Norwest Surfboards Surf Store, 3/52 Robinson St, Carnarvon. Tel: 08–9941 4884. Run by local tube junkie Paul Donda who also shapes Norwest Surfboards.

Red Crab Surf Shop, Christmas Island. Tel: 08–9164 7176.

Accommodation

Cocos (Keeling) Islands

Until recently, the Cocos Islands were virtually inaccessible but now twice weekly flights from Perth give adventurous surfers the chance to sample some of the powerhouse waves that pound the West Island's sharky waters.

West Island Lodge, West Island. Tel: 08 9162 6695. Rooms from $35–$70 per night.

Private houses are also available. Ring Genesis Travel, 49 Phillimore St, Fremantle. Tel: 08–9430 6166 regarding accommodation on Cocos and Christmas Islands.

Christmas Island

Lying 2623 km northwest of Perth, Christmas Island is famous for its red crabs that take over the entire island during their annual breeding migration, but little is known about the island's surfing potential. Accessed via twice-weekly flights from Perth, apparently there are waves on the island and who knows what you might score during December to March when the larger swells arrive.

Christmas Island Resort, Tel: 08–9164 8888. Rooms from $165–$245 per night.

Christmas Island Lodge, Tel: 08–9164 8585. Twin share rooms from $85 per night.

Exmouth

Potshot Hotel Resort, Murat Rd, Exmouth. Tel: 08–9949 1200. Homestead and resort rooms from $60– $115 per night.

Yardie Creek Homestead, Yardie Creek. Tel: 08–9949 1389. Close to Yardie Creek's awesome lefthander and the waves at Graveyards. Camp sites from $70–$80 per week. Caravans from $250–$300 per week. Chalets from $350–$450 per week, sleep up to 6 people.

Lighthouse Caravan Park, Yardie Creek Rd, Vlamingh Head. Tel: 08–9949 1478. Easy access to some of the area's best reef and beach breaks at Surf Beach and along Wreck Rd. Camp sites from $16 per night. Vans from $40 per night. Chalets from $85–$120 per night. All rates for two people.

Pete's Backpackers, cnr Murat and Turnscott Crescent Exmouth. Tel: 08–9949 1101. Rooms from $13 per night.

Gnaraloo

Gnaraloo Station Homestead, Tel: 08–9388 2881. Camping grounds from $8 per night. Shearers quarters from $15–$25 per night. Fishing Lodge from $18–$30 per night. Homestead from $18–$30 per night. Three Mile Camp, right on the beach overlooking the waves at Tombstones.

Carnarvon

Carnarvon Caravan Park, Lot 4, Robinson St. Tel: 08–9941 8101.

Carnarvon Backpackers, 50 Olivia Tce. Tel: 08–9941 1095. Rooms from $12 per night.

The Batavia Coast

Surf Shops

Kalbarri Surf Shop, Shop 4, 42 Grey St. Kalbarri. Tel: 08–9937 2076.

Scalpel Sail & Surf, 41 Urch St, Geraldton. Tel: 08–9921 3159.

Stone Surfboards, 968 Chapman Rd, Glenfields, Geraldton. Tel: 08–9938 1849. Run by respected local shaper Mark Stone.

The Corner Surf Shop, Shop 13, Town Towers, cnr Cathedral Ave and Chapman Rd, Geraldton. Tel: 08–9921 3127. Run by senior surfing champion Ian Salmond.

Accommodation

Kalbarri

Kalbarri Tudor Caravan Park, 10 Porter St, Kalbarri. Tel: 08–9937 1077. Camp sites from $12–$20 per night. Vans $30 per night, while cabins $30–$50.

Kalbarri Beach Resort, cnr Grey and Clotworthy St . Tel: 08–9937 1061. Units sleep 2–7. Rates from $85 per night and $455 per week.

Wagoe Farm Chalets, Wagoe Beach. Tel: 08–9936 6060. Chalets sleep 5–9 with rates from $35–$45 per night and $160–$220 per week.

The Houtman Abrolhos Islands

Situated 60 km west of Geraldton, the Abrolhos Islands are a surfing and diving paradise. Surrounded by relatively uncharted and treacherous waters, a few charter boat operators take surfing trips out from Geraldton. The best waves are found on the Easter and Wallaby groups and Force Five Charters specialise in surfing trips.

Force Five Abrolhos Adventures, 3 Trigg St, Geraldton. Tel: 08–9921 6416. Rates from $290 per day, all costs inclusive.

Geraldton

Abrolhos Reef Lodge Holiday Units, 126 Brand Hwy. Tel: 08–9921 3811. Rates from $60–$70 per night.

Ocean West Cottages, cnr Hadda Way and Wilcock Dve, Mahomets Beach. Tel: 08–9921 1047. Cottages from $60–$85 per night.

Grantown Guest House, 172 Marine Tce. Tel: 08–9921 3275. Rates from $23 (single) and $45 (double) per night.

Mahomets Village Holiday Units, Wilcock Dve, Mahomets Beach. Tel: 08–9921 6652. Units sleep 2–6. Rates from $62–$96 per night.

Sunset Beach Caravan Park, Bosley St Geraldton. Tel: 08–9938 1655. Vans from $30 per night. Cabins from $35 per night. Park homes from $50 per night.

S Bends Caravan Park, Tel: 08–9926 1072. Camping sites from $11 per night. Chalets from $40 (daily) and $240 (weekly). On-site vans from $26 (daily) and $156 (weekly). Right on the waves at Flatrocks.

Greenough Rivermouth Caravan Park, 4 Hull St, Cape Burney, Greenough. Tel: 08–9921 5845. Camp sites from $14 per night. Cabins $42 per night, while vans $26 per night.

Dongara

Denison Waterfront Cottages, 68 Pt Leander Dve, Pt Denison. Tel: 08–9927 1104. Rates from $55–$78 per day, $350–$600 per week.

Old Mill Hotel, Brand Hwy, Waldeck St. Tel: 08–9927 1200. Rates from $45 (single) and $55 (double) per night.

Dongara Backpackers, 32 Waldeck St Dongara. Tel: 08–9927 1581. Rates from $12–$15 per person, per night.

Dongarra/Denison Beach Caravan Park, 250 Ocean Dve, Port Denison. 08–9927 1131. Located right on the Port's breakwall lefthander, the park offers park homes, caravan and tent sites. Camping $12 per night.

Central West Coast

Holiday mecca for jaded Sydney folks and home to a sizeable local surf-mad population, the Central Coast offers heaps of great surfing locations.

Surf Shop

Lancelin Surf Sports, 127 Gingin Rd, Lancelin. Tel: 08–9655 1441.

Accommodation

Wedge Island
The beauty about this place is you've only got two options—park your swag under the stars or go luxury and BYO five-star tent.

Lancelin
Lancelin Caravan Park, Gingin Rd, Lancelin. Tel: 08–9655 1056. Over half of the 180 sites are powered and offer separate toilets, laundry and hot showers. Camping sites are $10 daily for a double, while the on-site vans are $35 for a double.

Lancelin Lodge, 10 Hopkins St, Lancelin. Tel: 08–9655 2020, Fax: 08–9655 2021. Described as the 'Hilton of backpackers', the Lodge has 40 beds from $13 per night. They can also arrange 4WD trips to the Pinnacles.

Ocean Front Holiday Flats, Gingin Rd, Lancelin. Tel: 08–9655 1029. All 8 one and two bedroom flats sleep up to 6 and offer shower, TV and cooking facilities. BYO blankets and linen. Weekly rates from $170.

Windsurfer Beach Chalets, Hopkins St, Lancelin. Tel: 08–9655 1454. With ocean frontage, all 6 chalets are fully self-contained. Rates start at $40–$50 for a double.

Lancelin Accommodation Service. Tel: 08–9655 1100. For beach house rentals.

Yanchep
Lodge Capricorn Hotel, Two Rocks Rd, Yanchep. Tel: 08–9561 1106. All 28 units have separate bathrooms, TV, in-house movies and are air-conditioned. Double rooms range from $100–$130. The Clubs' 37 chalets, which accommodate 4 to 6 guests, costs $465 per week.

Club Capricorn Chalets. Located right on 'The Spot', the area's best surfing location. This is a great place to stay with a group of friends. Chalets sleep 4–6 from $465 per week.

Yanchep Lagoon Lodge Guest House, 11 Nautical Crt, Yanchep Lagoon. Tel: 08–9561 1033. Overlooking the Indian Ocean, the 4 rooms have basic facilities including room service. Rooms are $50–$60 for a double per night, and $60–$80 including a light breakfast.

Two Rocks Harbour View Apartments. Tel: 08–9561 1469. Overlooking the Indian Ocean and Two Rocks Harbour. Units sleep 4-6 from $290–$380 per week.

Perth Metro

Home to a series of excellent beaches, the waves north of Sydney have been a breeding ground for two generations of devotees.

Surf Shops

Bare Nature Surf Shops, 185–187 High St, Fremantle. Tel: 08–9336 4400. Also at 337 Stirling Hwy, Claremont. Tel: 08–9284 4401.

Capital Fashion, Level 1, 81 Market St. Fremantle. Tel: 08–9431 7997

Colin Earle Surf Supplies, Rear 101, Cambridge St, West Leederville. Tel: 08–9388 1021. Board repairs.

Cordingley's Surf City, Shop G4, The Esplanade, Scarborough Beach. Tel: 08–9341 5688.

Cruel Sea Surf Shop, Unit 4, 32 Prindiville Dve, Wangarra. Tel: 08–9309 9567.

Crystals Surf Shop, Shop 126, Rockingham City Shopping Centre. Tel: 08–9528 1770.

JP Surf, Shop 18–20, Hillarys Boat Harbour, Sorrento Quay, Sorrento. Tel: 08–9448 8599. Stockists of all major labels and accessories.

KJ Water Sports, 10 Whyalla St, Willeton. Tel: 08–9457 4122. Wetsuit repairs and alterations.

Rottnest Dive Surf and Ski, Thompsons Bay, Rottnest Island. 08– 9292 5167.

Salty Dog Surf Shop, Shop 16, South Tce Piazza, Fremantle. Tel: 08–9430 8808.

SOS Sail & Surf, 1 Quarry St, Fremantle. Tel: 08–9430 7050. Malibu specialists.

Star Surf Shop, 332 Murray St, Perth. Tel: 08–9321 6230. Centrally located.

Sunover Beach, 114 Park Rd, Mandurah. Tel: 08–9535 7533.

Surfscene, 105 High St, Fremantle. Tel: 08–9335 1289. Open 7 days a week.

The **Power Station**, Shop 1, 575 Canning Hwy, Melville. Tel: 08–9330 5535.

The **Sands Surf Shop**, Shop 4, Sands Shopping Center, Mandurah Tce, Mandurah Tel: (08) 9535 3804.

The **Surf Boardroom**, Shop 3, Ocean Plaza, cnr Scarborough Beach Rd and West Coast Hwy, Scarborough. Tel: 08–9341 6843. Shop 9, 279 Canning Hwy, East Fremantle. Tel: 08–9339 8611. Shop 13a, Grove Plaza Centre, Stirling Hwy, Cottesloe. Tel: 08–9384 8188.

Town & Country Surf Shop, 229B Queen Victoria St, Fremantle. Tel: 08–9430 7955.

Vidlers Surf Sports, 14 Station St, Cottesloe. Tel: 08–9384 2416, Fax: 08–9385 2426.

Accommodation

Trigg and Scarborough
All Seasons Observation Rise, 183 West Coast Hwy, Scarborough. Tel: 08–9245 0800. Two and three bedroom apartments overlooking the beach. Includes pool, gym and tennis courts. Off peak rate for a two-bedroom apartment (sleeps 4) per night is $190, while peak season is around $240.

Scarborough Starhaven Caravan Park, 18 Pearl Pde, Scarborough. Tel: 08–9341 1770. 30 sites, 300 m from the beach. Daily rate for a double is $15, and $85 weekly. On-site vans are $23–$35 daily for a double, and $175 weekly. The weekly rate for the 2 holiday units is $280.

Indigo Lodge, 255 West Coast Hwy, Scarborough. Tel: 08–9341 6655. Newly renovated with ocean views, the Lodge offers boogie board hire and free pick-up. Rates per person, per night are $12 for a dorm bed, and $18 for a twin share.

Cottesloe/Swanbourne
Cottesloe Beach Chalets, 6 John St, Cottesloe. Tel: 08–9385 4111. 24 two bedroom units (sleep up to 5) are self-contained and have access to a restaurant, pool and private parking. Daily rates from $105–$140.

Cottesloe Beach Hotel, cnr Marine Pde and John St, Cottesloe. Tel: 08–9383 1100. Beachfront location. Room rates per night are $50–$55 per person, and $70-85 for a double.

Cottesloe Waters Holiday Units, 8 MacArthur St, Cottesloe. Tel: 08–9242 2660. Overlooking the ocean, 9 one- and two-bedroom units (sleep 1–6) supply everything. Daily rates are $55–$90, or $350–$595 weekly.

Fremantle
Esplanade Hotel, cnr Marine Tce and Essex St, Fremantle. Tel: 08–9432 4000, Fax: 08–9430 4539. A huge hotel with 259 rooms, 2 restaurants, fitness centre, 3 spas and 2 heated swimming pools. Rates per night range from $165 for a double and $210 for a studio with private balcony.

Fremantle Hotel, cnr High and Cliff Sts, Fremantle. Tel: 08–9430 4300. The 33 rooms in this popular watering-hole, provide the basic facilities and are serviced by a restaurant. Rooms per person are $50–$65 per night, or $65–$75 for a double.

Fremantle Village Caravan Park, cnr Cockburn and Rockingham Rds, Fremantle. Tel: 08–9430 4866. All 150 sites are powered, while facilities include kiosk, general supplies and separate laundry. Daily rates are $20 (double). Self-contained on-site chalets are $70 daily, and 6 park cabins are $50 daily (double).

Backpackers Inn-Freo, 11 Packenham St, Fremantle. Tel: 08–9431 7065, Fax: 08–9336 7106. Situated in this historic port and only 4 mins walk from the Rottnest Ferry. Hostel rates from $15 per night.

Mandurah
Coastal Holiday Homes, 4 Crystaluna Dve, Golden Bay. Tel: 08–9293 5393. Only 100 m away from the Indian Ocean, this cottage (sleeps up to 9) is self-contained and includes microwave, central heating and air-conditioning. Daily rates from $60–$90, and weekly from $250–$700.

Singleton Beach Guest House, 108 Foreshore Dve, Singleton. Tel: 08–9537 3427. Self-contained rooms include cooking facilities, room service, shared spa and security parking. Daily B&B rates from $40 (single) and $80 (double), while weekly rates start around $280 (single) and $420 (double).

Miami Caravan Park, Lot 2, Old Coast Rd, Miami. Tel: 08–9534 2127. All 140 sites are powered and include separate utilities, washing machine and hot showers. Daily rates per double are $14, and $90 weekly. On-site vans from $25 per night.

Lucky Caravan Park, 20 Henson St, Mandurah. Tel: 08–9535 3313. Adjacent to the beach, all 20 camping sites are powered and supplied by town water. Camping rates from $16–$21 per night. Park cabins from $43–$53, on-site vans $30–$45, and cottages from $48–$63 per night.

Melros Beach Caravan Park, Melros Beach, Mandurah. Tel: 08–9582 1320. Half of the 60 sites are powered and offers recreation room and kiosk. Daily rates for a double include $10–$15.

Rottnest Island

Rottnest may be less than 20 kilometres from the mainland, but it only takes a couple of hours for you to feel like you're on the other side of the earth.

Getting There
There are only two ways of getting to the island—either by sea or air, and once you're there, bicycles will be your main form of transport. A number of ferries which depart from Rous Head in Fremantle, Barrack Street Jetty in Perth, or Hillarys Boat Harbor, offer you a variety of styles and transit times. It takes roughly 20 minutes for the quicker boats, and prices range from $25–$35 for a same day return, or $30–$40 for an extended return. Rottnest Ferry Operators include: Boat Torque Cruises, Tel: 08–9221 5844; Oceanic Cruises, Tel: 08–9325 1191; and the Rottnest Express, Tel: 08–9335 6404. Departure times vary with the season, so contact a tourist information centre for updates. Rottnest Airlines can be contacted on 08–9334 2288 for information on flight timetables that depart from Perth Airport and land on the island airstrip.
Bikes (and helmets which are compulsory) can be hired from the island bike shop; for more information ring About Rottnest Bike Hire on 089-9221 1828.
    Two coach tours of the island are available, and tickets can be purchased at the Visitors' Centre. Contact Rottnest Island Bus Tours on 08–9372 9752 for further information.
    For a more extensive listing of accommodation on the island including villas, bungalows, houses and Tentland, contact the Rottnest Island Authority, Tel: 08–9432 9111, or the West Australian Tourist Centre on 1300 361 351.

Rottnest Lodge Resort. Tel: 08–9292 5161. All 79 units contain basic amenities such as refrigeration, TV and tea-making facilities. There's also a restaurant, pool and shared spa. Daily rates for a double from $130–$185.

Rottnest YHA, Kingston Barracks. Tel: 08–9372 9780, Fax: 08–9292 5141. Located 1.2 km from the ferry jetty and 1 km from the airport, the hostel has 52 beds and 9 separate rooms. Nightly rates from $19 per person.

South West
Surf Shops

Beachlife Surf Shop, 117 Bussell Hwy. Margaret River. Tel: 08–9757 2888.

Country Waves, Shop 12, Dunsborough Central Shopping Centre. Tel: 08 9755 3380.

Creatures Of Leisure, 11 Clark St, Dunsborough 6281. Tel: 08–9755 3408.

Hilzeez Surf Stop, 65 Queens St, Busselton. Tel: 08–9752 3565. Bunbury Forum. Tel: 08–9791 4717.

MC Board, Margaret River. Tel: 08–9757 9990.

Performance Surfboards, Injinup Rd, Yallingup. Tel: 08–9755 2109, Fax: 08–9755 2205. Custom-made surfboards and sailboards.

Wet Dreams Surf Accessories, Unit 2/226, Minchin Way, Margaret River. Tel: 08–9757 3722, Fax: 08–9757 3782.

Yallingup Surf Shop, 2 Valley Rd, Yallingup. Tel: 08–9755 2036.

Accommodation

Dunsborough
Bayshore, 374 Geographe Bay Rd, Dunsborough. Tel: 08–9756 8353, Fax: 08–9756 8354. Fully furnished and equipped two and three-bedroom villas; facilities include log fires, cafe, spa, tennis court and games room. Villas range from $100–$205 per night.

Dunsborough Resort Motel, 536 Naturaliste Tce, Dunsborough. Tel: 08–9755 3200. Fax: 08–9756 8540. Comfortable accommodation with swimming pool and BBQ area. Costs per night range from $75–$105 for a twin share.

Dunsborough Bay Village Resort, 26 Dunn Bay Rd, Dunsborough. Tel: 08–9755 3397, Fax: 08–9755 3790. Wide range of facilities including self-contained chalets and villas with in-house movies, Chinese restaurant, on-site diving academy and charter vessels. Priced from $38 per person per night (four share), and $55 per person per night (twin share).

Three Pines Resort YHA, 285 Geographe Bay Rd, Quindalup. Tel/Fax: 08–9755 3107. Facilities include 67 beds, 17 rooms and meals. Dorms start at $15 per person, twin share $35, and $50 for family rooms.

Yallingup
Canal Rocks Beach Resort, Smith's Beach Rd, Yallingup. Tel: 08–9755 2116. All of their 16 one and three-bedroom units are self-contained, including access to a tennis court and cafe. Doubles range from $135–$165 per night, and $660–$1155 per week.

Caves Caravan Park, cnr Caves and Yallingup Beach Rds, Yallingup. Tel: 08–9755 2196, Fax: 08–9755 2319. Equipped vans with TV, and minutes from the beach. Rates range from $43 double per night and $258 double per week for a park home, $39 per night and $234 per week for an on-site van, and $15 per night and $98 per week for camping facilities.

Caves House Hotel, Caves Rd, Yallingup. Tel: 08–9755 2131, Fax: 08–9755 2041. 10 units and 4 suites serviced by a restaurant, recreation room and tennis court. Prices range from $120 for a room to $175 for a suite. Caves House hotel section has 23 rooms, 1 suite and includes TV and tea-making facilities. Rooms from $65 to $175 per night.

Chandler's Smith's Beach Villas, Smith's Beach Rd, Yallingup. Tel/Fax: 08–9755 2062. Perched on a hillside overlooking Supertubes and Smith's Beach main break, the rammed-earth villas are ideal for groups of surfers. BYO food. Prices per night start at $75 (mid-week) and $90 (weekend), and $575 per week.

Yallingup Farm Cottages, cnr Caves Rd and Marrinup Dve, Yallingup. Tel: 08–9755 2261. Self-contained cottages, including a pot belly stove and microwave oven. Doubles around $55–$120 per night, and $420–$750 for a weekly rate.

Injinup
Camping Grounds

Cowaramup
Bettenays Red Gum Ridge, Harmans South Rd, Willyabrup, Cowaramup. Tel: 08–9755 5539. Their 3-bedroom chalet (sleeps up to 8) costs $70–$110 daily, and $440–$700 weekly.

Gracetown Chalets, Cowaramup Bay. Tel: 08–8755 5376. Run by surfers for surfers, the chalets overlook two of the southwest's best waves at North and South Point. Chalets from $350 per week.

Karriview Lodge, Caves Rd, Cowaramup. Tel: 08–9755 5553. Intimate accommodation with 6 rooms, shared spa, tennis court and golf driving range. B&B ranging from $70–$160 for a double.

Taunton Farm Caravan Park, Bussell Hwy, Cowaramup. Tel: 08–9755 5334. All 40 sites are powered, hot showers, camp kitchen and public phone. Two-person rates for the camping area start at $15 per night. Taunton's 4 cabins (accommodate up to 6) are $60 a double, while on-site vans are around $40 per night.

Margaret River
Situated 227 km south of Perth, the fertile land of Margaret River produces some of Australia's finest wines.

Captain Freycinet, cnr Tunbridge St and Bussell Hwy, Margaret River. Tel: 08–9757 2033. Facilities for the 62 units include a fully licensed dining room, telephone, TV, in-house movies and pool. Rooms start at $80 per person or $98 for a double per night, with child and family concessions available.

Gnarabup Ocean Grove Cottages, 66 Bauding Dve, Gnarabup. Tel: 08–9757 2072. Cottages include cooking facilities, lounge, and washing machine. Rates from $10–$15 daily per person, to $700–$1050 per week.

Margaret River Bed & Breakfast, 28 Fearn Ave, Margaret River. Tel: 08–9757 2118. Their 4 rooms (one of which has its own ensuite) has shared lounge, TV, video and BBQ. B&B start at $35–$40 per person, and $55–$65 for a double.

Margaret River Caravan Park, Margaret River. Tel: 08–9757 2180. In the heart of Margaret River, the Park has 60 powered sites and 10 on-site vans. BYO pillows and blankets. Peak rates for an on-site van start at $20 per person.

Margaret River Lodge, 220 Railway Tce, Margaret River. Tel: 08–9757 9532, Fax: 08–9757 2532. Doubles, twins, quads and dorms available, shared kitchen with full facilities. Pool, bike hire, surf/body board hire. Affordable accommodation from $13 per person, per night.

Surf Point Lodge, Reidle Dve, Gnarabup. Tel: 08–9757 1777, Fax: 08–9757 1077. Located right on the beach. 23 new rooms (ensuites available), TV and games room, surrounded by national parks, with courtesy bus to and from Margaret River. From $13 per person, per night, and $40 double/twin rooms.

Prevelly Park
Burnside Bungalows, Burnside Rd, Margaret River. 08–9757 2139. Two fully self-contained, limestone chalets bordering state forest and 5 minutes walk from the town centre. Rates from $60 per night.

Prevelly Ocean View Villa, Lot 121, Papadakis Ave, Prevelly Park. Tel: 08–9339 3613. The villas have ocean views and are situated 300 m from the beach. Doonas and pillows provided, but BYO linen. Units from $70 a night and special weekly rates.

Prevelly Park Caravan Park, Prevelly. Tel: 08–9757 2374. Facilities include 90 sites (50 powered), 20 on-site vans, 5 cottages, cooking facilities, kiosk and on site liquor outlet. Tent sites per person range from $9 per night to $63 per week, while on-site vans cost $67 a night and $465 per week.

Prevelly Villas, Vattos Way, Prevelly Pk, Margaret River. Tel/Fax: 08–9757 2277. Self-contained houses with easy access to beautiful beaches. Cabins between $90–$150 per night, $600–$1000 per week.

Sea Breeze of Prevelly Park, 40 Lakeview Cres, Margaret River. Tel: 08–9757 3684. Private self-contained accommodation, nestled between native bush and the sea. Includes TV and video, as well as an ensuite with a bath. Double rooms per night range between $55–$80.

Far South Coast
Surf Shops
Albany Surf Shop, 278 B York St, Albany. Tel: 08–841 5544.

Big Drop Surf Shop, 21 South Coast Hwy, Denmark. Tel: 08–9842 2183.

Last Frontier Surf Shop, Andrew St, Esperance. Tel: 08–9071 2463.

Mad Marty's, The Link Shopping Centre, Albany. Tel: 08–9841 8597.

Surf &Sound, 150-160 York St, Albany. Tel: 08–9842 2597.

Yahoo Surfboards, Unit 3, 1 Clark St, Dunsborough. Tel: 08–9756 8336.

Accommodation
Walpole/Nornalup
Billa Billa Farm Cottages, Hunter Rd, Walpole. Tel: 08–9840 1131. These 4 cottages on a beef and sheep farm have cooking facilities and pot belly stove. Daily rates between $50–$80, and $300–$500 weekly.

Coalmine Beach Caravan Park, Walpole. Tel: 08–9840 1026. Powered sites from $14 per night. Park cabins from $40–$55 per night.

Crystal Springs Camp, Walpole-Nornalup National Park, off South Western Hwy. Tel: 08–9840 1027. Limited facilities due to its location, including no power. Rain water and separate toilets are available. Sites for a double from $5 per night.

Glen Echo, Lot 12, Riverside Dve, Nornalup. Tel: 08–9810 1272. B&B rates per night from $35 (single) and $65–$75 (double).

Tingle All Over Budget Accommodation, cnr Inlet and Nockolds Sts, South Coast Hwy, Walpole. Tel: 08–9840 1041. Their rooms have shared cooking facilities, lounge and recreation area. Rooms from $14–$25 per person, or a twin room from $28–$36. Tingle also has a dormitory room (sleeps up to 6) from $13 per person per night.

Denmark

Karma Chalets, Lot 411, Lapkos Rd, Denmark. Tel: 08–9848 1568, Fax: 08–9848 2124. Fully-equipped chalets in a peaceful location, (2 include two-person spa baths). Rates from $70 for a double per night.

Ocean Beach Caravan Park, Ocean Beach Rd, Denmark. Tel: 08–9848 1262. Separate toilets and laundry for the 160 powered sites, with kiosk, tennis court and BBQ area. Sites daily for a double at $14, on-site vans daily $30–$40, while the cottages are $40–$55 per day.

Spring Bay Villas, Ocean Beach Rd, Denmark. Tel: 08–9848 2456. Self-contained villas which sleep up to 6 people and within easy walking distance to Ocean Beach. Double per night ranges from $80–$110.

Tree Tops, 21 Payne Rd, Weedon Hill. Tel: 08–9848 2055, or 08–9364 1594. This timber A-frame cottage is set in Karri trees with views of Wilson's Inlet. Fully equipped for 4 guests including linen, video and CD player. Nightly $100 (minimum of 2 nights), and $640 weekly.

Albany

Emu Point Chalets and Holiday Units, 9 Medcalf Parade, Emu Point. Tel: 08–9844 8889. Chalets from $45–$100 per night for 2 people or $295–$840 per week for up to 8 people.

Emu Beach Caravan Park, Medcalf Parade, Albany. Tel: 08–9844 1147. Cabins from $33 per night.

Middleton Beach Caravan Park, Middleton Rd. Tel: 08–9841 3593. Camp sites from $8–$15 per night. Cabins from $35–$55 per night, sleep up to 7 people.

Cheyne Beach Caravan Park, Cheyne Beach. Tel: 08–9846 1247. Camp sites from $11–$13. Vans from $26–$44 for 2 people. Cabins from $35–$50 per night. Situated on some very tasty beach breaks.

Bayview YHA Lodge, 49 Duke St. Tel: 08–9842 3388. Rooms from $12–$14 per night.

Esperance

Esperance Beachfront Resort, 19 The Esplanade, Esperance. Tel: 08–9071 2513, Fax: 08–9071 5442. Fully self-contained units, 5 minutes walk to town and jetty. Spa, BBQ area and on-site cafe. Rates per night start at $55 (single) and $65 (double).

Bathers Paradise Caravan Park, Westmacott St, Esperance. Tel/Fax: 08–9071 1014. Just 150 m from the water's edge. Camping sites from $14 daily per night. Park cabins are $30–$42 daily, while on-site vans are $25–$40 daily.

Blue Waters Lodge, Goldfields Rd, Esperance. Tel/Fax: 08–9071 1040. Newly renovated, the hostel has 100 beds and is located just 20 m from the seafront, overlooking Esperance Bay. Daily rates are $14 per person, and $35 for a twin share.

Esperance Bay Caravan Park, cnr The Esplanade and Harbour Rd, Esperance. Tel: 08–9071 2237. Separate toilets and laundry for the 40 sites (30 are powered) which are close to fishing charter departure jetties. Sites are $12 daily per double ($14, powered), while on-site cabins range from $32–$34 daily for a double.

Esperance Backpackers, 14 Emily St, Esperance. Tel: 08–9071 4724. One lodge unit accommodating 32 guests. Rooms per night are $14 per (single) and $30 (double). Weekly $80 (single) and $170–$180 (double).

Stokes National Park Camping Grounds, 92 km west of Esperance. Tel: 08–9076 8541. Don't be surprised if you're the only one on the beach, so take advantage of the raw Southern Ocean waves! Due to its isolation, there are limited facilities and no power. Sites are $5 daily for a double, and day passes are $5 per car.

Contributors

Mark Thornley
Raised on Western Australia's remote surfing coastline, Mark has spent most of his life in the ocean, either surfing, fishing, windsurfing or diving. A former editor of *Waves* surfing magazine, he was also Senior Editor of the hip pop culture-style bible *REVelation* magazine.

Now based in Sydney, NSW, Mark continues to write features for a host of Australian magazines including *Who Weekly, Black and White, Outdoor Australia, Inside Sport, The Good Weekend, New Idea, Surf Secrets, Underground Surf, The West Australian* and *Western Angler.*

Veda Dante
A former editor with International Masters Publishers, Veda has photographed and documented some of Australia's most spectacular travel destinations. Providing extensive coverage of health and lifestyle issues for publications such as *Australian Style* and *Outdoor Australia*, she was also Senior Editor of *Conscious Living* magazine before moving to Sydney NSW to pursue a variety of publishing projects including this book. A publicist for leading natural beauty care companies, she enjoys body boarding in her spare time.

Wayne "Rabbit" Bartholomew
A member of the famous Bronzed Aussies who expanded big wave surfing's performance horizons at Hawaii during the '80s, "Rabbit" is one of pro surfing's most legendary characters. As the National Coaching Director for Surfing Australia Inc, his contribution to Australian competitive surfing is unparalleled. Whether he's in front of a microphone or an 8-ft barrel, he still charges.

Andrew Buckley
Surfer, skater and outstanding young water photographer, Andrew Buckley is based at Narrabeen on Sydney's north shore. Here he continues to capture the radical antics of Australia's hottest young competition and free surfers for leading magazines such as *Waves* and *Surfer* in the United States.

Ricky Eaves
A freelance and landscape photographer, Ricky captures Tasmania's awesome scenery, wilderness and wildlife for a variety of magazines including *Australian GEO, The Bulletin* and *40° South*. When he's not shooting film, he's discovering new waves along Tassie's remote west coast.

Albert Falzon
Director of the seminal cult surf film *Morning of the Earth* and the international festival classic *Same As It Ever Was*, Albert is still making films, his most recent production being the *Metaphysical* video for Quiksilver. Loving life at his Eungai Creek farm on NSW's north coast, he surfs most days and is planning several creative publishing projects from his digital studio.

Ben Horvath
Editor of Australia's *Underground Surf* magazine, Ben has been a surfer since the age of seven. He still surfs everyday around Cronulla and NSW's South Coast and compiles the surf reports for the Sydney *Telegraph Mirror.*

Mick McCormack
One of Australia's first widely published water photographers, Mick continues to capture classic ocean imagery of NSW's south coast. Still contributing to some of Australia's leading surf publications, his unique, soulful style is still in hot demand.

Shaun Munro
Former touring pro surfer turned salty scribe, Shaun shares his infectious blend of new journalism with the readers of *Waves* surfing magazine. Now residing at Bondi, he remains a regular face at many hot free surfing sessions along the NSW coast.

Wayne Murphy
A regular columnist for *Tracks* surfing magazine, Wayne also works as an editor for Australian media baron Kerry Stokes. While devoting a lot of his time to junior competitive surfing throughout his home state of

Western Australia, Wayne is also a film-maker. He directed *Wave Rock*, an educational film starring aboriginal surfer Ken Dann.

Bill Morris
A Sydney fireman, Bill keeps his cool with impromptu surfing holidays and magazine-sponsored surf trips where he photographs leading pro surfers from inside the barrel.

Mark Newsham
Mark spends much of his time surfing and photographing the Wollongong area for *Waves* and *Underground Surf* magazine and documenting the remote surf regions of NSW's South Coast.

Neal Purchase Junior
A former international touring pro, "Purcho" now spends most of his time deciding whether to surf his world class local breaks of Kirra and Burleigh Heads (QLD), or duck off on an exotic surf trip with sponsor Hot Tuna.

Chris Rennie
Former editor for *Free Surf* magazine, Chris spends much of his time exploring the consistent waves of Victoria's Great Ocean Road. Having recently formed his own company Liquid Addictions, he now a consultant to the Board Sports industry, and writes and publishes works on surfing, snowboarding, skiing and skateboarding.

Glyndon Ringrose
Touring professional surfer and Victorian surf standout, Glyndon spends most of his time getting barrelled in the pristine lineups of his beloved Phillip Island.

Steve Ryan
Steve began taking photos of the Victorian coastline over 15 years ago. The former owner of the Bird Rock Café (an Australian surf icon), he started hanging his images on the café's walls before being approached by the surf media. Now enjoying a full-time lifestyle photography career, Steve submits his work to Australian and overseas surf publications.

Glenn Saltmarsh
Based on Tasmania's wild west coast, Glenn is a dock worker who spends his spare time surfing large, uncrowded waves in some of the world's most pristine wilderness tracts. Dedicated to encouraging competitive surfing in

his state, he has been instrumental in organising several national and international specialty surfing events within the Apple Isle.

Kevin "Twiggy" Sharland
Living in Western Australia's idyllic south west, Twiggy enjoys surfing Margaret River's powerful assortment of reef and beach-breaks while photographing resident surf superstars such as Taj Burrow and the Paterson brothers Jake and Paul. With a reputation for his water shots of some of Australia's remotest waves, Twiggy contributes to Australia's leading surf publications.

Brian "Squizzy" Taylor
South Australia's current senior state board-riding champion, Brian was the captain of the successful 1991 Australian Amateur Surf Team that toured Tahiti and the Carribean. Now coaching with Surf Culture Australia (a Surfing Australia licensed school), he enjoys promoting surfing in the community, taking coaching clinics and travelling around his state.

Ian and Eric Regnard
Tungsten is a photographic company created seven years ago in WA, by Mauritian-born Ian and Eric Regnard with the aim of supplying surfing photos to magazines. Today Tungsten (sponsored by Nikon) also specialises in windsurfing and body boarding, distributing images to Japan, Germany, Italy, France, South Africa, England, USA, Brazil and Australia.

Terry Willcocks
Living a laid-back surfing lifestyle at NSW's Byron Bay, Terry has been widely published in *Surfing World* and *Surfing Life* magazines and is renowned for his soulful surfing and lifestyle imagery.

Peter "Joli" Wilson
Surfing Australia's chief photographer, Peter is perhaps Australia's most widely published surfing photo journalist. Based on Queensland's Gold Coast, he travels throughout the world recording the latest free surfing and competitive evolutions on the world professional circuit. Currently the Senior photographer of *Surfer* magazine in America, his work has been featured in a variety of major surf advertising campaigns and with the assistance of wife Jan, he continues to supply freelance photographic services to the leading surf publications.

Acknowledgements

Firstly, thanks to Neil Ridgeway, former editor of *Tracks* surfing magazine and now editor FHM magazine for giving us the opportunity to do this book. Even though we've spent more time writing than surfing, we are grateful for the experience.

Thanks too must go to Rod Ritchie, Julia Walkden and the Periplus staff for their patience and understanding throughout all stages of this project.

Thank you to the individuals and organizations who helped put this publication together, including: the various State and Regional Tourism Commissions; Keith Curtain and the team at Surfing Australia Inc.; Fleur Hayes and Peter Carwardine, WA Tourism Commission; Ian McLean, Tasmanian Tourism Commission; Jill Clout, Savage Communications; South Perth 4WD; Wayne "Rabbit" Bartholomew; Ben Horvath; *Underground* surf magazine; John Foss, Surfrider Foundation; Pixie and Ed at Pinetrees, Lord Howe Island; Emma Shead, Trader Nicks, Lord Howe Island; Michael Legge-Wilkinson; Alby Falzon; Drew and Nicolette Sharp; Jack Finlay, *Surfworld Australia*; Nicole Reading, PPR Public Relations; Wayne Golding, Mambo; Adam Blakey and *Waves* magazine; Wayne Dart, *Tracks* magazine and Greg Perano.

Map Index

Index